TEMPLES OF INDIA

Ancient, Medieval and Modern

DR. K. RAGHURAM

INDIA • SINGAPORE • MALAYSIA

ISBN 979-8-89363-635-2

In loving memory of my wife…

Late. Smt. K. Kanaka Lakshmi (1954-2018)

CONTENTS

ACKNOWLEDGEMENTS

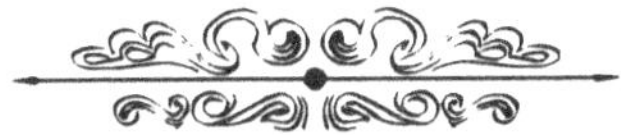

I want to dedicate this book to the memory of my beloved wife, the late Smt. Kanaka Lakshmi Kambhampati. I will always remember her unwavering support during our 48 years of association and invaluable advice throughout my academic journey with great fondness.

I would like to acknowledge my son, Rajani Kumar, for helping with his input on structuring the book, encouraging me to enhance the content with additional chapters, and, last but not least, translating my handwritten content into digital format and editing.

I thank my family members Vaidehi (daughter), Krishna Prasad (son-in-law) and Vasundhara (daughter-in-law), for encouraging me to write the book. I thank my brother K.V.S. Ramachandra and his sons Ramesh and Sreedhar for their valuable guidance, encouragement, and contributions during various stages of the publication work.

I also extend my sincere acknowledgements to our family well-wisher Sanjay Pulipaka for his expert guidance on various stages of the authoring and editing process.

I acknowledge with thanks the kind and unstinted assistance rendered to me by my friends and colleagues, Late Sri P.S. Nageswara Rao and A.V. Narasimha Rao (Professor of English).

Finally, I thank the publishers, Notion Press and their entire team who executed the publishing of this book.

PREFACE

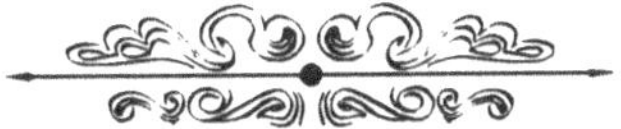

"Temples of India" is written to inform general readers, pilgrims, travellers, and those on a religious and spiritual journey. The book covers the temples of all states in India, and I have personally visited some of them, including ancient, medieval, and modern temples. Some ancient temples have decayed over time due to age factors or foreign invasions, while the Archaeological Survey of India protects others. Some temples are still active and regularly visited by pilgrims for performing 'Pujas' and celebrations. The information presented in the book is collected from reliable and authentic sources, both from India and abroad, with care taken at every stage of collection, arrangement, and presentation. The temple histories are written with priority given to legendary sources or 'Sthalapuranas' and include historical, mythological, spiritual, and philosophical aspects from ancient times to the present day. When visiting South Indian temples, one can see that they are preserved in their original form, maintaining their original glory. The chronological links between the temples are undisturbed, covering a vast period and wide area.

The Indian Temples are profound symbols of spirituality beyond being places of religious worship. They serve as repositories of Indian art and sculpture, a testament to our rich cultural heritage. The rites and rituals performed at these temples are not mere traditions but a living embodiment of the teachings of great saints and reformers like Adi Shankaracharya and Ramanujacharya. The temple deities, far from being stone idols, are believed to be living and vibrant Gods, their presence felt by all who visit. Chanting Vedic mantras is not just a practice but a way to infuse divine energy among the devotees, connecting them to a higher power.

In this context, it is important to acknowledge the profound influence of Grace Moley, a renowned figure in the US and Asia who was deeply moved by Indian religion, art, and sculpture. At the age of 80, she penned a book on Indian sculpture, a testament to her devotion. Her final wish, to have her ashes immersed in the holy river Ganges, speaks volumes about her connection to India. Similarly, despite our differences in religion or region, many great individuals have left an indelible mark on humanity. Inspired by their example, I have embarked on this journey to share the wonders of Indian temples with you through this book.

This book starts with an Introduction chapter explaining the growth of literature, Hinduism, various temple architectures, their evolution, and various dynasties. The rest of the chapters are organized by state for ease of reference. As there are several thousands of temples across India, this book is a humble attempt to list prominent temples across each state. As new temples continue to be constructed, this book focuses only on temples that were constructed approximately until the mid-20th century.

INTRODUCTION

India's religious and philosophical traditions are the richest, having excellent continuity and development. Since 3250 BC, Hinduism has been a philosophy that served the people's requirements, from a commoner to a philosopher. In short, Hinduism spans the complete spectrum of Indian culture, according to George Michell, an Australian historian. The origin of the religion goes back to the Harappa and Mohenjo-Daro civilizations, furnishing the information of worship of the "Mother Goddess". In other words, nature is personified.

The Harappa origin focused on the Dravidian, non-Aryan, and pre-Aryan versions. Of course, temples were not discovered, but the "Divine Mother" worship has extended to Shiva, Vishnu, Shakti, and minor deities. In other words, the system of worship gained significant momentum.

Growth of Literature

The Vedas:

The Hindu religion and culture are rooted in the Vedas, which contain stanzas (Mantras). In his book *"The Call of the Vedas" (Bhavans-1954)*, Dr Avinash Chandra Bose categorically explained the quintessence of the Vedas. The stanzas are found in different Vedas are as follows:

- Rigveda – 10,552
- Yajurveda – 1975
- Atharvaveda – 5,987
- Samaveda – 1875

<u>Explanation:</u>

'Vid' means knowledge; Veda is believed to be sacred knowledge. Rigveda is the oldest Veda, containing *Gayathri Mantra*. Yajurveda contains hymns revealing sacrifices. Atharvaveda's hymns contain mantras meant to conquer evil forces. Samaveda is useful during Yagnas and is also the source of music.

The Brahmanas: The hymns are written in simple prose on rituals and ceremonies.

The Aryankas: Deal with the instructions to be given in forests.

<u>The Upanishads:</u>

Like the Brahmanas, they are in prose emphasizing God. Brahman and soul come in this context. The Upanishads are the concluding part of Brahmanas or Vedanta. Indian philosophy is nothing but the Upanishadic knowledge.

<u>The Epics:</u>

Valmiki and Vyasa wrote Ramayana and Mahabharata, the two great epics. The impact of humanity is profound in moulding human life.

Ramayana contain 24,000 slokas (6 Cantos or Kandas), Mahabharata contains 1,25,000 slokas in 18 parvas. Bhagavad Gita is said to have been told by Lord Krishna on the battlefield. It occurs as an episode in Mahabharata. In times of crisis, it guides, and its message is universal. There is a famous and marvellous Sanskrit poem named "The Song Celestial" by Sir Edwin Arnold.

The epics exhibit a plethora of exciting roles or characters. For example, Rama and Dharmaraja for behaviour based on dharma; Hanuman, Bhima, and Arjuna for their bravery; Sita, Draupadi and Savitri for their love towards husband; Ravana and Keechaka for their lust; Mandodari and Sakuni for cruel advice.

<u>Philosophies:</u>

Advaita, Visistadvaita, and Dwaita are the different forms of interpretations of Hindu philosophy propounded and propagated by Sri Adi Shankaracharya, Ramanujacharya, and Madhvacharya. These philosophies are complementary but not contradictory. They tried to restore the past glory of Hinduism, which had been affected and eclipsed by Buddhism at the time.

Great philosophers of India

Sri Adi Shankaracharya, Ramanujacharya and Madhvacharya are considered a great trio of philosophers and propounders of Hinduism.

Jagadguru Adi Shankaracharya

Adi Shankaracharya strove hard to synthesise the diverse currents troubling India during his time to build unity and diversity. During a brief life of 32 years, he did the work of many long lives. He was a mixture of a philosopher, scholar, mystic, poet, and saint who lived in history as a practical reformer (*"Discovery of India"* by Pandit Jawaharlal Nehru).

There is no proper information about Shankara's era, and various sources indicate different timelines. These sources were written several centuries after Shankara's existence. Shankara was eight when he left Kerala. He walked over 1500 km, crossing forests, mountains, valleys, and rivers to reach Omkareshwar. There, he met his guru, Govinda Bhagavadpada.

Bhagavadpada, a great guru, redeemed Gaudapada, a disciple of Suka, son of Veda Vyasa, who was in the form of 'Brahma Rakshasi', by answering his questions on 'Advaita'. His guru taught Shankara 'Brahmavidya' (the secret of the Vedas, Puranas, Upanishads, etc.) and assigned him to spread Vedantic thought across the country.

Shankara defined Advaita, which people adopted. Sankara's commentary on Prasthana Triam ('Brahmasutras', 'Dasopanishads', and 'Bhagavat

Gita') is known as 'Brahmavidya'. 'Atman is the only reality that means 'sat' – 'chit' and 'Ananda'.

Shankara travelled all over India to preach 'Advaita' and establish 'non-dualism'. He visited Omkareshwar, Varanasi, Badrinath, Prayaga, Mahishmati(Bihar), Srisailam, Gokarnam, Sringeri, Rameshwaram, Tirupati, Dwaraka, Kamarupa (Asom), Puri(Orissa), Kashmir etc.

Shankara established four Matts for Advaitic learning: Sringeri, Dwaraka, Badari and Puri. His disciples were assigned there. He left his impressions on many splendid temples and holy places where he preached, renovated, and contributed to the traditions. At Badari, Puri, and Kasi, he established worship systems. He re-established the Badrinath temple of Lord Vishnu on the western bank of the Alakananda River, where Vyasa lived, compiled Vedas, and wrote Mahabharata and Brahma sutras. Shankara's last journey was to Kedarnath in the Himalayas. His Samadhi behind the temple is situated where his idol is placed. Unfortunately, there is no authentic information about how long he stayed there.

Ramanujacharya

While the devotees of Rudra or Shiva developed Saivism, the devotees of Vishnu developed Vaishnavism, which is also known as Bhagavatism. These sects are called Vaishnavas or Bhagavathas. The Dasavatara theory gained prominence.

Ramanujacharya, born in 1017 AD, was the first reformer to preach 'Bhakti' in the medieval period. Tamil Alwars inspired Ramanuja. Ramanuja was born at Sri Perambur. He criticized Advaita philosophy and said God is not 'Nirakara' but 'Saakara' to be worshipped. This cult is called Visitadvaita. Bhakti is the pathway to Moksha. The caste system was condemned, and all people were allowed to worship in temples.

Madhvacharya

Madhvacharya was born in 1238 AD near Udipi. At the age of ten, he became an ascetic. His philosophy is 'Dwaita', a dualistic theory. He propagated his philosophy and travelled extensively throughout India. Purnapragna and Ananda Tirtha were his followers. In Vaishnavism, Lord Vishnu was worshipped and described as 'Saakara'. God and devotees are 'Bimba' and 'Pratibimbas' only. Vyasa Tirtha summarized the teachings of Madhvacharya in the court of Sri Krishna Deva Raya.

Madhvacharya mastered several languages and fine arts, such as music and sculpture. He installed the image of Sri Krishna in the Udipi temple.

Prominence of Temples in Hinduism

For a staggering span of over 2000 years, Hinduism has held sway over India and much of Asia, standing as a formidable spiritual and religious force. In this expansive narrative, temples have emerged as pivotal players. A temple, in essence, is an artistic manifestation of Hinduism. These structures have graced the Indian landscape since ancient times. While some have been obliterated in the wake of foreign invasions, others stand as testaments to art and architecture. A few fortunate ones have been safeguarded and accorded the status of National and State-protected monuments by the Archeological Survey of India and State governments, in accordance with the Acts of the government of India and States of 1958-60.

Temples, the epicentres of sanctity, are strategically positioned on the riverbanks and atop mountains. Riverbanks, such as the Ganges, the Krishna, the Godavari, and their tributaries, have evolved into spiritual hubs housing these temples. Similarly, the mountain ranges, including the Himalayas, the Vindhyas, and the eastern and western ghats, have provided the perfect backdrop for the establishment of these sacred structures.

In the tapestry of Hinduism in India, life and religion are intricately interwoven. For several centuries, the temple has transcended its religious role to become a public institution, fostering socio-economic activity and serving as a centre of learning and employment. A myriad of professions, from dancers, musicians, florists, and cooks, to engineers, masons, architects, and record keepers, find employment in temple activities. The arts, in the form of dance, music, painting, drama, and sculpture, have thrived under the patronage of these temples.

The other aspect of the temple's activity is performing and promoting Dharma, which is visible in the conduct of the following activities:

- Satsanga
- Harikatha
- Bhakti
- Pilgrimage
- Gurupuja
- Meditation
- Japa and
- Loka Kalyana

Worship

Temple construction activities began to meet the religious and spiritual needs of the devotees, who desired to purify their hearts and control their passions.

The processes of worship are done according to the Sastras. In some ancient temples, worship is reinstated (some examples are Tanjore Brihadiswara temple, Somnath temple in Gujarat, etc.). In modern times, new temples are being constructed in India, besides the reconstruction and renovation of the ancient temples by the public, Dharmik organizations, and endowment departments of state governments.

Construction of the Temple

Temples are considered the epitome of religious architecture and were meticulously constructed in adherence to the sacred texts of 'Agamas' and 'Vastu', which are revered in Hinduism. These texts provided the blueprint for the Temple's design and layout. The construction process began with selecting a suitable site, followed by identifying the deity's image. Once the Temple was built, the Agamas dictated the worship timings, instilling a sense of sanctity and order for the devotees.

The Temples feature a Garbhagriha with a Vimana (the tower), Mandapa and Mahamandapa (for the purpose of Aaradhana), Gopura (the entrance tower), Pradakshinapada (the circumambulatory path around the Garbagriha), and Tirthas (Tanks).

The Temple, a microcosm of the universe, was often compared to the human body. The Garbhagriha, the innermost sanctum, was likened to the neck, housing the main deity. The front Mandapa, a spacious hall, symbolized the stomach, where devotees gathered for worship. The Prakara walls encircling the Temple were equated to the legs, providing stability and support. The gopura, the grand entrance tower, represented the feet, welcoming devotees into the sacred space. The main shrines, the Jiva in the body, were the heart and soul of the Temple. The Garbhagriha, dimly lit, housed the main shrine, while the temples also featured two other idols – the 'Moola Virat' and 'Uthsava Vigrahas'. Mother goddesses and minor shrines were also installed, adding to the Temple's spiritual aura.

Inscriptions, local legends, or Sthalapuranas were sources of information about the Temple's history.

Styles of the Temple

Styles of temple or temple arts differ from region to region, and they are to be classified as

1. Nagara
2. Vesara and
3. Dravida

<u>The Nagara style:</u>

This style of temple is Quadrangular from the neck to the top, and it is common in northern India.

<u>The Dravidian Style:</u>

The style is Orthogonal from the neck to the top (storied and rock-cut). This is mainly seen in Southern India.

<u>The Vesara Style:</u>

This style consists of structures that are round from the neck to the top.

Some states like Andhra Pradesh furnish all three types of temple architecture.

History and Temples

Northern India

Under the Guptas and their Successors:

The Guptas, who ruled from 319 AD to 467 AD, i.e., from Chandra Gupta I to Skanda Gupta, inaugurated the Golden Age in the field of Temple construction. The glory was extended to the 7th century AD. Later, the Hun and Muslim invaders destroyed the temples. Among the surviving, the following are marvellous.

1. The Dasavatara temple (near Jhansi)
2. The Vishnu temple at Tigawa (Jabalpur)
3. The Siva temple (Bhumer)

Dr V.A. Smith states, "Hindu Arts at its Best in the form of Temples during the Guptas". The creative vitality of the Guptas is reflected in the construction of the temples. After the decline of this dynasty, political unity in Northern India was lost, and minor dynasties cropped up but were of no use in the direction of temple construction activity. In the early 7th century, Sri Harsha succeeded in restoring the empire. During this post-Gupta period, temple architecture began to flower and flourish, popularly known as the stylish evolution. The Parvathy temple (Nachna) and the Dasavatara temple (Deogarh) were the best and preserved well. Over the Deogarh temple doorway is an icon of Vishnu seated on the Serpent, indicating the sanctuary's dedication.

The 5th and 6th centuries witnessed the emergence of a superstructure rising from the sanctuary's walls, which was a distinct characteristic of the "Northern Style." The Nachana temple has an upper storey. The temple of the Bhitargaon of the 5th century is a unique example of a brick building. This is set to be one of the complete 'Hindu Architecture' structures with a square sanctuary.

During the post-Gupta era, one may find a variety of forms of Northern Indian style of architecture (6th-7th centuries). The Western and Eastern zones of central India are to be cited for this type of temple. Two examples are mentioned below:

1. The Vishnu temple at 'GOP' in Gujarat, with a square sanctuary, had a passageway from four sides. Unfortunately, these types of temples are in ruined condition.
2. Mundeshwari temple at Ramgarh in Bihar is another one that has an octagonal shape.

<u>Northern style structures of 6th – 8th centuries:</u>

Some rock-cut temples of the early Chalukyas, Kalachuris, and Rastrakutas were discovered after excavations from the 6th—8th centuries. The cave temples had beautiful images of Siva and Vishnu (Aihole) at Ellora—Elephanta (750 AD) and Salsette (Western Deccan); historians expressed that these are stylish contacts with the North Indian architecture of the 6th—8th centuries. At this juncture, political changes took place. The Rastrakutas succeeded Kalachuris. Kailash temple at Ellora is best to be cited.

<u>Early Chalukyas (7th – 8th centuries):</u>

Apart from the political activities, the rulers had credit for architectural development. The temples of Badami, Aihole, Pattadikal, and Alampur were erected in different styles. In short, it was a blend of both Northern and Southern styles. The Durga temple of Aihole is celebrated as one of the finest of the early Chalukyas. Later, the Chalukyas established an independent line (early 7th century) known as Eastern Chalukyas. Alampur of the Telangana state is the best example of this temple style. (Swarga Brahma temple)

<u>Under the Kalingas and Eastern Gangas (8th – 13th Centuries):</u>

Orissan monuments are famous. Bhuvaneshwar temple offers the best example of the largest temple, followed by the Konark Sun temple and Puri Jagannath temple. Parusurameswara and Mukteswar temples were the earliest of the Bhuvaneswar group.

<u>Under the Pratiharas and Chandelas (8th – 11th centuries):</u>

The temples present central Northern Indian styles. Khajuraho presents 30 stone temples that are surviving. Rajasthani (8th—12th centuries) and Kashmiri temple architecture can be seen here.

Southern India

The South Indian temples evolved over a period of more than one thousand years, spreading over the rule of several principal dynasties and kingdoms:

1. The Pallavas (600-900 AD)
2. The Cholas (900-1150 AD)
3. The Hoyasalas (1106-1343 AD)
4. The Pandyas (1100-1350 AD)
5. The Vijayanagaras (1350-1565 AD)
6. Madurai (1600 AD Onwards)

<u>The Pallavas:</u>

The temple building activity has been continuous since the Pallavas up to the 17th century. The Pallavas ruled for over 300 years. The first 100 years are rock-cut, and the later 100 years are structural. Through the efforts of archaeologists, more than 60 temples have been excavated.

Rapid transition is noticeable from rock-cut to structural temples. Mahabalipuram and Kanchi are the centres of Pallavan architecture. Kanchi, also known as 'Dakshina Kaasi', had 108 temples. The Pallavan period is famous for cave temples and pagodas. Pallavan temples are both Saivite and Vaishnavite.

The Cholas:

The Cholas inherited Pallavan traditions in Art and Architecture. The temples of Tanjore and Gangaikonda Cholapuram are outstanding, and the Brihadiswara temples are magnificent in both places. The temple of Tanjore is the largest and highest and is famous for its rich carvings and fine ceiling paintings. This temple is an example of poise or dignity.

The Hoyasalas:

Belur Halibed reminds us of the work of Hoyasalas of Dwara Samudra. Ornamentation and sculptural skills are visible in Hoyasala architecture. They stood as unrivalled repositories of spiritualism expressed in plastic form.

The Pandyas:

The temples of Chidambaram, Sri Rangam, Rameswaram, and Madurai are the great works of Pandyas. They promote the religious and spiritual life of the people and attract millions of people from far and near.

The Vijayanagara:

Vijayanagara temples are distributed throughout the Dravidian land. They are many in number and popular for the richness of beauty found in the temple pillars and sculptures. Foreigners appreciate the temples as figurative drama in stone. The Vittala and Hazara Rama Swamy temples are just two examples of the Vijayanagara style. One thousand pillared halls became popular.

<u>Madurai and Nayakas:</u>

From 1600 AD onwards, a wave of temples and temple glorifications started, of which Sri Rangam is the largest. Temples are laid from east to west, but here, they are laid from north to South. During the Nayaka period of the 17th century, the temple's dimensions reached the highest watermark.

<u>Local Architectural Styles:</u>

Temples of Bengal and Kerala imbibed the local features in their architectural styles. The use of brick, bamboo and timber is distinct from other ways of construction. Further, Terracotta tiles are used to highlight the uniqueness of the roofs.

Gods, Goddesses, Minor Deities and practices of Temple worship

A great pantheon of Gods, Goddesses and minor deities unfolds Hinduism. The Gods are described in the great classics of Hindu religious literature, Vedas, epics, Puranas, and folk religion, revealing the powers of the divine forms. Temples have been built, which are characteristic of Hinduism and artistic expression. Practices of worship started, followed by ceremonies performed daily, occasionally, and annually.

Ganesa

Ganesa is known as the auspicious or 'Mangala Murthi'. It is customary to worship the son of Siva and Parvati on any auspicious occasion like Vidyarambha, Vivaha or any significant event. Ganesa's image plays a vital role in Hindu mythology and iconography. The deity is represented by a plump body, round belly, elephant head and trunk, followed by a little mouse. He possesses weapons like Ankush, Shankha and Pasha. The images of Ganesa in the most important temples are known as 'Swayambhu' or self-manifested. Every village, town or city would have the temple of Ganesa.

Siva

In Hinduism, the celebrated trio of Gods Brahma, Vishnu and Siva are considered the creator, preserver, and destroyer. The worship of Siva and Vishnu is quite common. Siva is also known as Maheswara and Mahadeva. This God is worshipped in the form of Linga. In India, he has been found since the earliest times. Another name for Siva is Pasupati, the lord of animals. Bull or 'Nandi' is his vehicle. Siva is the lord of dance or 'Nataraja'. He is the ascetic God of Kailasha. Parvati, or Umadevi, is his consort. Trident and bowl are his emblems.

Vishnu

He is seen sleeping in the milky ocean upon the Sesha (thousand-headed serpent). Garuda is his vehicle. Lakshmi is his consort. He is associated with 'Dasavataras'. Conch, discuss, and mace are seen with him.

Goddesses and Minor Deities

Parvati is also known as Shakti, who is said to be boundless (Aditi). She is supposed to be the mother of Gods. Durga riding a lion, Chamundi, Kali, etc., are the forms of 'Ugrarupa' (Wild). Gauri, Uma, and Mahadevi are the passive forms of Parvati. Her multiple appearances are found in the concept of Sapta Matrika. Lakshmi and Saraswati are the other prominent Goddesses.

Under the category of 'Minor Deities' come village Goddesses and Navagrahas. Gods and Goddesses are represented with emblems like rosaries, water pots, musical instruments, flowers, bows and arrows, swords, spears, etc. Birds and animals are also associated with the Gods and Goddesses—for instance, an elephant for Lakshmi, a Lion or Tiger for Shakti, a parrot for Meenakshi Amman, a swan for Saraswati, and a Garuda for Vishnu, etc.

Practices of Temple Worship

The worship and prayers of God are conducted in accordance with the puja principles outlined in the ancient texts, such as the Puranas or even earlier. In this sacred context, the priests play a pivotal role, guiding us in our devotion.

Before worship, devotees take a bath, and purification starts; then, temple worship starts, which is pious and powerful. Temple rituals consist of four stages on the common days – at sunrise, noon, sunset, and night. Hymns or mantras are recited with hand gestures. This process involves the awakening of God or Goddess, also known as 'Suprabhata Seva'. Oils, Camphor, and Sandalwood, are applied to them, and garlanding and 'Harati' are given, followed by 'Naivedyam' (offering of cooked food).

Our religious calendar is adorned with a variety of celebrations, both occasional and annual. These include the Utsavams and Brahmotsavams, which are special in our hearts. The highlight of these events is the Rathotsavams, which are grand processions. During these festive occasions, only Utsavalingas are displayed, adding to the spiritual fervour.

ANDHRA PRADESH (AP)

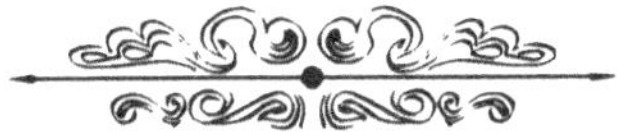

The state of Andhra Pradesh is the first in the list of states in India. The date of formation of the state was 1ˢᵗ November 1956. It attained the status of a separate state on 2ⁿᵈ June 2014. The state was split to create a separate Telangana state, and Amaravati was identified as the new capital of Andhra Pradesh. Telangana, Chhattisgarh, Odisha, Karnataka, and Tamil Nadu are the neighbouring states, and Yanam is the neighbouring Union Territory. The long coast is an asset of the state. The chief languages are Telugu and Urdu. Hinduism, Islam, and Christianity are the religions. Godavari, Krishna, Tungabhadra, and Penna are the rivers. The Eastern Ghats are the mountain ranges.

Figure 1: Andhra Pradesh – Maps of Major Cities and Temples

The state of Andhra Pradesh is rich in sacred temples. The temples represent different styles of architecture. The devotees represent their grievances to the Gods and Goddesses for redressal. Those suffering from ill-health pray for health, the healthy pray for wealth, and the wealthy pray for power. Those who are in power pray for the peace of mind. The temples in Andhra Pradesh represent various Gods. These temples had local legends or 'Sthala Puranas'.

Srisailam

Srisailam is the abode of Lord Siva (Mallikharjuna Swamy) and Parvati (Bhramaramba). This Temple is situated in the Kurnool District of Andhra Pradesh state in the thick and inaccessible forests (Nallamalai hills) of South India. This Mahakshetra is associated with the river Krishna, flowing as Uttaravahini (Patala Ganga). There are four gateways to Srisailam, namely Tripurantakam (Prakasam district) in the East, Siddhavattam (Kadapa) in the south, Alampur (Telangana State) in the west and Uma Maheswaram in the north.

Ancient Andhra desa was known as Trilinga desa, consisting of Draksharama (coastal Andhra), Kaleswaram (Telangana) and Srisailam (Rayalaseema). Puja or worship begins with 'Sankalpam' with the devotee's name, gotra and place "Srisalasya, Easanyastha Pradese, Srisailasya Uttara Digbhage". This Sankalpam applies not only to the God and Goddess of Srisailam but also to any deity. Mallikarjuna and Bramarambha are 'Swayambhus'.

Srisailam is one of the most popular Shivaite shrines in India. It is one of the 'Dwadasa (12) Jyotirlingas' while goddess Bhramaramba Devi is one of the 'Astadasa (18) Maha Sakthi Peethas'; indeed, it is a rare combination of the divine couple.

Sources to know about Srisailam:

Several sources, namely literary and archaeological writings, of Chinese travellers exist. 'Sthala Mahatyams' or local legends also add to the sources to learn more about this Maha kshetra.

Figure 2: Srisailam Mallikarjuna and Bhramaraba Temple

Literary Sources:

Literature in languages like Sanskrit, Telugu, Tamil, Kannada, and Marathi provides ample information. Going into depth are the following valuable sources:

Puranas:

Skanda Purana describes Srisailam. The description of Srisaila Mahatyam is known through Padma Purana, Markandeya Purana, Siva Purana, Aditya Purana, etc.

Epics:

Mahabharata mentioned the stay of Siva, Parvati, Brahma and other Gods at Sri Parvatha on the Srisaila mountain. Bath in the lake is equivalent to Aswamedha's sacrifice to the person and his entire race. In Bhagavata, Potana describes the Kshetra in the 80th chapter.

<u>Sanskrit and Telugu literature:</u>

Adi Shankaracharya's Sivanandalahari, Bhavabhuti's Malathi Madhavam, Bana's Kadambari, Sri Harsha's Ratnavali (Sanskrit works) and Jakkanna's Vikramarka Vijayam, Palkuriki Somanath's Basavapuranam, Srinadha's Harivamsam, Palnati Charitra, Sivaratri Mahatyam and Tallapaka Timmakka's Subhadra Kalyanam (Telugu Works) are some of the examples of ample sources of information about Srisailam.

<u>Archaeological Sources:</u>

Several inscriptions reveal the history of Srisailam. For example, according to the temple records, one of the inscriptions contains information regarding the construction of steps leading to 'Patalaganga' by the Kondaviti Reddi dynasty during the 15th and 16th centuries A.D.

<u>Writings of the foreign travellers:</u>

Chinese travellers Fahien and Heizmut-Sang have referenced the Sriparvata hill in the Krishna River valley.

<u>Stay of the divine couple at Srisailam:</u>

According to a legend, the divine couple came from Mt. Kailash to the earth in search of Subrahmanya Swamy, who was angry with them because his elder brother Ganesh outwitted him in the competition for divine fruit. Siva and Parvati consoled him, saying that he was the divine fruit, and they stayed at Srisailam.

<u>Growth and glory of Srisailam Under the rule of different dynasties:</u>

The habitational history of Srisailam dates back 40,000 years. Archaeologists confirmed this after testing the stone tools recovered from the site.

The earliest historical mention of Srisailam was made during the Satavahana Period (230 BC-220 or 225AD). Later, under the rule of different dynasties, growth and glory came to the limelight. Ikshwakus

(225AD–300AD) ruled Sriparvata or Srisailam. Pallavas (3-9th century AD) ruled Srisailam under Simhavarma. Vishnukundins (450 AD-616 AD) worshipped Srisaila Mallikharjuna. Kadambas and Telugu Chodas, too, were the staunch devotees.

Rastrakutas (Dantidurga 753 AD), Chalukyas of Badami (973AD) and Chalukya – Cholas followed the same tradition. Under the Kakatiyas (1000 – 1023 AD), Srisailam was patronized by Prataparudra Kondaviti Reddis (1325-1424 AD) ruled the region, and Prolaya Vemareddi patronized the Temple, and steps were laid down near Patalaganga (Inscriptional source). Great patronage was made under Vijayanagara rulers (1336-1565 AD). Harihara and Krishnadevaraya contributed much.

Mandapams were constructed in the chariot street. The sanctum sanctorum of the Temple was gold quoted along with vimana. Krishnadevaraya presented Golden Bull (Nandi) and Bringi. A row of houses in the car street was built. Steps were taken to provide income to the Temple. Minimum taxes on homes, villages, and tolls on horses, bullocks, and asses were remitted.

In 1660 AD, Shivaji came to Srisailam and did penance in the Bhramaramba temple. The deity presented him with a sword and blessed him. In 1667, he built a beautiful Rajagopuram on the northern side (Shivaji Gopuram). The Temple's endowment department has beautifully portrayed this episode in life-size.

The Temple's management was under Sringeri and Pushpagiri Maths. After independence, it was shifted to the A.P. Government's Endowments Department.

<u>Origin of The Temple:</u>

Two legends connected to the origin of the Temple are to be cited.

- Chandravati episode: Chandravati was the daughter of a Gupta king named Chandragupta. She was a great devotee of Lord Siva and used to offer daily a garland of jasmine flowers to the Lord and eventually married him. This is mentioned in the Skanda Purana and the temple records of the 16th century. According to the story, she went to the forest for penance with some cattle and herders. She was living on the income by selling milk. One day, she noticed that one black cow was not giving milk. The herdsman watched and reported that it gave up milk on a black stone image of Siva as a Linga. Chandravati witnessed and believed. Lord Siva appeared in a dream and told her that the black stone in the forest was his manifestation and that a temple needed to be constructed. Chandravati built the Temple and worshipped him with Jasmines. Since then, Siva has been known as Mallikharjuna.

- Chenchus or Tribals episode: Siva came to Srisailam on a hunting expedition, fell in love with a beautiful Chenchu woman and married her. Since then, Siva has been known as Chenchu Mallaiah. Chenchus has been given prominence in all the temple activities to date. They play a vital role during Sivaratri and Rathotsavam. Thus, it is a fact that anyone, irrespective of caste, creed, or sex, is allowed into the Temple's sanctum sanctorum. Historians opined that such Catholic worship is unknown anywhere else in Andhra except Srisailam.

<u>Site Plan of The Temple:</u>

The enclosure is square and measures 500 feet from east to west and 600 feet from north to south. The main temple structure is small and surrounded by several minor shrines.

Bhramaramba temple is situated in the west of the inner courtyard.

Mallikharjuna Swamy

Srisaila Mallikharjuna Swamy has been an important shrine in India since ancient times. Lord Siva is known as Mallikharjuna because of the following facts:

- Sri Maha Vishnu, Brahma, Indra and Brahmarshis worshipped this Swayambhu Linga with 'Mallelu' (Jasmines)
- Chandravati, daughter of Chandragupta, was a great devotee of Siva who offered a garland of Jasmines to the Lord daily. The Lord eventually married her.

The Swayambhu Linga of Srisailam is one of India's famous Dwadasa Jyotirlingas.

People firmly believe that the darshan of Mallikharjuna and Bhramaramba Devi of Srisailam and Sikhara darshan bless them with long life, health, wealth, and moksha or salvation. The following quote supports the above conviction of the people:

"Kasyanthu Maanamuktihi,
Smarana Darunachale
Srisaila Sikharam drustrya
Punarjanma Na vidyathe"

One gets salvation for him who dies in Kasi; at Arunachal, one gets simply by 'Smarana', but one who visits and sees the 'Srisaila Sikhara' will be relieved from rebirth.

Thus, the Asta Dasa puranas, epics, and writings of the world preceptor Adi Shankaracharya, supposed to be the 'Sivamsa Sambhuti', establish this kshetra's greatness and holiness.

Bhramaramba

Goddess Bhramaramba Devi, the consort of Mallikharjuna, is one of the 'Asta Maha Shaktis'. The neck part of her body fell here. The goddess is also 'Swayambhu' or self-manifested.

One of the episodes concerns Siva's marriage to a girl named Chenchu. When he left her, she cursed him to turn into a stone. Out of anguish, Parvati transformed the girl into a bee (Bhramaram), and hence, she has been named Bhramaramba; of course, she is also Parvati's Amsa.

In this context, another story is about the goddess killing 'Arunudu', a demon sending several bees.

Bhramaramba Devi of the Srisaila Kshetra protected all the people.

<u>Shrine of Vruddha Mallikharjuna:</u>

The stone Lingam of Siva (story cited above) is next to the Sanctum, which is said to be the oldest structure in the temple complex, dating back to 8000 years.

<u>Installation of some more Siva Lingams near the Sanctum:</u>

- Lord Sri Rama installed 'Sahasra Lingesvara Swamy' Shrine.
- Pandavas also installed some more Lingams
- Shrines of Arthanareswara and Veerabhadra exist.

<u>Adi Shankaracharya's visit to Srisailam:</u>

During his pilgrimage, the great Advaita philosopher Jagadguru Shankaracharya reestablished Hinduism throughout the country. He stayed at Srisailam for some time. Then he composed verses praising Mallikharjuna Swamy in his 'Sivananda Lahari'. Dwadasa Linga Stotram praises Bhramaramba. He wrote 'Bhramaramba Astaka'. In Shankara's words:

"Bhramaramba resides in Srisailam. She is Gayatri. She moves in the skies and is fond of music. She is majestic, having the royal Gail of an elephant. She is the daughter of the great Himavantha. She is beautified with sandal paste. She is worshipped by Ganga and Gautami. Her other name is Gomati".

<u>Temple Festivals and Sevas:</u>

The Temple management during a year is split between Pushpagiri Math (February – May) and Chenchus under a Jangam priest (June – January).

Sivaratri is the main festival, but it is not celebrated on a magnificent scale as in the past.

On the festival night, a big piece of unbleached cloth over 100 yards in length is wrapped around the prominent figure of Nandi and the pinnacle of the temple. This activity is done unobserved by anyone.

Goddess Bhramaramba's festivals come around a month or two after Sivaratri.

Daily Sevas of the Temple:

- Suprabhata Seva – 5:00 AM
- Maha mangala Harati – 6:00 AM.
- Abhishekam – twice – 6:30 AM-12:30 PM & 6:30 PM-8:30 PM
- Kumkumarchana – 6:30 AM – 12:30 PM & 6:30 PM. 8:30 PM
- Ganapati & Rudra Homams – By 7:00 AM
- Chandi yagam – 10:00 AM
- Kalyanam – Everyday at 7:00 PM
- Ekanta seva – 9:30 PM

Holy Places Around Srisailam:

- Pathala Ganga
- Paladhara – Panchadhara waterfalls
- Sikharesvaram – The darshan of temple Sikhara relieves from rebirth
- Sakshi Ganapathi Temple
- Adi Shankara's place of penance
- Hatakesvar Siva Temple

Veera Saivism:

Srisailam is one of the five Veera Saiva Maths, the principal seat of the Jangamas, who play a vital role in the temple activities. Jangamas are also called Lingayats, and they wear Siva Lingas around their necks.

Siva Kathas through Bas-Reliefs & Bronze Images:

Bas-reliefs: The Bas-reliefs of Srisailam are supposed to be the most valuable and wonderful. Lord Siva's different forms connected with the legends are beautifully portrayed. They are found outside courtyard walls (Southern & Eastern sides). They are:

1. In the story of Siva doing Bikshatana, Lord Siva cuts off one of the heads of Lord Brahma, which means Brahma hatya. The skull of Brahma sticks to his hand. To get rid of this (sin), Siva starts Bikshatana and reaches Brahma Kapala in the Himalayas, relieved of his sin and the skull of Brahma. This legend is one of the portrayals.
2. Marriage of Himavanta's daughter with Siva in disguise of an old man
3. Viswakarma is portrayed with the weighing Siva in one pan and all other Gods in another.
4. The story of Kiratarjuneeya
5. Parvati in the form of Chenchu figure
6. Dancing pose of Siva and Kali
7. Siva saving Markandeya
8. The Hindu symbol of eternity is depicted through a bas-relief of Sesha.
9. Siva in the form of Nataraj.

<u>Bronze Images:</u>

- In the dancing pose (Tandava), Siva reminds the cosmic energy.
- Siva and Parvati, called Soma-Skanda, are seated together on a lotus pedestal with the child (Skanda).

Tirumala Temple

Tirumala, the abode of Lord Venkateswara, is India's most visited pilgrimage centre. The history of the temple may date back to 2000 years. People believe that Lord Sri Maha Vishnu manifested himself at Tirumala to redeem them from miseries. Many people visit the holy place to get the darshan of Lord Venkateswara. He is known to the devotees as Srinivasa, Edukondalawadu, Venkata Ramana, Malayappa,

Balaji etc. Tirupati is a town at the foot of the seven hills. It is also cited with Tirumala. A cluster of temples is situated in Tirupati, the temple town, which includes the Padmavati temple of Tiruchanur, Govindaraja Swamy Temple, Kodanda Rama Swamy temple and others.

Location:

Lord Venkateswara temple of Tirumala – Tirupati is the famous Vaishnavite temple of India situated in Andhra Pradesh (Chittoor district). The region lies amidst seven hills in the Eastern Ghats range of mountains (Nallamalais). The holy Tirumala hill is 2000 feet above sea level. The Lord is said to reside in the Seshachala hills; hence, he is introduced as Seshachalavasa. The seven hills are supposed to be the seven hoods of Adisesha, the king of serpents. Thus, these hills are considered the form of 'Meruparvata'. In this context, a beautiful comparison needs to be cited.

While Tirumala hills represent the head of Adisesha, Ahobilala (Narasimha) is represented as the centre of Adisesha and Srisailam (Mallikharjuna) represents the tail end of the serpent king Adisesha. During the former Yugas of Krita, Treta, Dwapara, and Kaliguga, the abode of the Lord is differently named. In the Krita Yuga, the abode is known as Vrishabhachala, Anjanachala during the Tretayuga, Seshachala during the Dwapara Yuga and Venkatachala in the Kaliyuga.

Sources to know About the Lord and the Temple:

There are many sources, primarily literary and epigraphical. The first available reference is literary, which occurs in the Sangam poetry of Tamil Nadu of the first three centuries of the Christian era.

The original name of Tirumala is Vengadam. We have known about the kshetra since the 4th century through the songs and writings of Vaishnava saints (Alwars). Since the 9th century, epigraphy has played a vital role in providing a source of information. Thousands of inscriptions in the

Tirumala Temple, Govidaraja Swamy temple in Tirupati and Tiruchanur (the abode of Goddess Padmavati) furnish a detailed account of the Lord Venkatesa, Gavindaraja and Lord's consort Padmavati Devi. The information spreads between the 9th – 17th centuries.

Figure 3: Tirumala Venkateswara Temple

<u>Temple History:</u>

For comprehensive understanding, India's history is classified as ancient, medieval, and modern. The history classification regarding Tirumala and Tirupati throws light on historical and religious facts. The growth of the temple through the centuries is known.

The history of the Tirumala temple of the ancient period has been from the 1st century A.D. – the 9th century A.D. The source is mainly literature available in Tamil. The medieval period is based on inscriptions. The history is known from the 9th century to the 17th century A.D. From the 18th century A.D., up to date is the modern period. The growth or development is as follows: All great dynasties that ruled South India contributed richly to the temple's development. The Pallavas, the Cholas, the Pandyas, the Vijayanagar emperors and their successors, Nayakas, made rich offerings to the Lord.

<u>Patronage under the Vijayanagara:</u>

All the dynasties that ruled Vijayanagar, namely Sangama, Saluva, Tuluva, and Araviti, patronized the temple as per the epigraphical records. Rulers outdid one another in endowing the temple with rich offerings.

- Krishnadevaraya visited the temple for the first time on February 20, 1513, and was gifted a crown of nine jewels, a three-stringed necklace containing pearls and precious stones and 25 Silver plates. His queens, Chinnaji and Tirumaladevi, each gave him a gold cup.
- During his second visit on May 2 of the same year, he gifted the Utsavigrahas a sword set with diamonds, rubies, sapphires, a sword sheath, a pendant, two gold strings, and three crowns.
- On July 6, 1514, after capturing the Udayagiri fort, he visited Lord Venkateswara and performed the splendid ceremonial of the Lord, bathing his image with gold coins (30,000).
- In October 1515, on the occasion of Kalinga victory, he gifted 'Prabhavali'.

- In October 1516, according to the Kamalapurana inscription, Krishnadevaraya visited the Lord along with Tirumaladevi.
- His last visit was on February 12, 1521, and he gifted four costly jewelled ornaments. Tirumaladevi was also gifted an ornament with nine jewels.

<u>Patronage under the Modern Period (18th century A.D. – up to date):</u> With the decline of the Vijayanagar empire, there is a shortage of inscriptions in the temple. The British took over the management of all the temples in South India, including Tirumala – Tirupati (1801 AD). During the middle of the 19th century, the British desired to relinquish their management of temples. The administration of Tirumala-Tirupati was conferred to the then Mahant Sri Seva Dasuji (Hathiramji Math) in 1843 AD. Collector of North Arcot district issued a Sanad. Renovation activities started under the new administration, including Tirths, primarily Pushkarina.

The administration of Math ended in 1933. In 1951, the Religious Endowments Act came into force, followed by the Act of 1966 (A.P. Govt). After that, the Board of Trustees came into existence. In 1979, the TTD bill was passed, and the temple management became autonomous under the control of a Board.

<u>Sri Venkateswara Swamy Temple of Tirumala – Beginnings, Additions, Changes to Structures, Gopurams & Prakarams:</u>

When it was initially constructed, Lord Venkateswara Swamy Temple & Tirumala, it must have been a simple structure with a Garbhagriha and mukha mandapa and an Antarala and Pradakshina path surrounding it. Plenty of references are found in the inscriptions regarding the renovation, rebuilding, and addition of later structures. In the process, overlapping is noticeable in the walls of the original sanctum (13th century).

The temple's area is confined to two acres. It is 415 feet long and 263 feet wide and has three enclosures or Prakaras centred around the holy sanctum of the main deity. The inner Prakara has passages on the south, west, and north. The sanctum stands at the western end.

There is an open hall with sixteen pillars named 'Tirumaman' mandapa. Two giant bells are placed there. This structure was built in 1417. From this mandapa, the entrance is through a golden door popularly known as 'Bangaru Vakili'. On either side of the entrance are Jaya Vijaya (Dwarapalakas). 'Suprabhatam', the morning hymn, is sung before the door.

'Snapana mandapa', which has four pillars of the Vijayanagar times, is another structure the pilgrims reach via Rama Meda, Mukkoti Pradakshina. The stone step before the sanctum is called 'Kula sekhara padi'. The walls of the sanctum are supposed to belong to the 8th or 9th centuries (double walls).

<u>Structures, Gopurams, Prakarams and Images:</u>

Structures include the sanctum. The Prakara of the sanctum includes the Vimana Pradakshina. There is a mandapa and several rooms which contain shrines of Varadaraja, Narasimha, and Ramanuja, the saint. The Kalyana mandapa is a Vijayanagar structure, and we find the portrait of Annamacharya here.

The inner second gopura leads from Vimana Pradakshina to the first Prakara (Sampangi Prakara), similar to the first one. The first Prakara, which is more extensive, contains several structures. Krishnaraya mandapa contains some portrait bronzes of Krishnadeva, Tirumladevi, and Chinnaji. Another ruler, Tirumala, and his wife also stand here. Venkatapati, another ruler and Todaramal, his mother, and his wife are also seen here. Another structure worth mentioning is Ranga mandapa. For some time, the image of Ranganatha of Sri Rangam was preserved because of Muslim threats (14th century).

Tirumalaraya Mandapa is another one built in 1473, later extended and named 'Aina Mandapa' by the 16th century. In the open courtyard of this Prakara stand four mandapas constructed by Saluva Narasimha (1486-91).

Flagstaff and Balipeetha (Second gopura) are important. Outside the temple, 1000 pillared mandapa that existed are presently demolished, facing controversies and criticisms.

<u>The Idol of Lord Venkateswara:</u>

The idol of Lord Venkateswara is majestic, beautiful, and superbly executed. The Lord's arresting features give an overpowering sense of divinity. His facial expression and dark eyes indicate 'Sam Dristi', and his smile is tranquil.

Regarding the identity of the Lord, there was some dispute or controversy:

- The idol is a Vaishnavite or Saivite
- The idol is a Sakti idol

The supporting points of both Saivite and Sakti are as follows:

Saivite: The Lord's crown is richly adorned with flowing hair (Jatajuta) resting on the shoulders. Naga is depicted as coiled around Lord's right arm. Puja is done with Bilvadalas, which are used in the Sivarchana. There is a crescent mark on the head of the Lord. The crystal Lingam is present, which proves that the Temple is Saivite.

Sakti: Lord Venkateswara is also called as Balaji. Durga is known as Bala so that the idol may be Durga or Sakti. Galigopuram is known as 'Kaligopuram'. The use of sandal paste and turmeric indicates Sakti worship. 'Tomala seva' means 'Bhagavati Aradhana'. The chanting of 'Sukta mantras' indicates Sakteya worship.

The Alwars, Puranas, and the Sthala Purana say that Lord Venkateswara is the only god who can bestow happiness and salvation in Kaliyuga. The shrine is mentioned in the Varaha Purana and Bhavishyottara Purana.

Saint Ramanuja of the 12th century is said to have settled the above dispute between the Saivite and Sakti form of the idol and established the worship of Venkatesa or Srinivasa.

The idol of the Lord is standing with the left hand extending to the left thigh. The right hand is known as Varada hasta.

For Swamy's daily abhishekam, a silver idol named Kautuka is used. Snapana Srinivasa Murthy's idol is adjusted to Kautuka. In this temple, no minor shrines exist. The Original Sankhu-Chakras were not in the idol, but Ramanujacharya proposed placing them right after worship.

<u>Sage Bhrigu's Episode & Consequent Effects:</u>

Once, many Rishis assembled on the banks of the Holy Ganges and wished to perform a Yaga. Then Narada asked them to which deity they would offer the Yagnaphala. Then, the Rishis approached Sage Bhrigu to solve the problem. Bhrigu wished to identify who was the ideal among the trio of Brahma, Vishnu, and Maheswara. On this divine mission, the Sage first went to the abode of Lord Brahma, but Brahma could not notice the Sage since he was busy chanting Vedas. So, he went to Siva's abode. The Sage was also not seen since the divine couple were engaged in sports. The Sage felt that he was insulted in both places and proceeded to Vaikuntham and found that Lord Vishnu was in a similar posture with his consort Lakshmi. Thus, the angry Sage kicked Lord Vishnu on his chest, the dwelling place of Maha Lakshmi. Vishnu immediately got up, massaged the Rishi's foot and pierced the third eye (eye of ego) underneath the foot. Bhrigu realized his sin and returned to the rishis on the Yagnasthala. He declared that Sri Maha Vishnu was the most deserving deity to receive Yagnaphala.

Meanwhile, Sri Mahalakshmi left Vaikuntham for Kolhapur after Bhrigu kicked Vishnu at her dwelling place of Vishnu. Vishnu could not bear the separation; he also left Vaikuntham, wandered here and there, and finally came to Seshachala. At Lakshmi's request, Brahma and Siva took the form of a cow and calf. Lakshmi became a milkmaid and sold the cow and calf to the local king. The cow used to empty her on the anthill under which Lord Srinivasa stayed, thus nourishing the Lord every day. The king and cow herd, suspecting foul play on the cow not yielding milk, one day followed the cow and beat cow with a stick while it was amplifying under into the anthill. But the Lord resting underneath the anthill received the blow and cursed the king. However, the Lord, moved by the king's prayers for mercy, promised him that he would marry his daughter later. It was the same king who was later born Akasaraju.

According to the most popular legend, Srinivasa came to Earth and was adopted by Bahuladevi (Yasoda in her previous birth). Bhudevi's incarnation is said to be Padmavati, daughter of Aakasaraju, the local king who gave her to Srinivasa, and Kalyanotsav has been celebrated. All this happened during the absence of Sridevi when she was doing penance. Later, the three, namely Srinivasa, Padmavati, and Sridevi, meet on Venkatadri Hill. In the embarrassing situation, Srinivasa turned into a stone. Padmavati stayed at Alamelumangapuram (Tiruchanur), while Sridevi went to Kolhapur in Maharashtra.

<u>Customs of the Temple</u>:

The temple's customs to date include anointing the full image of the Lord with camphor and offering all the hair on their heads as a sacrifice to the Lord.

<u>Other Idols in the Garbhariha</u>:

1. Bhoga Srinivasa
2. Ugra Srinivasa
3. Koluvu Srinivasa
4. Malayappa (Utsavamurthi)
5. The Krishna idol
6. Idols of Sri Rama, Sita, Lakshmana, and Sugreeva.
7. Sudarsana

<u>Worship of the Lord:</u>

'Venkatachala Itihasa Mala' prescribes the main items for conducting worship. This work is divided into seven parts. The first three parts narrate the Vaishnava characters of the image. The other four parts deal with Saint Ramanuja and his disciple Anantarya's instructions.

Sri Ramanuja restored the worship rituals according to Vaikhasana Agama after performing the purificatory rite and repairing the Vimana over the main shrine (Anandinilayam). Saint Ramanuja restored systems already in existence and brought new change for the sake of permanence. Some of the reforms of Ramanuja are as follows:

1. Ablutions to the Lord were arranged every Friday as per the Vaikhasana Agama.
2. 'Urdhava Pundra' (Tilak) on the face mark of the Lord was prescribed (mixture of camphor) for four days. For three days, i.e., from Monday, white earth (Namam) is applied.
3. All the Jewels and ornaments are removed on Thursday. Venkateswara was to be dressed only with flowers.
4. The recitation of Nachiyar Tiruppavai was restored.
5. Vaikhasana priest named Bimbadhara was entrusted with the Temple work.
6. Two wells were restored for the temple's use, and the images of Srinivasa and Bhoodevi were set up there. Flowers used for the temple service should be thrown into the well.
7. Sri Ramanuja installed the image of Sri Rama as giving refuge to Vibhishana. The image of Sita was also installed. Sri Ramanuja also built the Sri Govindaraja Swary Temple at Tirupati.
8. According to a popular legend, the Sankha and Chakra were originally not in the idol (Controversy of Saivite or Vaishnavite). Sri Ramanuja proposed the Sankhu Chakras should be placed before the deity at night after worship.

9. After performing the last item of worship, Ramanuja said that garlands should be preserved in the temple of Vishwaksena, the garden deity.

10. Regarding the residents of Tirumala, the Saint said that those in Swamy Seva should only reside, and the rest of the people should reside in Tirupati.

11. Flowers should be grown but should be dedicated to the Lord only.

12. Killing of birds and animals on the top of the hill is prohibited. No one should be allowed to die on the top of the hill but brought down.

<u>Darshan of the Lord:</u>

The Lord's darshan has two types. First, there is a free darshan called 'Sarva Darshanam' for all the devotees. Second, there is darshan or seva on payment of a fee. To the temple, this is technically called 'Arjitam'.

Arjita Sevas in the Srivari temple of Tirumala are again classified into three types: daily Sevas, weekly Sevas and periodical Sevas.

Daily Sevas: There are eight sevas.

1. Suprabhatam – Everyday
2. Tomala Seva – Tue – Wed-Thu
3. Archana – Tue – Wed-Thu
4. Kalyanotsavam – Everyday
5. Dolotsavam/ Unjal Seva – Everyday
6. Arjita Brahmotsavam – Everyday
7. Vasantotsavam. – Everyday
8. Sahasra Deepalankara Seva – Everyday

Weekly Sevas: There are seven of them.

1. Vasantha Puja – Monday
2. Astadala Pada Padmaradhana – Tuesday
3. Sahasra Kalasabhishekam Wednesday

4. Tiruppavada Seva – Thursday
5. Melchat Vastram – Friday
6. Poorabhishekam – Friday
7. Nijapada Darsanam – Friday

Periodical Sevas: They are eight in number.

1. Float Festival – Feb/March
2. Annual Vasantotsavam – March/April
3. Padmavati Parinayam – May
4. Abhidheyaka Abhishekam – June
5. Pushpa Pallaki – July
6. Pavitrotsavam – August
7. Pushpa yagam – November
8. Koil Alwar Tirumanjunam – Yearly four times

Prasadams:

Food offerings started during the Vijayanagar period. Today, a variety of Prasadams are distributed and sold. Annaprasadams (Pulihora, Daddhojanam, Pongali), Vada, Laddu, Appam, Dosa etc., are some quoted.

Festivals (Utsavams):

Tirumala attracts large crowds from all over India as the Lord fulfils the desires of the devotees, and the devotees, in turn, fulfil their vows. Tirumala festivals attract devotees. The following are the festivals or Utsavams conducted:

1. Vasantotsavam
2. Kalyanotsavam
3. Unjala Seva
4. Brahmotsavam
5. Teppotsavam and
6. Pavitrotsavam

Vasantotsavam is celebrated for three or fewer days. Brahmotsavam is the most famous and essential festival suggested by Sastras and Agamas. Vasantotsavam and Brahmotsavam are crucial to drawing the crowds. Brahma started this festival, hence the name of Brahmotsavam. Before 966 AD, only one Brahmotsavam was conducted at Tirumala. In the 10th century, two Brahmotsavams were conducted. By about the 14th century, the Brahmotsav was performed three times a year.

On the day before the Utsav, Ankurarpana is done. Poornakumbham is installed. Brahmotsavam is an 11-day festival. The important days are the 5th (Garuda Seva), 8th (Rathotsavam), and 11th days (the Procession deity is taken to Swamy Pushkarini).

<u>Vahanams:</u>

On the auspicious occasions of the temple, Vahanams are used, and they are as follows:

1. Sarvabhupala Vahanam
2. Golden Garuda
3. Silver Garuda
4. China Sesha
5. Chandra Prabha
6. Gaja Vachana
7. Aswa Vahana
8. Simha Vahana
9. Hamsa Vahana and
10. Hanumantha Vahana

<u>Tirthams:</u>

There are several sacred Tirthas in the hills on the top and below. They are:

1. Swamy Pushkarini
2. Akasa Ganga (water taken for Abhishekam)
3. Kapila Tirtham (Tirupati)

<u>Architecture and Sculpture:</u>

The Tirumala temple is a masterpiece of South Indian architecture with a gopuram facing the east. This temple does not present a variegated pattern or mixture of different styles of architecture like several other South Indian temples. The structures and sculptures are beautiful. Matsyavatara, Kaliyamardana, Chaturbhuja Venugopala, Gajendra moksha, Srinivasa kalyanam, Mohini Vishnu, and Garuda, Gandabherunda, Surya Narasimha, Hanuman carrying Sanjeevani, Sri Rama Pattabhishekam are said to be beautiful sculptures. Of course, the Vijayanagara impact is noticeable in and out of the temple complex.

To conclude, Lord Venkateswara's glory and greatness are indescribable, and every day is a day of the festival in the Tirumala temple. This is popularly told in Telugu as 'Nitya kalyanam, Pacha Toranam'.

<u>Tirumala Temple – Role as a Spiritual cum Center of Social Activity:</u>

The Temples of South India are not only spiritual but also vital in playing the role of social activity. Uplift of humanity in all walks of life is the motto of Tirumala temple, which gave rise to the whole gamut of social activity. Several schools, colleges, and universities (Sri Venkateswara University and Padmavati University) were established to promote education. Sanskrit Vidyapeeth, a Centre for Vedic Learning, Music, and Fine Arts, was established. The institutions are funded by TTD (Tirumala Tirupati Devasthanam). The temple employed several people with varying professions like Devadasis (dancers), florists, musicians, cooks, accountants, engineers, masons, architects, etc. Therefore, the Tirumala temple became a centre of economic activity.

Tirupati

There are several notable temples in and around Tirupati. Some of them are listed below:

- Sri Govindaraja Swamy Temple: This is an ancient Temple. Saint Ramanujacharya consecrated the shrine of Govindaraja Swamy in 1130 AD. The deity is seen in the reclining posture of Sri Ranganatha in Si Rangam.
- Kodanda Rama Swamy Temple: Sri Rama's Temple was built to commemorate the visit of Lord Sri Rama, Sita, and Lakshmana to Tirupati after their return from Lanka.
- Kapileswara Swamy Temple: This temple of Lord Shiva is situated at the foot of seven hills. Sage Kapila installed the Siva Linga here, which is popularly known as Kapila Tirtham or Alwar Tirtham.
- Alamelumangapuram (Tiruchanur): The consort of Lord Venkateswara, Sri Padmavati Devi is here. The Goddess is seated on a lotus flown in the Padma Sarovar sacred tank.
- Srinivasa Mangapuram: The Temple is that of Sri Kalyana Venkateswara Swamy. According to the legendary source, after his marriage with Padmavati Devi, the Lord stayed here for some time before proceeding to Tirumala through Srivari Mettu. In the 16th century, Tallapaka Tiruvenkatanatha renovated the shrine.
- Narayanavanam: The shrine is of Kalyana Venkateswara. The Lord's marriage to Padmavati took place here. Akasaraju built the temple.
- Nagalapuram: Lord Veda Narayana Swamy is here. Vishnu's Matsavarataram form is seen here along with Sridevi and Bhoodevi.
- Appalayagunta: In this temple, Venkateswara idol is seen with Abhaya hasta.
- Venugopala Swamy Temple: At Karaveti Nagaram, Swamy is seen with Rukmini and Satyabhama.
- Vayalpadu: An ancient Pattabli Ramaswamy temple is here.

Sri Kalahasti Temple

Sri Kalahastiswara is the great Saivite temple about 36 km from Tirupati in the Chittoor district of Andhra Pradesh. Gnana Prasunamba is the consort of Sri Kalahastiswara. The temple dates from ancient times. It is said that Kalahasti is a part of Seshasaila or Mount Meru. The temple is located in the most beautiful surroundings; on one side, the Swarnamukhi River flows, and on the other, the town is bounded by hills. This magnificent temple of Sri Kalahastiswara is built beautifully by the great Vijayanagara ruler Sri Krishnadevaraya. Gopurams to the outer Prakarams further added beauty to the onlookers.

Legend:

A spider, an elephant, and a snake worshipped Siva; hence, God is named Sri Kalarhastiswara, and the town is named Sri Kalahasti. In ancient times, a spider worshipped the Lord by spinning a web over Siva Linga, a snake by placing a gem over it, and an elephant by washing the Linga with water. These three are said to have attained Salvation. The deity is believed to belong to Tretayuga, and Sri Kalahasti is known as 'Dakshina Kasi'.

Siva Linga in this kshetra is one of the five supreme Lingas, representing the five significant elements of Water, Fire, Air, Wind, and Earth. The Siva Linga of Sri Kalahasti is known as 'Vayu Linga' (Light flickering in the same temple's sanctum sanctorum).

The story of Kannappa:

Kannappa was a tribesman and a great devotee of Lord Siva who worshipped him in a rough way to earn Salvation. This episode is found in the great Sanskrit work of Adi Shankaracharya, namely 'Sivananda Lahari' and the Tamil work of 'Periya Puranam'.

Kannappa sacrificed one of his eyes as an offering to the Lord and was about to offer the other eye as well, but Lord Siva prevented him.

<u>Historic and Puranic References</u>:

The temple was built at the Kailasagiri by the Pallava kings and later by Tondaman Chakravarti. The Cholas renovated the temple. Kulottunga Chola superintended the Galigopuram in the main entrance (11th century A.D.). Outer Prakara was built in the 12th century by Veera Narasimha Yadavaraya. Vijayanagara rulers developed the mandapams. According to epigraphical sources, Sri Krishnadevaraya built 100 pillared mandapa in 1516 A.D.

The temple is supposed to have been dedicated to Dakshinamurthi (facing south).

As per the Puranic references, Skanda Purana may be referred to in addition to Saiva and Linga Puranas. Arjuna visited Sri Kalahasti and worshipped the Lord. Dhurjati's Kalahastiswara Mahatyam is another source.

<u>Kalahastiswara Lingam</u>:

The Siva Lingam is on a pedestal in the shape of an elephant's trunk with tusks on either side and a figure of the spider at the bottom. In addition, there is the appearance of a five-hooded snake. The Lingam is black (stone idol).

The spider's name is 'Sri', the serpent is 'Kala', and the elephant is 'Hasti'. Thus, the name of the town is Sri Kalahasti.

<u>Goddess</u>:

Gnana Prasunamba is the Goddess and is said to be Lord Venkateswara's sister of Tirumala.

<u>Paatala Vinayaka</u>:

There is an underground cell where Ganesa is worshipped as Paatala Vinayaka. The shrine is 35 feet beneath the surface, said to mark the level of the river. Almost crawling is needed to visit the shrine. The image was carved on a rough stone.

<u>Tirthas:</u>

Famous and sacred Tirthas are Harihara, Kalinga, Sahasra Linga, Markandeya, Mayura, Bharadwaja, Narada, Saraswati, Suka, Brahma, Manikarnika, and Tatwa.

Puranas also mentioned Swarnamukhi as a sacred one.

<u>Rahu-Ketu Pujas:</u>

People worship Rahu and Ketu Grahas to get relief from the evil effects. This system is quite popular in Sri Kalahasti.

<u>Festivals:</u>

Maha Sivaratri is the most important festival, lasting ten days during February-March. The fifth day is Maha Sivaratri.

Panchaaramas – The Saiva Aaramas

Dwadasa Jyotirlingas, Trilinga Dhams (Srisailam, Kalahasti, and Draksharamam), and Panchaarama are famous Saivite centres that attract millions of devotees, especially during Kartika Maasa. Panchaaramas are known for their puranic and spiritual significance. They are in Andhra Pradesh's East Godavari, West Godavari, and Guntur districts. Puranic sources reveal the prominence of the temples.

There are two versions regarding the formation of Panchaaramas.

- Tripurasura worshipped the Siva Linga. His devilish activities instigated Lord Siva to kill him. After his death, the Siva Linga was broken into five pieces, which formed Panchaarama kshetras.
- Kumara Swamy, son of Siva, killed Tarakasura, and from his stomach, Siva Linga split into five pieces, forming Panchaarama kshetras.

Whatever may be the story, the information of the kshetras is as follows:

Amaravati

Amaravati, the state capital of Andhra Pradesh, created on 2 June 2014, is famous worldwide as the seat of Buddhism and Hinduism.

Lord Siva is worshipped here as Amaresvara. Amaravati and Dharanikota, which are adjacent, were the seats of the ancient Andhra rulers. The Temple of Amaresvara stands on the banks of the river Krishna. The temple was built in the 11th century A.D. Siva Linga is made of marble and is 15 feet in height. Among the Pancharamas, the Siva Linga here is the tallest. There are two floors, and Abhishekams are performed from the second floor. It is said that Lord Indra installed the Siva Linga.

The temple has three Prakaras. In the first Prakara, the deities are Pranavesvara, Kasi Visvesvara, Uma Maheswara, Agasthesvara, Parthivesvara, Somesvara, Koralesvara, Veerabhadra, and Tripura Sundari Devi. In addition, there is a Kalyana mandapa on the way to the River Krishna.

In the second Prakara, Vignesvara, Kalabhairava, and Kumara Swamy temples are there. Navagraha mandapa and Yagnasala are there.

In the third Prakara, Srisaila Mallesvara, Kasi Visveswara and Surya temples are there. Venugopala Swamy is the kshetraplaka here.

Hiuen Tsang, a Chinese traveller in 640 AD, visited the place and called it 'Tenakachaka – Dhanyakalaka'. He said the Buddhist aaramas are almost vacant, replacing Hindu Temples.

Vasireddy Venkata Naidu constructed the town of Amaravati in the 18th century. Colin Mackenzie also visited the spot to study Buddhist sites.

Ksheera Rama Temple

This temple is situated in Palakol in the West Godavari district, about 8 km from Narsapur. Lord Siva is known as Rama Lingeswara because Lord Sri Rama installed this as he did in Rameswaram. Palakol is derived from the term 'Pala Kolanu', which means 'Pool of Milk'. According to a legend, a devotee of Siva named Upamanya was digging a Pushkarini chanting the Panchakshari mantra of 'Om Namahsivaya'. Surprisingly, he found milk instead of water, and it was used for Abhishekam and the Siva Linga daily during his lifetime. The Chalukyas constructed the temple during the 10-11th centuries. The Rajagopuram, with nine floors and 125 feet in height, is purely South Indian in style. The Siva Lingam, white, is 2 ½ feet tall. It is said that, before the commencement of Uttarayana and Dakshinayana, the rays of the Sun come through the second floor of Rajagopuram and touch Siva Lingam.

The other temples are Brahma, Visveswara, Gokarnesvara, and Goddess Lakshmi Devi. It is said that devotees are blessed with Punyaphala if they stay here for one day, which is equivalent to one year at Kasi.

Somesvara Temple

Somesvara temple is situated at Bhimavaram (Gunupudi) in the West Godavari district. Bhima I built this Pancharama kshetra during the 9th century. It is said that Chandra, the Moon God, installed this Siva Linga, which is five feet high. The Linga changes its colours to black, brown, and off-white on the new moon and full moon days. Perhaps this is according to Chandragamana. This kshetra is the pratista made by Soma or Chandra; hence, Siva is known as Somesvara.

Srinatha mentioned the Somesvara temple of Gunupudi, Bhimavaram, in his 'Bhimakhandam'. 'Pudi', 'Pundi', 'Poodi' means village. The temple, or 'Gudi', has a history since ancient times.

The temple constructed by Chalukya Bhima in the 9th century AD had two floors. Lord Siva (Somesvara) is on the ground floor, and Annapurnadevi is on the first floor. This arrangement is unique to this kshetra.

Kumararama – Bhimesvara Swamy Temple

Kumararama Bhimesvara Swamy temple, similar to Draksharama temple, is said to have been installed by Kumara Swamy. It also consists of two floors and is situated at Samarlakot in the East Godavari district, about 60 km from Rajahmundry.

The Siva Linga is 14 feet tall and known as Spatika Linga Bhimesvara. Bala Tripura Sundari is the Mother Goddess. Janandana Swamy is the kshetrapalaka along with Sridevi and Bhoodevi.

The eastern Chalukyas (892 – 922 AD) built this temple; epigraphical and literary sources provide ample information about it. The inscriptions (pillars) provide information about the temple's history of the 15th and 16th centuries and particulars. The temple faces east and has beautiful Gopurams. In front of the temple, there is a lake. The Maha Sivaratri festival is celebrated on a large scale and attended by thousands of devotees.

The other deities of the temple are Kalabhairava, Chandramoulisvara, Uma sahita Mrutyunjaya and Navagrahas.

Draksharama

Draksharama kshetra, one of the Trilinga kshetras and one of the Astadasa Shaktipeethas is a famous Panchaarama kshetra of Andhra Pradesh. One can reach this holy Siva Kshetra from Ramachandrapuram, Rajahmundry and Kakinada.

Bhimesvara Swamy is the deity of the place. The temple is famous for its architecture and historical importance. Draksharama attracts large numbers of pilgrims every year, especially during Sivaratri days.

Chalukya Bhima built the temple during the 9th and 10th centuries. During the reign bf Reddis (14th century), four Rajagopurams and five prakaras were constructed. The temple's campus is 12 acres. The Siva Linga is 14 feet tall. Manilkyamba is the main deity and one of the Shaktipeethas.

Among all the temples of Andhra Pradesh, this is the richest in inscriptions (381) between 1356 and 1434 AD.

<u>Name of Draksharama:</u>

The is from the name of Daksha Prajapati, who performed the Yagna. Parvati is his daughter. Though she was interested in attending the Yagna, Daksha never invited the divine couple. She attended, though uninvited, but she was insulted. Consequently, she jumped into the fire and ended her life. Siva became furious. Out of his sweat, Veerabhadra was born, and he killed Daksha.

The seven sages (Vasista, Bharadwaja, Kasyapa, Atri, Viswamitra, Gautama, Jamadagni) are said to have brought the waters from seven rivers to Draksharama and performed Abhishekam to Lord Siva (Sapta Godavari tirtha—Antarvahini of Draksharama).

Draksharama is also called southern Banaras. Vedavyasa is said to have established this temple; Veda Vyasa, cursed by Kasi Annapurna Devi, came here and worshipped Siva.

One of the other temples here is Sri Lakshminarayana Swamy (Sri Ranna as kshetrapalaka).

<u>Architecture:</u>

The Draksharama temple is a blend of Chola-Chalukyan styles reflecting Dravidian features.

Annavaram

Sri Veeva Venkata Satyanarayana Swamy temple of East Godavari district in the state of Andhra Pradesh is a celebrated one. The name of the Goddess is Ananta Lakshmi Satyavati. Though the temple is not ancient, it is very powerful. The temple is of recent origin. There is no Sthala mahatyam for the temple. There are no epigraphical records. Annavara Kshetra Vaibhavam has been narrated in Revakhandam of Skanda Purana. It attracts pilgrims in huge numbers.

<u>Location of the Temple:</u> The temple is located on the Ratnagiri hill. Ratnakara is the name of a sage who was the brother of Bhadra (Bhadradri temple). Ratnakara and Bhadra are the sons of 'Meru' (Lord of the hills). Lord Vishnu graced the hill as Sri Veera Venkata Satyanarayana.

<u>Annavaram:</u>

'Anina' means divine, and 'Varam' means boon. The Lord fulfils the wishes of the devotees, and hence, the place is known as Annavaram. The Lord is said to be Trimurthi aakrutudu (Brahma, Vishnu, and Maheswara).

<u>Construction of the Temple:</u>

The temple was built in 1893 by a Zamindar named Ramanaiah (the Lord appeared in his dream and ordered a temple). During the Kharanama year, on Sravana Suddha Vidiya, Makha nakshatra, the Mahanarayana yantra was installed by the monks from Badari.

The hill is small and encircled by green fields and a Pampa river. The temple is reached by 460 steps.

<u>The shape of the temple:</u>

The temple is chariot-shaped with four wheels in its four corners. At the centre, the Lord is installed (sanctum sanctorum). The temple is double-storied

<u>Role of Narada:</u>

Devarshi Narada was interested in helping humanity by relieving its sufferings, so he prayed to Lord Vishnu for Upadesa. Then, the Lord informed Narada to perform a vrata by the people to relieve suffering.

In this context, Satyanarayana vrata came into being performed by devotees, especially couples and newly married couples. People of all classes perform this Vrata for wealth, education, begetting children, relief from illness, and general prosperity. There are spacious halls to perform the Vratas; at a time, two to three thousand can perform simultaneously.

Bhishma Ekadasi is the auspicious day to perform the Vrata or on a Purnima day. Prasadam, made of wheat flour, is a speciality here.

Festivals:

Swamy Kalyana is performed on Vaisakha Suddha Ekadasi, and the Lord is taken to a procession in Garuda Vahana. Rathotsava, Pushpayaga, and Chakra Snana are the essential activities of the temple on this occasion.

Deri Navaratri, Sravan Suddha Ekadasi, Sitarama Kalyana, Kanaka Durga Yatra, and Teppa Utsavam are more festivals celebrated here.

Archana:

Every day, Archana is done both to the yantra and idols. There are Sri Chakra and Salagramas, which are also worshipped.

The other idols here (on the ground floor) are Aditya, Ambika, Ganapati and Maheswara.

Thus, Annavararm is gaining growing popularity not only in Andhra Pradesh but also all over India. There is no exaggeration to say that Annavaram is called the second Tirupati.

Vijayawada – Indrakiladri Temples of Malleswara and Kanaka Durga

Vijayawada is named after the Eastern Chalukyan king Vijayaditya – II (806-846 AD). There are various names for this place. Arjuna, the Pandava hero, intended to do penance; in this context, he was searching for a suitable location. Tribals Trikotiboya, son of Kaliyamaboya, showed the place named 'Pechachavada'. Its corrupt form is 'Vechchavada' and Bezzavada.

In Sanskrit, it appears as Vezzavada and Vijayawada. The spot where Arjuna's penance was was Indrakiladri Hill. Vijayavate is the name found in mythology; some inscriptions mentioned it as Rajendra Cholapura. According to another interesting story, at one time, huge boulders blocked the flow of the river Krishna. Then Siva dictated the river bore a hole('bezzam' in Telugu) through the rocks, hence the name Bezawada; thus, the historicity of Vijayawada is excellent, being the gateway of coastal Andhra Pradesh starting from the early Paleolithic age.

Malleswara Swamy Temple

Malleswara, also called Mallikharjuna Swamy, is said to have been installed by Dharmaraja as a token of the South's victory. Tribhuvanamalla, a Western Chalukyan king of the 10th century A.D., constructed the temple.

There are about one hundred stone inscriptions on the premises of this temple and the Indrakiladri hill. A Sanskrit inscription on the Kiratarjuna pillar narrates the legend connected with this place. The inscriptions provide historical information regarding Chalukya-Chola rulers and their chiefs. An inscription from the 10th century A.D. provides a sculptural illustration of Kiratarjuneeya's story—the penance of Arjuna to get Pasapatastra from Siva.

On the holy Indrakiladri, Durgadevi was present in the form of Mahishasura mardini is popularly known as Kanaka Durga. Lord Brahma performed a hundred Asvamedha Yagas, prayed to Siva with 'Mallika flowers', and requested that he stay here along with Kanaka Durga. Hence, Swamy is known as Mallikharjuna. Brahma's intention was fulfilled, and since then, he has performed the Kalyana of Sri Durga Malleswara Swamy. Over time, Adi Shankaracharya reinstalled Malleswara Lingam.

Arjuna, also called Siva as Malleswara. The Lord is also called Mahadeva Malleswara. Arjuna used to worship this Lord and his consort. Siva and his consort gave darshan to him and gifted Pasupata. Vijaya installed a Siva Linga named Vijayeswara on the southern part of Indrakiladri. On the Maha Sivaratri day, thousands of pilgrims throng these Siva temples, and Rathotsavams are celebrated.

Kanaka Durga Devi Temple

Kanaka Durga temple is an ancient one on a hill called Indrakiladri in Vijayawada. The origin of this deity is unknown. However, she is Swayambhu or self-manifest. She is also known as Chandi or the destroyer of the demon Durgama who was causing havoc in Dakshinapatha. The hill where Kanaka Durga temple is situated is known as Kanaka Konda.

Goddess Kanaka Durgamma is considered the patron Goddess of Vijayawada. This temple is said to be second only to the Tirupati-Tirumala temple. During Navaratri festivals, devotees come in thousands.

Durga Devi's idol is decorated with glittering ornaments and colourful and beautiful flowers. Devotees present the Goddess with expensive sarees. A gold-plated Vimana tops the Sanctum Sanctorum.

Ganesh, Nataraj, Sivakama Sundari, and Subrahmanya are the other shrines in this temple.

There is a mirror hall called 'Addala Mandapam'. A miniature replica of the Goddess is placed on a swing. Next to this is Malleswara Swamy temple.

Jagadguru Adi Shankaracharya installed Srichakra to appease the Goddess's furious look.

Festivals: During Asvayuja masa, from Suddha Padyami to Dasami, the Navaratri celebrations are conducted with pomp and glory. During the nine days of the Navaratri festival, the deity is decorated in nine forms. Kanaka Durga temple is one of the 51 Shaktipeethas in India.

Krishnadevaraya's patronage: According to an inscription of 1518 AD, Krishnadevaraya constructed Antaralaya, Ranga mandapa and Bhoga mandapa to the Devi.

Sri Narasimha Kshetras or Temples of the State

Most Sri Narasimha kshetras or temples in India are located in the Telugu-speaking Andhra Pradesh and Telangana states. However, some are also situated in Tamil Nadu and Karnataka.

The deity, Narasimha, is half man and half lion. Lord Vishnu, out of the necessity of 'Dushta Sikshana' and 'Sashta Rakshana' and prayers of sages, took the form of ten incarnations (Dasavataras). Narasimhavatara is the fourth one. Vishnu's avatars are classified into three categories:

- Purnavataras (complete human form) – Rama and Krishna
- Emotional Avatars – Parasurama and Narasimha.
- Amsavatars (With the amsa of Sri Maha Vishnu) – Matsya, Kurma, Varaha, Vamana, Balarama and Kalki.

The Story:

Baala bhakta of Lord Vishnu, named Prahlada, was the son of a demon king, Hiranyakasipa, who was blessed with a whole life, not to be killed by man or beast inside or outside a palace, by day or night. Hence, Vishnu, adopting the form of a lion-headed man (Narasimha), came to the palace at dusk and hid in a pillar at the entrance, out of which he sprung and killed the demon king Hiranyakasipa. Some sculptures show this. Some show the demon king on the lap of Narasimha, tearing out his entrails (intestines).

The purpose of Narasimha's incarnation was to protect his devotees. Adi Shankaracharya prayed to him to protect him from dangerous situations. In this context, he wrote 'Karava lambana Stotra'.

People usually visit 'Pancha Narasimha kshetras' and 'Nava Narasimha kshetras' in the Telugu-speaking Andhra Pradesh and Telangana states.

Sri Varaha Lakshmi Narasimha Swamy of Simhachalam

Simhachalam, once called Samhagiri, is in the eastern ghats near Vishakhapatnam or Vizag. It is the abode of Sri Varaha Lakshmi

Narasimha Swamy and is one of the most ancient and famous temples. Devotees call him Simhadri Appanna.

<u>Background of the name of the God:</u>

Jaya and Vijaya were the dwarapalakas in Vaikuntham, the abode of Lord Vishnu. Once, Four Kumaras (Sages Sanaka, Sanandana, Sanatana, and Sanatkumara) cursed the Dwarapalakas as they had not allowed the sages for the darshan of the Lord. Consequently, they became demons, namely Hiranyaksha and Hiranyakasipa. The first one attempted to take away Lakshmi Devi, and Varaha Swamy (3rd incarnation of Vishnu) saved her. The second one, Hiranyakasipa, the father of Prahlada, tortured his son for the offence of 'Harinamasmarana'. Hence, Narasimha (4th incarnation of Vishnu)_protected Prahlada by killing Hiranya without violating his boons.

The Swamy's head is in the form of Varaha, on the chest, Mahalakshmi, and in the lower part of the body, Narasimha. Hence, the Swamy is called Sri Varaha Lakshmi Narasimha. At the request of Prahlada, the Swamy was so named and stayed on the hill of Simhachalam, which is like a sitting lion.

<u>Sthala Puranam:</u>

The temple's Sthala Purana was divided into 32 chapters. Veda Vyasa's Skanda Purana was the original one.

The Sthala Purana consists of the foundation of the temple and the Temple of Hiranyakasipa and Prahlada. This source also mentions the renovation of the temple in such temple times. In this context, the story of King Pururava and Urvasi is told. (The king pleased Brahma and got Pushpaka Vimana). Urvasi recollected her previous birth and her visit to Simhachalam. She wanted to renovate the temple, finding out Swamy's image. Pururava, after a deep meditation for three days, found the whereabouts of the Lord in an anthill. Thus, the temple was renovated and gates were opened for worship. According to the spiritual voice of

Aakasavani, the Lord's feet are not visible because they are hidden on earth, and the sight of the Lord will attain salvation.

<u>Simhachalam in History:</u>

There are several epigraphical sources of this holy place. Here is the chronological order:

- 1099 AD: Kulothunga's inscription mentions his victory and Swamy Seva.
- 1137 AD: Velanati chief Gonka II covered the image of the Lord with gold.
- Several inscriptions of Eastern Gangas provided information on the construction of the Mukhamandapa, Natyamandapa, in 1267 AD.
- There is also evidence of rich contributions to the temple by the Templekings of Rajahmundry.
- Vijayanagara king Krishnadevaraya visited this temple twice in 1519 AD and offered jewellery (Pachchala haram is one among them)

<u>The Temple:</u>

- A Gopuram and Mukha mandapa surmount the shrine.
- There are 16 pillared Mandapa (Natya mandapa) and a stone car drawn by two horses.
- On the veranda, there are sculptured scenes from Vishnu Purana.
- There is a Kalyana mandapa with 96 carved pillars where Lord's Kalyanotsav is performed on the 11th day of Sukla paksha of Chaitra masa every year.
- There are different forms of the Narasimha Swamy here.

<u>Kappam Sthambham:</u>

Kappam Sthambham, or the pillar of tributes to the Lord, is an attraction in the temple. Since there is a yantra of 'Santana Gopala', people believe that those who do not have children will beget them after embracing this pillar.

<u>Chandana (Sandal) Yatra Festival:</u> This activity is the highlight of temple festivals. On the 3rd day of the Sukla Paksha of Vaisakha (Akshara Tritiya), the Sandal paste, which covers the whole body of the Lord, is removed. The Mulavirat of the Swamy in the shape of 'Siva Linga' is always seen.

It is said that the weight of the Sandal paste is 12 mounds. Only on one day, i.e., 12 hours on Vaisakha Suddha Tadiya (May), is the paste removed, and devotees have the fortune of looking at the Swamy in Nijarupa (Nijarupa darshan). This occasion is called the Chandana Yatra or festival.

<u>Other Deities of the Temple:</u>

Along with Simhadri Narasimha, the other deities are Aandal, Narayana, Tayaru, Alwar, Lakshmi, Simhavalli, and 7 Sita Rama.

Tripurantaka Swamy is the kshetra palaka of the temple.

Sri Ramanujacharya, the prophet of Vaishnavism and propounder of 'Visistaadvaita' philosophy, visited Simhachalam in the 11th century A.D.

Antarvedi

Sri Lakshmi Narasimha Swamy temple of Antarvedi is in the East Godavari district. This place is said to be the site of Maharshi Vasista's ashram. He installed the idol of Sri Lakshmi Narasimha. It is one of the 108 sacred shrines of Lord Narasimha. A tributary of the holy river Godavari, popularly known as Vasista Godavari, is near the temple. In 2005, the shrine of Vasista was consecrated.

Lord Brahma celebrated Vedic yagna here, and the temple was rebuilt here. Beautiful sculptures attract the pilgrims.

Uniquely, the Lord's shrine faces west instead of east. Sri Lakshmi is seated on the Lord's lap. The shrine was rebuilt in 1923.

Other shrines are Siva, Rama, Hanuman, Garuda, Sri Venkatachalapati, Sridevi, Ranganatha Swamy, Santhosha Gopala Swamy, Kesava Swamy, Alwars, Chaturbhuja Anjaneya Swamy.

The festivals of the temple are Nrusimha Kalyanam on Magha Suddha Dasami, Nrusimha Jayanthi and Vaikuntha Ekadasi. People attend in large numbers on all these auspicious days.

Akiripalli

The temple is situated in Nuzvid of Krishna district. Vyaghra Narasimha is the deity also called Sobhanachala Swamy. The Lord is in a cave on top of a hill. Malleswara is also here. Varaha Pushkarini is a holy tank attached to the temple. There are temples dedicated to Rajya Lakshmidevi and Alwars. Under the hill, there are temples of Venkatachala Swamy and Venugopala Swamy.

Legend or Sthala Purana:

In Krita Yuga, a king named Subhavrata lived a pious life and did penance to please Hari and Hara. The Gods were pleased, and the king turned to a hill named Sobhanadri. According to his request, Siva and Vishnu took their residence on the Sobhanadri hill.

Properties of the Temple:

Revenue sources were created through the issue of orders at different times to maintain the temple and its services.

- Akeripalli was declared a free Agraharam to Lord Sobhanesvara in 1626 AD (a copper plate was issued to this effect).
- Venkata Apparao issued a grant in 1697 AD to maintain the temple's services.
- Two Kaifiats were issued:
    - The village was dedicated to Paidimalli Dharmanna for the worship of the temple

- ○ Another one was issued by a local zamindar, endowing some villages for the purpose.

<u>Pushkarini of Akiripalli:</u>

The Pushkarini is named Varaha Pushkrini. A legend provides information. During his 3rd incarnation (Varaha Swamy) as Adi Varaha, Lord Vishnu dug this tank.

The village name Akiripalli is also derived like this: 'Ki' represents Varaha, and after the construction of Pushkrini, the name is confirmed as Akiripalli.

The Pushkarini's extent is said to be one hundred acres. There are regular steps on four sides for devotees to take a dip before darshan.

Further, the holy water from this Pushkarini is used for the worship of the Lord.

Pushkarini is used as 'Bindi Tirtham' and also Tirunalla (Teppotsavam) thrice a year during Kartika, Magha, and Phalguna masas. There is epigraphical evidence of this Pushkarini in Indrakiladri (Vijayawada).

<u>Significance of Ratha Saptami:</u>

The temple performs the occasion using a temple car. The flowers for the Lord are supplied from a 7-acre flower garden.

Akiripalli temple is famous for its unity with Vishnu and Sivatatvas, which attracts many devotees.

Vedadri (Sri Yoga Lakshmi Narasimha Swamy)

This temple is situated on the banks of the holy river Krishna near Jaggayyapet (18 km) in the Krishna district.

Brahmanda Purana narrates the Sthala Purana of Vedadri Sri Yoga Lakshmi Narasimha Swamy.

<u>Background:</u> A demon named Somasura snatched away the Vedas from Lord Brahma and hid in the ocean. Lord Vishnu represented the issue

by Brahma, in the form of Matsyavatara killed Somasura and rescued the Vedas.

Then, Veda Purushas requested the Lord for protection and stayed on Vedadri hill. But Vishnu gave Abhaya and promised to do so in the Narasimha incarnation. Until then, he ordered Veda Purusha to hide in the Krishna River as Salagrama Parvata. Veda Purusha translated Vishnu's words into action.

Vedadri is known as Pancha Narasimha Kshetram, as five forms of Narasimha—Vira Narasimha, Salagrama Narasimha, Jwala Narasimha, Lakshmi Narasimha, and Yoga Narasimha—are worshipped at this temple.

Legend:

During Narasimha's incarnation, after killing Hiranyakasipa and saving Prahlad, Svayambhu settled on Vedadri Hill as Jwala Narasimha, as per the word given to Veda Purush.

In the form of Salagrama, the Lord stayed in Satyaloka per Brahma's request but was later installed on Vedadri.

Sages like Rushyasringa worshipped Yoga Narasimha. This kshetra is supposed to be one of the 'Pancha Narasimha kshetras' (the other 4 being Mangalagiri, Ketavaram, Vadapalli and Mattapalli in the Nalgonda district of Telangana state).

During Kaliyuga, Vyasa said that without yagna-yagas, one could get moksha by visiting and worshipping Vedadri Narasimha, where nature is chanting Veda mantras, a rare phenomenon.

Temple Built:

Reddi Rajas built the temple's prakaras. Poets and Vaggeyakaras like Yerrapragada, Srinatha, and Narayana Tirtha visited and worshipped the Lord of Vedadri. Vaikhasana Agama Sastra is followed in temple activities. Mukkoti Ekadasi during Dhanurmasa is celebrated with utmost devotion and dedication.

<u>Other Deities:</u>

Visvesvara and Navagrahas exist. Kshetrapalaka is Visvesvara. Devotees strongly believe that those who do not have children will be blessed with children, and the visit and worship will cure their diseases of Vedadri deva.

Mangalagiri

In the Guntur district of Andhra Pradesh, Mangalagiri Narasimha Swamy temple is among the important temples. It is near the Kanaka Durga temple of Vijayawada. This temple is situated on a hill called Mangalagiri, which means happiness and prosperity. The history of this kshetra is mentioned in 'Brahma Vaivarta Purana'. The mountain of the Swamy is part of the eastern ghats and appears as if an elephant is lying on it.

God is known as 'Panakalaswamy' of Mangalagiri. People from all over India visit the Narasimha Swamy temple of Mangalagiri. The deity is worshipped here as Srimannarayana in Narasimha Swamy's incarnation (the 4th). Jaggery water or 'Panakam' is given to the Swamy. The Jaggery water is poured into the mouth of the Swamy, and the Lord shows that he is satisfied when half of the water is thrown back as Prasada to the devotees. A gurgling sound is audible during this process as if he is drinking. This phenomenon has been happening since time immemorial. The peculiarity is that no single ant is seen near the sanctum sanctorum. Because of this characteristic, the temple was named Panakala Narasimha Swamy temple. The temple is said to be since Krita yuga. Historically, the date is the post-Kakatiya period, i.e., 1558 AD.

<u>Sthala Purana and the Legends:</u>

1. There was an ancient king named Pariyatra. He had a son named Hrusvasringi. He was born with several bodily deformities. To cure them, the king and his son went on a pilgrimage. The king stayed at Mangalagiri for three years, and his son did penance. The king

wanted to take his son back. Sringi declined his father's request, assumed the shape of an elephant, and became the mountain Mangalagiri, which became the abode of Narasimhaswamy.

2. Lord Vishnu, as Lakshmi Narasimha, killed a demon 'Namuchi' with his chakra and protected the people. Hence, the people worshipped the Lord in the four yugas. In Krita Yuga, the Lord was offered honey. In Dwapara yuga, he was worshipped with ghee. In Treta Yuga, offerings were in milk and, finally, in Kaliyuga with Jaggery water or 'Panakam'. The offering of Panaka is made by pouring into the mouth of the Swamy with a conch (Sankha), and only half of the quantity is accepted while the rest is left to the devotee as Prasada. The idol's face is sculpted on the hill.

3. Sri Rama could not attain liberation even though he was the incarnation of Dharma. To obtain mukti, Lord Rama was advised to visit this kshetra, also called 'Totadri'.

4. Maha Lakshmi was born in Ksheera Sagara Madhanam. Devatas constructed a Pushkarini here, bringing water from holy rivers. She happened to take a bath in it and became the consort of Narasimha, hence the name Lakshmi Narasimha.

There is another temple at the foot of the hill. Its origins go back to the time of Dharmaraja. Sri Anjaneya was the kshetrapala of the temple. Sri Rama ordered Hanuman to stay at Mangalagiri forever for the 'Loka Kalyana', and Anjaneya obeyed and took his abode there.

History:

Sri Krishnadeveraya visited this place as per the epigraphical source.

Galigopuram:

On the lower temple's eastern gate is a beautiful Galigopuram built by Vasireddy Venkatadri Naidu around two centuries ago. The Galigopuram has 11 floors and is solidly constructed. Ancient Ratha is also there, with beautiful carvings depicting scenes of the three great epics.

<u>Festivals:</u>

Twelve days of Brahmotsavam in March and Vaikuntha Ekadasi, Sri Rama Navami, Hanuman Jayanthi, Narasimha Jayanthi, etc., are celebrated, drawing many people.

Ketavaram

Situated in the Guntur district and Mangalagiri is another Narasimha Kshetra in the same district. Sri Vajralayya Lakshmi Narasimha is the deity. Along with his consort, Lakshmi Devi as Chenchu Lakshmi, Swamy as Swayambhu is present on a hill of 600 steps.

There are three Narasimha temples in the same village, Ketavaram. The second temple, meant for festivals, is near the foot of the hill, and the third one is on the bank of the river Krishna.

Ketavarma was the king, and by his name, the place is known as Ketavaram.

<u>Legend:</u>

The Shepard informed the king about the Swamy's existence, and Devi's Swayambhu (Self-manifested) Murthis constructed the temple. The lord's Utsava Vigrahas and diamonds were discovered when the workers dug a koneru.

Another legend refers to Vasireddy Venkatadri Naidu, who became a staunch devotee of Narasimha. According to Vaikhasana Agama, all the festivals and Pujas are conducted in the temple. Kalyanotsavam and Rathotsavam are the main festivals, and people attend in large numbers.

Malyadri

Sri Lakshmi Narasimha Swamy (Jwala Narasimha) settled on a hill called Malakonda or Malyadri. According to a legend, Sri Maha Vishnu ordered a Vanadevata to create a beautiful mountain and natural scenery with water, flowers, plants, fruit-bearing trees, birds, etc., for his residence and consort. Vanadevata created the entire thing in the shape of 'Pushpamala'; hence, the place is known as 'Malyadri'.

The temple is in the Prakasam district. Lord Brahma worshipped the Swamy. Sage Agastya did penance here, and Jwala Narasimha appeared before the sage. At his request, he assured him to stay on this hill.

Darshan to the devotees is only on Saturday. According to the sage's request, the remaining days were allotted for devotees and sages to worship. Mahalakshmi, along with Narasimha, is in the temple, which has 200 steps.

There are other temples, such as Sivalayam and Venkateswara Swamy temple. Narasimha Jayanti is celebrated on a large scale here.

Singaraya Konda (Varaha Narasimha Swamy)

Situated in the Prakasam district and 30 km from Ongole-Addanki, this is also called Singara Konda. The temple had 60 steps. The five-storied Galigopuram invites the devotees from southern Dwara. Sri Lakshmi and Andal Devi are also there to bless people.

The place is also known as Southern Simhachalam. Varaha Lakshmi Narasimha's idol is installed in the sanctum sanctorum. Sri Krishnadevaraya built the temple during Vijayanagar rule. The king gave lands for the temple's maintenance and festivals.

Daily and annual pujas lasting nine days are performed. Narasimha Jayanti during Vaisakha masa is a big festival. During Margasira Vaikunta Ekadasi and during dhanurmasa, Andal kalyanam are performed. Yogananda Narasimha is also buried in a cave nearby.

Vedagiri

Lakshmi Narasimha Swamy of Vedagiri in the Nellore district is famous as an ancient Temple on a hill called Narasimhakonda. The name of the place is Vedagiri due to its history. 'Vedadhyana' and 'Veda pathanam' continuously occurred at this place. Sage Kasyapa is associated with this place. He performed yagna, and for that purpose, he created Tretagnis in three locations: Jonnavada (Ratnagiri), Ranganayakulapet of Nellore (Talpagiri), and the third one is Vedagiri. After the performance of the Yaga by the Sapta rishis, a great spark (Jyoti) entered a cave, which finally became Narasimha. The Rishis installed the deity.

According to epigraphical sources, Narasimhavarma Pallava constructed a temple between 870 and 915 AD. The 7 Homagundams became seven Pushkarinis. Govindaraja Swamy is also worshipped here.

A five-storied Galigopuram was there southwards. In the sanctum sanctorum, there are Utsavigrahams of the Swamy, Sridevi, and Bhoodevi. The other shrines are Godadevi, Ananta Padmanabha, Vishvaksena, and Alwars. Sri Adi Lakshmi Ammavaru is also installed.

The chief festival of the Temple is Brahmotsavam, which lasts 11 days. Daily Pujas are common.

<u>Significance of the Temple:</u>

The temple has existed since Krutayuga, and it was renovated several times.

<u>Idols:</u>

There are two idols of Narasimha. The first one is 6 feet in height and is in the cave; the second one, installed by Sage Kasyapa, is 3 feet in height and, along with Sri Lakshmi, is also 3 feet in height.

Penchalakona

Sri Penchalakona Penusila Lakshmi Narasimha Swamy is in the Nellore district, 80 km from Nellore. Narasimha here is self-manifested or Swayambhu. A beautiful waterfall falls from the top of the hill and reaches the Kandaleru reservoir. The Lord married Lakshmi Devi of the Chenchu community. The stone containing the Lord and his consort is interwoven called Penusila, the term later known as Penchalakona. It is said that sage Kanva did penance here. The Lord is believed to be the saviour of the devotees. Protection of Prahlada from Hiranyakasipa is a best-cited example. The Temple is an ancient one. Hanuman is the Kshetrapalaka of the Temple. Rajagopuram is imposing.

The Temple is also known as Chatravata Narasimha Kshetra, one of the Nava Narasimha, and this is said to be the emotional one (Avesa avatar). Among the festivals, Narasimha Jayanti and Brahmotsavams are important. On Suddha Chaturdasi, Narasimha Jayanti during Vaisakha masa is celebrated. Brahmotsavams are celebrated for five days.

Penna Ahobilam

Penna Ahobilam is situated in the Anantapur district, and Sri Lakshmi Narasimha Swamy is the chief deity, which is an ancient one and self-manifested. Sadasiva Raya of the Vijayanagar Empire built this temple during the 14th century. The right footprint of the Lord is said to be the main one of the worship, and the Lord is behind this. There are Gopurams on the Eastern and Western sides.

There are references to this Kshetra in Brahmanda Purana and Padma Purana. The Swamy, like the Lord of Ahobilam, is depicted in Ugrarupa. Sages like Rishya Srunga Uddalaka worshipped the Lord, and the temple has been famous since Tretayuga and Dwapara yugas.

History:

Rajendra Chola, who built Tanjore Brihadisvara Temple, repaired the Gopurams of the temple and Panchaloha Utsava Vigrahas were presented to this temple (Narasimha, Lakshmi and Bhoodevi). Later, Vijayanagara rulers took an interest in developing the temple in the Dravidian style. The temple is called Penna Ahobilam due to the holiness of River Penna. Brahmotsavams are celebrated for 12 days.

Kadiri

Sri Lakshmi Narasimha Swamy temple of Kadiri in Anantapur district is one of the 'Nava Narasimhas'. There are two Narasimha Kshetras here, one in the town and another on a hill called 'Khadri'. One can reach this place from Kadapa and Hindupur.

After killing Hiranyakasipa, Ugra Narasimha appeared as 'Soumya Murthi' at the request of the sages. The feet of the Lord are on the hill (Khadri). The town is called Kadiri because the Kadiri tree is associated with the Lord.

The region is holy since Vedavyasa propagated Vedas here and hence called Vedaranya. Sage Bhrugu brought three Ancha murthis here.

During the Chalukyas and Vijayanagara rulers, several inscriptions reveal the temple's history. Durga Devi or Amrutavalli was worshipped here.

The temple was constructed during Veera Bukkaraya's reign (probably 1274 AD). The Temple campus is vast, with 275 acres of land and four sides with beautiful Gopuras. There are Upalayas of Sri Rama and Govindaraja Swamy. Near Narasimha, there is the image of Prahlada.

The temple consists of three parts: Garbhalaya, Antaralaya, and Mandapa. Pujas are performed daily according to Vaikhasana Aagama Sasstra. Since Prahlada is there, the deity is also called Sri Prahlada Varada Narasimha.

The Tirthams:

Some tirthas include Bhrugu Tirtham, Draupadi Tirtham, Kunti Tirtham, Pandava Tirtham, Vyasa Tirtham, etc.

Festivals:

Brahmotsavams are celebrated for 15 days, and many devotees attend Rathothsavam. The Ratham was made some 133 years ago and weighs 540 tonnes. It is 37.5 feet high and 16 feet wide, and the Peetham is 540 tonnes.

Ahobalam or Ahobilam

According to Sthalapurana, there are two versions regarding the origins of the name Ahobila.

- Ahobala: The Ugrakala of the Lord, who killed Hiranyakasipa, was witnessed by devatas, who praised him as 'Ahobala'.
- Ahobilam: Great cave where the Lord stayed.

This Narasimha Temple in the Kurnool district is very ancient. Although there are several places where this Lord is worshipped, this place is unique in that it worships all nine forms of Narasimha.

1. Jwala Narasimha
2. Ahobila Narasimha
3. Malola Narasimha
4. Kroda (Varaha) Narasimha
5. Karanja Narasimha
6. Bhargava Narasimha
7. Yogananda Narasimha
8. Chatravata Narasimha and
9. Paavana Narasimha

All these are in Yeguva (Upper) Ahobilam. The two parts on the top of the hill are called Vedadri and Garudadri. A tirtha flows as 'Atarvahini'. On the hill's southern slope, the Lord appears as Ugra Narasimha. The Temple is magnificent, with a mandapa and gopura. Nearby, there is 'Guha Narasimha'.

There is also a pillar that is said to be the same pillar Hiranyakasipa kicked, asking his son whether Vishnu is present in that pillar. From the same pillar, the Lord emerged as Ugra Narasimha and killed Hiranyakasipa. Kroda Narasimha (Varaha) shrine is also nearby.

Santarupa Narasimha is Malola Narasimha, along with his consort Lakshmi. Kakatiya Prataparudra donated a golden Utsavigraha to the temple. The remaining Narasimha Rupas are also nearby. They are all worshipped here.

Ahobila Narasimha is self-manifested, or Swayambhu and this is the tiny idol. There are several legends about Narasimha, and one of them is related to Chenchus. Maha Lakshmi was born to Chenchus, and Vishnu, in Narasimha avatar, fell in love with her, i.e., Chenchu Lakshmi. Many folk songs came into existence in this context.

<u>Historical Backdrop:</u>

The Temple dates back to ancient times. The history is known through the inscriptions during the reign or visit of famous rulers:

Western Chalukya King Vikramaditya (1076-1106 AD) worshipped the Moola Vigraha of the Temple.

Kakatiya Prataparudra installed the Utsavigraha of this temple.

Vijayanagara Krishnadevaraya also visited this Temple and offered this deity a diamond necklace, wristlet, gold plate, and gold pieces.

Ahobilam is said to be a great centre of religious and spiritual activities. Nammalwar, Adi Sankara, Tirumangal Alwar, etc., praised the Lord. Sankara's Karavalambana Stotra is popular and portrays the Lord's greatness. The Upanishads and Bhagavad Gita also mention the Lord's greatness.

At the foot of the hill, the region is called 'Diguva (Lower) Ahobilam'. There is the Temple of Prahlada Varada Narasimha (an idol is installed blessing Prahlada), and the temple style is Vijayanagara. Diguva Ahobilam is the largest among the shrines of Ahobilam. In addition, several constructions like Amritavalli Sannidhi, Andal Sannidhi, Ranga mandapa, and Mandapas were constructed by Krishnadevaraya etc. The 'Yeguva and Diguva Ahobilam' mention was made in the 'Kasiyatra' by Yenugula Veeraswamy.

Figure 4: Ahobilam (Yeguva) Narasimha Swamy Temple

<u>Festivals:</u>

Brahmotsavams are celebrated for ten days from Phalguna Suddha Panchami to Purnima at Ahobilam.

Kapotesvara Temple of Chezerla

Chezerla of the Narsaraopet region of Guntur district is in Andhra Pradesh. Kapotesvara is a Siva Temple. The Temple is situated in the Chezerla village, surrounded by rocky hills covered by scrub jungle.

The story of this deity is connected to the great epic Mahabharata, which mentions Sibi's sacrifice. King Sibi sacrificed a part of his body to an eagle perusing a kapota or pigeon. Sibi tried to save the eagle from danger, which took refuge with him. This is perhaps the only Temple in India dedicated to Lord Siva as Kapoteswara.

<u>Temple Legends:</u>

Sibichakravarthi was the son of Mandhata, king of Kashmir, and the grandson of Yayati Maharaj. Sibi had two brothers, Mehadambara and Jeemutavahana. Mehadambara sought Sibi's permission to go on a pilgrimage. Sibi not only permitted his brother to go on a pilgrimage but also made arrangements for 1500 persons to go with him.

On his journey to South India, he visited 'Cherum Chorla', a holy place for yogis. He stayed there and died. His body was buried but did not perish due to his Tapascharya, or strength of penance. Finally, he assumed the form of a Linga as Mahadambesvara and worshipped. Sibi came to know all about this. Another brother of Sibi Jeemuta Vahana visited the place. He learned that his brother was converted into a Linga, and he, too, followed the same path as his brother and reached Kailasa. Sibi was informed about this. Sibi handed over his kingdom to his ministers and reached the place. He performed 100 yagnas. The Trimurthi (Brahma, Vishnu, and Siva) tried to test Sibi and transformed into a hunter (Siva), an arrow (Brahma), and Kapota (Vishnu). The story, as cited above, is well known. Finally, Lord Siva transformed Sibi's body into Linga. Thus, Chezela is full of Siva Lingas.

<u>The Temple:</u>

The Temple's architecture is excellent because it has three styles: Nagara, Vesara, and Dravida. The Vimana represents these three styles. This Temple is of the apsidal model (Hasti Prasta or elephant back). The internal walls and upper floors seclude the sanctum sanctorum. The Linga is made of white marble. Buddhist architectural features are found since the Temple came at a time of mutual tolerance between Hinduism and Buddhism.

There are several halls in front of the main shrine. A large Nandi faces the entrance, and there is also a carved image of Sapta matrikas. The main festival is Sivaratri, and all other festivals celebrated in the Saivaite temples are also celebrated, namely Toli Ekadasi, Ugadi,

Dasara, Brahmotsavarm (during Kartik masa), Jvala Toranotsav, Sankranthi, etc.

Devotees coming to this Temple believe their sincere prayers would be fruitful. The region came under Kondavidu Sima, and the rulers granted 360 acres of land (1517 AD) to maintain the Temple.

Mahanandisvara Swamy Temple of Mahanandi

The Temple is in the thick forest of Nallamalai hills in the Kurnool district of Andhra Pradesh, 6 km from Nandyal town. The location of Sri Mahanandisvara Swamy temple is famous for its scenic beauty. According to a legend, it was here that Lord Siva accepted Nandi's prayer to become his vehicle or Vahana. There are as many as nine Nandi temples, and the Maha Nandisvara temple is their most important.

Historical Prominence:

The Chalukya of Badami is said to have built this Temple in the 7th century. Later, various kings patronized this Temple successively. Inscriptional sources exist for the Temple during the Vijayanagara period, especially during Sri Krishnadevaraya and Narasimhadevaraya.

About the Temple and the Tank:

The Temple was built in Nagari style, and Vimana is an example. According to a legend, Rasasiddha of the north was associated with the construction of Vimana during the time of King Nanda.

The Temple is ancient and architecturally beautiful. There is a Tank in front of the Temple. The pool is 5.6 sq meters (around 60 sq. ft) with a mandapam in the middle. The water is pure and crystal clear. The pebbles underneath are visible. The source of water is unknown; perhaps it comes through mountain ranges. The water is just below the Swayambhu Lingam and enters the pool. The water is arranged so that the inlets and outlets provide plenty of water for irrigation. Mahanandi is known as Tirtha, and the water has curative properties.

The Mula Vigraha:

Siva is seen in Lingakara (Maha Nandisvara). It is like a rough, uncut rock, which is unique. It contains Saligramas. Therefore, Vaishnavas consider it the most valuable. Pilgrims can touch the Linga. A huge Nandi lies before the Lord's shrine (Mahanandi).

The Tank is known as Rudragundam, Vishnugundam, and Brahmagundam.

The Goddess is known as Kamesvari Devi. By the side of the main shrine, Adi Shankaracharya installed Srichakra in front of the deity. Besides the main shrines are three other small shrines (Sivalingas). There are nine Nandi temples nearby. They are:

1. Padma Nandi
2. Naga Nandi
3. Vinayaka Nandi
4. Garuda Nandi
5. Brahma Nandi
6. Surya Nandi
7. Vishnu Nandi
8. Soma Nandi and
9. Siva Nandi

The town's name 'Nandyal' is derived from the Nandi temples. According to the saying, one gets salvation by visiting Navanandis and the main shrines of the Lord and his consort from Sunrise to Sunset.

Mahanandi kshetra is well known for its sanctity and staunch faith.

Kotipalli Or Kotitirtham

Kotipalli is in the East Godavari district of Andhra Pradesh and is a famous seat of the ancient Siva Temple. Siva is worshipped as Sri Someswara Swamy, and the goddess is Sri Rajarajeswari Devi. Furthermore, the temple is unique for having both Siva and Vishnu shrines in the same building.

Siva is worshipped as Someswara, and Vishnu is worshipped as Janardana Swamy. Brahmanda Purana and Gowthami Purana are the sources of information. Kotipalli is a sacred pilgrimage centre confluent with the sea and surrounded by the holy river Godavari.

Indra, Chandra, and Kasyapa are associated with this place. Sage Kasyapa installed Sri Janardana Swamy's (Vishnu) idols and his two consorts, Sridevi and Bhoodevi. Indra installed Koteswara Lingam, while Chandra installed the Someswara Lingam and Sri Rajarajeswari Devi.

Sage Gauthami brought the holy waters of Kotipalli, and hence, it is known as Kotipalli Tirtha. Punyasnanam (Holy bath) confers salvation to the devotees. The temple had a massive three-tiered Rajagopuram. Draksharamam, Kakinada, Rajahmundry, and Ramachandra Puram are near this place.

<u>The procedure of worship:</u>

The Archakas bring holy water from the tirtha daily for the abhishekam of the Swamy. In the evening, the worship begins with Dhupaseva, followed by Asthanaseva and Pavalimpu seva. There is Somagundam in front of the temple. Regarding festivals, Dasara and Kartika Deepotsav are celebrated with pomp. Sivaratri festival is celebrated on a grand scale. Kotipalli is said to be one of the 'Asta Sameswara' Temples. Bath in this tirtha gives the fruits equivalent to that of Daana of one crore cows, one crore Kanyadanams, 100 Aswamedha Yagas and installation of crores of Siva Lingas.

Arasavalli

Arasavalli, in Srikakulam district in Andhra Pradesh, is well known for the ancient and powerful Lord Surya temple. Surya is represented by his three queens, Usha, Padmini, and Chaya.

<u>The Existence of Sun Temples:</u>

It is said that Sun Temples have existed since early times. Chronologically speaking, these are the temples:

- Marthanda Temple of Kashmir (9th Century)
- Modhesh Temple of Gujarat (1026 AD)
- Konark Temple of Orissa (1026 AD)

<u>Worship:</u>

The Suryaradhana is as old as the Vedas. The establishment of Lord Surya temples in A.P. is a rare phenomenon. Surya is found only along with other Navagraha. The worship of Suryanarayana has been prescribed since ancient days. Several puranic and historical sources reveal the benefits of 'Surya Upasana'. Sage Agasthya taught 'Aditya Hridaya' (Prayer) to Lord Sri Rama during his battle with Ravana.

Samba, son of Lord Krishna, worshipped God to cure his leprosy and was cured. To cure blindness, one poet, Maurya, of Sri Harsha's court, composed a Sataka during the 7th century A.D. To purify sins, the famous poet Bhavabhut suggested the early morning prayer of Sura to invoke the rising Sun.

Arasavalli Temple, as per a local legend, was established by Indra. Maya, the chief architect of the Gods, designed this beautiful Temple.

The Idol is beautifully carved out of black granite stone. Two lotuses are held in both hands, and Adisesha's hood is spread over the Idol of God. On the other side, the Lord's three queens were carved.

The prominence of God is that he is the embodiment of Brahma, Siva and Vishnu.

<u>Temple Reconstruction:</u>

The original Temple reached a decaying condition. Hence, it was reconstructed by Yelamanchili Pulalji Pantulr in 1778 AD. Subsidiary deities were added, namely Ambika, Vishnu, Ganesa, and Siva. This is followed by the worship of Panchayatana, which includes Aditya.

<u>Sun Rays touching Lord's feet:</u>

From March 9th to 12th and October 1st to 3rd (Uttarayana & Dakshinayana), the Sun's rays touch the feat of the Idol.

<u>Festivals:</u>

Kalyanotsava, Rathotsava, Surya Jayanthi, and Ksheerabdi Dwadasi are celebrated in addition to the daily Pujas. Devotees attend in large numbers to visit God and pray for relief from ailments like leprosy, blindness, and barrenness among women. The Lord is known as 'Kalivarada', a granter of the boons in Kaliyuga.

Sri Kurmanatha Temple of Srikurmam

Sri Kurmanatha Swamy temple is situated in the Srikakulam district of Andhra Pradesh. The village where the Lord is present is Srikurmam. Sri Kurmanatha is one of the Dasavataras of Lord Vishnu—Kurma is a tortoise. This is the only Temple in India with the name Kurmantha.

The Temple is beautiful, with mandapas sculptured, which are masterpieces of craft.

<u>Religious Backdrop:</u>

It is said that this Temple was originally Saivaite. Ramanujacharya, the proponent of Vaishnavite philosophy, changed it into Vaishnavite. Some references are found in a Sanskrit work named Prapurnamrita. Inscriptional sources are also available to this effect.

<u>Legendary Stories:</u>

Some legends reveal prominent persons' contributions. Narahari, fully known as Naraharithirtha, acquired the images of Rama and Sita. The stories of Krita, Tretayuga, and Dwapara yugas are connected with this place. The names of Narada and Durvasa are also mentioned contextually.

<u>The Deity of Sri Kurmanatha:</u>

Vishnu's incarnation deity is Kurmanatha. Sweta Pushkarni is holy converted into Kumas or tortoises. Vyasa also narrated the greatness of Srikurmam.

Vamsadhara River flows and joins the sea. Sage Narada uttered 'Kurma mantra'. Kurmanatha is decorated with the Sankha, Chakra, Gada, and Padma. The Lord created the Ksheera Samudra tank with his Chakra. Maha Lakshmi came to the sacred spot and resided. The place is known as Srikurmam or Kurmagundam.

King Suta built the Temple with golden walls. Narada and Brahma assisted him with Sudarsana mantra and Gopala mantra.

<u>Other Temples Around:</u>

Around the main Temple, there are many other temples:

- Sundareswara (Pippal village)
- Karpuresvara (Vamsadhara joins Sea)
- Koteswara (Banks of Langulya)

<u>Tirthas Around:</u>

- Vakra Tirtha
- Chakra Tirtha
- Sudhagundam and
- Asta Tirtha

<u>Blessings for the devotees:</u>

- Purifications of the sins
- Gets the same benefit by visiting Srikurmam as that of Mathura, Varanasi, Amaravati, and Ayodhya

- Bath in Sudhakundam helps the Pitrudevatas. A large number of pilgrims visit the Kshetra. The trip to Srikurmam helps get information about Kalinga Ganga rulers and their rule from the 4th to 14th century.
- To get relief from Sani dosha, one may perform Sahasranama Archana.

Festival: Jyeshta Bahula Dwadasi day is celebrated as a festival day.

Veerabhadra Swamy Temple – Lepakshi

Lepakshi is situated near Hindupur in the Anantapur district of Andhra Pradesh. Veerabhadra Swamy Temple is on a small hillock called 'Kurmadri' (Tortoise Hill). The Temple conveys that there should be no discrimination against Siva Kesavas.

Some episodes here are connected to the Ramayana story. Sri Rama and Lakshmana were searching for Sita, and on the way, they found Jatayu Pakshi (a bird). Ravana cut off the bird's wings, and Jatayu was waiting to convey this news to Rama. Then, Rama asked the bird to get up or 'Le Pakshi', which later became the name of Lepakshi.

Sri Rama installed Ramesvara Lingam. Anjaneya installed Hanuma Linga. In addition to these Siva Lingas, the other famous one is said to be self-manifested (Swayambhu) Papanasesvara Lingam. Skanda Purana mentions this Linga as one of the 108 Saivaite kshetra Lingas.

History crept into the temple construction during the Vijayanagara (16th century). The Temple is dedicated to Veerabhadra, a wrathful aspect of Siva. During Achyta Raya, the successor of Sri Krishnadevaraya, Virupanna was a treasurer. He had a brother named Veeranna. These two brothers built the Temple and installed Veerabhadra. Virupanna was charged with misappropriation of money during the construction of the Temple. Virupanna has forcibly plucked his eyes and crushed them against the Temple's walls, anticipating punishment.

<u>Design and Art of the Temple:</u>

Due to circumstances, the Temple's design is said to be irregular, such as Arthamandapa, Mukha Mandapa, additional structures, and the incomplete Kalyana Mandapa.

Veerabhadra is the main shrine. Lepakshi is a storehouse of paintings and sculptures – Its murals claim an honoured place in the annals of Hindu aesthetics.

Sculptures and Paintings are found on various Pillars; ceilings are no exception in this regard. There are 38 sculptured columns (Kalyana Mandala). With 42 pillars, there is a hall of creepers (flower designs). Even the Prakaras have been converted into sculptures like that of:

- Ganesa (2.3-meter image)
- Huge Siva Linga (5.5 meters)
- Seven-hooded cobra (Tallest in India)

Furthermore, Lepakshi is known for its murals that tell tales. Arjuna winning over Draupadi in the bow and arrow contest, the story of Kiratarjuneeyam, Ravana, and Atmalingam's episode, outwitted by Bala Ganesh, is an outstanding example.

Veerabhadra's mural painting on the ceiling (7.6X4.3), Asia's largest, is appealing.

<u>Huge Nandi:</u>

Lord Siva's vehicle is the bull or Nandi. The Nandi of Lepakshi is the second largest in Asia (monolithic), and Ganatesvara's statue is the largest (Sravana Belgole). Some others are Tanjore Nandi of Bruhadisvaralayam and Chamundesvari Temple (Mysore).

Vontimitta (Kodandarama Swamy Temple)

Vontimitta is about 25km from Kadapa in Andhra Pradesh. The place is known for Kodanda Ramalayam, which was built on a raised place of

160 feet. Sri Rama, Sita and Lakshmana images have been carved from a single rock. The place's name is derived from 'Vonti', which means single, and 'Mitta', which means high ground. There is also a story related to two decoits, Vontadu and Mittadu, who became devotees and turned their lives after the darshan of the Lord. Sri Rama, Sita, and Lakshmana come to Vontimitta before they meet Hanuman. These two brothers created water tanks with arrows, later called Rama tirtha and Lakshmana tirtha. Jambavanta installed the idols. There is no Hanuman idol because Rama visited the place before he met Hanuman. The temple existed during the Chola period when Vijayanagara rulers developed it.

The entrance is through the five-storied Rajagopuram. The temple consists of a sanctum sanctorum, Antaralaya, and a Mandapa. In the Sanctum Sanctorum, Sita, Rama, and Lakshmana deities are installed. As cited above, there is no Hanuman idol. Later, a separate temple was built opposite Rajagopuram. There are Kalyana mandapa, Rangamandapa (with 32 pillars), and Ramalingesvara Sannithi on the temple campus.

Tavernier, a French traveller, visited the temple in 1652 and described it as one of the grandest pagodas in India. The construction is splendid architecturally, with a towering gateway. The temple is a symbol of a glorious past. However, some of the art pieces are missing, giving scope for suspicion of wanton destruction.

Vontimitta village is also known as Ekasilanagaram, which reminds us of Bammera Potana (1450-1510 AD), the author of the third great epic Bhagavatha. Of course, there is a controversy regarding the nativity of Potana since Warangal or Orugal is also known as Ekasilanagaram. This was a time when Sataka Sahityam was in a swing. In the court of Praudhadevaraya, there was a poet named Tippakavi who wrote Raghuveera Sataka. The poet was a staunch devotee of Kodandarama of Vontimitta.

<u>Festivals:</u>

Sri Rama Navami is celebrated on a grand scale, and Navaratri Utsavams are celebrated. The Kalyanam falls on Chaturdasi, followed by Rathoatsavam. According to a local legend, the Nawab had a vision of Rama in his dream and was devotional. The Muslims here are also active in participating in festive occasions.

Dwaraka Tirumala (Chinna Tirupati)

Dwaraka Tirumala, popularly known as Chinna Tirupati, is the seat of Lord Venkateswara, who is self-manifested. Svayambhu provides an alternative to Tirumala-Tirupati. During Kritayuga, Tirumala is said to be Vrushasaila and Dwaparayuga, it is known as Seshasaila or Chinna Tirupati or Dwarka Tirumala of West Godavari district in Andhra Pradesh.

Dwaraka Tirumala is a holy place for Siva and Kesava. Adisesha's penance became fruitful, and both Siva, as Mallikharjuna and Kesava, as Venkateswara, stayed here.

Dwarka is the name of a sage who did penance, and consequently, Lord Venkateswara told the sage to install his idol here by bringing it from an anthill.

<u>Two Mualavaras:</u>

Two Mulavaras exist here.

- The deity of Venkateswara is only half visible above the waist (the original). The story of Bali is linked here, stating that Bali desired that the feet of the Lord should rest on his head. Hence, the half-visible part is seen.
- Si Ramanujacharya installed the second image behind the Svayambhu idol in the 12th century. The interpretation is that offering worship to a half-visible idol is not desirable.

The Temple's development is phase-wise. The Vimana, mandapa, gopuram, and prakaras are formed. Of course, the later additions were made during the 18th and 19th centuries. The Temple is on a small hill, approachable by steps. The statues of Ramanuja, Annamaiah, and Alwars have also been installed.

The Siva Temple:

Mallikhaijuna Swamy temple is situated on a hill shaped like Adisesha. The Siva temple is on the hood, while Vishnu's Temple is on the tail.

Kshetra Katha & Mahatyam:

Dwarka Tirumala was said to be Vidarbha desa and later Velanadu (the land between the Rivers Krishna and the Godavari).

Brahma Purana is the sourcebook of this kshetra. During Tretayuga, Ajamaharaj and his wife, Indumati, celebrated the marriage of Lord Venkateswara and Padmavati. This episode justifies the Temple as an ancient temple. In addition to this puranic source, there is archaeological evidence of a pillar inscription of Khanda Raya. The Temple was renovated in the 18th century by Dharma Apparao.

Pampa River is the Uttaravahini here. Vishnu created Sudarsana Tirtha, which is the present 'yerra kalva'. Konda Mallesh is the Kshetra Palaka, and Anjaneya is the Kshetra Rakshaka. Historically, the region is famous for different dynasties of Satavahanas, Ikshvakus, Brihat Palayanas, eastern Chalukyas, Salankayanas, Vishnukundins, Kakatiyas, Velanati Cholas, Reddis, and Vijayanagara kings, etc.

Pujas and Festivals:

Two Kalyanotsavams are being celebrated every year during Vaisakha and Aswayuja maasas. Vaisakha is famous for Svayambhu Murthi and during Asvayuja masa to the complete idol installed by Sri Ramanuja.

On the Artha mandapa, there are deities of Mangatayaru and Andal (Sridevi and Bhoodevi). Every Friday, visesha kumkuma pujas are performed.

The archanas are done according to Vaishnava traditions. Auspicious days of worship are as follows:

- Every Friday and Saturday
- Amavasya and Poornima
- Ekadashi
- Sri Krishnastami, Sri Rama Navami, Velgudi, Sankranti and Dhanurmasa.
- Teppa Utsav on Kartika dwadasi day

Devotees visit the Temple and all its festivals from the nook and corner of the country.

Ryali

Ryali, once known as 'Ratnapur', is situated in the East Godavari district of Andhra Pradesh at the confluence of Gautami—Vasista Godavari. Ryali is known for the Jaganmohini—Kesava temple, which is rare in India. The temple is said to be from the 10th or 11th century. Though it was demolished, it was renovated in 1936.

The temple had a beautiful scenic atmosphere. The place called 'Konaseema' is considered a pastoral paradise.

Temple's episode:

During the Ksheera Sagaramadhana episode, Devas and Asuras come together to churn for nectar in the ocean. When the nectar came out, the asuras snatched the 'Amrita patra' and ran away. In this context, Lord Vishnu took the form of Jaganmohini, a woman of dazzling beauty. When the asuras looked at her astonished, Mohini distributed nectar to the devas first and said nothing was left. Then, a flower from Mohini's hand fell at this place, i.e., Ryali. In the Telugu language, it means 'raale' (fell).

The story is interpreted in another form. King Vikrama, at that time, had a dream, and Lord Vishnu asked him to go by a chariot, and where it stopped, he should dig, and he could find the idol of Jaganmohini. So, the king translated the words of the Lord into action and saw the beautiful idol of Jaganmohini and Kesava Swamy.

The idol is of black stone. The idol in the front appears as Vishnu and Mohini in the back. Lord Vishnu appears in the true form with Conch, Discuss, Gada, and Padma. A perennial stream flows underneath the feet of the idol, which is said to be the source of Akasa Ganga.

The temple is facing east. Sanctum sanctorum, Garbhalaya, Antaralaya mandapa are there. Sridevi, Bhoodevi, and Satyanarayana Swamy are present.

Pujas and Visesha pujas are celebrated daily and on auspicious days.

Markandesvara Swamy Temple (Rajahmundry)

Rajamahendri, or Rajahmundry, is a town on the banks of the holy Godavari River. Markandeya was an 11-year-old boy who was a great devotee of Siva. With Siva's help, he outwitted Yama, who granted him a long life. The shrine is installed here where the episode occurred.

The Temple was patronized by various dynasties like Eastern Chalukyas (Rajaraja Narendra), Cholas and Reddis.

Sarangadhara Temple

In Rajahmundry town, there is another temple of Sarangadhara, a devotee of Siva. As a punishment, Sarangadhara lost his hands but got again due to the grace of Lord Siva, whom he worshipped on the advice of a sage. Sarangadhara was the son of great king Rajaraja Narendra and Ammangadevi.

Mukhalingam

Mukhalingam is a village in the Srikakulam district of Andhra Pradesh that is well known for its temple, Sri Mukhalingesvara or Madhukesvara.

The temple dates from the 9th and 10th centuries. According to Percy Brown, *"Mukha Lingam consists of a small group of Temples, namely Mukha Lingesvara, Bhimesvara, and Somesvara."*

The foundation dates from the time of the old capital. The rulers are said to have been quite in touch with the movements in the south and the west. Though the buildings are from centuries ago, they are currently very much restored, and the renovations appear to have not deviated from the original structures.

The Sthalapurana mentioned the temple during the time of Sage Agastya, who crossed the Vindhya mountains. The mountain ranges are supposed to be very high, causing difficulty for the Sun and Moon in their regular movements, creating confusion about the day and night concept. Hence, Agastya, at the request of the Sages, crossed Vindhya and asked to stay back in the bowing posture till he returned. Another episode is about Agastya marrying Lopamudra, bringing her into life in his kamandala while crossing, and later, her amsa remains as river Kaveri. On his way south, Agastya wished the darshan of Maha Siva in the form of Kasi Visvesvara. Kumara Swamy said the Lord is present in the 'Madhuka trees' grove in the Linga rupa. Hence Siva is known as Madhukesava and 'Sri Mukhalingesvara'.

The Temple of Mukhalingesvara is a Panchayatana temple, which is a temple of five shrines. The other four are in different corners. Chalukyas, under Vimaladitya, built the temple. Puranas speak about Bhima's name in the construction. The carvings are like scrollwork patterns, reminding of the Gupta style in the north and northwest region of the 7th century.

<u>Somesvara Temple:</u>

The Moon God installed this linga in the temple, which was built by the ruler of the Ganga dynasty on the banks of the Vamsadhara River. Rudrakotesvara Temple is another one.

<u>Bhimesvara Temple:</u>

Mahabharata hero Bhima installed The Bhimesvara Linga. Later, Kalingas constructed the temple reflecting the Chola style, which is visible here.

Subrhmanyesvara Temple of Mopidevi

Mopidevi village is near Pedakallepalli in the Krishna district of Andhra Pradesh. It is 30 km from Machilipatnam. This is the seat of Sri Subrahmanyesvara Swamy, along with Srivalli and Devasena. Skanda Purana in Sahyadri khanda, this kshetra and kshetra mahatyam has been narrated.

Sage Agastya's reference is cited in the context of Subrahmanyesvara. The Sage saw the deity in 'Valmika' with extraordinary radiance.

Mopidevi is otherwise known as Mohinipura. The deity is seen in the form of a linga, which is the speciality of this kshetra. The temple is facing east.

<u>Festivals:</u>

The temple is crowded and festive during Naagulachavithi, Subrahmanya Shasti, and Mondays and Thursdays. Santi kalyanam is performed every day. Special pujas are performed on Krittika Nakshatra to Rahu and Ketu for disease relief. The blessings of the day to devotees are Santanaprapti, eyesight, relief from ear diseases, Women's welfare, education, prosperity, relief from skin diseases, and mental peace.

Peda Kallepalli Durga-Parvati & Nagesvara Swamy Temple

Pedakallepalli is 24 km from the district headquarters of Krishna district – Machilipatnam.

In ancient times, the temple was known as Kadalipura (near the sea). Holy river Krishna flows through east turns as Uttaravahini and then eastern side and joins the sea. Skanda Purana narrates the significance of the kshetra and the benefit of attaining 'Janma Rahitya' for those who dip in the river Krishna here. Padma Purana is another source of information about the temple.

There are similarities between Kasi kshetra and this kshetra. There is Ganga in Kasi and Krishna in the Pedakallepalli. Kalabhairava is common in both places. Madana Gopala Swamy is the kshetra palaka of this temple. Siva Linga is self-manifested spatika Linga.

The Temple of Sri Durga Nageswara and Parvati is said to have been built in 1292 AD.

Local Legend:

It is said that eight serpent kings installed Siva and began to worship amidst 'Kadalivana' to get rid of a curse. Siva was pleased and named the place Kadalipura. Later, the term became Kallepalli. From the Siva Linga, Sri Durga, Parvati, and Nagesvara came out. The kshetra is well known as Nagesvara kshetra. There is a lake known as Naga Kundam.

Significance of the Kshetra:

This Kadalikaranya is one of 18 famous forests in India. Sri Durga of this kshetra is one of the Navadurgas. Janameyaya performed Sarpayaga here. 'Satya Stambha' is another monument.

Festivals:

Everyday pujas and Special pujas are performed. Ugadi and Sravana Purnima are important to perform 'Laksha Kumkumarchana' to Durgadevi. Sri Krishnastami, Mahasivaratri, Kalyanotsavam, and Rathotsavam are celebrated with pomp, glory, devotion, and dedication.

Venugopala Swamy Temples

Lord Sri Krishna, the eighth incarnation of Lord Sri Maha Vishnu's Dasavataras, is a great puranic hero with universal appeal and wide popularity. He made a deep impression on Indian life. Exciting episodes of Krishna appear in Vyasa Bharata Bhagavad Gita with 18 chapters, which is a direct speech of Krishna to Arjuna on the Kurukshetra battlefield; of course, the message is not only applicable to Arjuna but to the entire humanity irrespective of the age in which they live. Lord Krishna is also famous as Venugopala, a flute player. His music makes peacocks dance, and lotuses blossom.

There are separate temples for Venugopala in Andhra Pradesh and a few in Telangana state. Some of the temples provide information about the deity and its architecture. Krishnatatva is understood by those who study Him with Bhaktitatva.

Sri Movva Venugopala Swamy Temple

Krishna district of Andhra Pradesh consists of Venugopala Swamy Temples. Movva Venugopala temple is 8 km from Challapalli. The temple is said to be the 'pratista' by Sage Maudgalya as per Sthalapurana. After penance, the sage installed the idol of Sri Venugopala with sand.

Sri Venugopala is decorated with 108 Salegrama silas (chains). Venugopala Swamy is the God, and Rukmini and Satyabhama are the temple goddesses.

The episode of Varadaiah:

Varadaiah belonged to the time after Annamacharya. He was before the great saint singer Vaggeyakara Tyagaraja. Sage Maudgalya blessed Varadaiah, and consequently, he, too, was established as a great Vaggeyakara, otherwise known as Makari Kshetraiah. He visited several kshetras in India and composed several 'Padas' praising Venugopala. His Kirthanas or Padas had the makuta of 'Movva Gopala' dedicated to Venugopala.

Other temples are Rajya Lakshmidevi and Godadevi. Khadganjaneya Swamy temple is situated on the western side. During Magha masa, Brahmotsavams (three days) are celebrated.

Rukmini – Satyabhama Venugopala Temple (Hamsaladeevi)

The River Krishna merges with the sea here, and the place is known as Hamsaladeevi. Venugopala Swamy Temple, along with Rukmini Devi and Satyabhama, is situated here.

<u>Birth and Passage of River Krishna:</u>

Born in the western ghats (Sahyadri range), it travelled 360 km in Maharashtra, 482 km in Karnataka, and 612 km in Madhya Pradesh before finally merging with the sea. The place is known as Hamsaladeevi. A dip in the Krishna River here is as good as in the Ganges. Even a crow gets the shape of a swan; hence, the region is known as Hamsaladeevi. The temple pillars are similar to the Chola-Pandya style of architecture.

The temple facing the east had five stories: Rajagopuram, Mukhamandapa, Antaralaya, and Garbhalaya, which are the temple components. The self-manifested (Svayambhu) idol, along with the installed idol, is also to be seen in the sanctum sanctorum. Rukmini, Satyabhama, and Venugopala utsavamurtis also present.

Sri Lakshmi Narasimha and Janandhana Swamy also exist in the Mukhamandapa. Near this temple are temples of Bala Tripura Sundari, Annapurna, and Kasi Visvesvara.

Kalyanotsava in Magha masa is celebrated. The temples are attractive during Krishnastami and Dhanurmasotsav. During Kartik masa, devotees come in large numbers to dip in the sea, visit Swamy, and pray.

Nemali – Venugopala Swamy

Nemali is the name of the village situated near the borders of the Krishna and Khammam districts of Andhra Pradesh, located in Gampalgudem Mandal. The idol is of Salagrama sila (blue and black colours).

According to a local legend, Lord Krishna is said to have left his 'Nemali pincha' here before his Avatara samapti; hence, the village's name. The idol is in 'Tribhangi Akriti' and Svayambhu. The Lord appears to be beautiful. Nitya pujas and Brahmotsavams (six days during Phalguna masa) are celebrated. Krishnastami is celebrated on a large scale.

Gudivada Venugopala Swamy Temple

This temple is an ancient one. Kakatiyas under Ganapatideva patronized this temple. Unfortunately, the temple was destroyed during Muslim invasions.

Meduru Venugopala Swamy Temple

This temple in the Krishna district is also famous. On Vaisakha Purnima, festivals are celebrated for three days, Brahmotsavams. God is said to be powerful, but the temple's details are unknown, except for Gajapati's contribution to the temple.

Rajahmundry

Rajahmundry was once the capital of the eastern Chalukyas. It became famous because of Nannaya, who was patronized by Rajaraja Narendra, the king who ordered him to translate the Mahabharata into Telugu. The Kshetra palaka of Rajahmundry is Venugopala Swamy.

Sage Parasara served the Swamy and installed him on the banks of the Godavari River in Dwapara yuga. Later, the temple came into existence. In 1323, the Mughal army destroyed the temple. But the idol was protected by the Archakas (priests) and reinstalled in the same place. Reddi kings constructed the temple. They donated a village named Anaparti for the maintenance of the temple. The zamindars took up the temple renovation in successive years.

Bobbili

Near the Bobbili fort, Sri Venugopala Swamy is said to have existed as self-manifested or Svayambhu. The zamindars of Bobbili constructed the temple and the five-story Rajagopuram. Mandapas are also constructed where the temple festivals are celebrated. Bobbili is a historical place in the Vijayanagaram district.

Krishna Patnam

This port town is 25 km from Nellore, the district headquarters. There are several temples here, the Sri Venugopala Swamy temple being the most important. Since the 12th century, the town has become popular and is known by different names, such as Kulottunga Cholapuram, Grandhapura, etc. The temple style is similar to that of the Pallavas. According to a source, Vijayanagara rulers built this temple. The episodes of Ramayana and Bhagavata are beautifully portrayed in this temple.

Karvetinagaram

Roughly 50 km from Tirupati, near Puttur, the temple of Sri Venugopala Swamy exists in Karvetinagaram. The kings built the temple in 1719 AD. The temple is situated on a vast campus. Five-storied Rajagopura welcomes the devotees. The sculpture is simply superb. The idols of Sri Venugopala, along with Rukmini and Satyabhama, are installed for the darshan of the devotees. Daily pujas and special festivals are performed on special occasions.

Salakamcheruvu Temple of Satya Venugopala Swamy

The ancient temple of Satya Venugopala Swamy is in the Anantapur district. The idol is 5 feet in height. According to archaeologists, this was similar to that of Arthanarisvara, which dates back to the 16th century.

Satyabhama is represented as a heroic lady, and the Lord is playing the flute. Beneath the idol, cows are seen listening to Venugopala's flute music, a rare specimen of Sri Venugopala's idols.

Chennakesava Swamy Temples

In India, Lord Sri Rama Temples are many among Vaishnava temples, compared to other forms of Vishnu. On the other hand, Chennakesava Temples are few. But most of these few temples are situated in Andhra Pradesh.

Markapuram

Sri Lakshmi Chennakesava Swamy temple of Markapur in the Prakasam district of Andhra Pradesh is the most important one and is said to be India's first and foremost Chennakesava temple. Sri Maha Vishnu is self-manifested, or Swayambhu murti as Chennakesava, and its history is ancient. "Chennakesava" means beautiful. The place of Markapur is called differently in Kritayuga, Tretayuga, Dwaparayuga, and Kaliyuga. The names were Gajaranya, Madhavapuri, Sopanamani, and Marikapuram in the successive years. Presently, the name of the town is Markapur.

The Rajagopura is nine stories high. Vijayanagara rulers constructed the temple and allotted sufficient Manyams for its maintenance. Sri Krishnadevaraya, after the victory of Dhanya Kataka, came here, stayed for some time, and worshipped the Lord.

Description of the Mulavirat:

Mulavirat of Chennakesava is represented in a standing posture, possessing Sankhu, Chakra, Kaumudi, and Adisesha in his hands. This is a rare one. Dasavataras are carved on "Makaratorana". Sridevi (goddess of wealth) and Bhudevi (The Earth) are on either side of the Swamy. Sridevi is also known as Rajya Lakshmi Devi. Ranga Mandapa, or Madhya Mandapa, was constructed by Sri Krishnadevaraya. The temple has a large campus, and the height of Galigopuram attracts pilgrims along with Dhwajastambha.

The enclosures are Asthana Mandapa, Mukha Mandapa, Antaralaya, Garbhalaya, Yagnasala.

Other Murthis of the Temple:

Godadevi, Venugopala Swamy, Ranganayaka and Ramanujacharya are the other Murthis of the temple.

<u>Archanas and Other Activities:</u>

The temple activities include Nagara Sankeerthana, Gita Pathanam, Abhishekams, and Special pujas for Rajya Lakshmi Devi. Brahmotsavams are celebrated for 15 days in Chaitra masa. Krishnastami, Dasara, and Sankranti are also celebrated. Rathotsavams and Teppotsavams are unique attractions for devotees who come from different places.

Macherla

Chennakesava Swamy Temple of Macherla is a historical temple in the Guntur district in Andhra Pradesh. The area was formerly famous as 'Palanati Seema', and the temple is situated on Chandra Vanka's banks, a River Krishna branch. Geographically, it adjoins a forest region of Srisailam and Nagarjuna Konda. According to Mackenzie, it is the milk land where light cream-coloured marble is available. Ample epigraphical and historical sources raved about the region's history and the temple.

Mahadevachela was another name for Macherla and became famous for its Chennakesava Swamy Temple.

According to historical sources, Kartavirya Arjuna built the temple in 1113 AD. Later, the Haihaya dynasty (Anuguraju) rebuilt it. Finally, during the 13th century, Brahma Naidu renovated the temple.

This temple was initially a Saivaite temple (Adityesvara) but was later converted into a Vaishnavite temple by Brahma Naidu. In the Kesava temple, the traces can be seen looking at the platform. The temple is extensive and has several other deities. Parasurama installed Siva linga by the side of the main temple in the same complex. The pillars and sculptures reveal the stories of the great epics of Ramayana and Mahabharata. Kakatiya sculpture is found here. Chenna Kesava temple seems to be a replica of an Indian Temple, a blend of art, music, poetry, and painting, and in short, the temple is beautiful. The oneness of Siva and Kesava is found here.

Lakshmi Devi is in the Antaralaya. Garutmanta and Anjaneya are on either side of the Dhwajasthambha. Rangamandapa and Galigopuram have been renovated recently. There is a pillared Dhwajasthambha inside (17th century). From Chaitra Suddha Purnima, Brahmotsavams are celebrated for 16 days. Deepotsavams from Kartik Purnima are performed for five days, and the devotees attend in large numbers.

Rathotsavam is a unique attraction in which Hindus and muslins participate and pull the Chariot, which speaks about Hindu-Muslim unity.

Karampudi

Karampudi is nearby Macherla (Palnadu). Brahma Naidu constructed the Chenna Kesava Temple of Karampudi. The temple faces west. Garbhagriha, Antaralaya, and Mandapa are the three parts of the temple. In the sanctum sanctorum, Lord Chenna Kesava and his consort Rajyalakshmi Devi are installed. Daily pujas and special pujas are performed at festivals.

The famous 'Palnati yuddham' was fought here. The weapons of the war heroes like Brahma Naidu, Kannamadasu, and Balachandra are displayed here. The Temple sculpture is beautiful.

Kakumanu

In the Guntur district, there is another Chenna Kesava Temple at Kakumanu, which dates back to ancient times. The Cholas are said to have built this temple, which was later renovated thrice. Sridevi and Bhoodevi are represented, along with Chenna Kesava. Sri Venkateswara Venugopal Swamy and Garudalwar are installed here. According to Vaikhanasa tradition, daily and special pujas are celebrated. Kalyanotsavams are celebrated on a large scale.

Eluru

Chenna Kesava Temple of ancient times is in Eluru (West Godavari district). As per an inscriptional source, the Vengi Chalukyas constructed the temple during the 10th century. Later, Zamindars of Nuzividu renovated the temple two centuries ago and patronized this kshetra. Along with Chenna Kesava, there is a Siva temple on the same campus that reminds one of 'Advaita,' which means there is no difference between Chenna Kesava and Siva.

The temple's Galigopuram, with its beautiful sculptures, attracts pilgrims. In addition, daily pujas, special pujas, and festivals draw devotees to the temple.

Dharmavaram

Dharmavaram in the Anantapur district is another place for an ancient temple of Sri Lakshmi Chenna Kesava Swamy. The Galigopuram (entrance to the temple) is built in the Vijayanagara style. Dhvaja stambha, Sabha mandapa, mukha mandapa, Antaralaya, Garbhalaya are the components of the temple.

Chenna Kesava is seen with four hands possessing Abhayamudra, Sankha, Chakra, and Gada. Important temple celebrations are Brahmotsavas (11 days) from Vaisakha Suddha Saptami, Kalyanotsava on Ekadasi, and Rathotsavam during Asvayuja masa. Ammavari Navaratri festivals are also celebrated.

Talpagiri Ranganatha Swamy Temple of Nellore

Nellore is a District headquarters known for famous temples, and Talpagiri Ranganatha Swamy Temple is the most famous among the Vaishnavite Temples. The temple is on the banks of the Penna River. Among the Ranganatha Swamy temples in India, this is one, and it is a historical temple.

According to Sthalapurana, it was built during Janamejaya of the Mahabharata. The Cholas and Vijayanagara rulers patronized the temple.

Lord Ranganatha is Lord Vishnu in a reclining posture on Adisesha. His consort is Ranganayarkamma, the form of Sri Lakshmi. Another noteworthy point in this context is that Tikkanna of 'Kavitraya' did the translation work of Mahabharata sitting in this temple.

Devotees believe this temple is 'Vaikuntha'. The Rajagopura is seven-storied, and its height is 95 feet. 7 Kalasas covered with gold attract the pilgrims. On Mukkoti Ekadasi, the devotees enter the sanctum sanctorum through 'Uttara dvara'. According to a Sthalapurana, there is a reference to Sage Kasyapa, who did yagna, and from the Yagnakundam, holy fire came out in three directions. One is the Ranganatha Swamy temple of Nellore. The Lord is seen lying on Adisesha, keeping his head on the southern side.

<u>The historicity of the temple:</u>

The idol was installed by the Pallavas (7th century). By the 12th century, the temple was constructed and further extended by Rajaraja Narendra – 2. During the 13th century, Jatavarma Sundara Pandya allotted lands to the temple. The temple inscriptions provide information about this temple.

According to Vaishnavite scholars, Sri Ranganatha Swamy temples in Srirangam (Tamil Nadu), Sriranga Patnam (Karnataka), and Ranganayaka of Nellore (Andhra Pradesh) are famous.

<u>The Idol:</u>

There is a story connected to the idol's shifting from the Udayagiri Fort temple to Nellore through Penna during Muslim aggressions. The shifted idol was first installed in the Sangamesvar temple in place of the Siva Linga.

<u>The Temple:</u>

Garbhagriha, Antaralaya, and Mandapa are the three parts of the temple. The 'Padukas of the Lord' and Sri Ananta Padmanabha Swamy are to be seen in the Mandapa. In The sanctum sanctorum, the main deity reclining on Adisesha, Sridevi and Bhoodevi are present.

The devotees also visit Sri Ranganayaki Tayaru Sannidhi on the campus along with 'Andal Sannidhi'. Three Mandapa—'Noorukalla mandapa', 'Alankara mandapa', and 'Addala mandapa'—are meant for the devotees' darshan.

<u>Pujas:</u>

Nitya pujas, Visesha pujas are performed on festival days. Brahmotsavams are celebrated from Phalguna Sukla Dasami to Bahula Panchami. Vahana Sevas are performed during this period. The Ratha Yatra is another occasion for devotees to participate in large numbers from different corners of the state.

Ainaville Sri Siddhi Vinayaka Temple

Sri Siddhi Vinayaka Swamy temple, situated in the East Godavari district of Andhra Pradesh, is a very popular Svayambhu temple of Ganesa from ancient times. According to some sources, it was built by the 'Devatas'.

Ainavilli Vinayaka temple is a centre of people's beliefs and spiritualism and an excellent spot for scenic beauty in the Konaseema region. The temple is located at a strategic point and can be reached from any famous town in the district, namely Amalapuram (14km), Rajahmundry (55 km), and Kakinada (72 km). Going by ferry from Kotipalli (10 km from Draksharamam) would be enjoyable.

<u>Vinayaka Idol and The Temple:</u>

The idol is said to be a Svayambhu or self-manifested. Vyasa Maharshi, the author of Mahabharata and later Daksha Prajapati, also worshipped the Lord. The image of Sri Siddhi Vinayaka is gold-plated.

The temple had two small gopurams. Through the southern gopura, we can visit Sri Vara Siddhi Vinayaka directly. From the eastern gopura, we can have the darshan of Visvesvara on the same campus.

Tue Sanctum is part of the entrance, and the gopuram is three-tiered.

<u>Upalayas of the Temple:</u>

There are sub-shrines in the temple. Vishnu, known as Kesava Swamy, flanked by Sridevi and Bhoodevi, Sri Annapurnadevi, Kalabhairava, Visvesvara, and Ayyappa (later addition) are the sub deities. Kalabhairava is the kshetra palaka.

<u>Festivals:</u>

Ganapati Navaratri festivals are celebrated during Bhadrapada masa. Daily pujas and special pujas are celebrated on Chavithi, Dasami, Ekadasi, and other auspicious days.

People worship Siddhi Vinayaka before starting any vital family Subhakarya for the Siddhi of their beliefs.

Bhavanarayana Swamy Temples

Bapatla

Bhavanarayana Swamy Temple, situated in the Guntur district, is one of the ancient Vaishnavite temples. Bhavanarayana Swamy is famous in this region, and hence, the town of Bapatla was known as 'Bhavapuri' in the good olden days and later became 'Bhava patla' and then 'Bapatla'. The Swamy is said to be self-manifested.

According to a source, the temple was installed in 594 A.D. in the year 'Pramadicha' on Plalguna Suddha Purnima. In ancient times, the great sages performed Yagnas or Homas by reciting the 'Astakshari mantra'. In the Dwapara yuga, Lord Vishnu is said to be in the Ksheera Vriksha in the form of Adisesha.

This historical temple has 76 inscriptions, the first of which was in 1023 AD and the last in 1618 AD. The temple style is similar to that of Rajaraja Chola I (roughly 11th century) and consists of Garbhagriha, Antaralaya, and Mukhamandapa.

The other temple deities are Santakesava Swamy, Jvala Narasimha Swamy, Sri Rama, Anjaneya, Ranganath, Gauridevi etc. The mother goddesses and Alwars also existed. Si Krishnadevaraya visited the temple.

In the town's eight directions, there are the grama devatas of Vallalamma, Kunchalamma, Sankaramma, Singaramma, Dhanakondandaramamma, Mulakaramma, Nagabhushanamma, and Bobbalamma.

In the sanctum sanctorum, Bhavanarayana Swamy and his consort, Rajyalakshmi Devi, give darshan to the devotees.

<u>Pujas:</u>

Along with Nitya Pujas (daily), there are grand festivals of the temple like Brahmotsavams (Vaisakha Suddha Saptami to Purnima) and Rathotsavams (Purnima). On this occasion, 'Santi Kalyanam' is celebrated. On the other auspicious days, the following Utsavas are celebrated:

- Kodandarama Kalyanotsav
- Tiru Nakshatra Utsav (Sravana Purnima)
- Devi Navaratri (Asvayuja masa)
- Garudotsav (on chiluka Ekadasi)
- Uttara Dwara Darsan (Vaikunta Ekadasi)

People attend in large numbers each occasion of the temple activities to pay their respectful prayers.

Ponnur

Si Sakshi Bhavanarayana Swamy Temple is situated in the same district, which is also an ancient one. The Swamy is said to be self-manifested, and the temple belonged to the time of the 12th century (Velanati Chodas – Rajendra Choda, i.e., 1119 AD)

Ponnur was known as 'Svarnapuri' and 'Chakra Tirtham' during the older days. The first inscription belongs to 1119 AD, and the last in 1551 AD. The temple consists of Girbhagriha, Antaralaya, and Mukha mandapa. There are 12 idols of Alwars. Jaya – Vijaya idols are in front of the entrance.

Along with Bhavanarayana Swamy, his consort Rajya Lakshmi gives darshan to the devotees. The temples of Kasi Visvesvara and Kasi Visalakshi are on the same campus.

The secret of the Vedic lore is 'Ekam sat' – this is truth and knowledge. The proof of this is visible in the Bhavanarayana Swamy Temple of Ponnur since Vishnu and Siva are present, revealing that both are the same to protect the devotees.

Bhavanarayana Swamy is represented with four hands (Sankhu, Chakra, Abhaya, and Kati hastas). He is seen pleasant with his crown and 'Tirunaama'.

Daily pujas and Brahmotsavams (Vaisakha Suddha Saptami—it begins and lasts nine days) are celebrated with pomp and are attended by thousands of pilgrims.

Kamakshi Temple of Jonnavada

The Kamakshi Tayi Temple of Jonnavaada, once known as Jannavada, is near Nellore. Tikkana became Somayaji by performing yagna here. Sage Kasyapa also performed yagna and installed Siva as Mallikharjuna. According to a legend, Sage Narada narrated the powers of Sri Kamakshi Amma to the devatas, which enabled them to kill a demon named Vrishaparva under the leadership of 'Indra' to save the world.

Kamakshi Amman Temple is considered a 'Shakti Peetha'. Devotees strongly believe that the goddess is a 'Kalpavalli', fulfilling their wants, protecting them from all the fears of evil forces, and blessing them with health and happiness.

Adi Shankaracharya visited the goddess and laid Srichakra. The temple is said to be in existence since 1150 A.D.

There are Upaalayas for Vinayaka, Mallikharjuna, Subrahmanyesvara, Navagrahas etc.

<u>Pujas and Utsavas:</u>

Nitya Pujas, Visesha Pujas and Utsavas are being celebrated. In addition, Brahmotsavams are celebrated during Vaisakha masa.

In Andhra Pradesh, Sri Kamakshi Temple is very popular next to Kanchi Kamashi Temple in Tamil Nadu.

Mulasthanesvara (Siva) Temple of Nellore

One of the ancient Temples of the Nellore district is Mulasthanesvara (Siva) Temple. Siva appeared in a dream to the Andhra king named Mukkanti Reddy and told him that he was at the root of an amla tree (Mula). Hence, the king found the Siva Linga at the root of the Amla tree and constructed a temple. 'Nelli' means Amla tree in Tamil; thus, the town's name is Nellore. The temple is from 1400 AD. The author of the Mahabharata translation, Sri Tikkana Somayaji, is associated with the Mulasthanesvara and Nellore. The temple celebrates daily, Visesha pujas and festivals. Maha Sivaratri is the main festival of the temple.

Trikutesvara Temple of Kotappa Konda

The Siva temple is a hill temple near Narasaraopet in the Guntur district. Trikutadri means three Sikharas, namely the Brahma, Vishnu, and Rudra Sikharas. The hill known as Kotappa Konda is 1587 feet high. On the southern side of the temple, a river, 'Ogeru,' flows. There are eight tanks or Pushkarinis, and devotees dip there to get rid of their sins before Swamy darshan.

The episode of Daksha Prajapati is related to this temple. After Parvati self-immolated by jumping into the fire, Lord Siva reached the mountain and did penance. Kalyanotsavas are not performed here since Siva was grief-stricken.

Sri Krishnadeveraya visited the temple and granted Kondakapu village's revenues to the temple. Madhava Varma (Vishnukundin king) built this temple. Sivarati is celebrated grandly. The height of this Kotappa Konda is nearly 1600 feet. The temple's height is 687 feet. The Zamindar of the Guntur district (Narsaaraopet) built the steps to get into the temple.

Vara Siddhi Vinayaka (Kanipakam)

Kanipakam of Chittoor district was known as 'Vihara Puri' during ancient times. The deity is a self-manifested one, having centuries of history, and the temple is situated on the banks of the Bahuda River.

The speciality of this place and temple is that the region is crime-free, and nobody tells lies. Any criminals should take an oath before Vara Siddhi Vinayaka that they are innocent. Therefore, the people are God-fearing and stick to the truth.

The temple is said to date from the 11th century (Kulottunga Chola I). Later, the Vijayanagara rulers continued the work.

The episode of Dumb, Deaf and Blind Brothers:

There are three brothers with deformities of dumbness, deafness, and blindness. These three are digging a well to get water and notice the sound of a stone, the idol of Vara Siddhi Vinayaka. The crowbar hit the idol, and blood started oozing out. The three brothers lost their deformities since they brought to light the idol for the darshan of the devotees. Later, a temple was constructed, and Ganesa was decorated with ornaments. Peculiarly, the body of the Lord is growing, year by year, unable to wear the ornament (waist). The devotees broke several coconuts for Lord's abhisheka, and the water flowed up to

1/4th acre of land. Daily Pujas and Ganesh Chaturthi celebrations are performed.

<u>Other Shrines:</u>

Siva and Vaishnava shrines exist on the campus. Manikantha, Varadaraja Swamy, and Veeranjaneya Brahmotsavams are celebrated for 21 days from Vinayaka Chavithi. Rathotsavam is also celebrated.

Hamsa, Nemeli, Mushika, Sesha, Vrishabha, and Gaja Vahana Sevas are performed as Vahana sevas.

Sri Mavullamma of Bhimavaram

The temple of Sri Mavullamma, a village deity given the status of Mother Goddess, is situated in Bhimavaram town of West Godavari district. It is near the 'Sunday Market'. The district headquarters is around 90 km from Elur.

<u>The Deity:</u>

The deity is said to be self-manifested. The name is Sri Mavillamma temple because the temple was built where the idol was traced out amidst mango groves. The temple is said to be in existence for one thousand years. Although historical sources have been available since 1880, Maachiraju and Appanna built the temple in this location (present vegetable market).

Floods damaged the original temple and idol, which was later renovated. The idol is in the form of 'Raudra Swarupini', which was later changed to 'Santa Swarupini'.

<u>Pujas and Festivals:</u>

Nitya pujas are performed every day during the early hours. Every day, Laksha Kumkumarchana and Chandi Homam are performed. Sri Mavillamma is decorated beautifully as 'Saakambari' on Aashadha Suddlha Poornima. Being a village deity, Jaataras are organized during

Jyeshta masa. During Dasara, Navaratri Utsavas are celebrated with pomp. Devotees participate in large numbers from nearby villages to offer their prayers and pujas. Since the merchant community organizes the temple, the temple is sound financially, and the income is also good. Another festival of 40 days is organized from January 13th every year.

The deity is decorated and worshipped as 'Asta Lakshmi'. Daily pujas are: Praatahkala, Saayamkala pujas, Baalabhogam, Sahasra kumkumarchana, Panchahaarati (evening), Veda Paarayana etc.

In praise of Sri Mavullama, there is a Sataka written by an author named Aakondi Visvanatham.

ARUNACHAL PRADESH (AR)

Till 1972, Arunachal Pradesh was known as the Northeast Frontier Agency (NEFA). On 20th February 1987, it became a separate state. Having an area of 83,578 km, Arunachal Pradesh had Asom and Nagaland as the neighbouring states. Bhutan, Myanmar, and China are the neighbouring countries. The people here have varied and colourful ways of life in the beautiful background of the dawn-lit mountains.

Arunachal Pradesh is called the land of the rising sun. P.K. Bandyopadhyay, in a poetic way, described the state as follows:

"The beauty is unique with snowcapped mountains, countless roaring streams, the murmuring rivulets, and the majestic forests."

Thousands of blooming flowers inspire and elevate the hearts of onlookers. The scenic beauty is quite inexhaustible. The people worship the Sun and the Moon. In Arunachal Pradesh, a large number of tribes and sub-tribes live. It is estimated that there are 100 ethnic groups.

Christian missionaries entered the region of Arunachal Pradesh. The role of the missionaries in changing traditional cultures and religious beliefs was faster during the British regime. Before their entry, Hinduism existed, and people were devotedly committed. Arunachal showed traces of sporadic efforts in Sanskritization. Some examples include the archaeological site of Malinithan at Likabali in Siang, Akashi Ganga and the famous Parusuram Kund near Tezu and Lohit.

Temples

Temple of Malinltan (Western Siang)

The temple is situated on a hill at Likabali. The temple is said to be from the 14th century. Some idols of Surya Rath, Iravat, Ganesa, Kartikeya, and Durga were found in the excavations. Siva's consort, Parvathi, invited Krishna and saved Rukmini (after Krishna saved Rukmini from Sisupala) for a happy stay. Parvathi is known as Malinidevi here. She is Durga Devi.

Parasuram Kund

Parasuram Kund is situated in the Teju district. According to a legend, Sage Parasuram became free from the sin of matricide (killing mother) after a dip in this kund. The axe fell away. Lohit River originated from this spot. Every year, the Makara Sankranti festival is celebrated, and pilgrims visit this holy place in large numbers.

Parvathi Mandir of Akasiganga

The Temple of Parvathi belonged to the 8th century and is said to be a Shaktipeeth. This place is near a river flow called Akasiganga or Akshaya Ganga.

Dibang Valley (Bhishmaknagar)

Bhishmak was the father of Rukmini, who married Lord Krishna.

Siva's Cave Temple (Dopurji)

A five-thousand-year-old Siva temple, which came to light in 1962, is there. It is also on a hill with scenic beauty.

Thus, Arunachal Pradesh is very much within the Indian mainstream with all its multi-colour and spectacular land and people.

ASOM (AS)

On 26 January 1950, the State of Assam or Asom was formed, with Dispur as the capital. The area of the state is 78,438 Sq.km. The neighbouring states are Meghalaya, Arunachal Pradesh, Nagaland, Manipur, Tripura, and Mizoram. Bhutan and Bangladesh are the neighbouring countries. Asom, the frontier province of India in the Northeast, has had a rich heritage since ancient times. Asom was known as 'Prag Jyotisa Pura' according to Ramayana and Mahabharata. 'Prag' means Eastern, and 'Jyotisa' means a star. The modern name of the state is a recent one. 'Lawhitya' and 'Kamarupa' are the other names in epigraphical and scriptural sources. Being attracted by the abundant natural resources and food materials, Tibeto Burmans migrated to this region. They named the place Assam, which means peerless and unique.

A story tells that Prag Jyolisa Pura was founded by Naraka, who was killed by Satyabhama (Krishna). It is said that 'Ahoms' (Assamese) entered India from Southeast Asia; hence, the name Assam derived from the term 'Ahom'.

The erection of temples in Assam dates back to an early period. Inscriptional and literary sources established the existence of Gods such as Sica, Surya, Vishnu, and Devi. However, due to earthquakes and invasions, most of the temples were destroyed. Though there are some legends, they are also incomplete in providing information. However, the existing temples provide little information, which enables devotees and tourists to visit and worship the deities.

Temples of Asom

Kamakhya Temple

The temple is situated on a hill three miles away from Gauhati, about 800 feet above sea level. The goddess's name appears outside the early literature. The hillock where the shrine stands is called 'Nilachala', which means blue. The Kamakhya Temple of 'Hari Kshetra' is essential for 'Shakti' (Tantric worship of female spiritual power). This temple is the first of the 'Astadasa Shakhi Peethams'.

"Kamakhye Kamadevi
Neelachala nivasini
Mataha – Matru saptaka
sevitha kalyana dayini – Hari kshetre
Kamarupe Prasanna bhava Sarvada"

Association of the name with a Legend:

Kamakya temple is one among the Ashtadasa Shakti Peethas. The 'yoni' of the goddess fell on the hill. Hence, this Shakti Peetha – Kamarupa Pitha (Kamakhya) is also known as 'Yoni Peetha'.

Curiously, the temple is unique compared to the Devi temples in other parts of India. No image of the goddess is found here. There is a cave within the temple, in the corner of which stands a block of stone on which the symbol of a yoni is printed. The devotees offer flowers and leaves here. As per the tantric worship, goats, pigeons and occasionally buffalos are beheaded.

By the end of the mother goddesses' menstrual cycle, the temple celebrates. The temple opens after three days. The celebration is known as 'Ambu Vaci' (Menstruation ritual) once a year in the first part of the month of Ashadha on Ekadasi day.

During Fairs & festivals, the shrine of Kamakhya wears a colourful look. Durga Puja, Ambuvaci and Debadhari are the festivals.

According to Kalika Purana, the deity is mighty, and she can take whatever form she wants. (Kamarupa) For instance, one form stands on the white lotus with a yellow garland in her hand (Tripura Sundari). In another form, she is seen happy sitting on the lion (Tripura Bala). In the form of the Ugramurthy, she appears standing on a dead body with a sword in her hand (Tripura Bhairavi). Whatever her form, she is said to be more beautiful or 'Lalitha Kanthika'.

By The side of 'Yoni Peetha,' the idols of Lakshmi and Saraswati are installed. The temple was demolished several times during invasions, and by 1565, it was renovated. In the renovated temple's sanctum sanctorum, there are no images of Gods or Goddesses. There is a 'Soubhagya Kundam' to bathe before the deity's darshan. Another one is 'Parvathi Kundam', where devotees dip in it.

The temple faces East, but the Goddesses' yoni form is on the northern side. On the same campus, there are idols of Ganesa and Visvakarma. The following temples are in the temple complex. They are:

- Kali
- Tara
- Bhuvaneswari
- Bhairavi
- Dhrumravati
- China Masta

Siva's forms are five types:

- Kurmesvara
- Siddhesvara
- Heruka
- Aghora and
- Koti Linga

In the same way, Vishnu to be seen in three forms:

- Kedara
- Gadadhara and
- Panduranga

Asvakranta

Asvakranta is a Vaishnavite shrine in North Guwahati. It is opposite Guwahati, and one must go there by motorboat on the Brahmaputra River. Asvakranta means 'ascended by horses'.

Here, the story relates to Narakasura vadha. Krishna camped here before the war with Naraka. Vishnu placed Naraka as the living of Pragjyotisa pura. Naraka ruled righteously for some time. Then Sonitpur was ruled by Bana, who was a staunch Saivaite. Naraka's character was utterly spoiled after his contact with Bana, resulting in his neglecting a Goddess, Kamkhya and harassing Brahmins. In addition, Sage Vasishta was refused permission to visit Kamakhya temple, after which the sage cursed Naraka to be slain by his father, Vishnu. At the same time, Vasishta said that the goddess would remain hidden during Naraka's lifetime. Naraka's rule became unbearable. Sri Krishna joined the army and stabled his horses on the rock opposite Guwahati. Krishna killed Naraka, and the latter installed his son, Bhagadatta or Bhagirath, on the throne. Peace was established in Kamarupa, and a Vishnu temple was built where he stabled his horses. This is 'Asvakranta'. Several small holes in the nock near the Brahmaputra River are believed to be the footprints of Krishna's horses.

The Temple:

Vishnu's image as Anantasayana is a reclining statue of excellent artistry.

Description of the details of The Deity:

A tortoise, a frog, and a piece of waterweed support Ananta, upon which Vishnu is seen reclining. Of his four arms, the lower left is thrown on the serpent's body while the lower right is stretched along the right thigh. The four-faced Brahma is depicted as sitting on the lotus, which has sprung out from the navel of Vishnu. Devi (Maya) and the two demons, Madhu and Kaitabha, stand in one corner. Nagakanyas are kneeling with folded hands and are extraordinary sculptures of high artistic excellence.

<u>Significance of the Place:</u>

Yogini Tantra narrates the greatness of this pilgrimage or Tirtha. Mantra, Homa, Pinda and Meditation are possible here. One will be freed from the greatest sins by a visit to Asvakranta. Even the dust of this place sanctions salvation. The residents of Asvakranta attain more Punya than the residents of Ganga or Pushkar.

Vasishta Ashram

This Ashram is situated around 10 miles from Guwahati amidst beautiful surroundings. There are three river streams: Sandhya, Lalita, and Kantha. A bath here increases longevity. Siva's temple is attached to the Ashram, constructed by Ahomes during the second half of the 18th century (the king was Rajeswar Singh). Regarding the architectural features, it is plain, resembling other temples of Asom.

Umananda

Umananda is situated on the peacock island of the Brahmaputra River. Siva sprinkled 'Bhasma' and imparted knowledge to Parvathi. Manmadha or Kamadeva interrupted Siva's meditation and became a victim of Siva's anger, resulting in Manmadha becoming Bhasma. Hence, the place is called 'Bhasma Kuta'.

Umananda is the temple deity. When it falls on Monday, Siva's worship on Amavasya is auspicious. The annual festival is Siva Chaturdasi.

The temple was built in 1694 by Ahom ruler Gadadhar Singh. However, the temple was damaged after two centuries due to the earthquake. Later, it was reconstructed.

There are sculptures of Surya, Ganesa, Siva, and Devi, followed by Vishnu and his ten incarnations. The sculptures reflect the mastery of the Assamese artisans.

Navagrahas

The temple is on a hill in the southeastern part of Guwahati. It contains nine phallic emblems of Siva covered with clothes of different colours sacred to the nine planetary Gods. – Surya, Chandra, Mangala, Budha, Brihaspathi, Sukra, Sani, Rahu, and Ketu.

The temple was built in 1752. The earthquake destroyed some parts of the temple, but later, they were repaired, and a tank was dug.

Temple of Pandunath

This temple is in Guwahati. Lord Vishnu is seen here in the form of Pandunath. Five stone slabs indicate the five Pandava heroes.

Manasadevi Temple

The temple is situated on Neelachala Mountain near Kamakhya Temple. The deity is said to be powerful. The Goddess is said to be the sister of Vasuki, the Serpent king. The emblems of snakes are carved into sculptures. Therefore, people believe that visiting this temple will not have any effect on snake bites.

Sukresvara Temple

The temple is located in Guwahati, on the bank of the Brahmaputra River. Sukracharya built his Ashram here and set up a Siva Linga (Sukresvara). This temple was built in 1744 (Ahoms), and the Siva Linga is one of the largest ones in India.

Hajo

It is situated northwest of Guwahati and was a great centre of culture. There are two temples at Hajo: Hayagriva and Kedaresvara. However, the focus is on the Hayagriva Temple.

Hayagriva Madhava Temple figures prominently in Assam because of Vaishnavism. From early times, the worship of Vishnu and the Dasavataras was prevalent. However, in the subsequent centuries, Vaishnavism declined; again, during the 13th century, it was revived and played a vital role in the Bhakti cult.

Hayagriva means 'Vishnu with horse head'. The worship is still prevalent in Assam. The temple at Hajo is built on a hill (Manikuta).

Santiparva of Mahabharata is the source of this story. While Vishnu was sleeping and Brahma was on the lotus, two demons named 'Madhu' and 'Kaitabha' took the Vedas from Brahma and went to Rasatala. Brahma prayed to Vishnu for the recovery of the Vedas. In this context, Vishnu assumed Hayagriva's form, recovered the Vedas, and gave them to Brahma. The two demons were killed.

The Hayagriva Temple at Hajo is said to be one of the existing Pre-Ahom temples in Assam.

<u>The Temple Art:</u>

A flight of stone steps to the hillock leads to the main precincts of the temple. The temple is built in stone with a pyramidical roof. Reconstruction was also done.

The temple has three parts: Basement, Middle portions, and Sikhara.

A row of elephants appears in the basement mouldings (16" in height). This artistry is identical to the style of the Kailasa cave temple at Ellora.

The Garbhagriha is square (14 feet), and the Sikhara is pyramidical. The exteriors feature sculptured figures. Dsavataras, including Buddha (9th), are also noticed here.

Krishna Temple (Tejpur)

Krishna's temple is on a mountain at Tejpur, and it is said that Krishna is 'Svayambbhu'. Krishna's grandson, Anirudh, married the daughter of

Banasura at this place. According to local legend, Krishna killed Bana here.

Surya Temple (Surya Pahad)

The temple is on the hill. The source is the Kalika Purana. On a pillar, the Murthis of Aditya and Kasyapa are found.

Sivasagar Temple

Siva Temple is situated amidst three temples with golden domes. A tank is also there (Sivasagar).

This place is said to be important because of Parasurama's penance after killing kings and leaving his weapon axe.

BIHAR (BR)

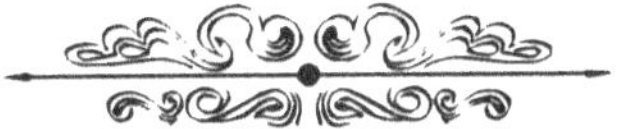

Bihar was formed on 26 January 1950. The state bifurcated on 15 November 2000 to create Jharkhand. The capital is Patna, one of India's oldest cities, and it has multiple names. Pataliputra, Kusumapura, and Pushpapura are the ancient names of 'Palibothra', the name given by the Greeks. Chinese named it Pa-Lin-fon. During the later Mughal rulers, it was Azimabad. There are several references to Pataliputra in Ashoka's rock and pillar edicts.

Sisunaga, Nandu, Maurya, and Singu dynasties ruled Bihar and Pataliputra. Later, it came under Andhras, Guptas, Palus etc.

Bharatiya Vidhya Bhavan has listed the important temples of Bihar, such as Patanduri Temples, Mangala Gauri, Vishnupada, Gaya Kshetra, Gadadhara, Hariharanatha Sita Rama, Rama, and Mundesvari. Moreover, the temples of Bihar are given to help people understand that there is a cultural affinity with Nepal, Bengal, Orissa, U.P., and M.P.

Patna Devi temples of Patna

The name Patna is derived from the Patna Devi temples situated here. There are two temples, Bari Patna Devi and Choti Patna Devi.

The Bari Patna Devi temple is in the Maharajganj area of Patna, and the Choti Patna Devi temple is situated at Patna City Chowk.

<u>Legends regarding the temples:</u>

The story of Dakshayagna is well-known and has already been cited. Parvati or Sati put an end to her life. Siva came to know of this, took her dead body on his shoulder, and began dancing (Siva Tandava). At the request of the gods, Vishnu intervened and started cutting Sati's body into pieces with his Chakra. Wherever the major limbs of the body of

Sati fell, the places became Maha Sakthi Peethas. The places where minor limbs fell became called Upapithas (the remaining 51). It is believed that some portion of the right thigh of Sati and the 'Pat' (cloth) fell near Maharajganj and Chowk, for which Mahakali, Mahalakshmi and Maha Saraswati came into existence (three small images in the temple).

The temple of Bari Patna Devi faces the north. The deities are standing on a 'Simhasan' (black stone make).

Choti Patna Devi temple is southeast of the famous Sikh temple of 'mandir. It houses images of the Sun god and Vishnu.

Like most temples, it has a chamber of other images. There is a statue of Parvati (a 100-year-old stone) and a small temple of Siva (constructed in 1950).

<u>Architecture of the temples:</u>

The temples have been reconstructed occasionally, using marble and mosaics in the Brahmanical Style.

Visiting hours are between 6 AM to 10 PM. Tuesday is important for devotees. The newlyweds and the newborn babies are brought for the blessings of the deities. A Mela is called in who sings songs.

On special occasions of Vijaya Dasami (Saptami, Ashtami and Navami), many devotees come to offer prayers. Prasad and Aarathi are followed during the prayer timings. Reciting hymns and ringing bells are the usual practices.

Temples of Gaya:

Sri Mangala Gouri Temple:

The temple is located on the banks of the river Phalguni. The region is a confluence of rivers Phalguni, Madhura and Sweta. Therefore, the region is imbibed with holiness. The 'Mangala Gauri' temple is on the Mangalagiri hill and faces the eastern side. The temple is one of the

"Astadasa Shakthipeethams". The deities' Vakshasthala' or breast fell on the spot (story of Dakshayagna, Sati ending her life, Siva roaming about with his consort's body and Devatas unable to bear this situation and Vishnu cutting the body into pieces with his Chakra and a part of the body fell on this mountain).

Another name of Mangala Gouri is Sarvamangala Devi. Space is limited in the Sanctum Sanctorum allowing just two or three devotees at a time. Ganesh Mandir is before the Sanctum Sanctorum 'Mangalagouri' is seen as 'Rakshasa Samharini'. A "Homakund" and a "Mandapa" are on the temple's campus. Finally, Nandi and Siva's images are presented.

The other temples in this region are Dasavataras, Mahishasura Mardini, Ahalyadevi, Janardhana, and Mahakali.

'Vasantha Navaratri', 'Sarannavaratri' and 'Maha Sivaratri' are special occasions when festivals are celebrated with grandeur.

Vishnu Paada temple:

The temple of Gaya is at the confluence of three rivers: Phalgani, Madhura and Swetha. The idol of Vishnu is beautifully styled as 'Gadadhara'. The speciality here is the footprints of the Lord covered with silver. The legend says that Lord Vishnu stood on the head of Gaya.

Indore Queen built the temple in 1787 with a Rajagopura of 30 feet in height. On the side of the river is a 'mandir', which speaks about the Ramayana story. During Vanavasa, when Rama was not there and the time of the Tithi was crossing, Sita Devi offered Pindapradan to her father-in-law, Dasaratha, here. The witness is 'Vata Vriksham'. Hence, Sita granted the tree a long life along with the river Phalguni.

Gaya Kshetram:

Kasi, Prayaga, and Gaya (Tristhali) are the three great holy kshetras, and people perform Pindapradan for their forefathers for their permanent Moksha or Salvation. The place 'Gaya' is named after a demon, Gayasura, who sacrificed his body to Lord Brahma to perform Yagna with Lord Vishnu as Gadhadhari Stord on his head, and the Yagna was successful.

Surya temple, also known as Dakshinarka temple, is 75 km away from Patna, which is also mentioned in the Vaayu Purana. The temple is said to have been constructed by Kaktiya Prataparudra during the 13th century. Offerings to the ancestors (Pindapradan) are made at the Suryakund or Dakshina Maanas tank, which is before the Dakshinarka temple.

Vishnu granted Gayasura a boon so that the place would acquire holiness and go with his name as "Gaya." So, Vishnu's footprints remained there, and all the devatas stayed there. This temple is called Vishnupaada temple.

Gadadhara Temple:

Gadadhara temple is an old temple of Lord Vishnu in Gaya. Vishnu is represented with four hands and is known as 'Gadadhara'. A legendary source explains how Vishnu killed a demon named 'Heti' with a 'Gada' taken from Lord Brahma.

Here is a connecting story. There was a demon named 'Gada', a great devotee of Brahma. Brahma asked for the bones of this demon since they were powerful. The demon sacrificed his life. So Brahma ordered Viswakarma to prepare 'gada'. Vishnu took the same one to kill 'Heti'.

Hariharanath Temple (Sonepur):

Sonepur is considered a holy place at the confluence of the Ganga and Gandaki rivers. There is a Siva temple here, which was supposed to have been built by Sri Rama on his way to Janakpur to win Sita. However, the region Tirhut division is associated with the Rama and Sita cults. There is no reference in Ramayana. The present temple is not old and Birlas reconstructed this temple.

The Gajendramoksha episode (Srimad Bhagavata) happened here only. "Gangasnan' and mela on 'Kartik Purnima' are the notable activities.

Sita Rama and Urmila Lakshman Mandirs of Baxar:

These temples are situated in Midhilanagar, 15 km from Janakpuri. There is also the ashram of Viswamitra where Rama was taught the 'Astra sastra vidya'.

Mundesvari Temple: (Shabad District)

Mundesvari is seen with many hands riding on a buffalo. There is also a Siva linga with four faces. Though goddess Durga appears to be Mahishasura Mardini, she is not in the act of killing.

The temple's location is beautiful, with a view of hills and plains. Mundesvari temple is the earliest specimen of the 'Nagara style', which is rarely found. The Sankaracharya temple at Srinageri during the 18th century is another example.

CHHATTISGARH (CT)

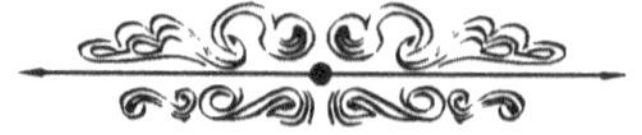

Chhattisgarh was carved out of Madhya Pradesh as the 26th state on 1 November 2000, with Naya Rayagarhpur as the capital. The state's area is 1,36,034 sq. km. The neighbouring states are Madhya Pradesh, Odisha, Telangana, Maharashtra, Uttar Pradesh, and Jharkhand.

Geographically, the state is situated in the heart of India. Mahanadi, Indravati are the important rivers. Hinduism is the major religion in the state, which is known for the Siva, Vishnu, and Devi temples.

Siva Temples:

1. Siva temples of Korba: This lakeside town is famous for its ancient Siva temple. Raja Vikramaditya, also known as 'Jayameyu', from the Banna dynasty built it in 870 B.C., and the temple underwent renovations in the 11th and 12th centuries.

2. Kankeshwar or Chakreshwar Mahadev temple at Kanki is an ancient temple believed to have been built by the Korba Zamindars around 1857 A.D.

3. Gandheshwar Mahadev temple of Shirpur: This ancient temple is situated on the banks of the Mahanadi River. The idols of Siva, Nataraja, Narayana (Garuda Narayana), and Mahishasura Mardani are appealing.

Vishnu Temples:

1. Rajiv Lochan Temple: This temple, which is said to date from the 8th century, is situated in Rajim town in the Raipur district. Sri Maha Vishnu is the chief deity. Other deities in the temple are Vamana, Narasimha, and Trivikrama. Kshatriyas are the pujaris in

the temple. Lord Vishnu's Idol is beautifully made of black granite and decorated with flowers.

2. Balaji temple (Raigarh): This temple is also ancient. The temple's walls are carved with the different stages of Sri Rama's life. Near the Balaji idol, several 'Salegramas' are brought from the Gandaki River of Nepal.

3. Syammandir (Raigarh): This is also said to be an old temple of Sri Maha Vishnu. Festivals are celebrated on a grand scale during Ekadasi and Janmashtami.

4. Lakshman Mandir (Shirpur): This is situated on the bank of Mahanadi and was built in the 7ᵗʰ century A.D. The speciality of the construction is that it was built using bricks. Of course, the temple is in a degenerated condition. Lakshman, brother of Rama, has a temple, which is the speciality of this place.

5. Sri Rama in the temple of Banjarimata: BanjariMata is none else but Durga Devi, and in this temple, Lord Sri Rama was installed during the 15ᵗʰ century.

Devi Temples:

1. Dantesvari: In the district of Dantewada, the temple of Dantesvari is situated during the olden days. It is said to be one of the 51ˢᵗ Sakthipeethas (tooth of Sati) located at the confluence of Shankini and Dankini. The Chalukyas built the temple during the 14ᵗʰ century. Dantesvari is said to be the family goddess of the Kakatiyas. The idol is sculptured on black granite. The construction of the temple consists of a sanctum sanctorum Mahamandapa. Garuda stupa is in front of the main entrance of the temple. Navaratri (Dasara) celebrations are performed a large scale here.

2. Sivani: In the district of Kankar, the temple, which is also of ancient times, is situated. Kali mata is the main deity that is said to be a form of Durgadevi (one side Kali and the other side Durga

– a speciality of the idol). The festival of Dasara is celebrated on a grand scale here.

3. Bamblesvari Temple: Near Durgapur, the temple of 'Bamblesvari' is on top of a hill (1600 ft high). She is said to be the goddess Durgadevi.

4. Banjarimata Temple: Durga Mata is said to be Banjarimata, situated in the Raipur region some 500 years back.

GOA (GA)

The area of Goa is 3,702 km. Panaji is the capital. Goa was liberated from Portuguese rule, and the date of formation of the state was 30 May 1987. Karnataka and Maharashtra are the neighbouring states.

Historical background:

Goa was ruled by many rulers from Ashoka (3rd century B.C.). Kadambas ruled for a long time. Velho (Vehla), today's little village of Goa, was their capital. Adil Shahis of Bijapur (Bahamas) ruled the old Goa region in the 15th century. By 1510, the Portuguese arrived and defeated the Bijapur kings (Information available from the Goa State Museum of Panaji).

Significance of Goa:

Goa is styled as the "Rome of the East" and has the charm, grace and divinity of temples. Rivers Gomati and Aghanashini, later known as Zuari and Mandovi, flowed here and joined the Arabian Sea. A peaceful environment prevailed with the western ghats and dense forests (both are green).

Goa is considered a land of holy temples, but this aspect is less known and needs to be publicized. Although the area of Goa is small—60 km by 105 km—there are more than 30 temples. These temples are not merely places of worship but also centres of people's activities.

The invaders destroyed the ancient temples. Hence, the newly built temples have existed for five centuries.

Temples of Goa:

During the construction of the temples, prescribed rules are carefully followed, including installing the deity. A few notable aspects of temple construction in Goa are:

1. The temple construction starts with laying the foundation stone in the decided place.
2. The middle portion of the temple area is called 'Garbhagriha', where the base stone or 'Adharasil' is kept. Over that 'Nidhikumbha' (pot), a tortoise, a lotus, gold, and silver are deposited. The whole thing is covered by 'Brahmasila'. All this activity is aimed at the smooth completion of the temple construction. Indirectly, it is the prayer to Mother Earth.
3. Stones, bricks and food are to be procured freshly.
4. In the next stage, preparation and installation of the main deity and the Parivar deities starts.
5. A temple should primarily be provided with plentiful water. For this purpose, it should be constructed on the bank of a river or in a tank filled with spring water.
6. Deepa Sthambhas are also set up facing the shrine.

Contributing to building the earlier temples in Goa (Former Gomantak) goes to the migrant Saraswat Brahmins. Saraswats came to Gomantak(Goa) less than a thousand years ago. But some say they belong to the epic period of Parasuram (the 6th incarnation of Vishnu). References to Gomantak are found in Mahabharata (Bhishmabarva), Harivansa and Skanda Puranas. Sage Kashyap undertook penance at Gomantak to overcome the sins of Parasuram, i.e., the massacre of Kshatriyas. Kashyap invited learned Brahmins from different parts of the country to perform yagnas. Among them were Saraswat Brahmins from Kashmir, the banks of the Sindhu and Saraswathi rivers, and Bengal.

The beauty attracted the Saraswats, and the serenity of the Gomantak region made them desire to stay there as their native homes. So, Parasuram gave them 96 villages to them for their settlement and sadhana. Unfortunately, no traces have been found today. Historically speaking, Chalukya kings received religious traditions during the 7th century A.D. This resulted in the regaining importance of Hindu temples.

The main Saivaite deities in Goa are Mangesh, Mallikarjuna and Saptakoteswar. Famous Vaishnavites temples are Damodar(Vasco), Narasimha Damodar(Velinge), and Devaki Krishna (Chodna in Marcel). The Devi temples, like Shanta Durga, are also noted in Goa and are located at Kavale.

Saivaites Temples

Shri Mangesh Temple at Priyol

The Siva Temple in Priyol is the Mangesh temple, one of the most powerful deities of Goa. This temple is between 'Panda' and 'Panaji' in a hilly region. The original temple was situated at "Kusasthali", on the bank of the river 'Zuari', which was demolished around 1560 by the Portuguese. It is said that the idol was brought to Priyol by the devotees, and a temple was constructed. A constant stream of devotees came from the different corners of the country to worship. The temple is not large, but it has become noted for its elegant and well-proportioned structure.

<u>Mangesh and the legend:</u>

Siva and Parvathi played a game of dice in the mountain abode in Kailash. Siva lost everything to Parvathi, including his mountain home. Therefore, he left the place and reached Sahyadris in 'Goapuri'. He stayed at Kusasthali. Parvathi also left Kailash and incidentally reached Kusasthali. She saw a fierce tiger (Siva in tiger's garb) covering her. Panicked, she called out, "Trahi mam Girish" (Girish means Siva). Siva came and consolidated her.

The word' mam Girish' later became 'Mangarish' and, eventually, Mangesh. At the exact spot of this tiger's incident, Siva left his symbol, 'The Linga', which was spotted by a cowherd. A small temple was built, but Muslims and Portuguese damaged the shine. Later, the temple was rebuilt.

Associate deities of Mangesh are Lakshmi Narayana, Surya Narayana, Mulkeshwar(cowherd), Veerabhadra, Kalabhairava and Sankari.

The Mangesh temple opens at 5:00 A.M., and the last Arathi is at 10:00 P.M. Abhishek of Siva has different types: 1. Rudra, 2. Laghurudra, 3. Maharudra, and 4. Stirudra.

For Abhishek, a patra flows over the Lord through the horn of a bull covered with silver.

Coconut, flowers, bananas, and Gandha are offered to the Lord on Sivaratri, the day of a special festival. Bells are rung, and the chanting of "Har har Mahadev" is heard. Rathotsav is a significant event here.

Mallikarjun of Kanakona

Another noted Siva temple is Mallikarjun of Kanakona, south of Goa. Tribal communities are the worshippers here (Kunbis). During the last century, the priests were non-brahmins(Gaudas or Kunbis). Later, they invited Brahmin priests to discharge priestly duties. But the non-brahmins continued their priestly duties. Hence, they asked the Brahmin pujaris to be for eight months only, and the remaining period would be left over for Gauda pujaris. Though the Gauda pujaris are not proficient in Sanskrit texts and puja systems, they have strictly observed the priest's code of conduct. Special utensils, Artis, and the tortoise-shaped wooden seat are needed for worship.

About the Temple:

Mallikarjuna temple is as old as the Mangesh temple of the 16th century. The place is quiet, with tribal, rural surroundings.

Temple appearance:

The temple's spacious compound is under excellent maintenance. Parivar devatas exist; some are two feet high, and the rest are more significant.

The temple plan comprises 1. Mukhamandapam, 2. Sabhamandapam, 3. Antaralaya, and 4. Garbhagriha. The temple prioritizes cleanliness. Sayings like 'Cleanliness is Godliness' are written in Marathi.

<u>Musical instruments:</u> Nagara, Tasha, Turhi and Cymbals are kept in Mukhamandapa.

<u>Vahanas:</u> Horses/elephants are kept for performing seva.

<u>Art:</u> Carved wooden pillars exhibit the art of murtis, and the Dasavataras are also made of wood. The Dasavataras are carved beautifully. Brass lamps are present traditionally.

Dwarapalas are present on the doors of Antaralaya. Brass bells are fixed up above the entrance. In short, one may find artistic refinement in all the carvings and portrayals. Silver cover doors are fixed to the main shrine. However, the luxurious look is missing compared to the Saraswat temples of Ponda.

The main deity is Siva Linga, who wears a silver 'Kavach'. Excellent items are offered to the deity for Naivedya. On special occasions, Naivedya consists of Kheer and Vada. The temple has two major festivals: Shimoga, celebrated during March, and Sivaratri, which draws large crowds.

Sapta Koteswar at Naroa

The Temple of Sapta Koteswar was built in the mid-16th century in the beautiful location of Nature on the forested slopes of 'Bicholim' (Naroa). The deity is identified with Khandoba, the folk deity of Karnataka and Maharashtra. Sapta Koteswar is also known as 'Yelakoti Mahadeva' and is worshipped by everyone. He is also known as 'Mailar' by the Chalukyas and Hoyasala rulers who ruled Karnataka and Deccan.

<u>Justification of the name of Sapta Koteswara:</u>

Mahadeva, or Siva, had an army of 7 crores, and he led the armies as commander to fight demons. There are great devotees of Sapta Koteswar among the kings; one such is Kamaladevi, wife of Kadamba king Sivachitra (1155 AD). Another was King Jayakirita (1210 AD), who struck gold coins in the name of the God' Shri Sapta Koteswara Labhdevara'.

<u>Attacks, Restorations, and renovations on the temple:</u>

1. The first recorded attack on the Sapta Koteswar temple in Goa was during 1356-66 by Bahmani kings – The temple was destroyed, but the Linga was rescued by the devotees and protected in a field. The deity was re-established after three decades by the rulers of Vijayanagar.
2. The Portuguese were the next to attack the temple. They threw away the Linga and converted the sanctum sanctorum into a chapel. An Italian traveller by the name of Giuliano de Medici appreciated the art of the temple. The figures are marvellous in black stone.
3. The Linga later travelled to the kingdom of Bijapur Sultans by their efforts. The area is Nae Naroa, a new abode of Sapta Koteswar.
4. Shivaji used to visit the deity when he was at nearby places. The poor condition of the temple prompted him to order reconstruction (According to an inscription above the temple's entrance). The Temple foundation was laid on November 13, 1668.

The Linga in the Garbhagriha is of the shaft type known as 'Dhara Linga'. Images of Vaishnavite deities like Gopinath and Vithoba are present. Of course, the presence of Vaishnavite deities in Shaivaite temples is common in the temples of Goa. In the Antaralaya, one can see several stone images, such as a large Ganesh.

The Panchayatan of Sapta Koteswar includes Lakshminarayan, Bhagawati, Kalbhairav and the Moolpurush. Kalbhairav is the senior 'gana'.

<u>Archanas of the Temple:</u>

The daily puja activities begin at daybreak. 'Arati and Archana, with the recitation of mantras, take place at noon. The Naivedya (Bhog) consists of plain dal and rice topped with ghee. During the night, the deity is offered only fruits.

Archana of the Panchayatan consists of Abhishek with oil to Kalbhairav and Naivedyam of rice topped with ghee only. Bhagawati is offered 'Arati' with Deepam and flowers but no 'Naivedyam'. Womenfolk worship her on Tuesdays and Fridays.

Sivaratri is the main festival. Bhajans, followed by reading from Puranic texts, is the activity. The deity is offered Bel Patra, Oak flowers, and fruits. 'Mangal Arati' during the night with numerous Deepams performed. The lamp tower in the courtyard will be lit. Night stay and worship followed by bhajans are the usual activities on Sivaratri.

Harijagaran, religious discourses, and bhajans mark the auspicious occasion during the 'Kartik masa' (Full moon night). 'Arati' is taken around the temple complex, and Prasadam, made of dried coconut chips and beaten rice, is distributed to all the devotees.

Vaishnavite Temples

The Vaishnavite Gods are worshipped in Goa, along with Saivaite deities. Damodar (Vasco), Narasimha (Veling) and Devaki Krishna (Chorao) are the Vaishnavite deities. One speciality is that all the Vaishnavite deities are not always in the form of Vishnu but are Lingas (An example being the temple of Damodar at Vasco). Here, they are worshipped with the mask of Vishnu. The mask will be removed only at the time of Abhishek.

A large temple for Vishnu (Lakshmi Narayan) is situated in the Shanta Durga temple at Kavalem. Priests and workers are allotted separately to serve God. Lakshmi Narayana is a part of Panchayatan of Shanta Durga Devi. Vishnu is seen in a standing posture; Lakshmi is invisible here.

Vishnu has the usual symbols of Padma, Chakra, Sankha, and Mace in his four hands. The annual festival falls on Krishna Panchami in Jeshta masa. Special puja is performed on Ekadasi. Vishnu is offered Tulasi leaves in puja.

Devaki Krishna is one of the notable Vaishnavite deities a goa.

Devaki Krishna Temple

Devaki Krishna is one of the notable Vaishnavite deities in Goa. The temple is near a tributary of the Zuari River and Ponda hills. It had a spacious compound surrounded by coconut palms, jackfruit and mango groves. Tranquility prevails here.

Devaki Krishna is a migrant deva, like other deities of the Ponda area, is 300 years old. Religious persecution forced the Mahajans to shift the deity to Karnataka. But The Sonde Raja promised to provide protection and build a temple. In this context, they brought the daily to Marcela and built the temple. The temple attracted several artists and musicians. Several small structures of Devaki Krishna and panchayatan came into existence.

The image of Devaki Krishna brought by its Mahajans from Choodamani (known as Chorao in current times) is ancient. Due to constant abhishekas, the features of the idol are lost. Hence, a new murti was ordered. The idol of Krishna was carved from black Shaligram stone and installed in 1979.

The Murti has four hands, each holding a butter ball (symbol of Pridhvi, the earth), a Sankh (Conch), a Padmac(flower), and a chakra (disc). The old Murti consigned has been to the temple well. Devaki Krishna is the personification of the mother-child relationship.

Worship:

The devotees perform special Abhishek to the deity with Panchamrit. The daily offerings are dal, rice and payasam (milk preparation is essential). The naivedya during the night, prepared by a priest, consists of fruit, dry coconut, moong, chana, jaggery and cardamom. The Arati is conducted by beating the drum and blowing the Conch-shell.

Festivals:

Mondays of Sravana masa are special. Monday is typical for Mahadev, Sravan, and Bhadrapad, as well as for Vishnu and Krishna. This speaks about the Saivaite influence at the Vaishnavite temples.

Srikrishna Janmashtami is the most important festival. The shrine is decorated with lights and flowers. A Special Abhishek is performed. Music and devotional songs are played when the daily is in full swing. Prasad is distributed to the devotees.

Worship of the Seshasai Vishnu is another important festival at This Temple. Go-puja is another festival. Navaratri is celebrated with great devotion.

Devi Temples:

In Goa, the worship of 'Devi' or Mother Goddess is amply evident, in addition to the worship of Saivite and Vaishnavtite deities. The Shakambari aspect of Devi worship is visible during the pujas of Navaratri celebrations. She is the mother par excellence who sustains the life of all inhabitants of the earth, whether humans or animals. She is the embodiment of knowledge, learning, and music.

Shanta Durga Devi Temple (Kavale)

Shanta Durga Temple is nearly 80 Km from Panaji. Initially, the deity was worshipped at 'Kaloshi'. However, the idol was moved to Kavale in Ponda after the Portuguese destroyed the Temple in 1564. The Temple was rebuilt in 1738. After over two and a half centuries of reconstruction, it looks fresh or almost new.

Shanta Durga is a widely worshipped deity in Goa. Her incarnation may be explained with peace and power. Every village and hamlet of Goa contains her form. Devotees call her a 'mai' or mother.

The Temple was built in the style of the 12th century (Simplicity and beauty). The Deepa Stambha is unique in its dignity. During Peswa Bajirao's time, the efforts of the minister Naro Ram became fruitful in getting endowments for the maintenance of the Temple. The Temple plan contains Mukhamandap, Sabha mandap and sanctum sanctorum. The deity has various Vahanas, such as 'Palakis' and 'Asanas. 'Agrasalas (pilgrims' hostels) are also constructed. Temple had a tank for the celebration of festivals.

Daily activities:

The dawn starts with music at the shrine, played by an instrument called 'Chaughada' in combination with Shehnai. Pujas begin at 6.30 AM. Cleaning the shrine (Nirmalya Visarjan) is the starting point for worship. It is followed by 'Abhishek' and 'Kumkumarchan'. The activities continue till the night 'arati'. The temple staff are engaged in all the temple activities. Their services include cleaning, lighting lamps, preparing articles for Abhishek and puja, playing musical instruments, and Hari Katha and Pravachan.

The Murthy of Santa Druga Devi is in the shape of a Linga. In front of this is a murti of the Goddess sitting, raising her right hand to bless devotees. Her ornaments are the golden crown, Mangala sutra, necklace, bangles, bracelets, hair bun-like ornament, anklets, diamond earrings, and diamond tiara (on festive days).

Four Utsava murtis of Devi are prescribed for various occasions.

Bhogas (Naivedya):

At noon, the Bhogas are observed. Pujaris cook food that includes rice, dal, chapati, curd, ghee, and sweets. At night, only fruit offerings are made. This Bhoga concludes with the slogan "Santa Durga Jagadambe

Udayasty". Arati is a part of the activity. After the day's puja, the Utsavamurthi is taken to the bed chamber with two lamps. A special light called 'Nandadeep' (traditional brass lamp) hanging from the ceiling burns the entire night.

<u>List of festivals:</u>

Festivals are celebrated from Chaitra to Phalgun. Rathotsav and Navaratri are the major festivals.

The Temple stands with a message stating that Siva and Kesava are equal. To the devotees, the Goddess is 'Santamurthi', standing between Vishnu and Siva.

Kalika Devi (Kasarpal)

This temple is believed to be more than a thousand years old. It is now an almost shapeless piece of stone. It is believed to have been Chaturbhuji, Trisul and Dhal in the two left hands, lotus flower, and Khadga in the right.

Since the idol is shapeless, a new one was installed some seventy years back, carved out of Shaligram stone. The goddess is not a destroyer but a compassionate one. Navaratri is a significant festival of the temple.

Santa Durga Devi is one of the Panchayatan Temples, and the other temples are in Ramanath region, 35 Km from Ponda in the state. Lakshminarayana, Siddhanath, Bethal and Ramnath are the deities the devotees worship.

GUJARAT (GJ)

The state of Gujarat, situated on the western coast of India, has a rich history, character, and glory. Gujarat derived its name from the Prakrit word 'Gurjara ratta', which means 'the land of Gurjaras'. The Gurjaras were an immigrant tribe that entered India along with the Huns. The name Gujarat has been popular since the 10th century.

The state was formed on May 1, 1960. Rajasthan, Maharashtra, Madhya Pradesh, Daman-Diu, Dadra, and Nagar Haveli are the neighbouring states, and Pakistan is a neighbouring country. The Arabian Sea had its coastline. The area of the state is 1,96,024 sq km. Gandhinagar is the capital. Gujarati is the primary language. Hinduism and Islam are the main religions. Sabarmati, Maha Narmada and Tapati are the rivers. Gir range mountains are well known.

Temples of Gujarat are the added beauty of the state. They have physical prosperity as well as religious base and historicity. Temples may be classified as Siva, Vishnu, Krishna, Surya, Shakti, Mahalakshmi, Rukmini, Kali, etc.

Siva Temples

Somnath Temple

The Legendary or celebrated temple of Somnath in Gujarat is believed to have been built by 'Soma' (the moon God). It is one of India's most ancient temples, with references to Puranas, epics like the Mahabharata, and the writings of Al-Biruni.

Figure 5: Somanath Temple

Somnath's famous phoenix-like temple stands in neat gardens above the beach, 6 km southeast of Veraval. The sea below gives it a nostalgic charm. Locals compare the temple that rose again after repeated destructions to a mythical phoenix, which is a unique bird of the Arabian desert that burned itself on a funeral pyre every few centuries and rose from the ashes with renowned youth. They believe the bird leaves an egg so that another phoenix can rise.

<u>Puranic/Epic and Historical Backdrop:</u>

Somnath temple has been razed and rebuilt multiple times. Soma, the moon god, is believed to have constructed a gold version of the temple, which Ravana rebuilt in silver. Krishna built the temple with Sandalwood, and Bhimdeva, the Solanki ruler, constructed it in stone.

During his reign of 24 years (1000-1024 AD), Muhammad Ghazni from Afghanistan raided India 17 times, out of which seven times on Somnath. The most important one was in 1024 AD. The Muslim soldiers took sufficient water and food for seven days. Thirty thousand camels were used in the task of the Somnath expedition.

<u>Sources of revenue – Staff and the description of the Temple</u>

The temple had the financial resources of 10,000 villages. Every day, 1000 Pandits and 500 dancers performed their duties. Somnath was installed on a platform of 56 pillars. Nityabhishek is being performed. A vessel is hung above the Linga with a golden chain of 200 maunds (a maund means 38 kilograms). The vessel is intended for abhisheka (water is poured).

Mahmoud Ghazni looted and carried away a camelload of jewels, gold, and other valuables. During this period, 70,000 Hindu defenders died, and the temple was destroyed.

The rebuilding work continued for centuries. The temple was again razed in 1297, 1394 and finally in 1706 by Aurangazeb. After the 1706 demolition, the temple was not rebuilt until 1950. The current symmetrical structure was built according to traditional designs on the original coastal site. It is painted creamy and appears to be a fine sculpture. A large black 'Sivalingam' is installed.

Somnath is one of the 12 (Dwadasa) Jyotirlingas in India, and it is the first one.

"Saurastra dese (Gujarat)
visadete Ramye.
Jyotirmayam
Chandra kalavatansam.
Bhaktipradhanaya
krupavatheernam.
Tham Somanatham Saranam Prapadye."

The meaning of this sloka is devotees' worship and surrender to Somnatha of Gujarat, who is the embodiment of knowledge and is as beautiful as the moon, which is kind enough to bless them and ignite the feeling of devotion among them.

Nageswar Temple

Nageswar Temple is 12 km from Dwaraka in Gujarat. It is one of the 12 Jyotirlingas. Naganath and Nagesvari are the Gods and Goddesses. The source of this temple is Sivapurana.

"Yamye Sadange
Nagaretinamye
vibhushitangam, Vividhaischa
Bhogen
sadbhakti, mukti Pradayani
Samekam
Sri Naganatham Saranam Prapatye"

Yamye means southern direction. Seeking protection of Nageswara, who was beautifully decorated, provides bhakti and mukti or salvation. This is the substance of the above-cited 'Sloka'.

Figure 6: Nageswar Temple

Though there is an ancient temple, another great temple was constructed. Women are not supposed to touch the Linga but are allowed darshan. A big Siva idol, a rare one not found elsewhere, is installed by the side of the temple.

Siva Temple (Bhadbhut)

Lord Siva, also known as Mahadeva, is present in the temple (Bhareswar). This is located on the northern side of the Narmada River.

Patan group of Temples

The town of Patan is 112 km from Ahmadabad. During the 10th century, it was a great seat of Saivism. On its bank was a great lake (Sahasra Linga Talab), and it was said there were 1108 Siva temples.

Vishnu and Maha Lakshmi Temples

Swami Narayan Temple and several Vaishnavite temples are situated in Ahmadabad. Siddhapur Maha Lakshmi temple is one of the 108 Shaktipeeth temples described in the Devi Bhagavatam. Bindusarovar is famous and one of the five great Sarovars.

Sri Krishna Temples

Lord Vishnu's ten incarnations are popular in Hinduism as 'Dasavataras'. Krishnavatara gathers around several legends. He is the hero of the great epic Mahabharata, in which he delivered the celebrated sermon of the Bhagavad Gita, which contains 18 chapters (Astadhyayi).

Dwaraka

Lord Krishna founded Dwaraka after migrating from Madhura with his Yadava clan about 3,400 years ago. In ancient days, Dwaraka was known as 'Dwaramati'. Dwaraka became the capital of Krishna's empire. The place attained sanctity, drawing millions of pilgrims.

Archaeological excavations brought the present Dwaraka to light. Some more (5) are said to be submerged in the sea.

Janmashtami festival is the biggest festival during August / September, drawing people from different parts of the country. Dwarka is one of the four maths established by Sri Adi Shankaracharya in the 8th century to spread Hinduism. Krishna's temple, established by Krishna's grandson, exists. One enters by Swarga Dwara (heaven) facing the Gomati River and leaves by Mokshadwara (Liberation). The speciality of the temple is that it was said to be built in one night (with Supernatural help).

On the west coast of the Arabian Sea, Dwaraka is also the seat of one of the Dwadasa Jyotirlingas, Nageswar. The five-floor Krishna Temple is also known as Jagat Mandir and Dwarakadhiish Temple.

The other temples near Dwaraka are Rukmini Mata, Vamana Murthy (Porbandar), Balarama, Jambavati, Satyabhama, Sudhama (Kuchela) Temple, etc. Bet Dwaraka had its significance. It is 5 km from Dwaraka. The golden idol of Krishna attracts elders and children.

Balak Tirth

The hunter's arrow struck Lord Krishna's foot, and he obtained 'Niryan' here, at the confluence of the rivers Kapila, Saraswathi, and Hiranya.

Surya Temple

Modhera Temple of Sun God was built in 1026 A.D. (Solankis). The temple is the finest in Indian temple architecture. Though the temple was ransacked, the structure exists to convey the grandeur.

Shamalaji Temple

This Temple is a Vaishnavite temple. The Idol Vishnu is made of black stone. It is known as Gada Tirth because the idol carries a mace (Gada). The Temple is in the Solanki style.

Shakti Temple

Ambaji Temple near Mount Abu is a Shakti Temple. Navaratri celebrations are popular.

Kali Temple

Pavagad Hill temple (550 meters in height) is that of Kali. The area is in Champaner, Pavagad, a World Heritage site. A Ropeway facility is provided. Further, one must climb 250 steps to reach the temple.

HARYANA (HR)

The area of Haryana is 44,212 Sq. Km. Chandigarh is the capital. Hindi and Punjabi are the chief languages. Hinduism, Islam, and Christianity are the major religions. Ghaggar and Yamuna are the main rivers. The lower Shivalik range of mountains forms important mountains. The state was formed on November 1, 1966.

Neighbouring states are Punjab, Himachal Pradesh, Uttaranchal, UP, Delhi, Rajasthan, and Chandigarh (UT).

The most famous place, Kurukshetra, has a spiritual history and many temples. The temples are of Lord Siva and Devi.

Kurukshetra (Thanesvar)

The importance of Kurukshetra in the epic or spiritual history of India may be briefly illustrated as follows:

"Kurukshetra is a place where Lord Brahma created the universe, and Lord Krishna delivered the Bhagavad Gita on the 18th day of the battle of Mahabharata."

Several things came to light when peeping into the depth of the historical backdrop of Kurukshetra.

Lord Brahma created 'Brahma Sarovar' (1170 meters in length and 546 meters in breadth). He made penance, followed by the creation of the universe. Kurukshetra is 155 km from Delhi. Through the great war of Mahabharata, the name of Kurukshetra came to the limelight.

Episode of Kurukshetra:

A king named Kuru came to this holy place where eight rivers flow: Sarasvati, Vaitaruni, Madhusrava, Kausiki, Drustadvati, Mandakini,

Vasu, and Ganga. Kuru made a plough and then requested Siva and Yama provide Nandi and buffalo to fill the land there.

Then Indra questioned him about what he was doing there. Kuru replied, 'I am growing eight crops.'

1. Truth (Satya)
2. Kindness (Daya)
3. Pardon (Kshama)
4. Charity (Daana)
5. Cleanliness (Shuddha)
6. Austerity (Nishkama)
7. Conduct (Brahmacharya) and
8. Devotion (Yoga)

Kuru said that the seeds are within him. Vishnu also questioned the same, and Kuru replied the same. Then Vishnu asked for evidence. Kuru offered his body, and Vishnu cut off his body, and he was brought to life by the Lord for his sterling character. He blessed Kuru that by his name, the place Kurukshetra would become popular and famous.

Further, those who die here will get 'Swarga Prapti'.

Hence, Kurukshetra became Dharmakshetra. Gita addressed the place as 'Dharmakshetre, Kurukshetre'. The Mahabharata war, the victory of the Pandavas, and the defeat of The Kauravas (Kuru was the founder of the Kaurara dynasty) took place here. Lord Krishna's Gitopadesa to the Arjun, Bhishma on 'Ampa sayya' waiting for 'Uttarayana Punyakala' to breathe his last. Arjun, using his arrows, brought Tekt Patala Ganga.

Sages like Vasishta and Vishwamitra attained Divayatva here. Valmiki and Vyasa wrote great epics that were gifted to humanity. World preceptor Shankaracharya visited this place. The place is holy, with several lakes and temples, old and new.

Siva Temples

- Thaneswar: Siva Linga, along with Trisul, is found in a lake at Thaneswar, and a temple was constructed. The attractive idol of the same campus is Lord Brahma from the naval of Sri Maha Vishnu, for which there is a separate temple.

- Bhootesvar Temple: Hari Kailash Temple and Jwala Maheswar Thirth are more temples on the bank of a Lake in the Jind district of Haryana.

- Sainik colony temple of Faridabad: A big Siva Linga (21.25 ft) exists here. There is also a cave where Lord Siva is found doing penance, and an idol of his consort is by his side. Daily worship, Abhishekas, and festivals are celebrated here.

Devi Temples

- Jwalamahesvari Devi Temple (Jind): On the banks of river Jayanthi, this ancient temple is roughly 120 km away. This temple is said to have been built by Pandavas in Mahabharata times. They worshipped the Mata for their victory in the Kurukshetra war.

- Manasadevi Temple (Mani Majra): The temple is just 10 km from Chandigarh and is also an ancient temple. Satidevi's head part fell here; hence, this is also said to be one of the Shakti Peethas, and the Devi is known as Manasa Devi. Maharaja Gopal Das Singh constructed this temple during the 8th century. Along with Manasa Devi, Lakshmi Devi and Vaishnavi Devi idols are also there. Ganesa and Subrahmanya Swamy are also installed. During Phalguna masa, a mela is celebrated every year.

- Ambadevi Temple (Ambala): The town Ambala had its name due to this Goddess. The devotees worship Ambadevi as Durga and Bhavani.

- Sithaladevi Temple (Gurgav): This Devi is said to be the form of Satidevi, and this place is also considered one of the Shakti Peethas. Devotees worship the Goddess to get relief from chronic diseases.
- Jayanthi Devi Temple (Near Chandigarh): Formerly in Himachal Pradesh, this temple is on the banks of the Jayanthi river and attracts devotees.
- Devi Temples (Kaital): The Salivahana kings built these temples of Devi with red stone in the 7th century. Daily Pujas are performed.

HIMACHAL PRADESH (HP)

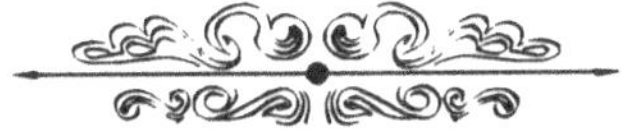

The Himalayas or Himachal, 'The abode of snow,' are mighty, mysterious and the most fascinating of all the mountains in the world. The state is named Himachal Pradesh, as it is part of the great Himalayan mountain range. Before the independence, several principalities or small states existed under the control of the Rajas. Of course, the final control was that of the British. In free India, the integration process has been completed, and the new state of Himachal Pradesh came into existence on 25 January 1971 with Shimla as the capital (once a hill station under the British). Punjab, Haryana, and Uttarakhand are the neighbouring states, and China is the neighbouring country. The area of the state is 55,673 km. The flowing rivers are Ravi, Beas, Chenab, Sutlej, and Yamuna. The history of this area is the history of the people who settled in the wilderness of the Himalayas since time immemorial. Himachal Pradesh is also known as the "Apple state of India" since the state is forward in producing superior-quality apples.

Himachal Pradesh is universally acclaimed for its scenic beauty. With valleys full of apple orchards, apricots, cherries, and strawberries, the state is styled as the "fruit bowl of India."

The state's fauna and flora are fantastic, fascinating, and unique. Rare species are noticeable. Maple, Bamboo, Mulberry, and broad-leaved varieties are found.

Under the fauna of the state, rare species like Kalij, Kokla, Monal, and Snow Cock deserve mention. Small mammals like Himalayan squirrels, wolves, blue sheep, musk deer, yak, black bear, and brown bear are found in the various parts of the state. National Parks, zoos, and wildlife sanctuaries were established to protect flora and fauna.

Regarding the population, Hindus are the predominant compared to people of other faiths.

Mount Kailas – Manas Sarovar

Mount Kailas is the holiest place to the devotees of Lord Siva, Vishnu, and Devi, or 'Shakti'. It is considered one of the 51 'Shaktipeethams'. It is the place where the right hand of Sati Devi (consort of Shiva) has fallen.

The Manas Sarovar, or the recent Mount Kailash Yatra, consists of two spots to be visited. One is 'Kailas Giri' and the other 'Manas Sarovar'. The speciality of this place is that there is no temple or idol. The devotees must concentrate their minds and thoughts on the holy place and the deities because Kailash is the dwelling place of Lord Shiva and Parvathi. One of the greatest devotees of Shiva, Ravana, did great penance to get the 'Atma Linga' of Shiva and succeeded in getting it. The world preceptor Adi Shankaracharya succeeded in obtaining four 'Shiva Lingas' from Shiva and installed in four directions in India, namely:

1. Puri (Govardhan Matt)
2. Sringeri (Karnataka)
3. Sarada Matt (Dwaraka, Gujarat)
4. Uttarakhand (Badari – Jyothir)

Devi or Shakti Temples

1. Nainadevi Temple: This Temple is situated at Nainadevi on the top of a hill. According to a legendary source, the eyes of Satidevi (Parvathi) have fallen here, which is connected to the episode of Daksha Yagna. Therefore, the goddess's name is Nainadevi'. The temple is small and covered with gold-quoting shikhara. The deity is not in the form of an idol. It is shaped like a round stone decorated with golden eyes.
2. Chamundi Bhagavati Temple: This is situated in the 'Naggar' region. The deity is said to be one of the 'Sapta Matrikas' and the true incarnation of Durga.

3. Chamunda Temple: The Temple is situated in a valley named Chamunda. The deity is said to be one of the 'Nava Durgas'. The deity is Chamunda. The temple has a spacious compound. The temple is built with three floors. There is Mukha Mandapa and Sanctum Sanctorum. This idol is also of stone form with the shape of a coconut but decorated with eyes, eyebrows, and mouth. The deity killed two demons named Chanda and Munda; therefore, she is called Chamunda, as per legend. According to puranic sources, she is said to be a form of Parvathi Devi. Near this temple is a Shiva temple named Nandikeswara. There is also a ten-foot image of Hanuman known as 'Sankatamochan'.

4. Jwala Mukhi Temple (Goddess of Light): The place's name is Jwalamukhi, and the temple's name is Jwalamukhi. This is a famous holy place on the top of a hill. This is said to be one of 51 Shaktipeetha. The tongue of Sati Devi has fallen here. The deity is said to be in the form of a flame (Jwala). There are nava Jwalas(9). Shiva is known as 'Unnata Bhairava'. Vidyeswaridevi is also present here. A golden trident of 40 feet is to be seen here. Regarding puja, 'Arati' is given to the deity five times daily. There is a tradition here saying that girls below ten are worshipped, treating them as the form of 'Mata' (Puja is called Kanne puja). People believe that they will be happy and prosperous by following this tradition. Ranjit Singh installed the gold dome of the temple.

5. Taradevi Temple (Jwalamukhi): This temple is situated just opposite the Jwalamukhi Temple. In recent times, it has been built on modern lines with sculptural details. The deity is popularly known as the deity of 'Dasa Mahavidyas'.

6. Kali Temple: In Ghoshi town, the temple is at 8500 feet at sea level. The age of this temple is said to be one and a half centuries. There are three idols Kali, Syamala and Chandi. The deity is considered to embody "Shakti" and "Durga Devi". People attend and worship her in large numbers.

7. Vajreswari Temple of Kangda: There is a Puranic source about this old temple. The goddess is known as Vajratara and Vidyeswari or Vijayeswari. Some 7th and 8th-century inscriptions are traced here, revealing temple history. Foreign invasions and earthquakes destroyed the temple. The deity is said to be powerful as per the six Chakras: Aagna, Visuddha, Anahata, Manipuraka, Swadhistana, and Mooladhara. As per Puranic sources, war occurred between Shiva and Jalandhara (demon). Vishnu was also involved, and after Jalandhara's death, the place became popular with 64 Kshetras. The name of Kangda: In The war, Jalandhara's head was cut off (Kan). The place is Gad (Kota or fort). Therefore, the place is 'Kangada', later known as Kangda. The body of Jalandhara is as hard as vajra, and hence, the deity of this place is known as Vajreswari. The festival is celebrated here in Pongal the next day (Lohri). Bhairana and Kapali Bhairev temples are also here near the Vajreswari Temple.

8. Chinta Purni Devi Temple: The place's name is Chinta Purni, and it is associated with the deity's name. This temple is a Shakipeeth; Devi is one of the 'Nava Durgas' forms here. The devotees' difficulties or problems (Chinta) are solved by worshipping her with utmost faith and devotion. The temple is built on the slope of a mountain. The walls are covered by golden sheets with beautiful designs. The deity is in the form of a 'Pinda' and not an idol. There is another name for this deity – 'Chinnamastika'. To kill the demons, she came to save the people. The festival or 'mela' is celebrated every year from March to April, July to August, and September to October.

9. Valley of Parvathi Devi (Kulu): This is the place where Parvathi Devi's earring was lost. The serpent king brought this and handed it over to Lord Shiva. Dasera celebrations are performed grandly.

10. Hidimba Temple (Manali) or Dhungri Temple: The story relates to the Mahabharata. Hidimba was the wife of Bhimasena. A temple is constructed here. According to the inscriptions, Hidimba or

Himadevi temple was built in 1553 AD. This is an ancient stone and wood temple. The construction of the temple is novel, with four stores. The temple is built of wood and has beautiful carvings of dancers. Ghatotkacha is worshipped in the form of a tree near the temple.

11. Nagini Temple: The Rajputs of Noorpur took a particular interest in this temple 1000 years ago. People believe that they are saved from snake bites. The temple is situated in Badwar, a village in the Kangda area.

12. Solani Devi (Solan): Solan is the name of the district. Devotees worship the deity in the form of Durgamata.

13. Tripura Sundari Temple (Naggar): The temple was built in the Pagoda style. Umbrella-shaped 'Gopura' is the speciality here. The Idols of Ganesh, Vishnu and Brahma are installed beside the main deity, Tripura Sundari.

In the Himalayas, a variety of shrines are found. Several village Gods are being worshipped. In addition to the above-cited Devi or Shakti Temples, the temples of the village gods reflect the faith of the people at large. The temple committees manage such types of temples, and the village temples are the nucleus of the village activities.

Saivaite Temples

1. Baijnath Temple: Baijnath, or Vaidyanath Temple, is an ancient Shiva temple in the small town of Bajinath. It was built in 1204 AD by two local merchants. The style of the temple combines the northern and Orissan. The Vimana is 50 feet high, and on it exists a round-shaped Sikhara. Sculpturally, this temple is beautiful. The sculptural art of devata murtis is found on the pillars. The walls of the temple contain art representations. Among the artistic works are the murtis of Mahishasura Mardini, Kali with eight hands, meditating Shiva, The Nandi, elephant, etc., which are to be cited. In the sanctum sanctorum on a marble platform, Shiva is in the

form of Linga with Nagabharana. Behind him, Parvathi's murti is seen.

2. Mani Mahesh Temple: Mani Mahesh is on the top of a hill, and there is an ancient Shiva Temple on it. This temple is compared to Manas Sarovar. The temple is situated in Barmore in Chamba. The temple had a tank (lake).

3. Bhootanath Temple (Mandi): An ancient temple of Shiva is in the Kulu valley. Bhootnath is also Arthanareeswar. Nandi and Simha idols are also present.

4. Pancha Vaktra Mahadev (Mandi) is another Shiva temple. Shiva has five faces and ten hands.

5. Bijili Mahadev (Kulu): The Temple is at the confluence of the Parvathi and Beas rivers. This Mahadev is mentioned in the Rigveda. The temple is in the shape of a Pagoda. During Sravana masa, festivals are celebrated for Shiva and Parvathi.

6. Manikarnika Shiva Temple: This area is said to be where Shiva and Parvathi enjoyed the scenic beauty of Kulu Valley (also cited above as 'Valley of Parvathi Devi '), and at that time, the goddess lost her earring. It is believed that the Serpent king, 'Adisesha', took it and disappeared. Shiva ordered the 'Ganas' to search for it, but they failed to find it. Hence, Shiva opened the third eye and performed Tandava, resulting in the fall of gems. Hot springs in this temple area are believed to have formed when Sesha, after Lord Shiva's Tandava, threw up the jewels from under the water, creating hot springs. Parvathi's earring 'Manikarna' fell here; hence, the place is known as Manikarnika.

7. Kulantha Peetham: Manikaran Shiva lived here. A hot spring lake is here. Devotees use the water not only for baths but also for cooking. It is said they could obtain 'punya lok' by doing so. Narada talked about Shiva's greatness in removing the evil qualities of the devotees.

8. Baxunag Temple: This is a place of waterfalls where Shiva stayed for some time, and a temple was constructed. Lakes and

Kunds existed. The holy waters make sinners free from their sins.

9. Sarahan—Srikhand—Mahadev Temple: Shiva meditated here near a hill. The Pandavas visited this place and worshipped Swayambhu Shiva.

Vaishnavite Temples

1. Chamba Temples: Lakshmi Narayan temple, Radhakrishna temple, Lakshmi Damodar temple, etc., are in Chamba. The biggest temple is Lakshmi Narayan Temple, which was built in the 10th century. The smallest temple is Radhakrishna Temple, which was built in 1828 AD. Lakshmi Damodar Temple has the deities of Lakshmi and Narayan.

2. Barmore: The Narasimha Temple, also called Brahmapuri, is situated here in the Chamba Valley. It is part of the Chaurasi temple complex.

3. Raghunath Temple (Kulu): It is near the Beas River and was constructed during the 17th century by Raja Jagat Singh. The main idol was brought from Ayodhya.

Other Temples

There are several other temples in Himachal Pradesh worth mentioning. A few are mentioned here:

1. Kangda – Masrur temple complex consists of several rock-cut temples resembling the Ajanta and Ellora temples. Sita, Rama, Lakshman, and Shiva are the important ones.

   a. Veerabhadra Temple: Veerabhadra destroyed Daksha yagna and cut off Daksha's head. Veerabhadra temple is here.

2. Bhunter: Mahadev and Jagannath temples are located here.

3. Barmore: The Chaurasi temple complex consists of 84 different Shiva, Narasimha, and Ganesh shrines. Raja Sahil Verman is believed to have built these temples in the 7th century.

4. Pandava's Temple: This temple is located at Nadaan on the banks of Beas.
5. River temples for Ganga & Yamuna at Kulu are also to be visited.
6. Triveni Sangam: Confluence of Dhaumya Ganga, Vyasa Ganga and Soumya Ganga.
7. Jakhu Temple: Situated on Jakhu hill, a small shrine of Hanuman is in this temple. Hanuman's funny relief murals are portrayed. There is a 33-meter-high Hanuman's statue here.
8. Old Manali – Manu Maharshi Temple is built here, and he is in a meditation posture.

Architecture Of the Temples

The temple architecture in Himachal Pradesh offers a variety of styles and shapes. There are six categories:

1. Cave
2. Sikhara
3. Pagoda
4. Mandap (Dome)
5. Flat Roofed and
6. Gompa

The history of temple architecture in Himachal Pradesh goes back to the 6th and 7th centuries. A roof and Pagoda-style fusion are also found in the upper Sutlej region.

Himachal Pradesh has a proud possession of temples and stone and metal sculptures. The metal images of Lakshmi Devi, Narasimha, Ganesh, and Nandi are rare art pieces.

JAMMU & KASHMIR (JK)

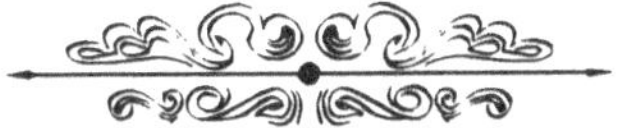

Jammu & Kashmir was initially formed as a state on 26 October 1947, when Maharaja Hari Singh signed the instrument of accession in favour of the Indian Union.

Jammu and Kashmir Reorganization Act 2019, passed in both houses of Parliament in August 2019, provided provisions to reconstitute Jammu & Kashmir as two separate Union Territories: Jammu & Kashmir and Ladakh.

Jammu and Kashmir are universally known for nature's beauty, which includes mountain ranges, waterfalls, valleys, and great Hindu temples. Blue waters on one side and green carpet-like landscapes on the other attract many people and tourists, both Indian and foreign. Amarnath and Vaishnavi Devi temples attract spiritualistic pilgrims.

Amarnath

In Jammu and Kashmir, there is a Hindu Pilgrim Mountain named 'Amarnath', the seat of Lord Shiva. This is a cave and an ancient seat of God supposed to be 5000 years old. The distance from Srinagar to Amarnath is 141 km, and from the sea level, it is 3888 Mts. The distance from Pahalgam is 46 km. The pilgrimage starts from Srinagar and reaches the destination via Pahalgam, Chandanwari, Seshnag and Panchatarani. The right time for 'Amarnath Yatra' is July to mid-August.

Discovery of Amarnath Cave and the Shepherd Boy – A Story:

A shepherd named Bhuta Malik happened to meet a sage or an ascetic who gave him a bag containing coal, and the latter disappeared. Bhuta Malik started searching for the 'sadhu' but failed. To his great surprise, he found gold coins in the bag and the cave or 'Guhalaya' containing 'Hima Linga' of Lord Shiva.

<u>Permission Required:</u>

Pilgrims need to get permission to go to Amarnath from the Government since it is a tight security zone with the borders of China on the north, Tibet on the east, Pakistan on the west and the southern side, our States of Himachal Pradesh and Punjab exists. Hence, the region is controlled by the Military, Paramilitary and CRPF.

<u>The Journey:</u>

The journey to Amarnath is difficult. Still, one can forget it by looking at the panoramic beauty of the hills, valleys, rivers, and sub-rivers on the way to Amarnath.

One route to the destination is by road. Another route starts from Sonamarg to Baltal and Amarnath – a hilly way that is difficult (14 km). 'Dolis' are available for the aged women and children.

<u>Classification of Shiva Lingas – Special reference to Amarnath:</u>

- Kruta Yuga – Ratna Linga
- Tretayaga – Swarna Linga
- Dwapara Yuga – Rasa Linga
- Kali Yuga – Parthiva Linga

Shiva Lingam of Amarnath is a natural stone covered with snow (Himam). Hence, it is known as 'Hima Lingam'. In the Planet Publication from Singapore, these lines throw light on the Amarnath deity:

"The stone lingam becomes opalescently encrusted with ice, and it is believed to wax and wane with the moon's phases."

The shape of Shiva Linga is that of a conch ('Sankhakruti') with a height of 5-8 ft, depending on the formation of snow on the stone Linga.

The devotees take baths in the river, have darshan of the Lord, pray, and take stone powder as a 'Vibhuti', which they consider Prasad. They find the difference in the growth and disappearance of the Linga during Jyesta—Aashada masas (increase) and Sravanam vanishing or disappearance.

<u>Source about Amarnath:</u>

The book 'Raja Tarangini' reveals the history of the 11th-century AD Kashmiri kings and The Kshetramahatyam of the temple. Suryamathi, the queen of Kashmir, presented a 'Baana Linga' and golden Trident (Trisul) to the temple.

<u>Puranic Story of Amarnath Cave Temple:</u>

One day, Parvathi asked Shiva to reveal the secret of birth and death cycles when they were in a pleasant mood in the Himalayas. Shiva said this secret cannot be revealed amidst living ones before them. Before going to the cave, Lord Shiva left his associates Nandi at Pahalgam, Chandra Vanka (crescent moon) at Chandanwari, snake at Seshnag and Ganga at 'Panchatarani'. In this context, they searched for a convenient place and found the cave of Amarnath. Some doves were there then but flew away with the sound of Shiva's 'Dhamaruka'. Of course, there were two eggs of the doves unnoticed. Shiva narrated the secret of the birth-death cycle to his consort. He said the newly born ones (coves) will not have the birth-death cycle. Hence, people believe that they are present to date in the cave.

In the Amarnath cave, there is not only Shiva Linga (Hima Linga) but also Parvathi, Ganesa and Bhairava Murthy (Himma Lingas). They, too, grow and decrease on Purnima and Amavasya days. Devotees will be thrilled by having the darshan of Himalingeswar-Amarnath to eliminate their sins.

Vaishno Devi Temple

Sri Vaishno Devi or Sri Vaishnavidevi is considered to be 'Adi Shakti' with the 'Amsa' of Maha Saraswathi, Maha Lakshmi and Mahakali in the form of a 'Pinda' settled in the cave temple on the mountain named 'Trikuta' in Himalayas. The temple is at 'Katra', 50 km from Jammu. The distance to the temple is 14 km, and the path is challenging, i.e., a steep trek. For those who cannot go up to the mountain, there is the facility of horses and 'Dolis'.

The devotees pray Vaishnavidevi, saying 'Jai Mata Di'. They believe the Goddess will bless them with 'Dharma, Artha, Kama and Moksha'. The token system is there for the darshan of Mataji.

Local Legend:

The existence of Vaishnodevi, Sri Rama's Vanavasa, Vaishnavi's approach, and her merger with the divine Ramachandra relate to Vaishnavidevi's history.

The story or history of this Goddess began in the Tretayuga. The incarnation of Jagannatha, known as 'Shakhi Swaroopini', combining in herself Maha Lakshmi, Mahakali and Maha Saraswathi, was born to Ratnakar Sagar as a daughter. She was named 'Vaishnavi'. Ratnasagar was the ruler of the Rameswar region and the surrounding areas. As she grew, she became a devotee of Mala Vishnu and said she would marry him only.

On the way to Lanka, Lord Sri Rama came to Rameswaram, and then Vaishnavi requested him to merge her with him. Lord Rama said he would oblige her request if she recognized him. After Ravana Vadha, Rama came to her on the way to Ayodhya like an older man. Vaishnavi could not recognize him, so she could not fulfil her desire. Of course, Sri Rama advised her to stay at Trikuta Parvatha in the Himalayas, bless the devotees who visit her and offer prayers. Further, he said in Kaliyuga, he would marry her as Kalki. Vaishnavidevi remained on Trikuta Parvatha as per the word given to Lord Sri Rama.

There are also sub-stories of Sridhara, a great devotee of the Goddess and Bhairava. The latter was chasing Vaishnavidevi and came up to the cave (Trikuta). Vaishnavidevi cut off the head of Bhairava. The demon-like Bhairava requested her to pardon him, and the Devi said that the devotees, after her darshan, should visit Bhairava for the completion of the pilgrimage.

A new way was built, making it easier to visit the Devi. In front of the cave is the idol of Vaishnodevi, her Vahana—Simha's idol. We find three Devatasilas indicating Saraswathi, Lakshmi, and Kali. The main God's 'Pinda' is covered with red silk cloth and decorated with ornaments. Three golden Chatras (umbrellas) are kept behind, along with golden crowns. The Deepakanti makes the atmosphere more holy and beautiful.

The temple is open almost throughout the day and night (except sometime in the morning and evening). As per statistics, more devotees visit this spot next to Tirupati.

Other Temples:

Ramalayam – Anjaneya idol, Bhairavaghat reminding Bhairava (Pinda form). Anjaneya is decorated with a red cloth, while Bhairava is decorated with a black cloth. There is a 'Homa Gundam' where 'Vibhuthi' is available. Sarannavaratri and Vasantha Navaratri are performed every year during September to October timeframe.

Other Temples of Jammu and Kashmir

Surya Temple:

The temple is at Marthand, 68 km away from Srinagar. Kashmiri king Muktaditya built the Surya temple in the 7th – 8th century AD. The temple is the most beautiful, with 84 pillars. This temple was built in a square shape with limestone and bricks. It is said that Kasyapa Mahamuni resided here. The Sun temple of Marthand is a backdrop of snow mountains. The beauty of the Kashmir valley is visible from this place. A British historian, Sir Francis Younghusband, appreciated the sculptural beauty of the temple.

Siva Temples:

- Baramullah: Siva Temple was constructed in 1915 by the queen of Kashmir, Mohini Sisodia. Siva and Parvathi idols were installed.
- Puramandal: This place is 50 km from Jammu. It is considered a Gaya Temple. Siva is worshipped as Umapathi along with his consort Umadevi.
- Suddha Mahadev Temple: This ancient temple of Shiva is located 16km from Jammu on the way to Srinagar. The consort of Siva is called Suddha Mahadevi. Trisul is worshipped here, which killed a demon named Suddhantar.
- Basukinath Temple: This ancient Shiva temple is famous near Srinagar. The idol of Shiva is in black marble. The Trisul sent to Amarnath is from this temple, which is on the banks of the river Jhelum.
- Budha Amarnath: This ancient temple is located 236 km away from Jammu-Kashmir at Rajpura Mandi on the banks of the Loran River. Festivals are celebrated on Sravana Pournami.

Nageswar Temples:

- Nageswar Mandir of Verinag is near Srinagar, the birthplace of river Jhelum. Ancient Siva temple named Nageswar and Nageswaridevi is situated here.
- Anantnag – Adisesh Temple: This is also an ancient temple and is located 56 Km from Jammu. Lord Vishnu slept on Adisesh, and this Anantnag is significant in this way.

Raghunath Mandir:

Situated in Jammu, this temple was built in 1835 by Gulab Singh. His son Ranbir Singh continued the construction of the temple. This is a big temple with a spacious campus. There is a separate temple for

Rama – 'Raghunath Alay'. There are several temples here. Separate idols of Lakshman – Bharat-Satrughna are also installed along with 'Sita's idol. Among several temples are Matsya, Kurma, Varaha, Narasimha, Hanuman, Radhakrishna, Lakshmi Narayan, and Siva. Gayatrimata's temple is also to be seen.

<u>Kali Temples:</u>

- Bhadrakali temple: This temple is located on top of a hill 40 km from Almora. Here, we find a confluence of the rivers Bhageswari, Sarayu, and Gomathi. Nearby is a great Siva Kshetra—Vaidyanath.
- Spituk Kali's Temple: This temple is in Leh, close to the Spituk monastery. The deity's face is covered throughout the year except on 'Sankranthi' day.

<u>Siva Vishnu Temple (Avanthipur):</u>

These two Temples are dedicated to Siva and Vishnu. King Avanti constructed the Siva (Avantiswara) and Vishnu (Avanti Swamy) temples during the 9th century. Vishnu is represented with six hands. Sridevi, Bhoodevi is in 2 hands and Sankha – Chakra – Gada – Dhanus is in the four hands.

<u>Raksh Sthal of Janmu:</u>

This place is where Ravana Brahma did penance.

JHARKHAND (JH)

Jharkhand is a state created from part of Bihar on 15 November 2000. Its area is 79,714 sq km, and Ranchi is its capital.

The neighbouring states are Bihar, Uttar Pradesh, Chhattisgarh, Odisha, and West Bengal.

Ranchi Temples

- Jagannathupur Temple: Similar to the Puri Jagannath Temple, this temple on a hill was built by a king in 1691. In size, it is tiny compared to the Puri Temple. Ratha yatra is conducted here.
- Angrabadi Temple: This temple is situated at a distance of 40 km from Ranchi. This multi-Gods and goddesses temple consists of images of Sita, Rama, Hanuman, Siva, and Ganesa. The name of the temple has been changed to 'Amreswartham'.
- Chinnamasta Temple: The temple is built on a hillock on the riverside or confluence of the Damodar and Bhairavi (or Bhera) rivers. This temple is known for tantric worship. Goddess Kali is the centre of worship. Of course, there are sub-temples of Goddesses known as 'Dasamaha Vidyas'. They are:

  - Taara
  - Shodasi
  - Bhuvaneswari
  - Bhairavi
  - Bhagala
  - Kamala
  - Maatangi
  - Dhoomavati and
  - Kali

Festivals are celebrated on 'Maha Sankranti'. People from Bihar, Jharkhand, and West Bengal attend in large numbers.

Dewri Temple: This sandstone temple is 60 km from Ranchi and is dedicated to Durga Devi (another name: Solhabhuji).

Deoghar Temples

Deoghar is considered the abode of Gods, having a picturesque location. To the north of the town is a wooded area called Data Jungle. In the northwest, there is a wooded hill called Nandan Pahar and beyond that, there is a range of hills known as 'Trikuta Parvatha'. There are two rivers, Yamunajor and Dharua. With its scenic beauty, this place is attractive. The Temples of Baidyanath or Shiva are the most important of all the temples of Jharkhand, attracting pilgrims in large numbers all year round.

Three import fairs are held on occasions of Sri Panchami, Sivaratri and Bhadra Purnima. There is a legend about Ravana's request for Mahadeva to come to Lanka. Still, Siva did not accept the request but asked him to take one of the 12 Jyotirlingas on condition it should not be deposited on earth, failing which it would be fixed to the spot forever. In the guise of a Brahmin, Lord Vishnu came forward to hold the Linga when Ravana asked for relief. When Ravana turned back, the Jyotirlinga was fixed firmly, and The Brahmin vanished. Ravana attempted to move the Lingam but could not.

Consequently, he used to come from Lanka and worship the Lord daily, and the place is considered Deoghar. After Ravana's death, a hunter named Baiju worshipped the Lingam, and therefore, this is named Baidyanath.

Another one is the famous Maha Shaktipeeth (Daksha story reference), the heart of Sati fell at Deoghar.

Tapovan Temple of Deoghar:

Siva Temple, on the top of a hill, attracts pilgrims as Tapovanth Mahadev. There are caves around this temple, one of which contains Siva Linga. The image of Hanuman is also in the broken rock.

Radha Krishna Mandir:

About 1½ km from Baidyanath temple, the temple of Radha Krishna is situated at 146 feet in height and built beautifully. The mandir is similar to the Sri Ramakrishna Mandir of Belur. Special pujas are performed as per the Vaishnavite tradition.

Surya Temple:

At about 40 km away, the modern temple of Sun God has been built. A chariot of Surya with 18 wheels and eight horses drawing the chariot is well represented. This temple is different from other temples of the Sun God in other places.

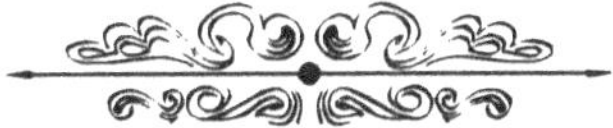

KARNATAKA (KA)

The State of Karnataka was formed on 1 November 1956. It was initially part of Mysore state. On 1 November 1973, the State was renamed Karnataka.

Figure 7: Karnataka – Map of Major Cities and Temples

The capital of Karnataka is Bengaluru. The State's area is 1,91,791 sq km. The neighbouring states are Kerala, Goa, Maharashtra, Andhra Pradesh, and Tamil Nadu. Hinduism, Islam, and Christianity are the main religions in the State. Jainism is also predominant in Karnataka.

Krishna, Tungabhadra, and Cauvery are the State's main rivers. The main mountain ranges in the State are the Western Ghats, Chitradurg Hills, Nandi Hills, Badami Hills, etc. Dussehra, Ugadi, Diwali, Navaratri Ramzan, etc., are the main festivals celebrated in the State.

The Temples of Karnataka are mostly ancient, and apart from their holy and religious aspects, they are unique in their rich architecture and beautiful sculptures. The Karnataka temples consist of the Gods and Goddesses, namely, Maha Ganapati, Siva, and Vishnu, in different forms such as Sri Krishna, Sri Ranganatha, Narasimha, Venkateshwara, Sri Rama, Subrahmanya, Chamundeswari, Annapurneswari, Mangala Devi, Mookambika etc.

Mahaganapathi Temples

Mahaganapathi is the most popular Daiwa or God in the Hindu pantheon. He is being worshipped in India and worldwide, from South America to Japan. Looking at the historical sources, the Indus Valley seals testify to the worship of Mahaganapathi. Adi Shankaracharya composed Pancharatnas on Ganesa. Its essence brings forth the image of God as well as the powers of God. Mahaganapathi likes 'Modakas'. He wears the crescent on his forehead. He protects devotees in all times of calamities and destroys their sorrows. In Buddhist art, Ganesh had a place. Ganesa is worshipped with different names in different countries:

- Rome – Ganas
- Myanmar – Maha pina
- Mongolia – Dotkar
- Tibet – Tosktrak
- Cambodia – Prak Ganesh

- China – Citlyang
- Japan – Kon-Kiten
- Mexico – Virakocha

The worship of Ganesha is considered a must before the commencement of any work, with a strong belief that he will destroy all the obstacles or Vighnas. He is also called the grain God, which speaks about his prominence in agriculture. In all the temples, the image of Ganapathi is found. Sage Vyasa worshipped Ganesha with 'Shodasa Namavali'.

Among several Ganesh temples in Karnataka, a few are mentioned here: Idugunj, Basavanagudi, Kubhasi, Sharava Ganapathi, Hattangadi Ganapathi and Gargeswari Ganapathi.

Idugunji Ganapathi

'Idugunji' was formerly known as 'Kunjaranya'. The nearest Town is Honnavar, and Gokarnam is 54 km away. The Temple is visited by more than a million devotees each year. Ganapathi is known as 'Dvibhuja Ganapathi'. The Ganesh idol here has no crown, snake, or Mooshika Vahana. The deity has three eyes. Ganesh is said to be Balaganapathi, who is wearing anklets.

<u>Legend:</u>

A Sage named Valakhilya and his followers did penance but could not succeed. At This juncture, Sage Narada advised praying to Ganesa. Narada took interest and brought the idol of Vinayaka made by Viswakarma on the advice of the divine couple of Kailasa. The sages followed Narada's instructions and did penance. In response, all the Gods, Siva, Parvati, Ganesa, Brahma, Vishnu, and others, came to the spot and left some powers. Narada installed the image of Ganapathi at Idugunji or Kunjaranya near the river Sharavathi.

Ganapathi informed the sages that he would stay here forever. Various Tirthams are here, and the devotees dip in them to fulfil their desires. God created Ganesa Tirtham.

<u>The Temple:</u>

The Temple is a two-tier structure. The sanctum is in a vast hall. The idol is having two hands (Dvibhuja Ganapathi). Lord Siva worshipped before conquering Tripurasura, Vishnu before tying Maha Bali, and Brahma worshipped before starting creation. Seshanag worshipped before carrying the earth on its head, and Parvathi worshipped before destroying Mahishasura.

Puja is performed three times daily (7:00 AM, 1:00 PM and 8:00 PM).

The car festival, held during January – February, Ganesh Chaturthi, Makara Sankranthi, and Karthika Deepotsava are the prominent festivals celebrated at the Temple. Thus, Ganesa is a universal God who is popular and powerful. He gives his blessings to remove obstacles in life simply by Praying.

Ganesh Temple at Basavana Gudi

The Ganesh Temple of Basavanagudi is located in Bangalore and is known for its ancient history and popularity. The temple features a 16-foot idol of Lord Ganesha that is worshipped and covered with 100 kg of butter, later distributed among the devotees after three days. This tradition is similar to that of Simhachala Narasimha Kshetra, where sandal paste is applied to the Swamy. It is believed that the size of the idol is increasing every year, similar to the Kanipakam temple in Andhra Pradesh. The temple celebrates various festivals and auspicious days in honour of Lord Ganesha.

Mahaganapati Of Kumbhasi

'Kumbhasi' is to be split into words 'Kumbha' and 'Asi'. Kumbha means the demon, and Asi means the sword. The place is 6 km from Kundapur (National Highway No 17). According to a legend, the Pandavas came to this place during their 12-year exile. Sage Gautama requested Bhima to kill a demon named Kumbhasura, who troubled him while he was in penance. Bhima heard a divine voice telling him to pray Maha Ganapathi. Bhima kept a sword in front of Ganesh and prayed. Bhima killed the demon. This is the reason why the place is named as Kumbhasi.

Kumbhasi is one of the sacred places, and the others are as follows:

- Kukki Subrahmanya.
- Koteswara
- Sankaranarayana
- Ananteswara
- Mookambika and
- Gokarna

Mahaganapathi is self-manifested, and the Temple is on the top of the hill. The Ganapati idol of Kumbhasi is growing. The roof of the Temple is to be removed over the head of the Lord.

<u>Darsan:</u>

The Temple is open throughout the day. Puja is conducted at 6:00 AM and noon and from 7:00 to 8:00 PM daily.

The idol is adorned with flowers. During a special puja, 1000 coconuts are offered as devotees believe their prayers will be answered.

Sharavu Maha Ganapathi (Mangalore)

The Sharavu Maha Ganapathi temple is situated in the heart of Mangalore town. About 900 years ago, there was a chieftain named Veerabahu in this region. In the vicinity was an ashram of Sage Bharadwaj, where a tiger and a cow stood. The chieftain aimed at protecting the cow from the tiger and shot an arrow ('Shara') at the tiger. Unfortunately, the cow died. The Sage advised Veerabahu to construct a temple for Lord Shiva on the spot where the cow was killed. The place has since been known as Sharavu, and Shiva is known as Sharabhesha. Parvathi came in a dream of Veerabahu and ordered him to install her idol and name her Mangala. The chieftain fulfilled Parvathi's order.

The Ganesa idol (Svayambhu one) was also installed in the same temple. Once, Tipu Sultan wanted to attack the place and camped near the temple. In the night, he dreamt that an elephant had trampled him. Tipu's followers said it was a warning from Ganesa, so he abandoned the idea of attacking the temple.

The temple celebrates many festivals, the most important of which are the Ganesa Chaturthi and Deepotsavam. Regular pujas are conducted daily.

Hattangudi Ganesa Temple

The temple is believed to have originated during the 9th century A.D. The idol of Ganesa is considered sacred, and if the rituals associated with it are not performed correctly, a liquid is said to ooze out of the idol's left ear and flow through the trunk. Devotees believe their wishes will be fulfilled if the flowers fall from the idol.

Gargeswari Ganapathi

The Siva temple of Gargeswari has an idol of Ganapathi. The Muslim population adores God. The temple is said to have been constructed by a sage, Garga. The Siva Linga is supposed to grow every year. Adi Shankaracharya laid the Sri Chakra here. Devotees perform Puja only in the morning hours. They firmly believe that Gargeswari Ganapathi is their protector.

Siva Temples

In the Hindu pantheon, Brahma, Vishnu and Siva are considered a 'Trinity': Brahma – is the creator, Vishnu – is the sustainer and Siva – is the destroyer.

Siva is considered a Pre-Aryan God, and the Vedic Aryans called him 'Neela Lohita'. Since pre-Vedic times, they have been worshipped in the Linga form. In the later stages, Siva is known as Rudra. As Pasupathi, he is considered the God of animals. Siva is all-pervading for music, dance, wisdom, and Yoga. He is the master. The Nataraja aspect is inducted in this context. The mantra chanted by the devotees is 'Om Namah Sivaya' – 'Na' stands for Brahma 'Ma' for Vishnu (Maha), 'Si' for Rudra, 'Va' for Maheswara and 'Ya' for Sadasiva. Siva is trinetra, having three eyes.

The third eye is supposed to represent 'Agni' and the other two for the 'Sun' and the 'Moon'. Kailasa is the abode of Sivas. He appears wearing the moon on his crest. His mudras of Varada and Abhaya symbolize his eagerness to protect the devotees. Hence, he is considered to be the remover of all fears. The following are a few important Siva Temples in the state of Karnataka.

Gokarna (Sri Samsthana Mahabaleswara Deva)

The temple is 53 km from Karwar, in the northwest of Karnataka state, bordering Goa. Goa means cow's ear. Siva is said to have emerged from the ear of a cow, which is Mother Earth. Gokarna is well-known for its association with the Atma Linga of the Ravana episode.

<u>Sthala Puranam:</u>

Ravana obtained the Atma Lingam from Lord Siva for installation in Lanka; Kaikasi, the mother of Ravana, desired to worship a million Siva Lingas daily. Some sages advised that worship of Atma Lingam was equivalent to worshipping many Siva Lingas. Siva gave the Atma Lingam to Ravana on the condition that it should only be set on the ground once he reached Lanka. All the Gods never liked the idea of Ravana carrying Atma Lingam and hence, according to the advice of Vishnu, approached Ganesh to play a role in saving the Atma Lingam. Ganesa encountered Ravana with Atma Lingam on a beach in the guise of a boy.

Ravana wanted someone to hold the Linga since it was time for noon prayer; he saw Ganesa and handed it over to him. Ganesa said the Linga was very heavy, and he could hold it only for a brief while. Ganesa called Ravana thrice, and when there was no response, he put the Linga down. Ravana rushed back and tried to pick it up but failed. A piece of the

Lingam fell in Murudeswara and was worshipped there as Agohara Lingam.

The original Lingam of Gokarnam is called Mahabaleshwar, and the temple had tiled roofing. The entrance to the Sanctum is wood-panelled and well-decorated with flower motifs. Atma Lingam is protruding a few inches from the ground.

<u>Pooja:</u>

Devotees perform Puja thrice daily, and they are allowed to touch the Lingam. The temple complex is enormous. Parvathi or Tamra Gowri is situated across the corridor. There is also Maha Ganapathi temple (as a boy diverted Ravana).

<u>Other Shrines:</u>

Apart from the Mahabaleshwar Temple, there are 20 smaller shrines, 30 Lingas and 30 Tirthas. Shrines for Brahma, Vishnu, Siva, Rama, and Agasthya are some of them.

Sri Manjunatha Temple (Dharmasthala)

Dharmasthala is Dharma's abode. Sri Manjunatha is Lord Siva. The priests in this temple are Vaishnavas and Madhvas. Heggades are the Jains, and they are the temple trustees.

The temple is located in the western ghats, 40 km from Mangalore. Its speciality is that both Hinduism and Jainism are involved here. Manjunatha is one of the best Jain deities. Manju means beautiful. Manjunatha is in the form of a Linga; simultaneously, there is one Tirthankar named Manjunatra. Hence, the place and the temple are adored by both Hindus and Jains.

<u>Sthala Purana:</u>

Dharmasthala was formally known as Kuduma eight hundred years ago. A Jain chieftain, 'Pergade,' lived long with his wife here. Some

Dharmadevatas came to this couple's house. They were fed and honoured. Pergade converted his house into a temple and dedicated his life to the propagation of Dharma. Vaishnavaite priests were appointed here in this Siva shrine.

Siva Lingam was installed, and a temple of Manjunatha was built. As per the Vedic rites, the idol was reconsecrated, and the place is known as Dharmasthala.

<u>Puja:</u>

Worship is allowed twice daily in the morning and evening. Devotees take baths in the river Netravathi and darshan in the temple.

<u>Festivals:</u>

The Laksha Deepotsava festival is celebrated in November – December. During this festival, one hundred thousand lamps are lit, discourses on Dharma are held, and one thousand devotees are fed every day.

The West Coast style was adopted for the temple's construction. A museum with sculptures, paintings, and manuscripts is available here.

The Manjunatha Cultural Center is a research foundation that collects ancient manuscripts in three languages: Kannada, Sanskrit and Tulu. Hospitals also cater to the needs of the people. Thus, the name of the place Dharmasthali is justified.

Murudeswara Temple

Murudeswara temple is 165 km from Mangalore, and its location is beautiful. In the episode of Atma Lingam of Lord Siva, the roles of Ravana, Ganesa, and Gokarna Kshetra are continued with the start of the Murudeswara temple. The Arabian Sea surrounds a massive temple complex on three sides around the Siva temple. This is a coastal paradise.

Sthala Purana:

Sootha Maharshi narrated the Murudeshwara's glory and the Atma Lingam episode to Sounaka and other sages. Ravana, angry with the Gokarnam incident, threw away the cloth covering the Atma Linga. The moment it fell here, it was transformed into Murudeswar Lingam. Mruda means happiness. The sea near the Temple is called Agni Tirtha. A lake known as kamandala tirtha (Brahma sprinkled water from his kamandala) is behind the Temple.

Mahabharata Story:

Pandavas visited this place. Dharmaraja ordered Bhima to get the Ganges for Abhishekam to Murudeswara. Bhima prayed to Siva to bring the Ganges but failed. Then he banged his head against the earth, and Siva appeared before him and blessed Bhima – Ganges flowed from where Bhima banged his head. This spot is known as 'Bhima Tirtham'. It is believed that a dip in these Tirthas will cure diseases.

Interesting details of the Temple:

- A 20-tiered Rajagopuram of 249 feet height welcomes pilgrims, which is said to be the world's tallest. This was taller than that of Sri Rangan and Tanjore Rajagopurams.
- Images of decorated elephants are at the entrance.
- On the hill, overlooking the sea, there is a gigantic image of Siva sitting in Padmasana posture. It is 123 feet high and is considered to be one of the world's tallest Siva statues. The meditating Siva is represented with four arms, one giving Abhaya to the devotees and the other pointing to the earth. The third holds a trident, and the fourth holds a small drum. Nandi sits in front of Siva.
- In front of Nandi, the images show Ravana giving Atma Lingam to Ganesa.

<u>Growth-Decline and Rise of the Temple:</u>

The ancient Temple was in ruins during the early 20th century. By 1935, the sanctum was on the verge of collapse. Later, people like RN Shetty took the initiative to renovate and reconstruct the Temple. Inspiration was drawn from Vivekananda Rock Memorial in Kanyakumari. In 1977, the services of hundreds of sculptors from Tamilnadu were solicited. The sanctum of the Temple was gold-plated. On the top of the hill, colourful life-size images of the Purana purushas are being installed.

- Vedavyasa dictating Mahabharata to Vinayaka
- Chariot of Sun God
- Krishna as charioteer to Arjuna on the Kurukshetra battlefield.
- The Atma Lingam episode is presented, and the sound and light show are arranged.

Abhishekams and festivals are conducted on the auspicious days of Murudeswara and chiefly on Maha Sivaratri.

Basavanagudi (The Bull Temple) – Bangalore

The Bull Temple (Basava) is an ancient temple situated in Bangalore. The Temple is dedicated to Basava, Siva's favourite vehicle,' Nandi'. Basava happened to be an object of worship. The Temple is the biggest, perhaps the only Temple dedicated to Nandi.

<u>Temple details:</u>

The Temple was built in 1586 by Kempe Gowda, the founder of Bangalore. Nandi is carved out of a single rock and is 6.57 meters tall and 5.1 meters long. Surprisingly, it has grown to 5 meters.

The area was meant for growing groundnuts in the field. The farmers found that thieves plundered their crops on every full moon night. But the story is different when they want to catch the thieves. They saw a huge bull, golden in colour, with shining eyes. Later, they found the bull missing. Later, they discovered a huge stone, Nandi, on a nearby hillock.

The villagers realized that it was no one else but the vehicle of Lord Siva, Nandiswara. Kempe Gowda built the Temple.

At the entrance of the hillock, there are a couple of bull horns on either side.

<u>The Temple:</u>

A five-tiered Rajagopuram was constructed, and a granite Dhwajastambham was installed in front of it.

Nanjundeswara (Sri Kanteswara Swamy) – Nanjangud

Nanjangud is situated on the banks of the Kabini, 20 km from Mysore, 80 km from Kerala, and 140 km from Bangalore, and there is a famous temple of Siva, known as 'Nanjundeswara' or 'Sri Kanteswara'. Parasurama installed the murtis of Siva (in the form of Linga) and Parvathi in this temple. Parasurama found the murtis about two km from the main shrine. According to Sthalapurana, Gautama installed the Lingam.

Nanjundeswara is the title of Siva for drinking 'halahala' or Poison during the churning of the ocean by the 'devas' and 'danavas' in quest of nectar. In the process, Poison emerged. Siva put the Poison in his mouth, and his consort, Parvathi, held his throat tightly to prevent it from entering the body. Poison is said to be lodged in Siva's throat, and this is the reason to call Siva Nanjundeswara (the Lord who consumed Poison).

<u>Sthala Purana:</u>

Sage Gowthama installed the Lingam at Nanjanguda. Parvathi is in a separate shrine. There are separate shrines for Subrahmanya, Ganapati, Chandikeswara etc. Nandi had a small shrine here.

<u>Temple And History:</u>

The temple is spacious and 128 meters long, 53 meters wide, supported by 147 columns. History is known through the following dates connected to the temple.

- Gangas built the temple in the 9th century.
- Hoyasalas renovated
- Hyder Ali (1761-82) and Tipu Sultan (1782-99) contributed to the temple. Tipu Sultan prayed to the temple's Lord to rescue his elephant's eyesight. Being convinced of the power of God, he called Him 'Hakim Nanjundeswara'.
- After Tipu, the Rajas of Mysore patronized the temple.

<u>Significance of the river Kapila:</u>

Parasurama took a bath in this river to get rid of his sin acquired by beheading his mother.

<u>Architecture of the Temple:</u>

The architecture of this temple is different from that of the other temples (West Coast style). The Gopuram is of the South Indian style. Instead of stone, wood is used. The temple tower is seven-tiered. The Gopuram is without figurines, and some additions were made in the later stages.

<u>Gifts to the Temple:</u>

The royal family of Mysore, Shringeri Muth, Sultans Hyder Ali and Tipu Sultan, gave the temple numerous jewels and other items. Among them are a silver cup studded with precious stones and an emerald necklace.

<u>Puja:</u>

Puja is performed twice daily, in the morning and evening. The car festival is celebrated for three days with pomp and glory. Many people flock to the temple complex to visit the Lord, which is decorated beautifully with jewellery gifted by rulers.

Maha Vishnu Temples

Brahma, Vishnu and Maheswara are the great trio of divine forms, and they are held responsible for creation, sustenance, and destruction.

God Vishnu is considered the embodiment of mercy and goodness. He rides on Garuda, and his consort is known for prosperity (Shri) and fortune (Lakshmi). Vishnu's incarnations or Avatars (ten in number) are purposeful, i.e., to punish evil and protect good. Whenever people need his help in any yuga, he is born—"Sambhavami Yuge Yuge."

Among the ten incarnations, the first three, Matsya, Kurma, and Varaha, are the animal forms. The fourth is Narasimha (partly animal and partly human). Among the remaining, the human form starts with Vamana (dwarf). Coming to the next avatars are the Rama and Krishna, the epic heroes. Remaining are Parasurama, Balarama and Kalki.

Vishnu is represented with Chakra, Sankha, Gada, Padma, etc., and 'Mudras' like 'Abhaya' indicate assurance to the devotees.

Srikrishna Temple (Udupi)

On the seacoast and 90 km from Bangalore, Udupi or Udipi is situated, and the place is famous for its Sri Krishna's Temple, Krishna Mutt, and Madhvacharya. A 5-tiered Rajagopuram of the Sri Krishna Temple attracts. Of course, it is recently built. Instead of gopuram, there is an arch, an entrance to the temple. Devotees should have the darshan of the Lord only through a window with nine holes denoting nine planets. Madhvacharya burnt the light by the side of Sri Krishna. Since then, it has been burning.

Sub-Shrines: Hanuman and Garuda are the sub-shrines brought from Ayodhya.

Madhava Sarovar is a tank. It is believed that Ganga water flows every ten years. Madhvacharya installed the Krishna idol in Udupi and the Balarama idol in a village near the seashore. Sri Krishna holds the churning rod (used for curds) in one hand and a whip in the other. He is seen with a beautiful smile, reminding his childhood activities at Gokulam.

Viswakarma made the idol and handed it over to Rukmini. Arjuna kept it safely after the Krishna avatar.

Chennakesava Temple of Somanathpur

Somanathpur is located 175 km from Bangalore and can be reached via Mysore. The Sri Chennakesava temple was constructed in 1268 AD by General Samanatha, who served under Hoyasala ruler Narasimha III (1254-91). This temple is considered the finest example of Hoyasala architecture. It is built on an elevated platform with three towers accommodating Janardhana, Kesava and Venugopala.

Figure 8: Chennakesava Temple of Somnathpur

The temple's themes are based on the epics of Ramayana and Bharata, with depictions of Krishna Leelas. Like in Belur and Halebidu, the names of the sculptors who worked on the temple are written. The corridors are elevated, and the platforms are raised, with beautiful sculptures carved into them. Visitors can see Krishna's 'Kaliya Mardana' and his playful interactions with the Gopikas. The ceilings are full of intricate carvings. It is believed that Acharya Jakkana was behind the temple's architectural excellence. Unfortunately, the temple has not been used for puja activities since Muslims raided it. It now serves as a monument and tourist attraction, preserving the memories of its past glory.

Sri Chennakesava Temple (Belur)

Belur, formerly known as 'Velapuri,' was the capital of the Hoyasalas, who ruled for about three and a half centuries from 1000 AD to 1346 AD. These rulers were known for their exceptional skills in building temples. Belur is located 40 km from Hasan and 220 km from Bangalore.

The Sri Chennakesava Temple was built by Vishnuvardhan, the Hoyasala emperor, in 1117 AD to celebrate his victory over the Cholas at 'Talakad'. The temple construction was completed after 103 years. The temple was built on a raised platform that consisted of the sanctum, a vestibule, and a Navagraha mandapa pavilion. The 5-tiered Rajagopuram was added later in the 14th century. The sanctum is star-shaped and has east, north, and south entrances. The hall's pillars reflect the Hoyasala art, and there are various female figures in dancing poses on the 42 pillars of the mandapam. The temple also has beautifully sculpted figures of 80 Gods and Goddesses, Brahma, Vishnu, and Siva.

The sanctum is crowded with figures and figurines, and the chief sculptor is Jakkanacharya. Chennakesava is also known as Vijayanarayana Swamy.

Sri Ranganatha Swamy Temple of Srirangapatna

Sri Rangapatna is located 15 kilometres away from Mysore and is home to the famous temple of Lord Ranganatha, a manifestation of Vishnu. Typically, Vishnu is depicted with his consorts, Boodevi and Sridevi, but here, there is an additional seated figure representing the Goddess Cauvery near Lord Ranganatha's idol. According to a story, the Goddess prayed to the Lord to be rid of the sins passed on to her by devotees who bathed in the Cauvery River. Ranganatha advised her to worship him, which is why her figure is present in the sanctum sanctorum.

There are three Ranganatha Swamy temples in the Cauvery River region: Srirangapatna and Sivasamudra in Karnataka and Srirangam near Tiruchirapalli in Tamil Nadu.

Sri Rangapatna was once the capital of Hyder Ali and Tipu Sultan and is now one of the most significant shrines in Karnataka. The temple's architecture is similar to the Hoyasala—Vijayanagar styles and the five-tiered Rajagopuram is in the South Indian style. The temple walls resemble a fortress. Sub-shrines include Ranganayaki Thayaar, Srinivasa, Narasimha, Hanuman, Rama, and Gopala Krishna.

Tippu Sultan was gifted a lot of jewellery and silver plates. His father, Hyder, also had faith in the Lord.

Puja is performed twice daily, and Garudotsava is an important festival in the temple. Sage Gautama had his ashram here, where he worshipped Ranganatha, and Sri Ranga Jayanti is celebrated in the temple.

Sri Veera Narayana Temple (Belavadi)

Belavadi is an ancient village home to several temples, the most prominent of which is the Sri Veera Narayana Temple. This temple is a fine example of Hoyasala architecture and is currently under the care of the Archaeological Survey of India. Belavadi was formerly known as Ekachakrapura. According to legend, this place is associated with the Pandavas, who lived here in disguise after escaping from the House of Wax.

The Sri Veera Narayana Temple has three shrines, one of which is the Veeranarayana shrine (Trikuta temple). The Lord here is eight feet tall and has four hands. The other two shrines are dedicated to Gopala Krishna and Yoga Narasimha, respectively. The temple is held in high regard and is worshipped with the support of the local community. Veera Ballala II built the temple around 1200 AD.

Narasimha Temples

One of the incarnations of Lord Vishnu is Narasimha. Lord Krishna, addressing Arjuna on the Kurukshetra battlefield, said that I am born from age to age to destroy evil and protect the virtuous. (Bhagavad Gita CL IV SLKS 7-8).

Hiranyaksha and Hiranyakasipu were the demon brothers. Hiranyaksha was killed by Vishnu when he attempted to take over the 'earth'. Hiranyakasipu wanted to take vengeance by killing Vishnu. But his son Prahlada was a great devotee of Vishnu. Vishnu, as Narasimha, emerged from a pillar and killed Hiranyakasipu. Narasimha Swamy temples in Karnataka are as follows, and they are the important ones:

- M.K. Hubli
- Torvi Narasimha
- Koppar Narasimha
- Jharani Narasimha
- Chintamani Narasimha (Kudli)
- Gulgunji Narasimha (T. Narasipur)
- Narasimha of Maddur
- Devarayanidurga Teamples

M.K. Hubli

The place is about 30 km from Belgaum. Once there, a jeweller named Yadappa Naika went on a journey after prayers to Lord Narasimha. He encountered some dacoits at M.K. Hubli, but surprisingly, they fell at his feet instead of attacking him. Naika asked them the reason for their strange behaviour. They replied that they were under spiritual influence for this action. He became a Madhva saint known as Yadavaraya (1560-1640). He settled down at this place where he met the dacoits. Narasimha came in his dream and said to collect his idol from the Malaprabha River. Yadavaraya went to the river, collected the stone (idol), and started worshipping, applying sandal paste to the idol. A Sage named Chavan performed Mahayagna to please Narasimha. He brought a stone from the river, drew the figure of the Lord with Sandal paste, and started worship. After the yagna, he deposited it back in the riverbed. Vijayanagara king discovered a Siva Linga along with the image of Narasimha. Puja is performed twice daily, and Narasimha Jayanti is the chief festival of the temple.

Torvi Narasimha

Torvi is near Bijapur and is famous for the Narasimha Temple and the renowned poet Kumara Valmiki, the author of Toravi Ramayana. Sage Durvasa, who is said to be the incarnation of Siva, installed and worshipped the idol of Narasimha with fresh flowers, fresh Tulasi leaves and sandal paste. The story is mentioned in the Toravi Ramayana.

The Narasimha idol is said to be powerful. Puja is performed by noon daily, and Narasimha Jayanti is celebrated here.

Koppar Narasimha

Koppar is just 15 km from Devadurg village, which is situated on the banks of the Krishna River. According to the legend, Narasimha appeared in the dream of the Bijapur Sultan and asked him to revive the glory of the shrine so that worship could be conducted properly. As a result, the Sultan renovated the temple and granted some villages the right to maintain it.

The name Koppar is derived from Karpara, who had the darshan of Narasimha penance. In the stump of an Aswatha Vriksha, several Saligramas and the Lord's idol were found. The Saligramas were arranged around the base of the fallen tree near the Narasimha idol, which had 16 hands.

Jharani Narasimha

The place Jharani is near Bidar. Narasimha of the stream is known as 'Jharan'. The Lord is self-manifested in a cave with water all around. The Saligrama appears like the back of an idol.

A demon named Jharasura terrorized people. People prayed to the Lord to save them. It is said that a fight took place between the demon and the deity, and the demon was killed. This story was found in Brahmanda Purana.

Puja is performed twice daily. Monday and Saturday are auspicious days. Narasimha Jayanti is the festival celebrated here.

Chintamani Narasimha of Kudli

From Shimoga, one can reach 'Kudli'. The deity is Chintamani Narasimha. People pray to get relief from illnesses and mental disorders.

The shrine is situated at the confluence of two sacred rivers, 'Tunga' and 'Bhadra'; commonly, the river is called 'Tungabhadra'.

Prahlada was indirectly responsible for his father's death. Hence, he wanted to do penance to get rid of the sin. Prahlada selected this place for penance. Further, a saint gave him a saligram of Narasimha and 'Mantra'. Prahlada worshipped Saligrama after bathing in the river, and Swamy appeared before Prahlada. Prahlada, at the request of the Lord, reduced his size to normal by pressing him with his thumb and forefinger.

Kudli is significant because Lond Sri Rama came here and installed Siva Linga. On Vasishta's advice, he performed 'Sraddha karmas' to Vali.

Puja at the temple is performed twice daily. Narasimha Jayanti is an important festival that is celebrated here.

Gulgunji Narasimha (T. Narasipur)

This place is 35 km from Mysore. Narasimha is a self-manifested God. The idol was found in an anthill. It was brought out along with a treasure and utilized for constructing the temple. According to Skanda Purana, Gulgunji (seed of the bead plant) is in the hands of the Lord. The Puja is done twice a day.

Narasimha of Maddur

Maddur is 16 km from Mandya. According to Mahabharata, Arjuna and Krishna came here and worshipped Narasimha, which Lord Brahma installed. Sage Kadamba also worshipped the Lord; the place is therefore called Kadambapura, and the river's name is also the same. Puja is performed from 8:30 to noon and 6:30 to 8:30 PM. Narasimha Jayanti is celebrated.

Devarayani Durga Temple of Narasimha

The place Devarayani Durga is 15 km from Tumkur. It is a Temple on the hill. One deity is Bhoga Narasimha, and the other is Yoga Narasimha. Rama visited this temple and created water with a shot of an arrow. Puja is done twice a day.

Venkateswara Swamy Temples

Among India's most essential and ancient temples, The Tirumala Temple of Lord Venkateswara occupies a unique place. He is considered as a family deity. There are many temples of this Lord of Seven Hills. In Karnataka state, there are also shrines dedicated to this God. Just two temples are covered here for the perusal of the readers and pilgrims.

Venkateswara of Kanakagiri

Kanakagiri got its name from a sage Kanaka muni. Maski is a Center of the Buddhists and the Center of Ashokan inscriptions, and the place of Kanakagiri, known for Lord Venkateswara, is situated in the Raichur district.

A local chieftain, Parasappa Naika, wanted the shrine of Venkateswara as popular as Tirumala and constructed it. Proudha Devaraya, the Vijayanagar emperor, donated grants to maintain the temple. The Puja systems are according to the Tirumala kshetra. Vaishnava priests are appointed. Here, the devotees offer their hair to the deity. Pushkarini, a sacred pond similar to Tirumala, is maintained.

Venkatachalapati is the popular name of the deity here. Puja is done twice a day, and all the Vaishnavite festivals are observed. There are idols of Vaishnavite saints and the deities of Hanuman, Ganesa, Saraswathi, and Lakshmi Narayana. Kanakagiri temple is a feast for the eyes.

Sri Venkateswara Temple of Karkala

This temple is situated approximately 37 km away from Udupi. The original idol was brought from Tirumala and installed in the temple in 1537. After performing puja, a cow and calf were brought here to wander, and the place where they stopped was chosen to construct the temple. The temple was renovated in 1699, as per the inscriptional source. The main deity is Srinivasa, and the Utsavar is known as Venkata Ramana. Religious discourses are conducted in the temple complex. The gopurams of the temple resemble those of a West Coast Kerala temple. The pujas, rituals, and Brahmotsavams follow the traditions of the Tirumala temple.

Sri Rama Temples

Kodandarama Temple of Hiremagalur

Hiremagalur is a place near Chikmagalur. According to the Puranas, nine saints lived here and performed penance near Siddha Pushkarani. The Prushkarani water cures snake bites.

The place became famous because it is associated with Sri Rama. He broke Siva's mighty bow and married Sita. But he was challenged by Parasurama to break another bow of Vishnu. When Sri Rama broke that bow, Parasurama realized that Rama was the Lord of Gods. Parasurama finally installed the idol of Rama. The place is, therefore, called Bhargavapuri, along with Hiremagalur.

Puja is performed in the temple in the morning and evening. The idol of Sri Rama is significant because it is holding a bow in the left hand and an arrow in the right hand. The Lord is not to be seen with either Abhayahasta or Varadahasta.

The temple construction reflects the engineering skills. It can be dismantled piece by piece and reassembled.

<u>Jatara:</u> By the end of February, the Jatara takes place. Harijans are respected in the temple and during temple activities.

<u>Janamejaya's Yaga:</u>

A distinguished ruler of the Lunar dynasty (Chandravansha) performed 'Sarpayaga' at Hiremagalur. Janamejaya's grants to the temple are referred to in the copper plates as per the 'Epigraphica Karnataka' source.

Temples of Avani

Avani is a small village on the Bangalore-Chennai highway. It is called the 'Gaya of the South' since funeral obsequies are performed, which are said to be equivalent to Gaya's.

Several inscriptions of the Pallavas, Cholas, Hoyasalas, and the Vijayanagara emphasize the prominence of the place. The temples of Valmiki, Sita, Lava, and Kusa are situated here. Valmiki Ashram is on the hilltop.

The place is associated with the Ramakatha, which happened after Pattabhisheka. In other words, the Uttarakanda of the Ramayana deals with the story of Sita, Lava, and Kusa. Therefore, the place is known as Kusa-Lava Puri.

Lakshmana left Sita at Avani. Lava and Kusa were born in Valmiki's Ashram. While performing Aswamedha yaga, Sri Rama left the 'Yagaswa'as captured by Lava and Kusa.

Rama's forces were attacked by Lava-Kusa (including Lakshmana and Satrughna). Rama was also about to be attacked, but Sita stopped. There is a temple near where Rama met Sita.

Sri Rama and his brothers installed Siva Lingas for the sin of fighting children. Lava and Kusa worshipped Siva Linga to expiate the sin of fighting their father.

Below the hill, there are several shrines to Siva, Parvati, Kamakshi, Ganesa, and Subrahmanya. Rama, Lakshmana, Bharata, Satrughna, Hanuman, Sugreeva, and Angada installed the Siva lingams here, which are known as Rama Lingeswara. One of the biggest is in Lakshmana temple.

Puja is performed here. Sivaratri is the major festival celebrated here.

Hanuman Temples

Hanuman is also known as Maruti or Anjaneya. He is more popular as 'Rama bhakta Hanuman', who opened his chest and showed Sri Rama, Sita and Lakshmana. Rama blessed him as 'Chiranjivi,' meaning living for all time to come. He was the son of Anjana Devi and Vayu Deva. When he was a boy, he went to protect Sun from Rahu. Indra, too, wanted to protect Sun by throwing his Vajrayudha. Still, it hit Maruti's chin ('hanu'); he has also been known as Hanuman since then. Being born with the 'amsa' of Siva, he was also known as 'Rudramsa sambhuta'. Hanuman is being worshipped in kshetras in Karnataka; some are mentioned here.

Mulbagal

In the Dwapara yuga, Lord Krishna suggested Pandavas install the image of Hanuman at Mulbagal. In the Kurukshetra battle, Hanuman was associated with the flag on the chariot of Arjuna.

Todarmal of Akbar's services worshipped the deity here. Hanuman is represented with a sword instead of a mace. Hanuman likes Ketaki flowers, and there are plenty in this region.

In the temple complex, there are several shrines dedicated to Venkata Ramana Swamy, Govindaraja Swamy (installed by sage Brugu),

Venugopala, Lakshmi Narasimha, Chennakesava, Varadaraja and Ganesa.

Outside the sanctum is a Hanuman figure with a chakra behind it. Puja is performed twice daily. All festivals, including car festival, are celebrated.

Wadagera

Hanuman is called reclining Hanuman. The place is 7 km from Yelandur. Sage Vasishta's penance is spoiled by a demon, and on listening to the prayers of the sage, Sri Rama asks Hanuman to deal with the situation, and Hanuman kills the demon. Sri Rama gave Hanuman a gift called 'Udugore,' which became 'Wadagera. '

Puja is performed to Hanuman in the temple only on Saturdays.

Other places depicting Hanuman with rare features:

- Maddur: In the presence of Rama, Sita and Lakshmana, Hanuman covered his mouth and nose with his right palm.
- Bangalore (Banswadi Temple): Hanuman holds a branch of the Asoka Tree.
- Banglore (Basavanagudi): Hanuman holds Chudamani.
- Tumkur (Bailu Hanuman): Statue in an open place.
- Mysore: In the Narasimha Swamy temple, Hanuma projects are on the right, and Varaha is on the left. The crown is with Hayagriva image and the back Garuda (All in a single stone)

Kadarmandalgi

This Hanuman temple is 100 km by road from Dharwad. The temple's speciality is that Hanuman is worshipped in three forms—Hanuman, Bhima, and Madhvacharya. These are supposed to be the reincarnations of Hanuman. Hence, Hanuman is worshipped in the morning, Bhima at noon, and Madhvacharya in the evening.

Shikaripur

This place is also called 'Huchappa' or 'Huchuraya'. People believe that worshipping Hanuman will cure mental diseases. Saligrama is fixed on the idol. Hanuman of Shikaripur has a Saligrama for the nose fixed by Vyasaraya.

Shimoga

Kote Hanumantha temple is located in the fort area of Shimoga, also known as Durvasa Kshetra. The temple houses a Siva Linga and a Maruti Yantra.

Chakra Tirtha (Yantrodharaka Hanuman)

Legend has it that Chakra Tirtha is located in Kishkindha of the Ramayana, situated on the banks of Tungabhadra near Kamalapur. Sugriva, who was driven away by his brother Vali, sought refuge on Rushyamooka mountain and was aided by Hanuman. It was at this place that Rama met Sugriva. Sita Devi, whom Ravana abducted, cast her jewels on the mountain.

There are two shrines of Lord Rama in this location – Pattabhirama and Kodandarama.

Vryasaraya, a Madhva saint, dreamed that Hanuman appeared and instructed him to install his image here. The figure of Hanuman has been fixed in a Yantra; the figure of Hanuman is drawn in the middle of a yantra in a padmasana posture. Bijakshara mantras (which number in the crores) are inscribed on it. Dwadasanamas are also written in the corners. Hanuman is shown holding a Japamala. Vyasaraya installed 720 Hanuman idols, starting with Chakra Tirtha. Hanuman is believed to destroy the fears and diseases and fulfil the desires of his devotees.

Subrahmanya Swamy Temples

Subrahmanya Swamy is the son of Siva and the embodiment of wisdom. His vehicle, the peacock, symbolizes pride. The message is that it should be controlled to achieve success. The serpent symbolizes the cycle of births and deaths. Skanda's six faces represent six chakras, symbolic of the kundalini. Rigveda mentions Subrahmanya in three contexts. The name of Subrahmanya is significant—'Su' means joy, 'Brahma' means supreme reality, and 'Nya' means Supreme Godhead.

Historically speaking, the worship of this deity goes back to Mohenjo-Daro during the Kushans and Guptas; it is also prevalent. Kumara Sambhava, the Sanskrit work of Kalidasa, the Indian Shakespeare, provides a peep into the birth of the Lord. Adi Shankaracharya wrote Subrahmanya Stotra.

Subrahmanya goes by several names, such as Kartikeya, Shanmukha, Saravana, Skanda, Swaminatha, Murugan, etc.

Subrahmanya Temples are usually located among mountains or Jungles. In Sri Lanka, a Murugan temple also exists. In the Karnataka state, the temples of Subrahmanya Swamy are classified into three categories: Adi (beginning), Madhya (middle), and Antya (End).

Two of the famous temples are to be mentioned here under.

Ghati Subrahmanya

The distance between Bangalore and Ghati is 56 km. According to legend, Subrahmanya once transformed into a snake and protected other snakes such as Vasuki, Ananta Karkotaka, Pingalaka, and Takshakaa from Garuda, the kite. As a result, all snakes were worshipped and granted protection.

The temple dedicated to Subrahmanya features an idol of the deity alongside Narasimha and Lakshmi. The idol is placed inside an anthill, and it is said that a cow once shed milk over it. A temple was built around the idol, and Puja was performed thrice daily. Worshipping the Lord is believed to bring benefits such as curing infertility and skin diseases.

Kukke Subrahmanya

The place is full of scenic beauty of creeks and mountains and is 110 km from Mangalore. Adi Shankaracharya mentioned about this shrine in his 'Subrahmanya Bhujanga Stotra'. Since the 8th century, worship has been going on. Kukke (Tamil) means child. Hence, Subhahmanyam is Bala Subhahmanyam. Inscriptions and copper Plates give us information about the temple. Images kept in a basket are worshipped, and Kukke originates from the existing worship system.

In Kritayuga, Tretayuga, Dwaparayuga and Kaliyuga, the temple enjoyed the patronage and worship of the devotees.

Lord Subrahmanya married Devayani, Indra's daughter, at Kukke. He installed Umamaheswara Lingam to get rid of the sin of killing Tarakasura. Among the temple rituals, 'Naga Samskara' is the important one.

Temples of Goddesses

Devi, Goddess, or the Mother Goddess are the different eternal forms of the universe. She is the creative force as well as the protective force. She embodies supreme knowledge, according to Devi Mahatyam of Thomas B. Coburn.

The concept and cult of the Mother Goddess is of indigenous origin. This cult is prevalent among the tribal. The worship of the Goddess in villages is quite common as village deities (Grama devatas). Importance is given to the female form of divine force in the context of putting an end to demons like Mahishasura.

The Purana Purushas and incarnations of Vishnu worship goddesses. For example, Sri Rama worshipped Durga before the battle with Ravana, Anjuna worshipped before entering the battlefield, Yudhishtira prayed in times of distress, Rukmini worshipped Durga to marry Krishna, and Brahma and Sive also worshipped the Goddesses.

The glorification of the Goddess is found in Rigveda, Puranas (Kali, Skanda, etc.), Mahabharata and Devi Bhagavatham. Saptamatrikas are the different forms of the Mother Goddess that emerged from the Gods.

<u>Sapta Matrikas:</u>

1. Brahmi (out of Brahma)
2. Maheshwari (out of Siva)
3. Kaumari (out of Skanda)
4. Vaishnavi (out of Vishnu)
5. Varahi (out of Varaha Avatara)
6. Narasimhi (out of Narasimha's incarnation)
7. Aindri (out of Indra)

The popular Goddesses are Durga, Lakshmi, Saraswathi, Mahakali etc. A few Temples of Goddesses are as follows:

Sri Chamundeswari (Mysore)

Sri Chamundeswari of Chamundi Hills is the supreme Goddess of Mysore. Mysore was initially known as Mahishuru. The area was ruled by a demon named Mahishasura, whom the Goddess Charnundeswari Devi killed.

Mahishasura had two followers, Chanda and Munda. These two demons attacked the deity. The goddess, with her terrifying aspect of Kali, killed both demons.

Mysore city was the Wodeyars' capital and the Vijayanagar empire's feudatories.

<u>Chamundi Hills:</u>

The hills are 1000 meters above sea level. In 1659, 1000 steps were built by Maharaja Dodda Devaraja.

<u>The Temple:</u>

Hoyasalas built the temple in the 12th century.

Vijayanagara rulers renovated it in the 17th century. Sri Krishnamaraja Wodeyar III constructed the Rajagopuram, which is seven stories high, in 1827. He presented the deity with a star-shaped necklace (Nakshatra mala).

<u>Nandi:</u> The unique attraction is the granite Nandi, which is 15 feet high and 24 feet long.

<u>The Devi:</u>

Chamundeswari is said to be the incarnation of Sri Durga, a fierce form of Shakti installed in the sanctum sanctorum. The idol is of pure gold. She appears sitting on a golden throne decorated with flowers and jewellery. There was a golden throne shaped like a lion.

About 6 km from the Chamundeswari Temple (Uttanhalli village), there is a shrine of Jwala Tripura Sundari, Chamundeswari's sister.

<u>Rituals of the temple:</u>

Rituals are observed in both the temples of Chamundeswari and Tripura Sundari Devi.

- Kannna Kannadi means display of Goddesses
- Bayi Biga is the second ritual. – Locking of the mouth
- Huyyu Vada is the third ritual, which means ceremonial cooking.

The Dasara festivals of Mysore are celebrated with pomp and glory for ten days. Vedic verses are chanted. After Dasara, a 'Jatara' is celebrated on a full moon day, along with a car and boat festival.

The Temple timings are from 6:30 AM to 2:00 PM, 3:30 PM to 6:00 PM, and 7:15 PM to 9:00 PM.

Figure 9: Chamundeswari Temple

Annapurneswari of Horanadu

Annapurneswari is known as 'Adi-Saktyatmata'. This deity's main seat is Kasi or Varanasi. Next to Kasi, there is another shrine in Karnataka at Horanadu.

The priests did not know the Sthalapurana. It is said that there were some old palm-leaf manuscripts. Unfortunately, they are unavailable, and it is said they were burnt in a fire accident. However, this temple is connected to a group of temples at 'Kalasa'. From Sringeri, this temple is 70 km, and from Kalasa town, it is just 7 Km. The distance between Bangalore and Horandu is 330 km.

Like Kasi, there are temples for Siva, Bindu Madhavi, Kala Bhairava, and Bhadrakali. The main deity, Annapurneswari, is near Siva, just like in Kasi. Sage Agasthya had installed the deity. For 400 years, a trustee has been looking after the temple activities. Renovation and expansion began after 1960.

Annapurneswari is well known for feeding devotees for several generations.

<u>The Temple:</u>

There is a massive arch at the entrance of the temple. The images of the deities Sri Lakshmi and Sri Saraswathi are to be seen. One must go through a series of steps to visit the primary deity. There is a tiled mandapa, and from there, one can go to the sanctum of the Devi. The goddess is decorated with gold ornaments. She stands on a Peetham holding a conch, a discus, a Sri chakram and a carving of Goddess Gayatri Devi.

<u>Puja:</u>

Puja is performed twice daily, in the afternoon and at night, and thrice during Dhanur masam. No cooked food is offered as Naivedyam, and devotees are prohibited from prostration.

The Kumkum used for worship is used to treat ailing devotees and treat diseases of plants and animals.

Mangala Devi (Mangalore)

The shrine of Mangala Devi is at Bolar, 3 km from Mangalore. The town is known as Mangalore because of this deity.

The Temple is quite an ancient one.

History:

This region was ruled by Kadambas, Vijayanagara rulers, Chalukyas, Rastrakutas, Hoyasalas, and the Portuguese. By 1799, it was under the English rulers. According to a Sthalapurana, the Temple was built by Goraknath. The people of this region worship Mangala Devi to get married and succeed in their business.

Festivals:

Dasara and Ganesh Chaturthi festivals are celebrated here with great enthusiasm. Mangala Devi is decorated with ornaments and flowers during the Dasara festival (Navaratridays). On the 7th and 8th days, the Devi is worshipped as Saradadevi and Marika Devi. The car festival is performed on Maharnavami day. Puja is performed thrice daily, but the most important is in the afternoon.

Mookambike of Kollur

Kollur is 140 km from Mangalore. Mookambike temple is supposed to be the sacred and most important one in Karnataka state, situated on the banks of the Souparnika river. Parasurama is said to have been installed as the deity of this temple. The deity is called Tejomayi, who grants the wishes of the devotees. Lord Siva installed Sri Chakra. Siva told Skanda that this supreme divinity is residing in the Jyotirlinga. Siva said Maha Lakshmi, Parvathi, and Mahakali reside here.

This deity, Mookambika, killed Mookasura. This region is significant because Adi Shankaracharya performed penance here. Secondly, a Sanjeevani herb fell here while Hanuman carried it to Save Lakshmana.

Mookambika has four arms. The upper left hand holds a conch, the right a discus. The lower left arm is the Abhayahasta, and the right is the Abhistha.

Puja is performed thrice daily. Chandihoma is also performed here as a special puja.

Festivals:

Dasara, Vanabhojana are the important ones. Pilgrims from Kerala and Tamilnadu also visit this temple.

Krishnadevaraya gave Devi an emerald necklace.

Mookambika Temple of Kollur is amid calm, peaceful and serene surroundings. The best in man can be evoked from every pilgrim, which provides a soothing effect on the mind, body, and soul.

KERALA (KL)

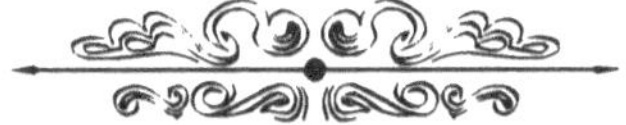

Kerala is beautiful between the sea and mountains, and it is green in the destiny of high trees and fertile land. Kerala state was formed on 1 November 1956. It was a Travancore Cochin state by July 1949. The Malabar merger took place on 1 November 1956, and the state's area is 38,863 sq km, with Thiruvananthapuram being its capital city.

Tamil Nadu, Karnataka, and Lakshadweep are the neighbouring states. The state's specialities are hill stations like Munnar and backwaters like Alappuzha, Kollam, and Kochi, which attract millions of tourists. Hinduism, Islam, and Christianity are the main religions of the state.

The number of temples where worship is conducted is estimated at 2,200. K.P.S. Menon opines that temples are houses of prayer, social clubs, and Cultural Centers. Saints, poets, and people have created a rich heritage of unique temples with ample courtyards and tiled conical roofs, as Mulk Raj Anand said.

The ritualistic arts of dance and drama (Kathakali, Mohiniyattam) and folk styles (Theyyam) are continuously enacted from generation to generation. The temple architecture of Kerala is unique and began in the early 9th century of Kulasekharas (as per Archeological Survey of India records). Another exciting feature of the Kerala temples is that they are higher than the coconut palm groves around them, surrounded by groves and tanks. Nothing is more beautifully picturesque than the Kerala state. In short, the Kerala temples are the nerve centres of all cultural activities.

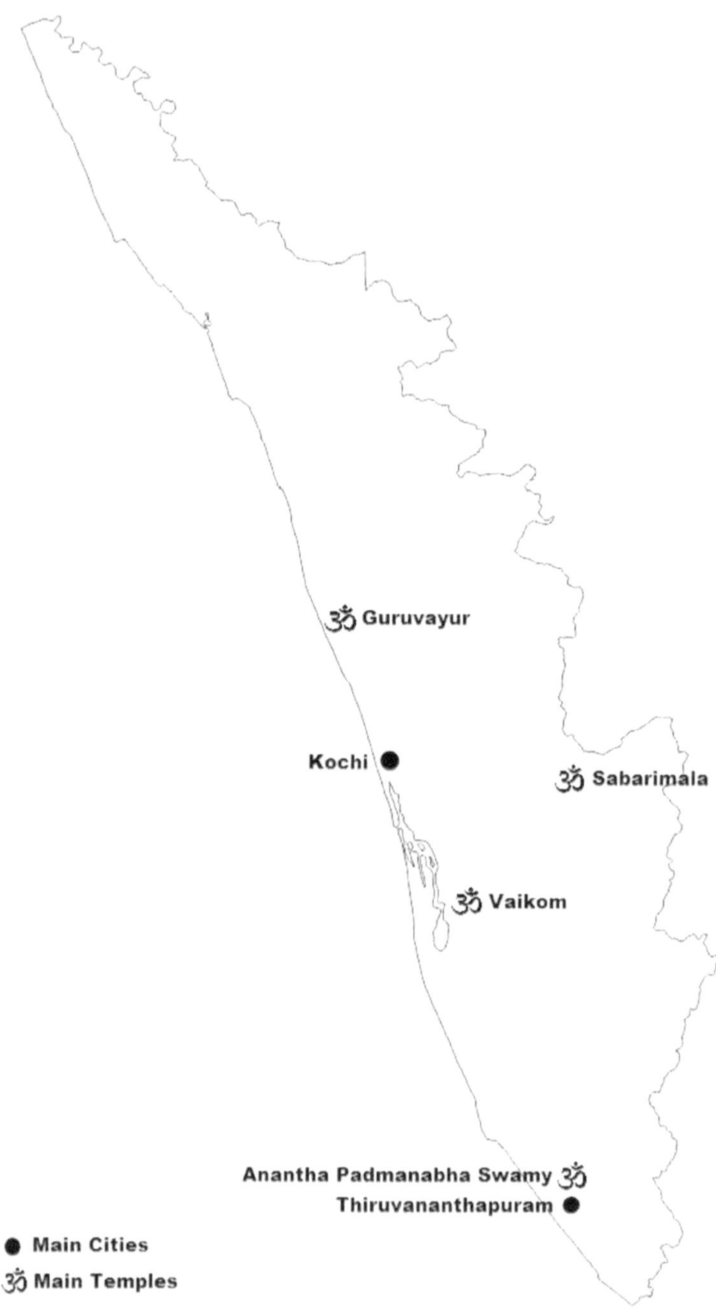

Figure 10: Kerala – Map of Major Cities and Temples

Trivandrum (Thiruvananthapuram) Anantha Padmanabha Swamy

Trivandrum derived its name from Tiru – Ananta – Puram (Thiruvananthapuram); Padmanabha Swamy temple is a landmark of Trivandrum. Lord Padmanabha reclines on 'Adisesha' or Ananta, which happens to be the place of the sacred serpent. Further, this place was also called 'Ananthapuri' during the Mahabharata times when Pandavas visited it during their exile or Vanavasa. Hence, the Lord of the Temple in Ananthapuri is known as Anantha Padmanabha Swany. This centuries-old temple is considered to be the spiritual heart of Trivandrum. The deity is said to be made of over 10,000 Salagrams (sacred stones), transported from Nepal by elephants. Sridevi and Bhoodevi stand by the side of Vishnu or Anantha Padmanabha, while Brahma is on the lotus, which rests from Vishnu's navel. The deity is visible from three doors in a row: face (southern side), navel (middle) and feet (northern side). Outside the inner shrine are smaller shrines of Krishna, Kshetrapala, Narasimha, Vyasa, Siva, Ganesa, Rama, Sita, Lakshmi, and other deities.

Figure 11: Author and his wife in front of Sri Anantha Padmanabha Swamy Temple during their visit in 2017

The Temple structure:

Fort walls surround the 100-foot-long seven-tiered temple structure. 'Rajagopuram' on the eastern side is said to be the gateway to the main deity. The temple's style is South Indian, with 350 pillars beautifully carved out of granite.

Sources:

The sources of information about the temple may be classified as puranic and legendary. The deity and the temple are known through Padma Purana, Skanda Purana, Bhagavatha Purana, Brahmanda Purana, Setu Mahatyam and palm leaf records. The antiquity of the temple is known through these puranic sources. Balarama's visit to the temple, a great Vaishnavite pilgrimage Centre, was mentioned in Bhagavata Purana.

The Legendary source throws light on Sage Dewakara, to whom the credit for the temple's prominence and the Lord's presence in Trivandrum is known. When Diwakara was in deep meditation, a boy disturbed him. The sage chased the boy, but the latter disappeared, saying he would be found only in the Anantha forest (Ananthakaadur). The sage realized that the Lord played with him in the form of the boy. The region is said to become a great kshetra, and the deity could be worshipped through three openings. (Vishnu's form of Aantha Padmabha, reclining on Adisesha, is too big an idol). As per Palm-leaf records, Diwakara set up the temple on the 950th day of Kaliyuga.

The historicity of the temple:

Padmanabha Swamy temple of Thiruvananthapuram is one of the 108 Vairshnaavite 'Divyadhamas' built in 3000 B.C., according to one of the legendary sources.

In 1749, Maharaja Marthanda Varma, after annexing principalities, placed his sword at the feet of the Lord in devotion, dedicating his kingdom to him. Since then, the rulers, the army, and the people have considered themselves as 'Dasas' of Padmanabha and acted as the temple's caretakers. The reconstruction work of the temple began and continued for about fifty years, ending in 1800 AD (encircling the shrines). Swati Tirumal (1813-46), the king and great music composer of 'Kritis', did excellent service to the temple.

During the reconstruction, 4000 masons, 6000 labourers and 100 elephants were engaged.

The Temple Flagstaff was built of unique teak wood engraved in gold and transported from a site 48 km away. The flagstaff was transported without touching the ground, and elephants made this marvellous feat possible. The sanctum sanctorum was also reconstructed. The wooden idol of Padmanabha became old and recumbent (lying on the ground) and hence was replaced with a new one moulded in shape by 'Salagramas' with a particular kind of mortar, the composition of lime and granite.

<u>Architecture of the Temple:</u>

The architecture may be summarized as a harmonious blend of Indigenous, especially Dravidian. Artistic excellence is found in sculpture and bronze. Art is realistic; for instance, Ganesa's image with his portly belly and stout diminutive lines is a masterpiece of realistic art. On his side stand three Brahmin priests performing puja.

Murals and wood carvings with themes from the epics and puranas are highlighted. The temple's mandapams reflect the beautiful sculptures. The best examples are the Navagraha Mandapa and Siveli Mandapam. On one side, they look like elephants; on the other, they resemble bulls.

<u>Details of worship at the temple:</u>

Worship systems like Prarthanas (prayers), Pujas (Archanas), and Naivedhyams (offerings) are the regular schedule of temple activities.

Since the size of the deity is very big to view and worship, sage Diwakara prayed to God Padmanabha to condense himself in size to facilitate the devotees for Prarthanas and Archanas, and his prayers were fruitful!

Tulu Brahmins of Diwakara's region are to perform the pujas, and it became a precedent. Malayali Brahmins or the Nambudris of Kerala are deputed to chant prayers. The Rigveda, the Yajurveda, and the Samaveda are to be recited. A ceremonial of 56 days is significant, and the Vedic recitation is compulsory on this occasion.

Naivedyam (Offering):

Diwakara had already stipulated the rules of offerings to the Lord. When he first saw the Lord, he is said to have offered an unripe mango and a coconut shell. Naivedyam is offered as rice in coconut shells.

Dress Code for the Devotees:

The dress code is strictly observed for men and women. Dhoti without upper garments for men and saree for women are implemented.

Temple Festivals:

Periodical, annual, and bi-annual temple festivals are celebrated with pomp and glory coupled with discipline, dedication, and devotion. They are attended by thousands of people, not only Keralites but also from every corner and nuk of the country. Foreigners also attend in large numbers.

Laksha Deepotsavam (Lighting festival) is a festival of lights celebrated every six years.

Temple festivals are celebrated twice a year in the months of 'Meenam' (March) and 'Tulam' (September / October). These festivals last ten days. Celebrations start with flag hoisting (Kodiyettam) and hunting (Pullavitha) and end with the immersion of the deities for bathing in the sea called 'Arattu' on the 10th day. The atmosphere is filled with celebration hoopla.

This festival marks the visit of the Pandavas during their exile to Ananthapuri. Towering effigies of the Pandavas in long red robes are placed before the temple entrance (eastern side). The idols are made of wood fibreglass. The colossal figures are set up to please the rain God Indra. Dharmaraja is seen sitting; Bhima, Arjuna, and Nakula's figures are the tallest, and that of Sahadeva is the shortest.

Folk arts are performed by 101 male artists dressed in war costumes, recalling the Kurukshetra battles of the Pandavas and Kauravas. Velakali is the name of the folk art. This custom was discontinued in 1941 and revived in 2011.

'Arattu' is the concluding event of the festival on the 10th day. The images of Padmanabha, Krishna and Narasimha are carried to the Arabian Sea at 'Shankhu Mukham' beach to give a bath by immersion. Princely families, armed police, and temple staff, with an escort of the government, attend to participate in the vast procession of thousands of devotees followed by elephants and horses. The images are brought back to the temple. Further, the ceremonial arts of dance – dramas such as Kathakali and Mohini Attam and folk styles like Theyyam are enacted generation after generation.

Lord Sri Krishna of Guruvayur

Sri Krishna temple in Guruvayur is one of the most famous temples in South India. From the point of income, it is second only to Sri Venkateswara Swamy Temple in Tirupati-Tirumala. Lord Sri Krishna was born on Krishnastami / Janmashtami day, probably 3000 years ago, before the birth of Jesus Christ in Mathura on the banks of the Yamuna. As an avatar of Sri Maha Vishnu, he appeared in Dwaparayuga. Krishna performed several miraculous deeds since childhood, including the killing of Putana the demon, the display of Vishwarupa by opening his mouth before Yashoda, lifting Govardhanagiri, Kaliya mardana, playing with Gopikas, etc. In the later years, he exhibited his skills as a warrior, statesman and Guru or teacher. Krishna's most important activities are participating in the Kurukshetra battle as a charioteer to Arjun, where he delivered the 'Bhagavad Gita' message to humanity and a philosophical elixir. The essence of the Gita is showing a way to Bhakti-Marga, the way of devotion; jnana-marga, the way of knowledge; and Karma-Marga, the way of action. Krishna passed these messages through Arjuna and his friend Udhava. Krishna is also the architect of Dwaraka.

<u>Journey of The Idol to Guruvayur:</u>

According to Sthala Purana, Sri Krishna manifested himself in the flesh and blood to the people of his times as the son of Devaki and Vasudeva. Among the Krishna shrines in India, the most famous is that of Guruvayur, known as 'Bhooloka Vaikuntha' Dattatreya acquainted the glory of Guruvayur to Janamejaya, son of Parikshit. Janamejaya worshipped the Lord of Guruvayur. Lord Brahma worshipped the image here and gave the idol to Vishnu. Sri Krishna brought the idol to Dwaraka. When he is to ascent to heaven (Swargarohana), the idol is given to Uddhava, his friend and devotee. Later, Uddhava was entrusted to 'Guru' and 'Vayu' Guruvayur derived its name from 'Ur' – the place and 'Vayu' who jointly installed the idol.

Guruvayur is known as the Dwaraka of the South. The idol of Sri Krishna is enchanting and endowed with four lustrous arms carrying the conch, the discus, the mace, and the lotus.

Sri Krishna appears in all radiance with the Tulasi mala and pearl necklace. The deity of Guruvayur is said to be a living deity who answers the prayers of pilgrims. In this context, the preaching of Krishna in Kurukshetra, i.e., Gita, deserves to be quoted:

"I am responsible for the welfare of those who think of me to the exclusion of all else and who remain devoted to me all the time."

<u>Some details of the Deity and Temple:</u>

The Temple was built by Vishwakarma, the celestial architect, in such a way that the first rays of the Sun fall at the Lord's feet, symbolic of the Sun paying his obeisance. The worship started 5000 years ago. The historical mention states it was the 14th century. The idol of the deity is said to be of rare stone, Patala Anjana, possessing healing qualities.

Narayana Bhattathiri, a great Sanskrit scholar and a noted savant of Kerala of the 16th century, composed 'Narayaneeyam' in praise of the Lord of Guruvayur, which brought fame to this Guruvayur temple. Narayaneeyam contains the essence of Bhagavad Gita, which shows the path to come out of the cycle of births and deaths and finally grants salvation.

The Puja systems:

The Temple follows the puja systems laid down by Adi Shankaracharya, who visited this Temple and composed eight slokas in praise of this Lord known as 'Govinda Asstakam'.

A bit of History:

By 1638, the Temple had been rebuilt entirely. Unfortunately, the Dutch raided the Temple in 1716 and looted its valuables, setting fire to the western gopuram. The Tower was rebuilt in 1747. Again, Tipu Sultan raided it twice and captured it in 1766 and 1789. Then, the main deity and the Utsawamurthy were reinstalled in September 1792 after Tipu's defeat at the hands of the English.

The Legends of the Leela of Lord Krishna of Guruvayur:

The Lord of Guruvayur is said to be powerful. He blesses devotees who surrender to him to get relief from their long-pending ailments or diseases. Hence, the Lord is called a divine healer. There are a number of instances—two popular ones need to be quoted. Anantha Rama Dikshitar was cured of leprosy. Chembai Vaidyanatha Bhagavatar, who lost his voice in a concert at Suchindram, regained it.

Offerings to the Lord:

There are 21 types of special pujas. The daily pujas start at 3:00 AM and stop by midnight. Abhishekams are performed. The Mula virat is applied with sandal paste, camphor, rose water or panneer, kumkum flower (Saffron). The Lord is taken in procession amidst the people on the elephant. On Sukla paksha Ekadasi, special prayers (Prarthanas) are arranged monthly (the day Gita was preached). Sri Krishnastami and other auspicious days are observed. Other shrines of the temple complex are Parvati, Ganesa, and Ayyappa. Forty-one days of Bhajans are arranged to fulfil their vows.

Bananas, Coconuts, Jaggery, etc., are offered as Naivedyam. The Tulabharam ceremony is a special activity here, and the devotees are weighed against bananas, sugar, jaggery, coconuts, etc., and Annaprasadams are distributed to the devotees.

<u>Art and Sculpture:</u>

The Mandapams are adorned with sculptures. Murals depicting Krishna Leelas or miracles are attractive on the walls of the temples.

Temples of Sri Rama

Triprayar

Vakkey Kaimal was a local chieftain who had a dream in which mysterious persons appeared and told him that four idols had been washed ashore in the nearby sea. Each was to be constructed as a temple at the allotted places. Kaimal, a great devotee of Sri Rama, hastened to the seashore and found the idols of Rama, Lakshmana, Bharata, and Satrughna lying there. They were installed in four places in temples as directed in the dream.

- Sri Rama – At Triprayar
- Lakshmana – At Moozhikulam
- Bharata – At Koodalmanikyam and
- Satrughna – At Payammal

These four idols resemble Lord Vishnu but are worshipped with different names.

When Kaimal consulted Pandits about installing Rama's idol at Triprayar, an unknown voice was heard saying that a peacock would fly high above the sky and the idol be installed at the spot exactly below. All were ready for installation, but there was no sign of the peacock. At this Juncture, a devotee holding a branch of peacock feathers appeared on the scene and performed the Pratista. Later, the peacock appeared. So, the altar (Balikkal) was installed as planned previously. Surprisingly, the Balikkal started moving. The Pandit had a nail on it and stopped its movement by chanting mantras.

In the temple sanctum, Sri Devi and Bhoodevi were installed by Viswamangala Swamy.

<u>The image of the Lord:</u>

Like the image of Vishnu, the idol is a four-armed one with Sankha (Conch) and Chakra (Discus) in the left hand and Kodanda (bow) and a mala (garland) in the right hand.

There is also an image of Dakshinamurthi facing South. The chief deity is believed to have a Siva aspect. Sri Rama possessed both the Saiva and Vaishnava aspects after killing Khara (Asura). Rama's image – one left hand possessing 'mala' indicates the aspects of Brahma. Thus, Sri Rama is said to be a 'Trimurthi Swarupa'.

There is an image of Ganesa outside the temple. Even though there is no Hanuman, the devotees visualize the image of Hanuman and bow before the mandapa (This scene is probably after the return of Hanuman after the search as Sita).

During the raids of Tipu Sultan, the temple and idol were also damaged.

<u>Rama's Idol – Captivating:</u>

Rama's idol presents a beautiful image with a sweet smile. The neck is radiant with a Kaustubha ornament and a Srivatsa mark. The chest is charming, and the shoulders are decorated with garlands, bracelets, and bangles. One cannot take one's eyes off.

<u>The Temple – Attractive</u>:

Architecturally speaking, the temple is one of the most attractive in Kerala state. The wood carvings are quite appealing. There is a beautiful copper-plated mandapa (namaskar mandapa) with 24 panels of wood carvings. On the walls, there are mural paintings. Episodes of the Ramayana are with grace and exquisite beauty. Outside the temple, there is an Ayyappa shrine.

<u>Performance of 'Kattu'</u>:

'Kattu' is performed for 12 days. The theme is 'Anguliyangam' – a conversation between Hanuman and Sita (taking a ring to be given to Rama).

<u>Festivals</u>:

Ekadasi and Poornima are the important temple festivals, which are from November to December and from March to April.

On Ekadasi, Sri Rama is taken in procession with 21 elephants. The temple is under the Cochin Development Board.

Other Famous Temples of Lord Sri Rama

After the Triprayar temple, two more foremost temples are to be cited. They are Tiruvilwamala and Tiruvangad. The image of Sri Rama at Tiruvilwamala is Swayambhu or self-manifested. Only a few temples in Lakshmana in India, let alone Kerala. There is one temple at Vennimala, 8 km from Kottayam. But it is less popular than Tiruvilwamala.

<u>Temple for Bharata at Irinjalakuda</u>:

Irinjalakuda is 20 km from Trichur, where the temple of Bharata is situated. Bharata is represented with four hands. He is worshipped only with lotus flowers and Tulasi and Bilwa dalas. There is also a tank or Koneru. Sri Rama visited the place after Vanavasa.

For Satrughna, there is a temple at Payemmal.

Sita-Lava-Kusha Temple:

The Temple is in a small town amidst coffee, pepper, and teak plantations. The town is Pulpally. Sita-Lava-Kusha temple is in lush green surroundings. Sita, the wife of Sri Rama, the incarnation of Dharma, is the daughter of Bhoodevi. She emerged from and disappeared into the Earth. Sita, along with her kids, lived here. The story is from Uttarakanda, one of the seven kandas of epic Ramayana.

After the killing of Ravana, Sri Rama returned to Ayodhya. The rule of Rama begins. Through the spies, he learned that one of his subjects blamed his character for bringing back Sita, who stayed in Lanka under Ravana's control. Lakshmana was asked to take her to the forests and leave her there. Being grief-stricken, she took refuge in Valmiki's ashram. Lava and Kusa were born there. After some time, Rama intended to conduct a yagna and sent the Yagna Aswam to establish his suzerainty. The twins caught hold of the yagna Ashwam. Satrughna, Lakshmana and finally, Rama came to get the horse released. War took place between them, and finally, Rama was informed about his sons. Sita called on Mother Earth and went along with her.

Valmiki Ashram is located at Pulpally. Pul means grass. Sita used to make a bed with grass for Lava and Kusa.

<u>The Temple:</u>

The Temple was built by a king who fought with Hyder Ali and Tipu Sultan. He was attacked by the British, who shot him on the banks of Pulpally in 1805.

The twins are worshipped here as child sages. Sita was known as Jadayudha Amma.

Sub shrines of the Temple are Ganesa, Siva, Ayyappa, Naga etc. The temple complex is vast, and the temples are of west-coast style.

The place is considered holy because of the Sri Rama, Sita, and Lava-Kusa episodes that happened here. Finally, Sita prayed to her Mother

Earth to take her back. Rama pulled her back by holding her hair (Jada). Hence, the Mother Sita is known as Jadayatha Amma.

The Ashram site is meant for a research project on the Ramayana. The Temple's management set up an international foundation for the study, research and conducting of seminars on the various aspects of Ramayana.

The Tamil Nadu border is just 50 km from Pulpally. Gooty is 125 km away, and Mysore is less than 150 km away.

The twins installed a Siva Lingam here and worshipped. Hence, the Siva Linga is known as Kusalava Puriswara.

Krishna Temple of Trichambaram

Trichambaram is 25 km from Kannanur district headquarters. Sri Krishna's Temple is said to be ancient, and here, Lord Krishna is worshipped in the most ferocious form. Trichambaram Krishna temple is known as North Guruvayur and is similar to Guruvayur temple in many ways.

Inside the temple is a temple for Goddess Jaladurga.

<u>The story about the temple:</u>

Kamsa arranged a wrestling display by 'Mustika', 'Chanura', 'Kuta Shala', and 'Toshala'. An arena had been erected for this purpose of wrestling. The purpose of arranging this show was to kill the Krishna brothers who had arrived from Brindavan. But they were blocked by an elephant named 'Kuna Layarada', which was brought to attack them. Krishna killed Assuras and proceeded towards the elephant, broke one of its tusks, and finally killed the elephant. Kamsa realized that all his plans to kill Krishna had become futile. Krishna caught hold of Kamsa and threw him to the ground, and killed him. Madhura, actually the spot where the happenings happened, was full of joy and happiness. In short, Madhura was agog with excitement.

The Lord was jubilant after the Killing of Kamsa. Lord Krishna at Trichambaram is considered to be in a posture after Kamsavadha, and the Roudra expression is visible on his face. Parasurama constructed the Krishna Temple, as in the case of several other temples in Kerala. Parasurama laid down the rules of the puja system and the festivals.

The temples of Vishnu and Sita existed in this Malabar Desa much earlier than the 11th century A.D., upholding the oneness of Siva Kesavas.

Customs of the Temple:

The peculiar custom here is the offering of 'Naivedyam' immediately after the temple's opening. Secondly, elephants are prohibited in the temple complex.

Temple Renovation:

The temple had undergone renovation after the Tipu Sultan's invasions. The temple architecture had distinct features.

The Krishna temple of Trichambaram contains excellent wood carvings with Bhagavatha themes. The renovation activities were completed in the 14th – 15th and 17th – 18th centuries.

The double-walled Garbhagriha has a beautiful stone image of Krishna decorated with ornaments. A pond and a Durga shrine surround the northern side of the main entrance. The water level in the pond always remains the same.

The Trichambaram temple is smaller than other temples like Vaikom. Though it is small, it looks like a beautiful rose. The crowds visiting the temple are limited, not like Guruvayur's. However, Trichambaresar grants the desires of his devotees like Guruvayurappan.

Temple festival:

The annual festival is in March. Elephants are not used in the procession. The images are carried on the heads of the priests.

Lord Siva Temple of Vaikom

A famous Siva Temple is near Ernakulam and Kottayam (less than 50 km), and the place is known as Dakshina Kasi. Life here revolves around the temple. Lord Siva is known to be Vaikatappan. The deity's origin goes back to Tretayuga, per the Puranic source. Lord Siva of Vaikom is the benign Lord or kindhearted. People of different castes and sects of faith, like Saivaite and Vaishnavite, go for the darshan of the Lord. , Hundreds of devotees enter the temple complex every morning and evening with 'Sivanama Smarana' of 'Namassivaya', 'Hara Mahadev', and 'Sambho Mahadeva'. The devotees firmly believe that Siva grants everybody's wishes, such as children, health, jobs, etc. Further, the deity is popular as Annadana Prabhu, the giver of food.

The Maharaja of Trivandrum invited all Vaikom (Nambudris) cooks to prepare food and items or Prasadam. It is believed that Siva partakes in food during festivals along with the Brahmins and devotees. Darsan of the deity is called 'Ananda Darsan'.

<u>Origin of the Deity and Temple:</u>

The history of the deity and the temple is based on the 'Vyaghrapuri Mahatyam' of the Bhargava Purana.

During Ramayana, a demon named Khara lived and performed severe penance to praise Siva. God granted him several boons and three Siva Lingas. The demon took hold of the two Lingas in each hand and the third in his mouth. On the way of his journey, he kept one linga of the right hand at a sacred place knee-deep in water, took a rest for some time, and afterwards tried to pick up the linga but failed to move it.

A sage named Vyaghrapada appeared there. Khara entrusted the Linga to the care of the Sage and proceeded to a nearby place named Ettumanur, where he installed the left-hand Linga. The one in the month was kept at Kaduthuruthy. Thus, the three Lingas brought by the asura were installed at Vaikom, Kaduthurthy, and Ettumanur, which became holy centres. It is said that the darshan of these three places is auspicious.

The place name:

The place name goes by the name of the saint Vyaghrapada, Vyaghrapada Puram or Vyoghrapuri, and Vaikom is finally named briefly.

The Sage was a great devotee of Siva and Parvati; the divine couple gave him darshan under a peepal tree near the eastern gateway of the temple. The spot is marked as another tree with a raised platform to light a lamp and perform pujas.

Parasurama's association with the Holy Place:

The idol and the temple are attributed to Parasurama, the incarnation of Vishnu. In Kerala, the Sage has constructed several Siva and Vishnu temples for the well-being of the Keralites. Parasurama embraced the Siva Linga at Vaikom in knee-dep water. The Linga is about five feet high, and the platform is two feet high. To enhance the power of the linga, he performed Puja by bringing Pandits.

Ashtami Festival of the Temple:

During Kartika masa (November – December), a unique festival is celebrated here on Ashtami day, to Vaikom Mahadeva. The festival is known as 'Vaikom Ashtami' (a 13-day festival); whoever offers a Bilwa leaf, coin, or lamp on the day is liberated and gets salvation or moksha. Special pujas, public feeding, music entertainment, dance and elephant processions are arranged.

Description of the Temple: According to Ronal Bernier, Vaikom Temple *"is situated amidst a flawlessly finished green setting. The roof is cone-shaped and covered with copper and dazzling gold."*

Siva Linga is decorated with flower garlands and jewels. Siva's three eyes and crescent are also decorated.

Details of the History and Architecture of the Temple:

The Vaikom temple is datable to the 11th or 12th century, according to historian K.V. Saunderarajan. Some additions, like the wooden panel walls in the 15th-16th centuries, were made later. By the 18th century, some more additions (murals) were made under the renovation activity.

Style of the Temple:

The Vaikom temple is said to be of the Indigenous style of temple architecture. According to Stella Kramisch, the temple's plan is circular. A Nandi image is placed in front of the sanctums. The temple faces east.

Flagstaff: A 317-foot-high gold-covered flagstaff is installed. The temple's area is nearly eight acres, and it has four imposing gateways similar to those of all the South Indian Temples.

Other Shrines:

Vanadurga temple, which is exposed to the sun and rain, exists.

Episode of Yakshi:

A demi Goddess of evil aspect was Yakshi, a Gandharva damsel cursed by sage Agasthya. She was roaming in the temple area and harassing people and animals. Sage Vyaghrapada showed people the path by installing Stambha Vighneswara on the northeastern side of the temple entrance. He ordered Trisuli to protect the victims who were one of his Bhootaganas.

Special Features of the Temple Activities:

'Arattu' is a particular activity, a holy bath ceremony. It is common in Kerala Temples, where it is performed in front of tanks or the sea. Parasurama, during his worship of the linga, bathed the deity with Sahasra Kalasam of holy water according to Vedic rites.

Thrissur / Trichur (The Vadakkunathan Temple)

The Siva Temple, or the Vadakkunathan Temple, is one of the most unique, ancient, and important temples of Kerala in Trichur town. It derived its name from the original 'Tiru Siva Perur'. During the time of Kulasekhara in the 9th century, this town was built around a hillock. Sri Vadakkunathan temple is a classic example of Kerala's style of architecture. The temple is popularly known as 'Tiru Kailasam'. Thrissur is located amidst a forest of teak woods. Vrishachalam is another name for Trissur or the place of Nandikswara.

The Temple:

Trissur is a holy place of Siva, and this is the oldest in Kerala state. The temple had a spacious campus of nine acres of land with beautiful sculptures carved in wood; Mahabharata episodes are the themes of the murals, attracting pilgrims and tourists. The temple walls look like a fort. The massive stone was raised for its construction. Four Gopurams exist on the temple›s four sides: north, South, east and west. There are other shrines of Siva, Rama and Sankara Narayana (Siva-Kesava Tatva) in this multi-complexed temple. Further, some more shrines of Parvati, Sri Krishna, Ganesa, etc., also exist on the campus.

Legend of Three Deities:

It is said that Sage Purasurama installed the deities of Siva, Rama and Sankara Narayana after he saw them after meditation.

1. Parasurama saw Siva in his original form.
2. Then he saw Maha Vishnu with four arms holding conch, disc mace, and lotus. The Lord is worshipped as Sri Rama. Almost all the temples in Kerala state represent the Lord, either Rama or Krishna, as Sri Maha Vishnu. This may be the 'Viswa Roopa' representation.
3. Sankara Narayana is the combined form of Siva and Vishnu, emphasizing that both are the same: *"Ekam Sat Viprah Bahudha vadanti"*.

<u>Significance of the Temple:</u>

The Siva Lingam is 16 feet tall, covered by cow's ghee, which looks like a mountain. The Maha Linga cannot be seen as it has been covered with ghee for 1000 years. The speciality is that the cumulated ghee emits no odour, although it is 1000 years old. At the apex are 13 gold crescents and three serpent hoods reminding devotees of Kailas Mountain. There are other shrines like Adi Shankaracharya, Parasurama and Ayyappa. It is said that the darshan of the Lord amounts to several holy shrines in India, especially Kasi and Rameswaram.

<u>Temple Highlights:</u>

- This temple of Vadakkunathan existed even before Jagadguru Adi Shankaracharya (788-820 AD), who established four mutts, the first of which was Vadakku Mutt.
- The Nambudri Brahmins, the traditional priests of Kerala, framed the rules and regulations of this temple and worship in the temple.
- In Trissur temples, the 'Kuttu' (Drama) art form is seen with large, beautiful structures of good artistry.

<u>Festivals (Sivaratri – Pooram):</u>

Sivaratri is the only festival that is celebrated. The deity is not taken out in the procession. Vadakkunathan temple is known for its festival, 'Pooram,' which thousands of people attend. The teak forest around the temple comes alive on this occasion. During this time, the idols of Gods and Goddesses of other temples are brought here on elephants, followed by musical instruments. Fifty richly caparisoned elephants are used for the procession, which is a colourful display.

<u>The Temple Timings:</u>

The temple opens in the morning and closes by 10:30 AM. It is also open in the evening from 4:00 PM to 8:30 PM.

The Government of India has declared this temple a national monument under the Ancient Monuments and Archeological Sites and Remains Act.

Siva or Rajarajeswara Tempe of Taliparamba

Taliparamba, the abode of Sri Rajarajeswara, is just 25 km from Cannanore, near Calicut or Tellicherry. The region is famous and holy because of Siva or Rajarajeswara Temple, Krishna Temple of Trichambaram and Siva Temple of Kanjraghat. These deities bless the devotees with high status, good nature, and long life.

Sri Rajarajeswara temple is one of the 108 ancient Siva temples of Kerala. It is said that Siva gave three Siva Lingas to Parvati for worship. The temple had an epic background of Ramayana.

On his return from Lanka, Sri Rama visited this place and offered prayers. Taliparamba was famous for learning and devotion. Parasurama brought 15000 Brahmins to this place (Source: Kerala Mahatyam), and they contributed to the uplift of the region in the above aspects.

Tipu Sultan attacked the temple, destroying a gigantic gopuram at the entrance. The attacks were so severe that many Nambudri families ran away in search of safe places.

The Temple:

The tower had a pyramid-shaped roof. The central shrine was an ancient one with two roofs. The temple does not have a flagstaff. According to the epigraphical sources, the temple and the tank were renovated in 1524 AD.

Offerings to the Lord:

The primary offering is ghee, available in small pots and used for abhishekams of the Swamy.

Monday is an auspicious day for prayers and abhishekams. Maha Sivarati and New Year's Day (Vishnu) are observed as annual festivals. Women are allowed only for Puja in the night. This restriction is not applicable at the Siva temple at Kanjraghat.

<u>Description of Siva Lingam of Taliparamba:</u>

The Siva Lingam is only three feet in height. It is decorated with a crescent, three eyes, and a nose (all made of gold), making the idol look much taller with lustre. The Siva Linga here reminds Siva of Kailash.

Sri Mahadeva Temple of Mammiyur

Mammiyur is within walking distance of Guruvayur. Sri Mahadeva Temple is an ancient temple that was later renovated. It is said that Udhava, the friend and devotee of Sri Krishna, handed over the idol of Maha Vishnu to the guru and Vayu in the Dwarka Temple. Parasurama led them to a place with a lotus tank. There, they felt the presence of Lord Siva. The divine couple, Siva and Parvati, welcomed them. Siva and Parvati stayed at Mammiyur. Siva named the place as Guruvayur. Wall paintings and sculptures are pretty. A visit to Guruvayur is considered incomplete without a visit to Mammiyur.

Sabarimala (Sri Dharma Sastha Temple of Ayyappa)

There are temples dedicated to Dharma Sastha as Lord Ayyappa. Two of the famous temples of Kerala State are well-known and well-established. They are the Ayyappa temple of Sabarimala and Sri Krishna's Temple in Guruvayur. Ayyappa temple is the oldest and the most visited one in South India. The Temple is in the western ghats amidst the Sahyadri mountain ranges.

<u>The Story:</u>

According to a Puranic source, The King of Pandalam (a line of the Pandyas), Rajasekhara, had no issues. He prayed to Lord Siva for a Child. Siva instructed Dharma Sastha (an emanation of the Mohini Avatar of

Vishnu) to be born as Ayyappa. On his way back from the king's hunt, he found a child on the banks of Pampa. A Yogi told him to bring him up as his own by naming him Manikandan (having a golden bell around his neck).

Manikandan or Ayyappa is also known as Hariharaputra, Son of Vishnu (Hari) and Siva (Hara). Thus, He is Siva's third son, the other two being Ganesa, Murugan, or Kartikeya.

Ayyappa was born from the charm of Narayana and Jnana of Siva combined with a glowing light (Tejas). He embodies the qualities of both Siva and Vishnu. The king and queen raised him.

Manikandan cast an arrow that fell at Sabari, the place selected by the Lord for the construction of the Temple; he then disappeared. Sabari is located northeast of the Pampa River, where Bhakta Sabari was doing penance, seeking Salvation.

The Temple:

The Temple was constructed by the king of Pandalam Rajasekhara, who was regarded as the father of Ayyappa. It is believed that Parasurama installed the idol in the sanctum sanctorum. The main idol was made of wood. The temple architecture is in the Kerala style. This Dharma Sastha temple of Sabarimala is situated in the reserved forest area in Perinad village of Ranni Taluk of Pathanamthitta district of Kerala. There are Maha Ganapati, Sri Rama, Anjaneya, and Parvati shrines on the upper side of the north bank of the Pampa River.

The Age of the Temple:

Historians and archaeologists say the Temple is 4000 to 4250 years old, but the popular belief is that it is 5000 years old. Sabarimala was previously known as Mathangamala, as sage Matanga is said to have lived here. Later, it became Sabarimala after Sri Rama met Sabari, Matanga's disciple. Lord Rama was in quest of Sita at that time.

<u>Sabari Pilgrimage:</u>

The pilgrimage is unique and aims to clean the body and mind. A devotee must climb the 'Padinettambadi' steps to reach the main Temple. He considers the 18 steps as 'Astadasa Adhistana Devatas'.

<u>Mandaladharana Diksha:</u>

Before proceeding to the pilgrimage, devotees must observe hard penance (Vritam) for 41 days. They must observe strict abstinence from worldly pleasures. Shouting of Ayyappa Saranam (surrender) – Swamy Saranam is a prominent pilgrimage feature.

There are three routes, and the easiest one is via Chalakayam near Pamba. Only Neelimala mountain must be crossed. The other routes are long in distance and consist of mountains, valleys, and forests.

During the Deeksha, the devotees are strictly advised to follow the code of dress, food, and behaviour.

- Under the guidance of a guru, 'Mala Dharana' is to be followed.
- The dress code is black, blue, or saffron. The colour differentiation denotes the number of times the pilgrimage takes place.
- Head bath twice a day. Apply Vibhuti and Chandan on the forehead.
- Satvika aharam to be taken
- Visit the houses of other devotees.
- Haircuts, shaving, and applying oil to hair must be stopped.
- Brahmacharya to be followed.
- Do not wear shoes or sleep in bed.
- Give up all bad habits (smoking, liquor etc.)
- Politeness is to be observed using Swamy or Ayyappa in the case of gents and Amma in the case of ladies.

After the completion of Deeksha, he takes 'Irumudi' (essential material needed for puja tied in a cloth bag) – coconut filled with ghee and the items for Lord's Abhishekam are the essential items to be taken. After reaching the Temple, the devotee must perform Puja.

The Temple is open only for a few days. The first festival lasts 41 days (November 15 to December 26). The next one is the Makara Vaisakha festival, which starts on January 1 and ends on January 14. The shrine is open to all males from any religion, caste, or sect, but women are allowed with specifications. (Protests came up in the backdrop of the recent Supreme Court's judgment to allow all women into the Temple without any restrictions.)

The glimpse of Ayyappa lasts only a few seconds. Those carrying Irumudi Kettu are allowed to darshan. Jewellery is taken from Pandalam to the Temple to adorn the Lord.

The procession of the devotees reaches on January 14. The holy Garuda makes 9 Pradakshinas just above the Temple and disappears. The deity is adorned with ornaments, followed by an Aarati. Immediately, the Makara Jyoti appears three times on the eastern side of the Temple up above the hills (not a single star appears in the sky during this time). Only a bright star, Makara Nakshatram, appears. The devotees become alert to look at the Jyoti, which they feel is the divine darshan of Lord Ayyappa. The feeling of ecstasy is notable among the pilgrims. The pilgrimage is considered a soul's journey to unite with the Supreme.

Kalady – The Birthplace of Adi Shankaracharya

Kalady is the birthplace of the world preceptor and proponent of the Advaita philosophy. This place inspires and purifies men in their thoughts, words, and deeds. A visit to the place promotes tranquillity, self-restraint, and values.

Shankaracharya was born in 788 A.D. to a Nambudri couple, Sivaguru and Aryamba. By the grace of Siva of Trichur, this philosopher was born.

Sivaguru, Shankara's father, died when Shankara was only three years old, and his mother brought him up. At the age of five, his thread marriage was performed. He was sent to a teacher, and he mastered all the subjects. He served his mother. Another miracle he did was change the course of the Periyar or Purna River to enable his mother to take her daily bath, making the distance shorter from his house. Another miracle occurred when Shankara bathed in the river; a crocodile caught his leg. His mother was terrified. Then Shankara told his mother that the crocodile released his leg from its jaws when she allowed him to enter the Sanyasa ashram. The mother agreed, and immediately, the crocodile released Shankara's leg. Shankara promised her that he would be with her in her last days and would perform the funeral rituals, which he did.

To attain spiritual enlightenment, Shankara set out in search of a preceptor. He met his guru, Govinda, on the banks of the Narmada River. Under him, he mastered Yoga, Vedanta, and other systems. He came to know what 'Brahman' means. Later, Shankara went to Kasi and wrote commentaries for various scriptures. He visited several temples on the way of his journey. Shankara's erudition and exposition attracted him, and several scholars followed him and became his disciples – Sanandana was his first disciple (Padmapada).

When Shankara went to the Ganges to bathe, an outcast came from the opposite direction. Shankara asked him to give him the way. The late questioned him: Whom are you asking—the body or the soul? Shankara was taken aback. It took no time for Shankara to realize that the outcaste who questioned him was Lord Shankara, and he prostrated at his feet. He prayed Shankara with five verses of an Advaitic hymn called 'Manisha Panchaka'.

Adi Shankara proceeded to Badari, where Vyasa did penance. He wrote commentaries to the Brahma Sutras (10 Upanishads). Commentaries on the Bhagavad Gita, too, came out from him. He spent the remaining years of his life there. He visited several centres of learning and pilgrimage in India. He established Sringeri, Badari, Dwaraka and Puri Matts in four corners of India. Disciples were trained to carry the Vedantic message.

Shankara visualized his mother's last moments and came to her as he had promised. He prayed to Lord Vishnu, and the Lord appeared before him. Shankara's mother entered eternal beatitude or blessedness.

He performed the last rites of his mother and resumed his spiritual mission. He proceeded to Kedarnath and disappeared at the age of 32.

<u>Installation of Shankara's Idol:</u>

Sringeri Sarada Peetham installed the idols of Goddess Saradamba and Shankaracharya at Kalady. Due to Adi Shankaracharya's contributions to Hinduism, Vedanta, the place of Kalady, became famous. There is a memorial there named Adi Shankara Bhagavad pada Mandapam.

In November 2021, a 12-foot-high statue weighing 35 tonnes was unveiled at Kedarnath, at Adi Shankaracharya's Samadhisthal.

Temples of Maha Ganapati

There are two beautiful temples of Maha Ganapati: one at Kottarakkar, 22 km from Quilon (also known as Kollam) town, and the other at Kasaragod, near Calicut.

Kottarakkar Maha Ganapati Temple

Kottarakkar temple is an ancient and self-manifested temple; only Hindus are allowed in. Lord Siva, Parvati, Murugan, Ayyappan, and Nagaraja are the other deities in the temple. Devotees worship all the deities, but the chief deity is Maha Ganapati. One dance form named Kathakali was born here, and its originator was Kottarakkar Tumburan. The first performance was given at this temple.

Kasaragod Maha Ganapati Temple

This temple is near Calicut, and the temple complex is spacious and big. The idol is also said to be self-manifested (Svayambhu). Its speciality is that the idol grows just like Kanipakam Vinayaka of Kanipakam, situated in the Rayalaseema region of Andhra Pradesh.

MADHYA PRADESH (MP)

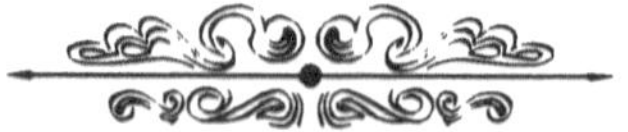

Madhya Pradesh was formed as a state on 1st November 1956. It was later bifurcated on 1st November 2000 to form Chhattisgarh. The state's capital is Bhopal, and it covers an area of 3,08,000 square kilometres. Madhya Pradesh shares its borders with Maharashtra, Gujarat, Rajasthan, Uttar Pradesh, and Chhattisgarh. The major religions followed in the state are Hinduism, Islam, and Buddhism. The Narmada is a famous river that flows through the state, and the Vindhya and Satpura are the prominent mountain ranges. Khajuraho, Omkareshwar, Ujjain, and Bhopal are famous temple towns. All Hindu festivals are celebrated with great enthusiasm and splendour.

Khajuraho Temples

Khajuraho Temples are superb examples of Indo-Aryan architecture. Khajuraho temples of Bundelkhand are the products of the Rajput times (Between 950 and 1050 AD by Chandelas). Khajuraho was founded by Chandravarman, the son of Moon God (Chandra). The number of temples constructed in a century (950-1050 AD) is estimated as 85.

Khajuraho was the capital of the Chandelas, and another name for this place was 'Kharjooravahaka'. Many Hindu and Jain temples are situated here. In the present context, Hindu temples are classified as Saivaite and Vaishnavaite. The temples are located in southern, eastern, and western directions.

Khajuraho's most striking and best-preserved temples are the western group.

<u>Southern Temples:</u>

1. Chaturbhuja Temple: This small Temple is situated just 3 km from Khajuraho in the southern direction. It was built by King Kirthivarne around 1100 AD. The temple consists of a pillared hall, Mandapa, and Sanctum sanctorum, where the idol of Sri Maha Vishnu, which is 10 feet high, is installed. The Shikhara is plain, but the walls contain different sculptures.

2. Dulhadev Temple: This is a Siva Temple of Khajuraho. It is said to be a complete temple because it contains Artha mandapa, Mandapa, Mahamandapa, Antaralaya, and Garbhagriha (Sanctum Sanctorum). The temple is 69 feet long and 40 feet wide. The temple and its complex are magnificent and full of rich sculptures. Salabhanjikas and 'Chakra Silpa' of the temple roof are the examples to be cited.

<u>Eastern Temples:</u>

1. Vamana Temple: Vijayapala built this temple around 1050 AD, which is 65 feet long and 45 feet wide. It is special because it reminds the Dasavataras of Sri Maha Vishnu on a five-foot platform. There are Antaralaya, garbhalaya, and mandapa. The main deity is Vamana.

2. Javeri Temple: This temple was built by Kirthi Varman. A unique feature is the construction of small Mandis for the different deities on the wall. Sculptural details are also to be seen.

3. Brahma Temple: This Temple was constructed on the bank of a tank. In this small temple, 'Chaturmukha Brahma' was installed.

4. Hanuman Temple: This is said to be the first temple built in Khajuraho. The Hanuman deity is 8 feet in height.

<u>Western Temples:</u>

Khajuraho's most striking and best-preserved temples are those within the fenced-off section of the western group of temples. They are estimated as 12 in number. The important ones are to be focused here. According to the inscriptional evidence, the temples are classified into two groups: The earlier notable temples are of the Chousath yogini, Mathangeswara, and Varaha. The latter comprises the rest of the temples.

1. Chousath Yogini Temple: These temples are said to be 64 in number and have 64 Yogini idols. Yogini temples in India are primitive in construction, having a quadrangular shape and not being circular. Since they are primitive, most of the temples are demolished. Only 32 are to be seen. Among them, three temples have the murtis of Mahishasura Mardini, Brahmani, and Maheswari facing east.

2. Matangesvara Temple: This is the largest and latest example of the first group. The deity is carved in black stone on an elevated platform.

3. The Varaha shrine: This is a pavilion built of red sandstone. As the preserver of order in the universe, Vishnu assumed human or animal forms (avatars) when necessary to correct some abuses. The Varaha, or the Boar incarnation, was the third form of Vishnu to rescue Earth from the ocean in which she had been submerged. Finally, she was saved by Varaha Murti with his arms.

The Latter Temples: The latter group of temples includes all other sandstone temples of Khajuraho. Lakshmana, Viswanatha, and the Kanchriya Mahadeva are the largest and most significant.

- The Lakshmana Temple: The temple's modelling is sensitive and massive. Further, it stands at the beginning of the finer and more developed series of Khajuraho temples. Visvanatha, Jagadamba, and Chitragupta have continued the same style. The peak of the style reached in the Kandriya Mahadeva, representing the grand finale and culmination of the architectural movement. Visvanatha temple is midway between the Lakshmana and Kandriya temples.
- The Kandriya Maliadeva Temple is the largest and loftiest of Khajuraho, similar to Visvanatha, measuring about 30.48 m each in length and height and 20.12 m in width. The shikhara is grand and ornamented.

- Two other fair-sized temples are the Vishnu and Jagadamba, measuring 72 feet by 58 feet. The Jagadamba temple may be cited as a good example of temple design. There are temples for Surya, the Sun God, and Chitragupta, similar to the Matangesvara temple of early times.

<u>Splendid sculpture of Khajuraho:</u>

"One of the most refined and finished manifestations of Indian architecture and sculpture in the Indo-Aryan style is found in the temples of Khajuraho in central India", as per Percy Brown.

The sculpture style is purely individual in character and rich in appearance. The sanctum is Sapta-ratha on plan and elevation with seven segments. This is supposed to be the most developed one in North Indian architecture. Further, the style harmoniously integrates sculpture with architecture.

Khajuraho temples had chiselled mouldings in two rows with elephants and horses, warriors and hunters, devotees, erotic couples, musicians, and dancers.

Two great Temples of Mahakaleshwar and Omkareshwar

One of India's 'Dvadasa Jyotirlingas', or sacred shrines of Lord Siva, is situated in Ujjain. The popular Mahakaleshwar is the stunning Temple of India. Omkareshwar, referred to as 'mini-Varanasi' with ghats, is also one of several holy places in our country. The 'Om' – shaped island is the sacred seat of Siva. Both Mahakaleshwar and Omkareshwar are situated in the western part of Madhya Pradesh.

<u>Mahakaleshwar (Ujjain):</u>

This Swayambhu, or self-manifested kshetra, is situated in a spacious campus facing south. This beautiful temple is constructed with five floors. The sanctum sanctorum and a lake show the way to Mahakaleshwar, and devotees can touch and worship the Linga. Ganesa, Parvati, and Hanuman idols are also there. Lord Omkareshwar, Nagendra, and Navagrahas are on the first floor. 'Bhasmabhisheka' is the specialty here performed by 4:00 AM.

There is a legend related to the dropping or falling of one drop of nectar (Amritabhanda of Ksheerasagara mathana story) at Ujjain. The other three drops were at Haridwar, Prayag, and Nasik. The other Temples of Ujjain are Harasiddhi (Siva – Parvati), Haragopal (Krishna), Ganesh, Durga, Kala Bhairava etc. Sandeep Ashram (Krishna – Balarama's Center of Education) is another exciting place.

<u>Omkareshwar Temple:</u>

This temple is located about 70 km from Khandwa and is also one of the Jyotirlingas (12). On the northern side of Omkareshwar village, the river Narmada flows along with Kaveri. On the request of Mandhata (founder of Ikshvaku Vamsa), Siva remained here as Swayambhu, named Omkareshwar or Amaresvar. Panchamukha Vinayaka with Sindhura is also here (renovated after the Muslim invasion). Here is a sloka about this place:

"Kaverika Narmadayoh Pavitre Samagane Sajjana taranaya, Sadaiva Mandhatrupure Vasantham Omkaramesam Sivamekamude"

Other Temples

Sun God Temples

In a small town, Unao, 17 km from Datia and 17 km from Jhansi, there is a famous 18th-century Sun God Temple, Unao Balaji Sun Temple. Holy water lakes are also built to relieve chronic diseases for those who bathe here. On a platform constructed with bricks, the God is installed as a 'Bimba' covered by brass. Twenty-one triangles are engraved in the shrine, representing 21 phases of the Sun. A unique festival is celebrated on the occasion of Pongal.

Three centuries before this temple, there was one Sun God Temple near Ujjain, but the Muslim ruler of Marwar destroyed it.

Some more Siva Temples

- It is estimated that there were 99 temples, 99 lakes, and 99 kilds near Khargam. Of course, they are all in decaying condition.
- Gondiyanagar is another place where there is a temple of 'Naagara', an ancient one. The 'Naaga' symbol is also found on the bottom part of Siva Linga.
- Bhajesvar temple near Bhopal was said to be constructed by Bhajaraj. The Siva Linga is made of marble.

Temples of Sri Rama

- Chitrakut – The distance from Allahabad is 90 km. Lord Sri Rama, Sita, and brother Lakshmana stayed in Chitrakut for eleven years out of 14 years of 'Vanavas' duration. River Mandakini flows, and devotees bathe in the river and then visit the temple for Ram Darsan.
- Anasuya-Atri (Sage) Ashram is also situated here. Temples for Sita Rama, Lakshman and Hanuman are here.

Devi Temples

- The Narmada Devi temple deserves to be cited because it is situated at Amarkantak, the birthplace of the holy river Narmada, called the 'Southern Ganga'. The Narmada is the biggest river to flow westward in the peninsula. Over 79 km through Madhya Pradesh, Maharashtra, and Gujarat States also benefit from Narmada's flow. River Narmada is said to have been born from the sweat of Lord Siva, and seven temples portray seven forms of the 14 Temples.
- Bhavani Devi Temple (Mandalesvar)—On the banks of the River Mahesvari, there is a temple of Bhavani, which is supposed to

be the seat of Shakhi Peeth. Further, the region is part of the Dandakaranya forest, where Rama spent some time as part of 'Vanavas'. Hence, there are some temples relating to the Ramayana episodes.

- Maatangeswar temple (Mahesvar) – Mahismati is another name for Mahesvar. Matangesvar is a Siva temple, and the Goddess here is svahadevi or Bhavani devi.

MAHARASHTRA (MH)

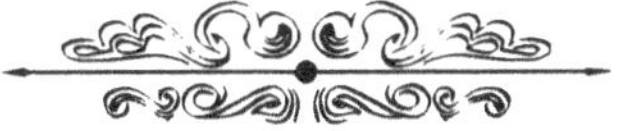

The state of Maharashtra was formed on May 1, 1960, after the bifurcation of Bombay into Maharashtra and Gujarat. It covers an area of 3,07,713 square kilometres and shares borders with Gujarat, Madhya Pradesh, Telangana, Karnataka, Goa, Nagar Haveli, and Chattisgarh. The Arabian Sea is a prominent landmark in the state, and Marathi is the chief language spoken here. The major religions the people of Maharashtra follow are Hinduism, Christianity, Islam, Parsi, and Jainism. The state is home to several rivers, including Godavari, Penganga, Manjira, Bhima, Varna, and Wardha, and mountain ranges such as Ajanta, Harischandra, Balaghat, Mahabaleshwar, and more.

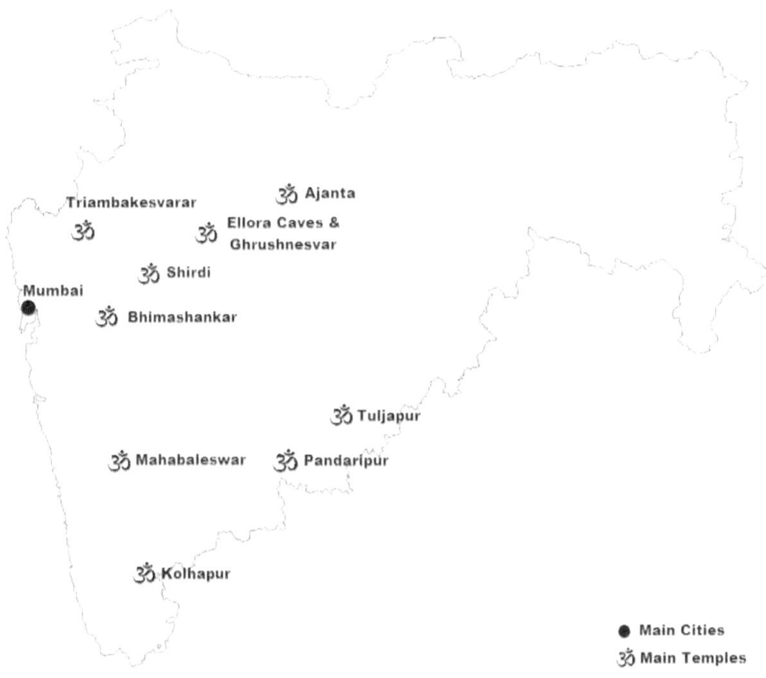

Figure 12: Maharashtra – Map of Major Cities and Temples

Ganesh Chaturthi is the largest celebration in Maharashtra. On the 10th day, millions of people come to the seashore of Chowpatty to submerge the largest Ganesh statues, making it a joyful mayhem. The capital of Maharashtra is Bombay, which is now known as Mumbai. Maharashtra is India's third-largest state by area and second-most populous state.

History of Mumbai:

Koli fishermen inhabited the Seven islands that formed Mumbai as far back as the 2nd century B.C. During 1534, this was under Portugal's control. The identity of Maharashtra was due to Shivaji (1627-80). In 1661, Catherine of Braganza married Charles II of England. Therefore, the region came under the possession of the British in 1665. Later, it was given on lease to the English East India Company. Below are the important temples of the State.

Ashta Vinayaka Temples:

Ganesh or Mahaganapathi is an auspicious deity of Hinduism known as 'Mangala murti'. Ganapathi, son of Siva and Parvati, is given utmost importance in any important work or auspicious occasion. Ganesh' Murthis' are either Svayambhu or self-created. Every town or village in India (including special reference to Maharashtra) would have Ganesh Temples compulsorily.

According to Mudgal Purana, eight images are mentioned, referred to as Ashtavinayakas. They are Vakratunda, Ballal, Heramba, Vighnesh, Bhalachandra, Chintamani, Sidhivinayaka and Mahaganapathi. Devotees visit these temples as an Ashtavinayaka pilgrimage.

1. **Mayuresvara Ganapati:** The most important Ganesh temple is Mayuresvara of Morgaon. This temple is the prime centre of the Ganesh cult, the foremost of the Astavinayakas. Ganesh is seen here riding a peacock; hence, the name of the Ganesa is Mayuresvara. This temple is built during the Bahamani reign using backstone. The temple's construction appears like a mosque

with four minarets, which was done on purpose to prevent any attacks on the temple during the Mughal era. This temple, too, had a local legend that says that a demon named 'Sindhurasura' was killed by Ganesh, who came to complete the work on a Mayur, the vehicle of his brother Kumara Swamy. The devatas, as well as the devotees, felt happy and worshipped him as Mayuresvar Ganapati or Moresvar Ganapati, who was a 'Swayambhu murthy'. On auspicious days of Vinayaka Chaturthi and Vijayadasami, celebrations are done on a large scale.

2. **Siddhi Vinayaka:** Ganesh helped Lord Vishnu fight a war with demons, namely Madhu and Kaitabhas. Since Ganesh entered the field here, the kshetra has been known as 'Siddha Kshetra'. Further, it is said that Lord Vishnu installed Ganesh here on the top of a hill. Siddhi and Buddhi are on either side of the main deity. The speciality here is that the trunk of the deity turns to the right side. The Good is represented as Chaturbhuja, and the Sanctum sanctorum is covered with gold plates.

3. **Ballalesvar Ganapathi:** This temple is located in Pali village in the Kolaba district in Maharashtra. Moraba Dada Phadnavis, the brother of Nana Phadnavis, erected the present temple of Ballal-Vinayaka. The deity is worshipped as 'Bala Vinayaka'. There was a devotee named Ballal, and Ganapati appeared before him, pleased by his Bhakti. Hence, the deity is known to be Ballalesvar Ganapathi. This temple is said to have been built during the 1770s.

4. **Varada Vinayaka:** Varada Vinayaka of Mahad is another Ashta Vinayaka not far from Pali. This is a very small village, and the temple is also small. In the sanctum Sanctorum, 'Akhanda Jyoti' has been burning since 1892.

5. **Chintamani Ganapati:** A large and beautiful Chintamani Ganesha temple is built at the confluence of the rivers Mula, Mutha, and Bhima. According to a legend, Sage Kapila got the diamond from Lord Ganesh, and this was known as Chintamani. The temple

belonged to the last quarter of the 18th century. The tirtha is also known as 'Kadamb Tirtha'.

6. **Girijatmaka Vinayaka:** Vinayaka, the son of Parvati is known as Girija suta. On the top of a mountain is a cave with a diety. Parvati (Girrja) did penance and got the child (the well-known Puranic story) to speak about this.

7. **Vighna Vinayaka:** The war between Vinayaka and Vignasura, the demon, took place at the request of the sages. Finally, the demon surrendered to Vinayaka and requested the deity to stay here in his name. A temple was constructed, and puja activities were devoted to it.

8. **Maha Ganapati:** 'Ganesa Purana' mentions The background of Maha Ganapati's existence. In the context of Tripurasura Samhara by Lord Siva, Narada, the great sage, advised Siva to pray Maha Ganapati as 'Sankata Vimochana Ganapati'. Siva followed Narada's advice and won. Hence Sankara installed Maha Ganapati at Ranjangaon.

Nasik Temples

Nasik is located on the banks of the Godavari River. The name Nasik is derived from the Ramayana episode where Lakshmana hacked off the nose (nasika) of Ravana's sister Surpanakha. There are ample references to Nasik and the temples around Nasik in Valmiki, Nannaya, Kalidas and Bhavabhuti's writings. Kumbhamela (once in 12 years) is the largest religious gathering in this region. Kumbhamela of Nasik is one of the four places, the rest being Ujjain, Prayag and Haridwar.

The story behind Kumbhamela:

'Kumbha' is referred to the 'Amrita bhanda'. Devatas and demons fought for nectar or Amrita during 'Ksheerasagara madhana'; some drops have fallen in the four places cited above.

Nasik is associated with Sri Rama's 'Vanvasa'. Places worth seeing are Brahmakund, Panchavati, Sundaranarayan Temple, Kalaram Temple, Kapalesvar Mandir, and Nilakantesvar Tapovan.

Siva Temples

The famous Saivaite shrines of Nasik are Triambakesvar, Mahabalesvar, Vaidyanath, Bhimasankar, and Grushnesvar. Four of the 12 Jyotirlingas are in the state of Maharastra.

Triambakesvar

This holy place is just 33 km west of Nasik. This is one of India's sacred Temples (Jyotirlingas). Godavari flows nearby. Triambakesvar is a famous religious Centre in India. Further, it is the source of the Godavari River. Sahyadri and Brahmagiri mountain range is just 2 Km. Sage Gautama stayed here. Lord Siva, known as Triambakesvar, is worshipped by thousands of devotees, and the temple is beautiful. Peshwas paid particular attention to the temple. About the God Triambakesvar, the holy river Godavari, the holy mountain range of Sahyadri and the blessings of salvation to the devotees are beautifully described in the sloka:

"Sahyadri seershe vimale vasanta Godavari teera Pavitra dese Yaddarsanath pataaka naasam prayati tam Triambakesam"

There are two Legends connected with Triambakesvar Kshetra. They are:

1. The originator of the Kshetra is supposed to be Sage Gautama. He was also the creator of the Great River Godavari (Gautami). Sage Gautama was one of the seven great sages or Rishis (Sapta rishis). They were: Gautama, Visvamitra, Bharadwaja, Atri, Vasista, Kasyapa and Jamadagni. Once upon a time, a terrible drought resulted in the deaths of humans, animals, and birds. Even devatas suffered from a lack of 'Havis' since yagnas could not be performed.

In this context, Sage Gautama did penance to please Varuna. Due to his blessings, Gautama dug a kund, and it filled with water. Further, he settled in the ashram with his wife Ahalya, produced plenty of agricultural products (Gayatri mantra's influence) and saved people from hunger. All this created confusion among the Pandits community, which resulted in jealousy. They made a cow and sent it to destroy crops. Sage Gautama drove the cow with his darbhas or grass ('Kusa' grass, and the place is known to be Kusavarta), and the cow died. Gautama was cursed with 'Gohatya'. He did penance to satisfy Siva and get rid of it, and the Lord appeared before him and said he would be present at Triambak. River Godavari, named Gautami to honour sage Gautama, would flow.

2. Siva came to Triambak as Triambakesvar because of a curse from Lord Brahma: Brahma, Vishnu and Siva are said to be powerful Trinity. Brahma and Vishnu, in a talk, felt that they had not understood Siva. Therefore, they searched Siva's head and feet ('Adi' and 'Anta'). Both started in opposite directions, but it was a complex task. Brahma wanted to play a trick on Vishnu. It said he had discovered Siva's head, citing a cow and ketaki tree as witnesses. Indra and other goods went to Sivaloka to verify the truth of Lord Brahma's statement. Siva told them that Brahma had deceived them and cursed Brahma that he would not be worshipped anywhere. Therefore, Brahma retaliated through a counter-curse, saying that Siva would stay in Bhuloka as a mountain. This is known as Brahmagiri – Triambak (3-eyed Giri), and at its base, Siva is seen in a miniature form as Triambakesvar.

<u>The Temple:</u>

The Temple of Triambakesvara Mahadeva is a magnificent one. The temple is built of local black stone. The temple is enclosed within a courtyard measuring 260 by 220 feet. Nandi is housed here. The sanctum sanctorum is square in shape. The Sikhara and miniature Sikharas are to be seen. The temple is a specimen of the North Indian or Indo-Aryan styles found in Maharastra. Peshwa Balaji Baji Rao (1740-1761) was behind the efforts. In the centre of the sanctum sanctorum is a slight depression full of water. In this water is the Swayambhu linga of Siva. Abhisheka goes on continuously. A golden mask is imposed on the linga. The five faces of the linga are decorated with golden crowns (Presented by Peshwa Sadasiva Rao – later carried away by the Delhi rulers). This is one of the most famous Jyotirlingas of this region.

The worship:

The worship of the god takes place daily and thrice a day. The Puja at each session is rich and consists of Abhishekas and Mahanaivedya—Peswa's allotted funds. At the time of each worship, a silver mask is placed. Regarding festivals, Sivaratris, Kartika Maasa, full moon day, Diwali, Dassera, etc., are celebrated.

Regarding historical references to this temple from earlier periods, very few are to be traced.

Nearby is a cave consisting of 108 Sivalingas (Gautama's installation). Pushkar Ghat, Kapalesvar temple, Cave for Maata site, and a mountain (Anjana), the birthplace of Hanuman, are also nearby.

Vaidyanathesvar

"Poorvottare prajvalika nidhane sadaa vasantham girija sametam suraasuradhita paada padmam

Srivaidyanatham tamaham namami"

With the name of 'Vaidyanath', there are four Sivalingas' in the country as follows:

1. Parli (Maharashtra)
2. Gangakhed (20km from Nanded, Maharashtra)
3. Keera Village (Punjab) and
4. Pathankot (Himachal Pradesh)

The Puranic Story is, of course, the same. This temple is one of the Jyotirlingas in the country. The temple is big. The Sikhara of the sanctum sanctorum is 60 feet high. Mukha mandapa and Sabha mandapa are in front of the Sanctum sanctorum. The Siva Linga is just two feet in height. His consort Parvati is also there in the sanctum sanctorum, the temple's speciality. The kshetra is famous for two episodes of Markandeya and Sati Savitri. The temple is known as 'Apurva Kasi Kshetra'. The replicas of Dwadasa Jyotirlingas are installed in the temple. People believe that the Lord of the Kshetra relieves them from diseases, known as Vaidanathesvar.

<u>Ravana Episode connected with the origin of the kshetra</u>:

In Thetayuga, Ravana's mother made Siva Linga with sand (Saikata Linga) on the seashore and worshipped the Lord. After some time, it was washed away, and Kaikasi, Ravana's mother, agonized over the incident. Ravana promised her to bring Siva's Atmalinga, proceeded to the Himalayas, and did terrible penance. Finally, he offered his nine heads by cutting off and proved his devotion to Siva. Siva was pleased with Dasakantha's devotion and appeared before him. Ravana asked his Atma linga to take him to worship in Lanka. Siva presented it with a warning that he was not supposed to put it on the ground at any cost in his journey. The devatas requested Ganesh to stop Ravana's activity since it would cause them terrible results. Ravana had to stop giving Arghya to Surya in the evening by giving Linga to a boy (Ganesh), requesting him not to put the Linga on the ground. The boy cried. He could not hold it anymore since it had grown in weight. Finally, he kept the Linga on the ground. Ravana tried to lift it but failed. The Siva linga is Vaidyanadhesvar. The same story was held to Gokarna Kshetra. The deities are Gokarnesvar and Tamra Gauri.

Grhusnesvar

"Ilapure Ramya Visalakesmin samulla samthamcha Jagatvarenyam Vande mahodaratara subhavam

Grhusnesvarakhyam saranam prapatye"

The 12th Jyotirlinga is Grhusnesvar, situated near the Ellora caves of Maharashtra. Grhusnesvara is the God, and Grhusnesvari is the Goddess of the Temple.

Legend:

A Brahmin couple lived in Devagiri. They were Sudharma and Sudeha. They had no children. One day, an ascetic came to their house, received their hospitality, and was pleased to bless them with a child. Sudharna married Grhusna, Sudeha's sister, and had a child. Grhusna was a devotee of Siva and worshipped him in the form of one lakh Lingas. Sudeha, out of jealousy, killed the child and was thrown into a lake. Sira came to the rescue of his devotee, Grhusna, and gave him life. Her patience and devotion guarded her and her child. Siva remained there as Grhusnesvar. According to a Puranic source, Lord Vishnu installed The Linga.

Historicity:

The ancestors of Shivaji constructed the Temple. Later, during the 1765-95 period, Ahalyabai, the queen of Indore, developed the Temple. The Temple is beautiful and different from the other temples. The temple campus is spacious, with a mandala with 24 pillars.

Bhimashankar

Bhima Shankar is the 6th Jyotirlinga kshetra in Maharashtra (Dakini – Khed region). The place is the birthplace of the holy river Bhima. The name of The God is Bhima Shankara, and the goddess is Kamalaja. Lond Brahma worshipped her with 'Kamalams'. Dhakini and Sakini, the evil forces, worship the deities. Siva was Bhima for them, and he was kind towards devotees by his blessings.

"Yam Dhakine Shakirika Samajaihi Nishevyamanam Pisithasanaischia Sadaiva Bhimadi Pada Prasiddham Tam Shankaram Bhaktahitam Namama"

There are three Siva Temples with the name of Bhimesvara or Bhima Shankar, namely:

1. Near Nainital in UP
2. On a mountain at Gauhati in Assam
3. Draksharama Kshetra in Andhra Pradesh

The Temple was constructed by Nana Fadnavis, the Peshwa (After Shivaji), during the 18th century.

<u>Tripurasura Episode:</u>

Tripurasura did penance to please Lord Brahma, obtained the latter's blessings, and became powerful. Indra, followed by goods and sages, feared this asura and his devilish activities. Being the victims of horror and sorrow caused by Tripurasura, they prayed to Lord Siva to relieve them from their suffering by slaying him. Siva promised to take up their cause if Indra practised penance before his jyotirlinga on the Sahyadris. Indra proceeded to start 'tapas'; Siva, being pleased, assured him that on the 7th day, from then onwards, he would kill Tripurasura. Siva assumed the gigantic form mounted upon Nandi wearing Trisula, and Dhamaruk proceeded to battle. His army of ganas and yogis like Dakini and Sakini accompanied him. Siva assumed Bhima form (He became known as Bhimesvera). The battle was stiff. Finally, Tripura fell, and it was a great relief and joy for Sages and gods.

<u>The Temple:</u>

The Temple of Bhimashankar is an unfinished restoration of a small old shrine. The sanctum sanctorum and Antarala form a separate block (belonging to a later period). The dome of the Temple has been removed to accommodate the new Temple.

The shrine consists of the artistic embellishments. The style of the Temple is Northern and Indo-Aryan. Bhimashankar temple is of great significance because it is the source of one of the holiest rivers in Maharashtra. A dip in the Tirth kund is supposed to liberate seven generations of a person's ancestors from sins. The Bhimashankara Mahatya provides the necessary information about this Saivaite centre. The Maha Sivaratri attracts thousands of pilgrims to this place. Lastly, the kshetra and its surroundings display the ruggedness and beauty of the Sahyadri and the dense jungles apart from the religious aspect.

Mahabaleswar

Originating from the Mahabaleshwar hills in Maharashtra, the Krishna River flows through the entire stretch of Andhra Pradesh and drains into the Bay of Bengal. Krishna River is a big river in South India. The Total length of the river is 1400 Km, of which 369 Km is in Maharashtra, 484 Km in Karnataka, and the remaining 611 Km in A.P. Five rivers of Venna, Koyna, Krishna, Savitri, and Gayatri had their birth in Mahabaleshwar. There is a Pancha Ganga temple at the confluence of these five rivers.

Mahabaleshwar temple was built in the South Indian Hemadant style of architecture by the Chanda Rao More dynasty in the 16th century. Sanctum Sanctorum has a Swayambhu or self-manifested Linga in the shape of Rudraksha, the only temple with Shiva Linga in the form of Rudraksha. The Linga is beautifully decorated with flowers.

Ellora and Cave Temples of Elephanta

Ellora

Caves of Ellora are 28 Km from Aurangabad. The total number of cavers is 34, belonging to 600 – 900 AD. The caves are the product of three religious systems: Hinduism, Buddhism and Jainism. Thirty-four caves based on religion are to be classified as Hindu – 17, Buddhist – 12 and Jain – 5. The carvings are the remarkable memorials of the respective faiths.

The richness of mythology had grown vastly around the Hindu pantheon. We may find and enjoy the visual grace in the execution of art and sculpture.

The Brahmanic or Hindu revival had produced the group of Ellora caves under royal patronage, which is to be witnessed through The Ellora caves as follows:

Hindu Caves:

- Cave No 14: The introduction to the new order is cave No 14. Goddess Druga, who worships nationwide, is found in the first Panel to the left. Next is Vishnu, the preserver, and Lakshmi, the consort of Vishnu or the goddess of wealth. The next wall is dedicated to Shiva and a series of goddesses, and the prominent one is Parvati (seen in other caves also).

- Cave No 15: This is a double storyed one. The courtyard consists of several small shrines and the temple priests' residences. The Department of Archaeology gives nameplates. The focus is mainly on Lord Siva. He is depicted with eight armed, warlike, slaying a demon, dancing the Tandava, the dance of destruction, playing dice with Parvati, another one rising out of the Lingam, destroying Tripurasura. The deity is Siva in the form of a Linga with Bull or Nandi in the centre passage.

- Cave 16: The best of all the Ellora excavations, Kailasa Siva's mountain abode is celebrated as one of India's most famous monuments. This is a rock-cut architecture of the highest technical skills of the 8th and early 9th centuries. In India's art history, this beautiful monument was created by hundreds of architects and sculptors. The Kailasha temple was constructed by King Krishna I of the Rastrakutas in 760 A-D. – a gigantic sculptural piece. This rock-cut Temple of Kailash is an engineering marvel representing Siva's Kailash, the Himalayan abode. A colossal elephant (lost its trunk), a victory pillar, and renderings of legends of Siva and Parvati are exciting. These are all in the northern court. Turning to the southern gallery, we find Lord Vishnu. Narasimha's form is seen tearing the body of Hiranya Kasipa, the demon king, with his claws. Another sculptural masterpiece is Ravana's lifting of Kailash on his head. There are several halls decorated well, including SivaLingam.

- <u>Cave No 17</u>: The pillars are enormous in this cave. It contains Siva Linga and the images of Brahma, Vishnu, Ganesh and Mahishasura Mardini.
- <u>Cave No 18</u>: Shiva Lingam exists in the interior of Garbhagriha.
- <u>Cave No 19</u>: Contains Siva Lingam.
- <u>Cave No 20</u>: Lord Ganesh, Mahishasura Mardini and Siva Lingam are worth seeing.
- <u>Cave No 21</u>: On a raised platform, there is Nandi. Beautiful figures of the river goddesses Ganga and Yamuna are also present. On a wall, there is the scene of Siva and Parvati Kalyanam.
- <u>Caves 22, 23 & 24</u>: Nothing special except Garbha grihas.
- <u>Cave No 25</u>: This huge cave contains a standing image of Sun God in a chariot drawn by seven horses.
- <u>Cave no 26</u>: This is nothing but a copy of Cave 21.
- <u>Cave No 27</u>: Contains the images of Balaram, Krishna, Vishnu, Varaha and Mahishasura Mardini.
- <u>Cave No 28</u>: It is an empty one.
- <u>Cave No 29</u>: It has a group of halls. A pair of stone Lions guard the entrance. Everything here is colossal: a huge Siva Linga with eight arms and another in a dancing pose.

Elephanta

The Elephanta caves are located near Mumbai. It is just 10 or 11 Km from the great Gateway of India. Formerly, this was a Buddhist centre, but it later turned into Saivaite. UNESCO declared this a World Heritage Centre. The caves are named Elephanta by the Portuguese (since there was the figure of an elephant in the early days). Huge mountains were turned into incredible caves, and temples were constructed in 60,000 sqft of circumference. The central theme of religion, rut, and sculpture revolves around Lord Siva.

The sculptural splendours are glorious, starting with the animal guardians of the temple, namely elephants in the early stages and later replaced by lions.

The period of the Elephanta temple is around 750 AD. It resembles Ellora's temple. The theme is 'Siva', as cited above. The different phases are artistically and sculpturally described in the language of stone. They are:

- Arthanareeswar (manifestation of Siva – the embodiment of male and female energies.
- Gangavatarana
- Marriage of Siva and Parvati.
- Lifting of Kailasa by Ravana.
- Siva and Parvati playing a game of dice.
- Siva is represented as Nataraj.
- Siva is represented as a sage or yogi.
- Asura Samhara (Andhakasura Vadha by Siva).
- The idol of Siva is Trimurthi, which is 17 feet in height. Here, Siva is represented as the incarnation of Panchabhutas of Earth, fire, water, air and Sky.

Devi Temples of Maha Lakshmi and Bhavani

Kolhapur

According to Hindu mythology, Karvir was the former name of Kolhapur. The abode of the great goddess Maha Lakshmi is well known all over India as Kasi of the South. Kolhapur has been a sacred place of Hinduism since historical times. It is also one of the 'Astadasa Saakti Peethams'. Mahalakshmi is also known as Bhavai and Analadevi.

The Temple:

The entrance of the temple is seen with two giant Dwarapalakas. Between 1760 and 1800, repairs were made to this holy centre thrice.

<u>Description of the Deity:</u>

The Goddess Maha Lakshmi has an extremely pleasant appearance. The image is carved in black stone, about three feet tall, and has four arms. In the lower right hand is a larger fruit. In the upper hand is a large mace. The upper left hand holds the shield, and the lower has a bowl. On the crown, there is a Cobra hood and a Siva Linga. The lion, her Vahana, is behind the Devi. The iconographic description of the present image goes back to the 13th or earlier century.

The temple has temples of Mahakali and Maha Sarasvati on the northern and southern sides. The temple of Maha Lakshmi has a Sri chakra. Golden Paadukas are also worshipped in the temple. Navaratri celebrations are held in the temple.

The campus has temples of Dattatreya, Vitoba, Kasi Visvesvara, Sri Rama, Radha Krishna, and others.

<u>Information of Karvir:</u>

A book by the name 'Karvir Mahatyam' states that this sacred place was the creation of Vishnu, who stays here in the Maha Lakshmi form and at Varanasi in the form of Siva, who grants salvation to the devotees.

Tuljapur (Bhavani)

The Bhavani temple is situated on the mountain ranges of Balaghat. For any Kshetra, 'Tirtha' is needed. In this context, 'Kallola' Tirth was created by Viswakarma at the command of Lord Brahma. Brahma decided to invite all the holy waters to come to the Yamunachala. Ganga, Yamuna, and Saraswati obeyed the command of the creator. All the Himalayan rivers, too, flocked together. The power of this Tirtha is great in destroying sins. The 'Tulja Mahatyam' says that a dip in this Tirth relieves people from their sins and cures diseases. Near The Tirthas are small shines of Siddhi Vinayak, Vitthal, Dattatreya, etc.

<u>The Temple and Image:</u>

The image of Bhavani Devi is variously known as 'Tulaja', 'Tvarita', 'Turaja', and 'Amba'; this image is a stone image of three feet in height. The Devi had eight arms carrying various weapons. The lowermost right hand holds the trident, the next a dagger, the one above this an arrow, and the uppermost right hand wield a Chakra. In the uppermost left hand is a Shankh, next is a bow, the third one carries a bowl, and the lowermost left hand holds the knot of hair on the head of a demon. The right leg is on Mahishasura's body, and the left is on the ground.

The lower left arm holds the head of a demon. The lion is the Vahana of the Devi. Ornaments of the Devi, like Earrings, Kundalas, Necklaces, etc., are carved on the image.

<u>The Goddess:</u>

The image is said to be 'Svayambhu', whose date of existence is the 17th or 18th century. The earlier reference to the goddess is from the copper plate grant of 1204 AD. Numerous records from 1650 AD onwards mention Bhavani of Tuljapur. The Maharashtra government bore expenses for daily worship under the advice of the Peshwas.

Around the temple, there are other images of Narasimha, Yamai, Lakshmi Narayana, etc. In the northeast corner, the Shakti of Bhavani exists, which is none other than Matangidevi temple. Rama and Lakshmana established two Siva Lingas known as Rameswar and Lakshmaneswar.

<u>Worship of the Goddess:</u>

The daily worship takes place in sessions: Early morning worship, afternoon worship, Evening worship and Late evening worship.

The procession is a part of the temple rituals, and the Navaratri festival is a special occasion. The image of the goddess is placed in an 'Ambari', which is placed on some of the Devi's Vahanas. A band of musicians follows the procession.

Festivals like Vijayadasami attract crowds. The Vahanas are made of wood—lion, horse, peacock, Nandi, Garuda, etc. Large crowds try to reach the deity to present the customary gold, the leaves of the 'Shami' tree. According to the local people's beliefs, the Devi promised to stay at Yamunachala—the Yamuna hill of the Sahyadris.

It is said that she foresaw Sri Rama's life story and decided to help him. Yamunachal was on her way from Panchavati to Rameswar.

The devotees pray the Devi to rescue them from the cycle of life and death, from the various calamities and finally to attain the Salvation. Dattatreya, Sri Rama and Saniswar are the other deities.

Dattatreya

Dattatreya is the incarnation of the Trinity (Brahma, Vishnu and Siva). He was the son of Sage Atri and Anasuya. Harivamsa provides information about the Datta incarnation. 'Kshama' or mercy was the chief characteristic of this incarnation. Dalla cult is called as Gurucharita. Datta appeared in several important incarnations: Narasimha Sarasvati and Sripada Sri Vallabha, his predecessor. Gangapur is related to Datta Sampradaya (50 miles southeast of Sholapur). Gangapur has not yet attained the form of a temple. It was initially an ashram or a Math of Sri Narasimha Sarasvati. People believe that Datta is in the form of Narasimha Sarasvati. Datta Jayanti falls on the full moon day of Margasira Masa.

Sri Rama (Ramtek)

Nagpur is considered the heart of India's orange country. Ramtek is 40 Km northeast of Nagpur. Sri Rama, Sita and Lakshmana spent some time in exile. Further, this place is marked by a cluster of temples that are over 600 years old.

Sani Singanapur

This is just 65km from Shirdi. There is no temple, but the idol of 'Sani' is a big pillar (black stone) or Linga. Only men wearing black clothes are allowed to perform puja after a bath. The place's speciality is that the doors are not locked.

Panduranga or Vithoba (Vittal) of Pandaripur or Pandharpur

The premier deity of Maharashtra is Panduranga Vittal. For the past thousand years, the deity has attracted people from various castes and communities. The Bhakti cult of Vithoba is a unique phenomenon in Maharashtra.

The temple in Maharashtra is Pandaripur on the banks of Bhima, and the Kshetra is known as Panduranga. This is considered as Southern Kasi by the Marathas.

The deity's origin is the 'Kanada' or 'Kanarese' region, and references are found in Namdev's (great saint and devotee of Vithoba) writings.

Historicity:

An inscription of a Hoyasala king, Someshvar, records a grant of a village in the Mysore state (1236AD). Padma Purana mentions a section of Pandaranga Mahatyam.

The deity Panduranga appears with his arms resting on the lips. The devotees please him with Bhajans.

The puja consists of worship with 'Tulasidal'. Every Wednesday, the devotees are allowed to touch the feet of the deity.

Anjaneya, Ganesa, Garuda Alwar, Rukmini, Satyabhama, and Radha temples exist. The temple complex also includes Navagrahas and Ashtadikpalakas.

Bhakta Pundarik Story:

Pundarik was the son of Janudev and Sathyavati, a Brahmin couple. He behaved like a self-centred man in their early years, neglecting his old parents. After some time, a significant change occurred in the sage Kukkuta's Ashram, where he got enlightenment due to the story narrated by Ganga, Yamuna and Sarasvati and the power of the sage due to his worship of his parents. This brought a change to Pundarik. Lord Krishna tested Pundarik's devotion and stayed there.

The temple's entrance is called Mahadwara, also called Namdev Dwara. Namdev was a great devotee of Panduranga. The other temples are Namdev, Rana, Venkataswamy, Hanuman, Kali, Tukaram etc.

People attend large numbers of festivals on Ashadha Suddha Ekadasi and Kartik Suddha Ekadasi.

<u>Role of Krishnadevaraya:</u>

The great king of Vijayanagara, Sri Krishnadevaraya, had taken the image of Pandharpur and established it in a temple. It is said that the king brought the image from Udayagiri on his way back from a victorious campaign. The intention behind this happened to be protecting the image from the neighbouring Muslim powers. However, Krishnadevaraya was a pious and faithful devotee of Sri Krishna or Panduranga.

<u>Worship and service of God</u>:

The worship and service of the God takes place five times a day:

1. Early morning (Kakad Arati)
2. Panchamruta Puja
3. Afternoon worship and Naivedyam
4. Dhupa – Arati (incense burning)
5. Shej – Arati (10-12 PM)

Apart from the daily pujas, there are several festivals. Gokul Ashtami is observed with great pomp and ceremony.

Shirdi Sai Baba

People are searching for peace and happiness at the dawn of the modern age. This resulted in the emergence of modern sects and religious centres. Worshippers are of two types, namely traditional and contemporary.

One of the modern religious sects of immense popularity during the 20th Century is the Shirdi Sai Baba sect, and Shirdi happens to be the busiest pilgrim centre. Shirdi Sai is worshipped as Guru, yogi and fakir. He is considered a saint by both Hindus and Muslims. Love, forgiveness, helping the needy, charity, contentment, etc., are some of Baba's teachings or the quiet essence of Hinduism and Islam religions. The Sai sect was confined to Maharashtra in the early times. After the 1990s, it became a national and international faith, showing the path of peace and happiness. Shirdi is thus the excellent pilgrim centre today.

Life of Baba:

The life of Shirdi Sai is neither known nor disclosed to anybody. He proposed faith and bhakti, combining Hinduism and Islam. 'Sab Ka Malik Ek' ('Oneness of God') is the saying of Baba. He used to sit under a neem tree and take shelter in an old and worn mosque at the request of the people. 'Bhikshatana' was the way how Sai could secure food. He maintained 'Dhuni' (sacred fire) in the mosque and used to give the devotees 'Udhi' (holy ash). He used to enjoy Kabir's songs.

His Philosophy:

Shirdi Saibaba opposed religious orthodoxy. He stressed the moral life, love, and faith, or 'Shraddha'. According to Sai, patience, known as 'Saburi', is an excellent quality. The Guru reiterates the three 'Margas' or paths of Hinduism, mainly Bhakti, Karma, and Jnana. The 'Oneness of God' is an idea borrowed from the Upanishadic philosophy. Sharing with others gives contentment, says Saibaba.

MANIPUR (MN)

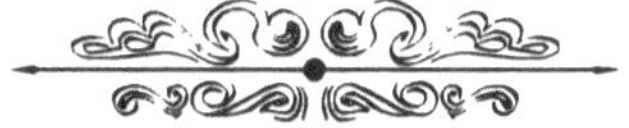

Jawaharlal Nehru described Manipur as a 'Jewel of India'. It is a land of majestic landscapes with vast fields and hills. The date of formation of the state was 21 January 1972. Mizoram, Assam and Nagaland are the neighbouring states, while Myanmar is the neighbouring country. Further, it is the meeting point between India and Southeast Asia. Imphal is the capital. One particular feature of the state is that hills constitute almost 90% of the total area of 22,356 sq. km. 29 Tribes are the state's inhabitants.

Manipur attained cultural and religious integration. The worship of the local Gods and Goddesses prevailed. Mainly, Vaishnavism gained popularity and propagation. Of course, priests were sent to villages to perform worship anciently. Culturally speaking, Manipuri is one of the classical dances of India – Male dancers perform acrobatics, and female dancers delightfully perform graceful movements.

Vaishnavite Temples

Bishnupur

Vishnu's temple is 27 km from Imphal and was built in the 15th century. When King Kyamba conquered the Kyang region, Chaopha Khe Khomba, the king of Pong, gave him a Vishnu idol. King Kyamba started worshipping Lord Vishnu and built a temple. This temple is now considered a protected historical monument. The temple's construction was done in Chinese style. Of course, the temple is in a ruined stage.

Govindji Temple

This temple, dedicated to the deity Radha Krishna, was built around the 18th century. Holi festival is celebrated on a grand scale with traditional dances. This temple is said to be an important Vaishnavite centre.

<u>Structure of the Temple:</u>

It is built with two golden domes. The deities are Balarama, Krishna, and Jagannadha. Originally built in 1846, the temple was renovated after the 1868 earthquake wreaked havoc.

Krishna's Temple

This temple was built in 1704 on the river banks of Manipur. Sri Krishna is installed on a three-foot-high platform. The idols represent various stages of Krishna's life from his childhood.

Other Temples

Pilgrims visit Hanuman Temple, Radha Swamy Temple, and Vanadevata Temple.

MEGHALAYA (ML)

Meghalaya was carved out of Assam on January 21, 1972, with two hill districts: United Khasi & Jaintia and Garo Hills districts. Meghalaya means the abode of clouds. Shillong became the capital of the state. This hill state has an area of 22,489 sq. km. Rare species of flora and fauna are found here. Meghalaya is very beautiful, and the beauty of the butterflies in the forests and meadows is lovely. The world's heaviest rainfall in Cherrapunji is a unique state record.

Apart from the beauty of Nature, which covers silent hills, streams, woods, and fields, spiritual centres, such as Jaintia Hills and the cave temple of Shillong, provide a religious atmosphere.

Jaintia Hills and Temple of Jainteswari

In the district of Shillong, there is Durga Devi temple, which is supposed to be five centuries old. This temple is also known as Nartiang Devi temple. The Tribes in this region are Khasis, Pnars and Garos. All these tribal groups worship the Goddess.

The temple was developed in phases. According to a local legend, the deity is one of the 51 Shaktipeethas. 'Shakti Puja' is the primary ritual. Parvati's left thigh fell here, so she is known as Jainteswari. The Puja system is different and a blend of Hindu and Khasi tribal traditions. Animal slaughter is common. During Pujas, on special occasions like Durga Puja, a Banana Plant is decorated, worshipped, and later immersed in the Myntdu river.

Cave Temple – Shillong

A cave temple of Siva known as Mahadev Khola Dham was discovered in Shillong by the military people. Small temples of Tulasi, Lakshminarayana and Gauri Shankar are also near the cave temple. People believe there is an underground way to Kamakhya temple from this place.

MIZORAM (MZ)

During the British days, Mizoram was known as Lushai Hills. The State of Mizoram was formed on 20 February 1987 as the 23rd state of our country. Tripura, Assam, and Manipur are the neighbouring states. Myanmar is the neighbouring country. It has an international boundary with Myanmar and Bangladesh running into 710 Km. Mizoram covers an area of 21,087 Km. The Mizors are pleasant and hardworking. Mizoram is to be portrayed with sparkling flora and fauna and rugged mountains. 'Selfless service for others' is their code of ethics. Regarding the religions of Mizoram, Christianity is a major religion, and Hindus constitute only 2.75% of the state's population as per the 2001 Census. Hence, no Hindu Temples are of great significance in the Mizoram state.

NAGALAND (NL)

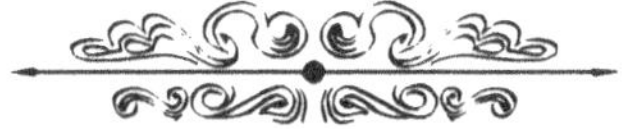

Nagaland has a majestic landscape and scenic grandeur. Its area is 16,488 sq. km. Several rivers passing through the Brahmaputra Valley have their sources in the Naga Hills. The people are divided into tribes and sub-tribes.

Nagaland was formed on 1 December 1963. Manipur, Arunachal Pradesh, and Assam are the neighbouring states, while Myanmar is the neighbouring country. Hinduism, along with Christianity, is the major religion.

<u>Name of the state:</u>

'Naga' is a generic name. According to Hutton, the word is a corrupt form of 'Noga' (Assamese), which means mountaineer. According to Edward Gait, the derivation of the term 'Nok' means folk. Some say the word is 'Nahangara', which means a warrior.

Dimapur is known for its temples.

Siva Temple

Situated in a village named 'Singrijan', the Temple was built in 1961. One villager went to a forest (Protected area) and brought a stone to sharpen his knife. When he started sharpening the knife, he found blood oozing out of the stone and intimated the same to the villagers. The same day, Siva appeared in his dream and said the stone was nothing but 'Siva Linga'. Knowing the incident, villagers began to worship, and later, they constructed a temple.

Kali Temple

The Kali Temple is said to have existed since 1956 at Dimapur-Kalibari. On the occasion of the Temple's Golden Jubilee, celebrations were performed, which included cultural programs, Dances, and Dharmic speeches. A library with religious texts was also opened.

ODISHA (OR)

Formerly known as Kalinga, Then Orissa, and presently named 'Odisha' (OR), the state has an area of 1,55,707 sq. km. Bhubaneswar is the capital. Orissa became Odisha in April 2010. Andhra Pradesh, Chattisgarh, Jharkhand, and West Bengal are the neighbouring states. The Bay of Bengal is the sea. Odiya (Oriya) is the chief language of the people. Hinduism, Jainism, Islam, and Christianity are the major religions. Mahanadi, Brahma Putra are the main rivers. Magnificent temples are famous nationwide.

Odisha is a well-known temple city. Once, there were 7000 Temples in Bhuvanesvar dating back to 2000 years. Only some remain today as places of worship, but other temples are famous as archaeological sites.

History of Orissa/Odisha & Temples

In the history of Odisha from 595 AD to 1435 AD, four dynasties ruled, namely:

1. The Sailodbhavas (575-730 AD)
2. The Bhumakaras (736-940 AD)
3. The Somavamsis (885-1110 AD)
4. The Imperial Gangas (1110-1435 AD)

Thousands of old temples exist, and of course, some are dilapidated. For the purpose of studying the temples of Orissa according to the date and style, they are to be grouped into three:

- Early Period (750-900 AD)
- Middle Period (900-1100 AD) and
- Later Period (1100-1250 AD)

Among the finest temples of not only Orissa but also in India, mention may be made about the temples – The Lingaraj Temple (Bhuvaneswar 11th century), The Jagannadh Temple (Puri-12th century) and the great Sun Temple (Konark – 13th century).

The Lingaraj Temple (Bhuvanesvar)

The Lingaraj Temple is just 60 Km from Puri. From the 11th century (1090-1104 AD), the Temple is the grandest and loftiest (above 36.50 m high). The architectural beauty of Bhuvaneswar is visible.

The Temple consists of the sanctum. The later additions are the halls for offerings and dancing. Fifty smaller temples and shrines surround the Temple. The main deity of the Lingaraj Temple is Tribhuvaneswar, which means Land of the Three Worlds. The name of Bhuvaneswar is derived from the name of the God.

The system of Puja (worship):

The granite block representing Tribhuvaneswar is bathed daily with water, milk, and bhang (marijuana). Two moustachioed yellow lions guard the main gate. Lingaraj temple appears with ten stories.

Other shrines and temples are:

- Muktesvar (A mixture of Hindu, Buddhist and Jain architectural styles)
- Siddesvar Temple is plain. Red-painted Ganesh is seen here.
- Kedaraguari Temple was rebuilt.
- Parasuramesvar Mandir of 650 AD is the Siva Temple.

Rajarani Mandir, built around 1100 AD, is supposed to be the most beautiful Temple in the world. The name of the stone used in constructing the Temple is "Raja-Rani" (Red Sandstone). This Temple is notable for its sculptural excellence.

Jagannath Temple (Puri)

Puri is a coastal town in Orissa situated by the seashore. It is one of the four holiest pilgrimage centres. Three others are Badrinath (North), Rameswaram (South) and Dwarka (West). Jagannadh temple is a mighty temple of Lord Jagannadh, his elder brother Balaram and his sister Subhadra. Jagannadh means Lord of the Universe. The images are wooden, painted in beautiful colours, sitting on a jewelled throne in the Temple's sanctum sanctorum. The deities are otherwise called 'Daru Devatas' (wooden). Lord Jagannath is said to be the incarnation of Vishnu. The Temple is said to have been built by Ganga ruler Chodaganga Deva in its present form in 1198, guarded by stone lions and a pillar crowned by the Garuda. The details related to Temple history are thrilling and informative. Six thousand temple employees and 20,000 people are divided into 36 orders and 97 classes. All are dependent on this great Temple of Puri Jagannadh for their livelihood.

Legendary Source:

According to popular legend, the Lord is worshipped by the Tribal people (Savaras). Viswavasu was the chief of the tribes. The legend says that a divine voice was heard from heaven, and Lord Jagannadh would construct his image and then be installed on the great throne.

In the guise of a carpenter, the divine architect, Viswakarma, carved out the images built in an unfished manner since the queen opened the doors out of curiosity. Later, according to divine instructions, the king installed the trio of images in a newly constructed Temple and worshipped them.

Temple Activities:

The temple activities are diverse, involving hundreds of temple staff for various purposes, such as 'Puja', 'Preparation of Prasada' and distribution, Car festival arrangements, other temple festivals, rituals, patronage of music and dance, etc.

King appointed hundreds of servants or Sevakas for the Temple's services. Their descendants also are performing their duties to this day. It is estimated that there are 36 rendering hereditary services, which include priests, potters (producing thousands of ritual vessels needed by the Temple daily), carpenters, devadasis (dancing girls), musicians and instrumentalists.

<u>Temple kitchen:</u>

The kitchen of the Temple is essential and plays a vital role. Preparation of Prasad and distribution to the devotees is a big task. It is being distributed to thousands of people every day. Jagannadha Temple had the most extensive kitchen in the whole country. The kitchen's capacity for cooking food (for offering God, known as Maha Prasad) is one lakh. Four hundred cooks prepare the food traditionally (without using garlic). Daily, 100 varieties of puddings are prepared. Devotees believe that Goddess Lakshmi supervises these activities. The food offerings or 'Naivedya' are offered to God in the morning, mid-day, Evening and at the end of the day. Devotees are served with Maha Prasad only in banana leaf.

<u>Lord Jagannadha – Actual references to the life of Lord Krishna:</u>

The history of the Temple describes the different stages of Lord Krishna. Krishna's journey from Vrepalle to Madhura to kill Kamsa is illustrated. The 'Niryana' of Krishna, the burning of his body, the leftover navel (Naabhi) part which was not burnt but thrown into the sea and later that was brought by Visvavasu, the chief of Savarars worshipped. (Neela Madhava Vigraha – A stone in the form of Vishnu coloured in blue).

<u>The four parts of the Temple:</u>

1. Bhoga mandapa
2. Natya mandapa
3. Mukhamandapa
4. Sanctum sanctorum

The four entrances:

- Eastern known as Simha dvara
- Southern – Aswadrara
- Western – Vyagra Dvara
- Northern – Hasti Dvara

Alokanadha, Narasimha, and Varaha temples have a well, and its water is used for Swamy's abhisheka.

The Cult of Jagannaddha:

The cult pervades the whole state of Odisha. Every house possesses the image of the Lord. Jagannadh is the deity of the king, who is the first servant of the Lord, Brahmins, scavengers, downtrodden, and ordinary men of all castes. Therefore, the cult is based upon love, affection, service, and sacrifice. In other words, it projects the idea of equality of all the humans brought before God, a unique feature.

Festivals:

Fifteen festivals are mentioned in the records of the Temple. The most important and famous is the car festival (Rath Yatra). Two or three days before the car festival, the wooden images of the deities are replaced by new ones after burning the old ones. Still, the naval part is kept as usual to the image of Jagannadh. This replacement of the new images is done with a festive look on the occasion between 'Chaitra' and 'Phalguna' maasas once in 12 years when Adlika Ashaadha masa occurs.

Three chariots are newly built during the car or chariot festival (Rath Yatra). Lakhs of devotees from all over India throng Puri. The car festival is a 9-day long festival. This festival begins in Ashadha (June – July), and the three deities emerge from the Temple. They are taken on a journey of 3 km in procession. The chariots are decorated. Three chariots are differently named:

1. Nandighosh (Jagannath)
2. Taladwaja (Balarama) and
3. Devadalan (Subhadra)

The images are re-entered in the Temple. Rath yatra is India's most incredible spectacle.

This periodic replacement of the images is a function, and it is called 'Nava Kalebara' (New embodiment of three deities).

The Sun temple of Konark (Black Pagoda)

The Sun temple of Konark in Orissa, once famous as the Black Pagoda, is undoubtedly one of the finest monuments of mankind, particularly in India. Sir John Marshall says, "There is no monument of Hinduism so spectacular and perfectly proportioned as the Sun temple of Konark.

The Sun Temple of Konark is a UNESCO World Heritage site. It is just 3 Km from the coast and visible from far out at sea. Sailors named it the 'Black Pagoda'.

Meaning of Konark:

Konark derives from the Sun God or Surya of the corner. 'Arka' denotes Surya, and 'Kona' means corner.

Sources:

Epigraphical and Puranic sources provide information about this place and deity. According to the Ganga inscriptions, this place is known as 'Konakona'.

Puranic Literature:

1. The Brahma Purana mentioned the name of Konaditya Kona, which means Southeast corner
2. Bhavishya Purana described Surya as Kona Vallabha.

3.   Varahamihara's Brihatsamhita placed Agneya disa (Southeast)
4.   Oriya Mahabharata of Saraladas says that Surya killed a demon called Arka

There are famous temples in this southeast direction, like Lingaraja, Jagannath, and Surya.

'Arka' is added for temples in other places, such as Lolarka Balarka (UP) and Kotyarka (Gujarat).

<u>Tradition of Sun worship:</u>

Sun worship in India has existed since time immemorial. There are epigraphical and Puranic illustrations about Sun worship from ancient times. Millions of people worship the Sun God, Bhaskara, or 'Surya Narayana' from the Sunrise. They feel his presence as a direct God or 'Pratyaksha Narayana'. They offer their prayers after dipping in holy river waters.

> *"Japakusuma Samkasam kasyapeyam Mahadhyutim*
> *Tamorim, Sarvapapaghnam Pratosmi Diwakaram"*

Sun Temples stand as centres of Sun Worship. In Gujarat, the Sun Temple of Modhera and in Kashmir, the Martanda temple are cited in texts. In Orissa, worship has existed since early times. Sun worship began in Kalinga according to 'Jaiminiya Grihasutra'. There is inscriptional evidence from the 6th century saying King Dharmaraja was a devotee of the Sun God (Sahasra Rasmi). Images of Surya of the successive centuries are Parasurameswar (7th), Vaital (8th), Muktesvar (10th), and Lingaraj (11th). The climax of the worship was reached when King Narasimha I built the Temple of Konark (13th century).

<u>Merits of Surya worship:</u>

The people believe that they will be saved from Bhaya (fear), Soka (misery) and Roga (illness).

There are three places of worship of Surya according to Skanda Purana:

1. 'Rising Sun' at Mundira or Udayachala (Mundiraswamy)
2. 'Mid-day Sun' at Kalapriya
3. 'Setting Sun' at Mulasthana, Maitreyavana or Multan.

All three are illustrated by Samba (Son of Krishna & Jambavati). Konark or Konaditya later replaced Mundiraswamy of Mundira.

<u>The mythological story of Samba:</u>

Samba Purana tells the traditional story of Samba regarding the erection of the first Sun temples at Mundira, Kalapriya, and Maitreyavana.

Samba, the son of Krishna, was proud of his handsome appearance, and once he ridiculed Sage Narada. Narada led Samba into a trap to take revenge and persuaded him to visit the bathing places of Gopikas. Meanwhile, Krishna came to the spot and cursed Samba to be affected with leprosy. Samba begged Krishna to get relief from it. Then Krshina asked him to proceed to Maitreyavana on the banks of Chandrabhaga river to install Surya to get rid of the skin disease. Samba did penance for 12 years and got relief from the disease by the grace of the Sun God.

It is believed that Samba brought mega pandits or Brahmins from Iran to conduct sacred rituals in the Sun temple (Multan). Hsuan Tsang, in the 7th century, and Alberuni, in the 11th century, referenced the temples. The name of this temple town is also known as Samba Pura.

<u>Historicity – Religious Prominence and Details of the Temple Construction:</u>

The Odishan king constructed the Sun Temple of Konark in the mid-13th century. Narasimhadeva I (1238-1264) wished to celebrate his military victory over the Muslims. But there is no exact date either for its beginning or completion. The Ganga inscriptions discovered so far have yet to shed any light on the date of construction. A Sanskrit work,

'Katakaraja Vamsavali', states that the Konark Temple was built in 1278 AD. The Temple was in use for three centuries. During the 16th century, the Sikhara (40m high) collapsed. The great Sun Temple is now in ruins.

<u>Konark Festival:</u>

Once a year, the people of Orissa celebrate the Magha Saptami festival at the Chandrabhaga and visit the Temple, which reminds them of how it was 800 years ago.

Irrespective of the historicity, several legends have developed around Konark over the centuries.

<u>The Main Temple:</u>

The Sun Temple of Konark is situated in a spacious compound consisting of the Deula (a general name for the Temple, especially the Kalinga style of architecture in Odishan temples), the Jagmohana (audience chamber), nata mandir along with the east and west axis. All the structures face the east.

Deula and Jagmohana are parts of architectural design and monumental chariots of the Sun God. Deula and Jagmohana stand on a platform (4m high).

The entire Temple was conceived as the cosmic chariot of the Sun God pulled by seven (7) mighty horses (representing seven days of the week). There are 24 cartwheels of stone (representing 24 hours of the day). The Temple was constructed so that the light of the dawn would illuminate the temple sanctuary interior and Lord Surya. Two stone lions crushing elephants guard the main entrance (Gaja Simha).

<u>Sculptural Art of Konark:</u>

The Temple of Konark is known for its monumental architecture and the excellence of its sculptures. Commenting on the wonders of artistry at Konark:

- Rabindranath Tagore wrote: *"Here, the language of man is defeated by the language of stone."*
- Ferguson remarks, *"no exaggeration for its size, the rich ornamentation of the building in the whole world."*
- Ananda Kumaraswamy: *"Konark temple is the perfect example of the adaptation of sculpture to architecture."*

Konark sculpture can be classified as cult images, human figures, erotic sculptures, animal motifs, mythological figures, floral, vegetable and geometric designs, etc. Sexual sculptures are connected with the dancing girls dedicated to the Temple. The Main Temple remained an outstanding monument of the archaeological monument. The ASI recommended large-scale repairs in 1952 but could not detect any causes for its ruins. The location of the Temple near the seashore, heavy monsoon rain, growth of vegetation on the Temple, sandblast, salt air, etc. hastened up the decay process. The figures of horses and elephants were placed on a mound.

PUNJAB (PB)

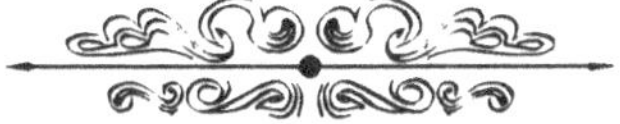

Punjab state, with a 50,362 sq. km. area, was formed in September 1966 with Chandigarh as the capital. Jammu and Kashmir, Himachal Pradesh, Haryana, and Rajasthan are the neighbouring states, while Pakistan is the neighbouring country. Punjabi is the chief language; Sikhism is the main religion, and the rest are Hinduism and Christianity. Beas, Sutlej, and Ravi are the rivers.

Punjab is well known for the golden temple of Amritsar, a holy place of the Sikhs. Further, Hindu temples of Gods and Goddesses attract the pilgrims. Ancient temples of Tretayug exist here. Temples of the epic times of Ramayana and Mahabharat are famous. Bade Hanuman is one of the important temples of Punjab.

Amritsar Temples

- Punjab is a state on the India – Pakistan border. The Golden Temple of Amritsar is a famous holy place for Sikhs. Similarly, another Hindu temple is called 'Drurgiana' and is in the same town as Amritsar. The model of this temple is similar to that of the Golden Temple, known as The Silver Temple, due to its large silver doors. This temple is also situated amid a Lake. The dome and the walls are covered with gold quoting. The deities of the Temple are Lakshminarayana, Durga, and Sarasvati (all marble-made); this temple is said to be from the 16th century, like the Golden Temple, but was rebuilt in 1921.
- Bade Hanuman Temple & Ram Tirth: This Temple is said to have existed since 'Tretayug'. Sundarakanda Parayana for nine days is common here. Uttara Ramayana's story is relevant to this place. Valmiki's ashram, Sita's stay at the ashram, the birth of Lava, Kush, Aswamedha Yaga by Rama, leaving Aswa, Capture by Lavkush,

who tied it up to a tree (Raavi). Hanuman's entrance and efforts to unite Rama and Lava Kush's story are the history of this place and Hanuman. The region is popularly known as 'Rama Tirth'. Hanuman dug a well here. There are temples for Sita, Rama and Lakshman. In the Valmiki mandir, Lava and Kusha had their education from Maharshi Valmiki.

Other temples of Punjab

1. Achaleswar Temple: In the district of Amritsar, there is a place called Barula, the Achalesvara temple of the olden days. This is the place where there is only one Kartikeya temple. Along with Kartikeya are Siva Linga, Parvati Mata and Kumara Swamy. Kumara Swamy remained 'Achala' (without movement) because he grew angry since Ganesa gained the power of 'Bhoo Pradakshin' simply going around the parents.

2. Siva Temple (Jalandhar): The speciality of this temple is that it was built by a Muslim nawab of the Lodi dynasty by the side of a mosque (Imam Nasar). This speaks well about religious toleration at a time of fanatism. The Sivaratri festival is celebrated grandly.

3. Dasuha Temple of the Mahabharata Times: Dasuha Temple was known as 'Viratnagar'. A story says that Bhima of the Pandavas dug a tank here called Bhimasarovar. Amid this lake is Krishna mandir. Around the lake are temples for Siva and Vishnu (Lakshminarayana). 'Semi Vriksha,' where Pandavas kept all their weapons during Agnathavasa, is said to be here only.

4. Devi Temple of 'Jvalamukhi': This is one of the 51 Shakti Peethas of Sati Devi (Vidyeswaridevi) on the top of a hill. The left hand's palm of the Devi fell here. Golden Trident (Trisul) of 40 ft is to be seen here. On all the auspicious days, festivals are celebrated. The Devi of Jvalamukhi is known differently as Vidyadevi, Visvamukhi, or Tripura Sundari.

RAJASTHAN (RJ)

The date of formation of Rajasthan is 1 November 1956. The area of the State is 3,42,239 Sq.Km., and Jaipur is the capital. The neighbouring states are Gujarat, Madhya Pradesh, Uttar Pradesh, Delhi, Haryana, and Punjab. Pakistan is the neighbouring country. The Geographical features of the State include deserts, rivers, and mountains. The Thar desert is the great Indian desert. Luni, Banas, Kali Sindh, and Chambal are important rivers. Aravali Range mountains are famous. Sambar Salt Lake is another important geographical asset. Hinduism is a major religion; the rest are Jainism, Islam, and Christianity.

Temples of Rajasthan consist of the major Gods and Goddesses like the great trio – Brahma, Vishnu and Maheswara, Vishnu's incarnations of Rama and Krishna, Devi, and Shakti Temples. Temples of Ganesa, Dattatreya and Sun Gods also joined The Hindu pantheon of Deities. One of the greatest and rarest temples of Rajasthan is the Pushkar Temple of Brahma.

The Temple of Brahma (Pushkar)

Pushkar is a prominent Hindu pilgrimage town in Rajasthan, 11 km from Ajmer. Devout Hindus visit it at least once in their lifetime. The town curls around a holy lake, which is said to have appeared when Lord Brahma dropped a lotus flower. This temple is one of the world's few Brahma temples.

<u>Holy Lake:</u>

The Holy Lake is a semi-circular area with 52 bathing ghats. The depth of the lake is ten meters. The holy dip on Sukla Paksha of Kartik masa (For the last five days) in this lake grants salvation according to the people's beliefs.

Brahma dropped a lotus flower, which fell at three places, and the holy water sprang up from all these three places:

1. Jyesta Pushkar
2. Madhya Pushkar and
3. Kanishta Pushkar.

Brahma dropped the lotus from his hand('kar'), and thus, the place is known as Pushkar.

It is said that there are 400 milky blue temples in the Town of Pushkar, which often hum with prayers. A few Temples were ancient, mostly desecrated by Aurangazeb and subsequently rebuilt.

Figure 13: Brahma Temple of Pushkar

<u>Brahma descending from Heaven (legendary sources):</u>

Lord Brahma felt there was no place for him on earth as all other Gods for worship. In this context, he dropped a lotus flower, which fell at three locations, and the great Pushkar Lake formed. Then Brahma thought of performing 'yagna' and began preparations. As the performer of the Yagna, he should be accompanied by his wife; Brahma asks Narada, his son, to bring Savitri. Narada went to Mataji and said she should go there along with Rishipatnis Indrani, Parvati and Lakshmi.

Consequently, Savitri was delayed for some time during this coordination process. In the meantime, the pandits advised Brahma to marry another girl so that yagnas could be commenced. Gayatri was brought (Gopa girl or a low caste girl – So she was put into a cow's mouth to make her holy. She was therefore called Gayatri) and proclaimed as Brahma's wife and started Yagna. Savitri came late and learned about the incident. She grew angry and cursed Brahma, saying he would not be worshipped anywhere except at Pushkar. She cursed Siva, Vishu, and Brahmins, went to Ratnagi(hill), and started penance.

<u>The Temple:</u>

The Brahmadeva's temple is said to be from the 14th century. During the reign of Aurangazeb (1658-1707), it was destroyed. It was again reinstalled (Pranapratista) in 1809. A Brahmin Woman 'Poondi Bai', daughter of Giridhar Das, set up the idol of Brahma. The present shape of the temple was given by Gokulchand Pareek, the minister of Daulatrao Sindhia (Gwalior king). The construction is made of marble.

In the sanctum sanctorum, Lord Brahma is sitting on a 'Swan' (vehicle) and is seen with four hands (Aksharamala, Kamandalam, Pustak and Darbhas). On his left side, there is Gayatri's idol. On the walls, there are beautiful pictures of Goddess Saraswati and other deities.

In the Puja system, only ascetics are allowed, not Grihastas. Festivals are celebrated on Kartik Pournami day. There is Brahmakund near the temple. According to the epics, Lord Rama and Lakshmana stayed in the Agasthya Ashram during their Vanavas and bathed in Pushkar.

Other Temples of Pushkar

The Temple of Savitri

On the western side of Pushkar town, there is Savitri Temple on a hill at a distance of 14 Km from Ajmer. Idols of Savitri and Sarasvati are installed (The story of Brahma performing Yagna and Gayatri is already cited above). The temple on The Ratnagini was built in 1690 by Ajit Sing (King of Marwar). Women devotees (married) will be blessed as 'Suvasinis'.

The Temple of Gayatri

This temple is also on top of a hill (Story already cited above).

Ajgandheswar Temple

This Temple is southwest of Pushkar. There is a story behind the existence of this Temple. A demon named 'Vashkali' did penance to please Brahma for about 10,000 years. Brahma granted him a boon, 'not to be killed by Gods or man'. The demon used to take a bath every day in Pushkar and had the darshan of Brahma. Then, it can only be used to take his food. With his natural devilish attitude, he raided Heaven and made Indra his captive. Indra approached Lord Shiva and prayed to return to his Heaven by killing the demon. Siva promised to do so.

Finally, Vashkali, the demon, was killed by Siva in the form of a goat with his horns. Later on, at the request of Brahma and other Gods, Siva wished to stay at Pushkar. Siva Linga emerged from the earth. He said that on every 14th day of Sukla Paksha of Karthika masa, he would be present in the form of Linga. Devotees shall be relieved of their sins if they prey on the above date.

Atpateswar Mahadev Temple

This temple is a cave temple near The Temple of Brahma. A bhikshu came with a scull in his hand to the Yagnavatika of Brahma and left it there. Though the scull was thrown away, several sculls were present there. Brahma realised that the Bhikshu was none other than Lord Siva. Brahma installed a Siva Linga 'Atpateswar Mahadev' and said those who perform Puja to this Linga will be free from rebirths.

Varaha Temple

The old Temple was 150 feet high. The Temple belonged to 1123-1150 AD and was reconstructed by Chauhan king Arunoraj after the Muslim raids and destruction. Again, the Temple was renovated during Akbar's time. Jahangir visited Pushkar in 1613 AD. Aurangzeb, too, destroyed the Temple. In 1727, the Temple was rebuilt beautifully again.

Other temples of Rajasthan

Vishnu and Krishna Temples

Udaipur:

Jagat Singh built a Vishnu Temple called Jagadish temple in 1651. It is in the Indo-Aryan style. The image of Jagannath is in black stone, and Lakshmi Devi is also present. A brass image of Garuda can be seen there.

Several Krishna Temples exist in Rajasthan.

- Jaisalmer: 187 km from Jodhpur, there is a Krishna Temple. It is said that Krishna dug a well here.
- Jaipur: Radhakrishna Temple of the 15th century was constructed near Jaipur palace, known as Jagat Siromani Temple. There is an idol of Vishnu behind the Radha Krishna idols.

- Khaata: At Khaata, 15 km from Jaipur, Krishna temple and Rukmini exist.
- Chitodgad: The Krishna temple, Kumbha Syam, was built in 1450 AD. Previously, Varaha Murthy existed; during Muslim invasions, it was destroyed, and later, the Krishna Temple was constructed.
- Nadh Dwara: This is 25 km from Udaipur. Krishna and Vishnu are worshipped here. Krishna is known as Nadhji. It is said that Krishna's idol was brought from Madhura, and Krishna was known as Govardhana Dharana and Deva damana.
- Kankroli: From Nadh Dwara, it is just 18 km distance. Krishna was installed here in 1678, and the temple is known as Dwarakaji.

Siva Temples

- Udaipur: Ekalingji Temple is a beautiful temple that is 50 feet high and 60 feet wide. It is supposed to be the famous Siva temple of Rajasthan. Sage Haritha did penance here. Mewad kings, who had a strong faith in Mahasiva, were the patrons of the temple. Siva Linga was carved with black stone. There is also Siva's idol with four faces. (Brahma – Vishnu – Siva and Surya). Adi Shankaracharya visited the temple and worshipped Siva and Parvathi.
- Dungarpur (Baneswar—Siva): Siva is worshipped as a Linga. A tribal festival is celebrated yearly from Magha Sukla Ekadasi to Magha Sukla Purnima. The temple was built in 1850.
- Vijaya Rajeswar: In Dungarpur, there is another Siva Temple by the name Vijaya Rajeswar, established around the 1920s
- Bhuvaneswar Temple (Dungarpur): This is said to be the swayabhu Temple of Siva. The tribal festival is celebrated on Holi.
- Pali (Samanath Temple): This ancient and beautiful temple was constructed in 1209 A.D. by Kumarpal Solanki, the ruler of Gujarat. The Siva Linga was brought from Saurashtra.

Brahma – Vishnu and Siva – Temple

In the Chitodghad region, there is Brahma-Vishnu and Siva temple. The trio of Gods are to be seen in standing posture.

Dattatreya Temple: (Aabu Town)

The Dattatreya temple is situated on top of a hill. Guru Dattatreya's holy feet are exhibited there. The deity is Brahma, Vishnu, and Maheswara in one form.

SUN God Temples

- Surya Temple (Jaipur): There is a hilly area in Jaipur (Galta Ji) where there is a Surya temple. Built in the Aravali Hills, 10 Km from Jaipur, Sun Temple is part of several temples built around the 15th century in Galav Ashram. The Temple complex here is beautiful, with natural springs filling several kunds. This temple complex is known as 'Monkey Temple' due to the many monkeys living here. There is a beautiful sculpture of a cow, and from its mouth, water flows. Devotees dip in the water and have a darshan of Sun God.
- Udaipur Temple: Udaipur is a town with a beautiful sunrise. The Mewar kings belonged to Suryavansa, so they built a temple for Surya Bhagwan (Suvarna Surya).
- Pali Temple: The Sun Temple was built in the 15th century and is known for its sculptural beauty. Its idols of Surya, in different forms, are installed here. One of the interesting sculptures is Surya's chariot ride with seven horses.
- Ranakpur Village Temple: The temple is in the same Pali district amid the Aravali mountains. Surya Narayan is the God worshipped by the people. The chariot ride of God is a unique attraction.
- Lohargala Temple: Ancient Sun temple is situated there, and 70 other temples exist according to the inscriptions. Hot springs are natural here; devotees dip in them and go for God's darshan. There is 'Surya Kund' here to merge the ashes of the dead.

Ganesh Temples

- Ghatiyala Mandir: Devotees travel from Jodhpur to visit the Mandir. This temple is known as 'Chaturdha Ganesh Mandir'. On a pillar, Ganesh Murthi is sculpted in four directions.
- Ranatambor Temple: The temple is accessible from Jaipur. Ganesh temple is on the top of a hill. The idol is damaged. Even then, devotees visit in large numbers to fulfil their desires. Therefore, he is known as 'Siddhidata'.

SIKKIM (SK)

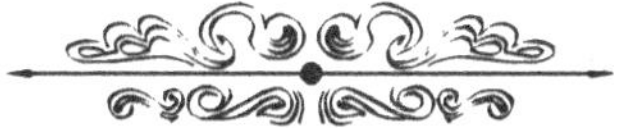

The area of Sikkim is 7096 Km. The capital is Gangtok, and the date of formation of the State is May 16, 1975. West Bengal is the neighbouring state. China, Nepal and Bhutan are the neighbouring countries. Among The two major religions of the state, Hinduism is one, and the second happened to be Buddhism. Teesta and Rangit are the rivers. Kanchan Junga is the highest mountain peak in India and the third highest in the world. The mountain, which has five faces, is adorned by the people. One can rejoice by looking at the Sunrise from the Tiger hill. The Kanchan Junga Mountain ranges spread from Sikkim to West Bengal.

Temples:

There is a small Siva temple just 40 km away from Gangtok on the banks of a lake that is 12000 feet above sea level. Teesta as cited above, is a river, a confluence of two sub-rivers. The region is beautiful with its greenery, valleys, and white stones. This is also Kanchan Junga's viewpoint.

Siddheswar Temple: The Temple is near the Siddheswar dam. Siva's idol is 108 feet in meditation form on the top of a hill. One interesting thing is that the models or designs of some of the great temples in India can be found here. Chardham temples, Puri Jagannath, Dwarala of Gujarat, and Rameswar Badrinath are some of the temples. The Siva temple was reconstructed in 2011 by Swamy Swarupananda of Shankara Peeth. It is also believed that Lord Siva lived in this area after the self-immolation of Parvati in the context of 'Daksha Yagna'.

Mahabharat Reference:

Kirateswar Mahadev Temple: The temple is on the river Rangit's bank. Arjuna of the Pandava brothers made penance in praise of Mahadeva.

Siva appeared to Arjuna and blessed him to win the war of corning' Mahabharata Sangram'.

Combination of Hindu gods in a Temple at Gangtok: The temple is in the heart of Gangtok. It was built in 1935. Shrines of Gods and Goddesses are installed here, and this was further extended in successive years.

Ganesh Idol: On a hill 6,500 feet high, Ganesh's idol is installed. The God is worshipped with a belief that the devotees are blessed with success in removing 'Vighnas' or obstacles in their activities.

Hanuman Temple: 6 Km away from Gangtok is a temple of Hanuman. According to the epic sources, Lakshmana became unconscious during the war between Rama and Ravana. Hence, Hanuman went in search of Sanjeevani to save Lakshmana. He brought the mountain of 'Sanjeevani' itself. On the way, he rested at this place (called Hanuman Tok). There are pictorial artworks related to the Ramayana incidents in the temple. The place is beautiful and scenic, with waterfalls.

TAMILNADU (TN)

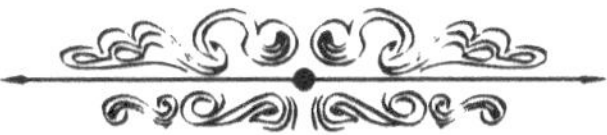

The region of Tamil Nadu exercised full powers under the British regime, with Madras' presidency being on par with the Bombay and Bengal Presidencies. After independence to create separate Andhra, this state has been bifurcated. On 14 January 1969, the state was renamed Tamil Nadu.

Figure 14: Tamilnadu – Map of Major Cities and Temples

Kerala, Karnataka, Andhra Pradesh and Pondichery are the neighbouring states. This state is formed with 32 districts, the capital being Chennai. The area of the state is 130058 km². Hinduism, Islam and Christianity are the main religions.Tamil is the state's chief language. Kodaikanal is a famous hill station situated on the Palani Hills. Kaveri is one of the state's major rivers. Temples of Tamil Nadu play a vital role in promoting rites and rituals in daily worship followed in the temples of Tamil Nadu.

Further, 63 Saivaite Nayanars and 12 Vaishnavite Azhwars (Or Alvars) dedicated their lives to the spiritual development of the people. Adi Sankaracharya and Ramanujacharya, the great saints, prescribed rules related to temples, which are still being followed today.

An attempt is made to focus on some important temples of Tamil Nadu. Madhura Meenakshi, Kanchi Kamakshi, Ganesha, Subramanya, and Ranganatha temples, along with many more, are covered in this book. Kasi in northern India and Rameswaram in southern India are famous for all the Hindus in India. One should visit these temples at least once in a lifetime. Rameswaram temple is located on Rameswaram island in Tamil Nadu. It is dedicated to Lord Siva, whom Lord Sri Rama has worshipped. The Temple has a set of corridors that measure 3850 feet, the longest in the world.

Rameswaram

The southernmost point of sacred India is Rameswaram. This temple city is situated in the Ramanathapuram district of Tamil Nadu. Rameswaram is as old as the great epic Ramayana. Only that of Kasi or Varanasi equals its importance as a place of pilgrimage. The shape of this island of Gods has been compared to Lord Vishnu's conch shell (Sankha), and further, it is well known as 'Gandhamedha Parvatha or hill'.

The glorious sunrise from the sacred waters of the Bay of Bengal and the Indian Ocean (famous for corals and conchs) is a beautiful experience.

Lord Rama, the Avatar of Vishnu, installed Lord Siva, popularly known as Ramanatha Swamy of Rameswaram.

<u>The Temple:</u>

Four famous Hindu temples are situated in the four corners of India: Badrinath in the north, Puri Jagannath in the East, Dwaraka in the west, and Sri Ramanatha Swamy in the south, the only Siva temple among the four.

Rameswaram temple is the southernmost of the 12 Jyotirlingas. It is believed that the pilgrimage to Kasi or Varanasi becomes complete only after one worships Ramanatha Swamy of Rameswaram with the holy waters of the Ganges and again visits Varanasi to worship Viswanath and merging sand collected from the sea at Rameswaram in the Ganges of Benaras.

<u>Phase-wise development of the Temple:</u>

The Ramanatha Swamy temple of Rameswaram is spread over 15 acres of land. The Temple's beginnings can be traced back to a thatched hut, and its development was phase-wise, finally reaching a glorious stage of architectural excellence.

Parakrama Bahu, the ruler of ancient Sri Lanka, built the stone structure. The east-facing Rajagopuram had a nine-tiered one with 126 feet in height. Another five-tiered Tower is at the rear. Long Corridors are supported by carved Granite pillars on a raised platform.

Much of the construction work took place between the 12th and 16th centuries. The long corridors belonged to a later period of the 18th century. At the entrance is a statue of one of the Sethupatis (Contributor to the Temple). There are beautiful paintings on the ceilings relating to the Ramayana episodes.

Journey of Rama to Sri Lanka in quest of Sita and prominence of places on the way:

- Vedaranyam: Footprints of Rama are preserved here by the archaeological department. To receive Sita by defeating Ravana, Rama came here to build a bridge across the sea to Sri Lanka led by an army of monkeys.
- Kattamvadi: The Archaeological Survey of India excavated and found traces of the old Road. The sea God obliged Rama's orders and became calm and quiet, giving the way.
- Pullaramyam: It became difficult for Rama and his army to proceed further into the sea because of the severity of sea waters. Hence, Rama was under deep meditation for three days, lying on green grass (Darbha) near the Temple of Adi Jagannadha. Adi Jagannadha blessing Rama presented a weapon of victory called 'Divya Chapam'.
- Miracle bridge: A floating bridge was constructed by Nala, the son of Viswakarma, to proceed to Lanka. The magic was heavy or light; even stone would float.
- Adi Setu: Even a squirrel helped along with 'Vanaras'. Rama petted it, and his fingers were seen on the squirrel's back at the location of Adi Setu near Jagannadha temple at Darbha Sayanam.
- Rama worshipped Ganesa and Navagrahas: while proceeding to the battle with Ravana, Rama worshipped Vinayaka and Navagrahas (Nava Pashanam).
- Dhanushkodi (Setu) is located at the confluence of the Bay of Bengal (Mahadadhu – Sanskrit name) and the Indian Ocean (Ratnakara – Sanskrit name), a centre for a holy bath. Lord Rama too bath (Vedalai). At Pamban, there was Bhairava Tirtha. 'Lakshmana Kunda' is another bathing point where Rama took a bath. To define Dhanushkodi, 'Dhanush' means the bow and 'Kodi' means the end. At Vivbhishana's request, Rama broke the Setu with one end of his bow.

<u>Pratista of Ramanatha or Rameswara Linga:</u>

There is a puranic background to the 'Pratista' or installation of Iswara Linga. After Rama killed Ravana, he returned to Rameswaram along with Sita, Lakshmana, and Parivaram. Then Agastya told Rama that the killing of Ravana, a Brahmin and great-grandson of Bhishma, amounted to 'Brahmahatya Patakam'. Hence, Agastya advised Rama to install Siva Lingam and worship. Then Rama sent Hanuman to Mount Kailas to bring a Siva Lingam. But, he could not return in time. Sita made a 'Saikata Lingam' (Sand) and worshipped. Soon after Hanuman returned from Kailas, he felt unhappy. Rama consoled him and worshipped that Lingam by installing it. Sita told Hanuman to remove the 'Saikata Lingam', and Hanuman wrapped his tail around the Lingam to pull out, but in vain. Hanuman realized his blunder and Leela of the Lord. Since then, worship has been done for the Siva Lingams, i.e., 'Saikata Lingam' and Hanuman's 'Viswa Lingam'. Puja to Viswa Lingam will be performed first. Today, worship and darshan of 'Spatika Lingam' are being introduced and have become a practice.

<u>Holiness and Significance of the Tirthams – (The excellent Bathing experience):</u>

A unique custom of pilgrimage to Rameswaram is the excellent bathing experience in various Tirthams outside and inside the temple complex to get rid of sins. The shore opposite to the Temple is 'Agni Tirtham'. The sea is calm and ideal for bathing. One has to take a bath here and then proceed to the 22 Tirthams of the temple complex. There are Puranic stories narrating Mahatmas who took a bath in Tirthams. Lord Krishna did so to get relief from 'Brahma Hatya Dosha', and Kala Bhairava also took a bath to be redeemed of the sin of cutting the 5th head of Lord Brahma.

Most of the 22 Tirthams are freshwater wells except two; one is the sea, and the other is a pond. Each of the Tirthams has a specific name as follows:

1. Maha Lakshmi
2. Savitri
3. Gayatri
4. Saraswati
5. Madhava
6. Gandhamadana
7. Gavatcha (Or Kavatcha)
8. Gavaya
9. Nala
10. Neela
11. Sankha
12. Chakra
13. Brahma Hatya Vimochana
14. Surya
15. Chandra
16. Ganga
17. Yamuna
18. Gaya
19. Siva
20. Satyamrita
21. Sarva
22. Kodi

The process of bathing in 22 wells is quite exciting and noteworthy.

There are specific hired persons with identity cards to help. They are fishermen outside the temple gate. They carry a small iron bucket, climb up the parapet wall of every well, skillfully throw the bucket inside the well and draw water. They pour the sacred water on the hands of Devotees. This custom has been followed for centuries with devotion and dedication. After completing this process, one should wear fresh clothes before Swamy Darshan.

<u>Temple architecture and festivals:</u>

Rameswaram Temple architecture is beautiful, reflecting the Dravidian style. The temple corridors are the longest in the world, measuring 3850 feet long, 17-21 wide, and 30 feet high. There are three Prakarams and four Gopurams. The ocean in front (east) is called Ratnakara, and in the west, Mahadadhi. Nandi vahana is as big as 12'X8'X9'. The towers are covered with mythological figures. The architecture is akin to the Egyptian style, indicating maritime trade.

Mahasivaratri, Vasantotsavam, Rama Linga Pratista Utsavam, Kalyanotsavam, Navaratri, Sanda Shasti and Arudra darsanam.

Divine Mother's Temple of Kanyakumari

The divine mother's temple of Kanyakumari is also known as Kanniyakumari or Kumariyamman temple. She learns her name to the town and district – Kanyakumari. The place is some 700 km from Chennai. Kanyakumari is a place of exquisite beauty of nature. It is a confluence of the Bay of Bengal, the Indian Ocean and the Arabian Sea. One can derive pleasure by looking at a magnificent sunrise and sunset.

Besides being a place of divine mother, Kanyakumari is historically significant. Long before Christ, the place attracted overseas travellers who called Cape Comorin.

1. After the third century BC, Herodotus wrote about Kanyakumari in one of his books.
2. Ptolemy, who lived 2000 years ago, referred to Kanyakumari in his book 'Kumaria Akron' and worshipped the divine mother.
3. Marco Polo, a Venice traveller who travelled in 1243 AD, visited this place to worship the deity in this temple. He said it was a glittering figure like a Pole Star, even by looking at it far away, 30 miles from Kanyakumari.

<u>Sources of the deity and the temple:</u>

Kanniya Amman, Bhagavathy Amman, or Devi Kanya Kumari appears to be a Hindu nun holding a rosary in meditation. The goddess's worship dates back to Vedic times. This divine mother is mentioned in the "Narayana Upanishad" and the "Yajurveda," "Skanda Purana," and "Mahabharata."

<u>Legendary Source:</u>

According to the Sthala Purana, the goddess was Parvati. She was reborn as Kanyakumari (Virgin Goddess) to fulfil the prayers of the Devatas to kill a demon, "Baanasura". The condition is only a virgin should kill him. In the meantime, a wedding is arranged between Kumari and Shiva before dawn. But Narada forestalled the wedding by crowing like a cock. Siva went back to Suchindram, his abode. Banasura was killed by Devi with her Chakrayudha (Discus). She stood like a guard at the tip of the Peninsula as our country's protector.

<u>The image of the goddess:</u>

The images are carved out of touchstone. In the afternoon, the priests cover the deity's face with a thick layer of sandalwood paste and put a red colour on her lips, making the deity appear to smile. She wears a brilliant diamond nose stud. The goddess looks exquisitely beautiful in the evening with the bright lamps. The door facing the sea is closed to prevent ships from coming closer to this rocky shore.

The Kanyakumari temple has a beautiful atmosphere of purity and holiness. The devotees chant Durga Suktam in the Sanctum ending with,

"Katyayanaya Vidmahe
Kanya Kumari dhimahi
Tanno Durga Prachodayat"

The images look much more beautiful and vibrant spiritually. Kanyakumari temple is always busy with a large number of worshipers from all parts of

India, namely Gujaratis, Tamilians, Marathis, Kannadigas, Telugus, and foreigners. Apart from the religious and spiritual points, there is another speciality here, which is the Vivekananda rock memorial. A tall statue of Tiruvalluvar on an adjoining rock attracts millions of people, giving messages.

Madurai

Madurai is the oldest city in South India. Meenakshi Sundareswar Temple is famous in Madurai and is one of the country's largest temple complexes (65,000 Meters), situated on the banks of river Vaigai. The temple is also known as Kadambavana Kshetra. Madurai I India is what Athens of Greece said by the Europeans. A century ago, Madurai was an excellent literacy seat in the famous 'Tamil Sangam'.

The goddess of Madurai is Meenakshi, one of the three powerful goddesses of India, and the rest are Kanchi Kamakshi and Kasi Visalakshi. She is self-manifested from sacred fire (Swayambhu) and fish-eyed. Jagadguru Adi Sankaracharya, the founder of the Advaita Philosophy of Hinduism, worshipped Meenakshi of Madurai and recited slokas. One of them:

"Sreevidyam (Parvati incarnation),
Sivavamabhaga Nilayam (keeping herself at Lord Siva's left)
'Hreenkara' Mantrojjwalam (Shines in Hrim mantram)
Sreechakrankita bindu Madhya Vasateem (Stays at Srichakra)
Sreematsabha Naayakeem (Queen of Sabha)
Sreemat sabha naayakeem (Queen of sabha)
Sreemat Shanmukha Vighnaraja Jananeem (Mother of Shanmukha
and Ganesa)
Sri Majjaganmohinim (Bewitcher of the universe)
Meenaksheem Pranatosmi Santatamaheem karunya varannidhim
(Ocean of grace)"

Legendary source of Madurai:

Kulasekhara, the famous king, was the builder of Madurai. As per the 'Sthalapuranam' or local legend, Indra worshipped 'Swayambhu Siva linga' in Kadambavana. This information reached Kulasekhara, a great devotee of Lord Siva. Siva appeared in a dream to him. Drops of nectar (Madhuram) fell on the spot (location of the temple) from Siva's matted hair. The place has been known as Madurai since then. Madhurapuri is the ancient name. From Madhram (Sweetness), the term Madhurapuri later became Madurai.

Figure 15: Madurai Meenakshi Temple

History of Madurai & History of the Temple:

Madurai was under the sway of the Pandyas and Nayakas. Pandyan kings were the earliest rulers of Madurai. During the 1st empire, the first king of Ceylon, Vijaya (500 BC), was the son-in-law of a

Pandyan king. Megasthanes referred to the Pandyan rule. There were commercial contracts between Madurai, ancient Greece and Rome. Ptolemy named Madurai as 'Modoura'. Madurai was considered as the Mediterranean emporium. Roman coins flowed to Madurai. Meenakshi (incarnation of Parvati) and Sundereswar (a form of Siva) are enshrined in twin temples of the Meenakshi Amman's Temple complex. During the 2nd empire of Pandyas (roughly 1190-1216 AD), Kulasekhara, as cited above, was the builder of Madurai and was succeeded by Malayadwaja. Meenakshi Amman was the daughter of this king and Kanchanamala.

The birth of Amman:

As per the source of 'Sthalapurana', Malayadwaja, the Pandyan King, had no sons; he performed 'Putrakamesti Yaga'. From the sacrificial fire, Goddess Meenakshi, a three-year-old girl with three breasts, came out. She had no physical origin. Hence, a 'Swayambhu' or self-manifested from fire. A spiritual voice ordered the king to teach the girl all the arts and fighting skills. The third breast would disappear when she cast eyes on her future husband (Siva). She started a military campaign, defeating enemies across the country. She went to Mount Kailash, and the lieutenants of the Lord were brought under her control. The prophecy came true. Her third breast disappeared. She married the Lord (Siva), He became Sundara Pandyan (1251-1272 AD). Ugra Pandyan was their son (incarnation of Subramanya).

The Golden Lilly Tank and the Gopurams:

Inside the temple, there is a sacred tank with golden lilies. It is said that, after taking a bath in this tank, Indra worshipped Siva with beautiful flowers to get rid of the 'Brahmahatya Pataka'. Please take a bath in this tank before Darshan of Amman. Spacious corridors surround the tank. Vedic scholars recite the slokas, which Shenoy has described as a feat of memory.

Gopurams or Towers:

The temple is unique, being one of the 17th-century architectural designs. Thirty of these constructions are grouped under the 'Madurai class of temples'. Meenakshi Temple is a double temple with two separate sanctuaries (Sundareswar and Meenakshi). The height of South Indian architecture is visible in the Madurai temple. This architecture is the aesthetic heritage of Tamil Nadu, as the Taj Mahal is to northern India. The temple complex is on six hectares of land with tall Gopurams and figures of Gods, Goddesses and demons. Only on the southern Gopuram, 1511, are such figures to be seen. The Gopurams, or the towers of the Meenakshi Temple, are the most noteworthy examples of post-Pandyan architecture.

By 1310 AD, there were 14 Gopurams. Allauddin Khilji sent Malik Kafur on a South Indian expedition, and Kafur raged 14 towers to the ground. Only two shrines remain. Successively, the later rulers of Madurai started and completed the construction of Gopurams and other architectural structures.

According to Percy Brown, The Madurai Temple was built mainly at one time. The architectural style is most typical of the 17th century. The double temple occupied the most significant space. The pool of the golden lilies is an artificial reservoir measuring 165' X 120'. From the Spot (Southern Gopuram's), the view of Amman's Temple is beautiful and looks with enhanced beauty.

Brief Account of the Gopurams (Towers):

There are nine towers. The four significant ones are the outer and remaining inner ones.

The Eastern Tower:

Typically, the 'Rajagopuram' of the eastern side of the Hindu temples will be the entrance. This practice is not to be seen in this temple because it was closed permanently due to superstition. He said that one of the temple servants jumped from the top of the Gopuram and died.

<u>The Northern and Southern Towers:</u>

The central shrine of Meenakshi Amman and Sundereswar's shrine is to be seen since the towers intersect a line. The Vimana of the main shrine can be seen from all the four corners.

<u>The Western Tower:</u>

Puranic stories are beautifully portrayed.

The entrance to the temple is through the Ashta Shakti on three sides of the sanctum sanctorium of Meenakshi temple since the Eastern tower is closed permanently. Shakti is depicted as Ichcha Shakti, Kriya Shakti and Jnana Shakti.

<u>Sculpture of the Temple:</u>

The richness of Madurai sculpture is visible and will be a feast to a pilgrim's eye. Temple pillars and Mandapams are to be cited in this context.

<u>Killikattu Mandapa:</u>

A parrot is a sacred bird; hence, Meenakshi Amman is seen with a parrot in her left hand, indicating peace and happiness. Her right hand indicates 'Abhaya' (protection). Other Mandapas include 'Dark Mandapa', Mudali Mandapa, etc.

Dwara Palakas are seen in dancing poses.

All the Gopurams or Towers contain all types of dancing poses. In other words, the temple of Madurai is an encyclopedia of the dancing poses in stone and wood.

<u>Further carvings and paintings on pillars are marvellous:</u>

1. Siva as Lingodbhava Murthi

2. Brahma in the form of Swan
3. Vishnu, that of a boar bearing the earth
4. Siva as Artha Nareeswara
5. Siva as Kalyana Murthi, i.e., the marriage of Meenakshi with Sundereswar
6. Yogic pose of Siva (Dakshinamurthi)
7. Three forms of Siva: Bhairava, Veerabhadra and Sabhapati along with Kaali.

The processional deities, Utsava vigrahas, are also beautiful. Figures of 63 Saivaite Nayanars are also depicted here.

Festivals:

Kalyanotsavam is celebrated on a grand scale. There was a 16-acre tank where the Goddess Meenakshi and God Sundereswar float festival is held annually in January/February.

Princes and devotees donate jewels containing precious stones, diamonds, emeralds, and Rubies. On festival days, the deity is decorated.

Kanchipuram Temples

Kanchipuram is an ancient city, and the Britishers called it 'Canjeevaram'. Situated on the banks of 'Vegavati', the town stands foremost among the seven ancient secret cities, the rest of the six being Varanasi, Haridwar, Ayodhya, Dwaraka, Mathura and Ujjain.

In the words of Kalidasa, Kanchi is the best among the cities, just as the jasmine flower amongst the flowers, Rambha amongst women and Grihastasrama among the Chaturasramas of human life. Coming to the learning or scholarship aspect, Kanchi comes next to Varanasi.

History:

Both literacy (Manimekalai) and historical sources say the city was 2000 years old. Under the early Cholas, Kanchi is the capital. Later the Pallavas (6-8th Centuries) contributed much to the building of the temples of Kanchi. The Cholas (10th-13th Centuries) and the Vijayanagar rulers (14th-17th Centuries) brought glory to this temple town (estimated as 1000), with this city standing as the first phase of the architectural form of the temple building. Later, this was considered and improvised during prosperous periods.

In Kanchi, both the sects of Hinduism, namely Saivaite and Vaishnavite, flourished side by side. The Saivaite stronghold is Sivakanchi (Big Kanchi) and Vaishnavite stronghold is Vishnu Kanchi (little Kanchi). According to Brahmanda Purana, Kasi and Kanchi are like the two eyes of Siva. Kanchi Kamakshi and Kasi Visalakshi are spoken of together.

Sri Kamakshi Amman Temple

Sri Kamakshi Amman, temple of Kanchi (Siva Kanchi), is an imposing temple and an important Shakti Peeth, along with Sri Meenakshi Amman of Madurai and Sri Visalakshi of Kasi. Kanchi Kamakshi is said to be the super Goddess of Parasakti. She has the amsa of Sarasvati, Parvati, and Lakshmi. She is worshipped as 'Parabhahma Svarupini'. She was first a Ugra Svarupini, but later, Adi Sankaracharya installed the Srichakram and persuaded the Goddess to become a Santha Svarupini. Adi Sankaracharya established the Kamakoti Peetham on the shrine's campus. Adi Sankara extracted a promise from Amman that she would not go out without his permission.

<u>The temple and its vicinities:</u>

The present temple covers an area of 5 acres. The Cholas constructed it. Other shrines of Bangaru Kamakshi Maha Sarasvati and Adi Sankara surround the temple's sanctum. Kamakshi Mata appears in a sitting posture (Padmasana), flanked by Brahma, Vishnu, and Siva. A Gold plate covers the Vimana of the temple. The outer Prakara has a tank, several Mandapas, and a 1000-pillared hall. The sacred tank is called Pancha Ganga.

<u>Temple Festival:</u>

The temple festival takes place in February and March, and the silver car festival is held on the ninth day. During October and November (Amman's birthday), daily pujas, Harati and Naivedyam, are offered to the Devi, and Go puja is also performed.

Sri Ekamabaranatha Temple

This temple is also known as Sri Ekambareswara temple and is situated in Siva Kanchi. This famous Siva temple is one of the 'Panchaboota Lingas' signifying the five elements. Ekambareswara is 'Pridhvi Lingam'. In Tiruvannamalai, Siva is known as 'Agni Linga', Jambukeswar as 'Jala Linga', Sri Kalahasti as 'Vayu Linga' and Chidambaram as 'Akasa Linga'.

Pallavas and Cholas contributed much to the development of this biggest temple. Pallavas renovated the existing temple. The Vijayanagara rulers maintained the temple well, and the present temple owes its existence to their patronage.

The Rajagopuram is towering and has a height of 190 feet. It was built by Sri Krishnadevaraya in 1509. The temple had towering Gopurams, long corridors and beautiful Mandapas, including the pillared hall.

<u>Significance of Ekambaranatha Temple:</u>

'Eka' means one, 'Ambra' or 'Amra' means Mango and ''Natha' means The Lord. Parvati traced Siva under a Mango tree; hence, he is known as Ekamra or Ekambareswara Swamy. All the devotees worship the mango tree. It has four branches representing four Vedas. Each branch bears mangos with different tastes, and the leaves are also different in appearance. Under this tree is a Siva Lingam, a composite of 108 small ones. There are two tanks, namely Kampa Nadi and Sivaganga. There is a Vishnu shrine in the Siva temple.

<u>Worship:</u>

Siva is worshipped in the form of Linga. Kamakshi Amman worshipped the Lord under the Mango tree. Parvati embraced the Linga and protected it during floods in the Vegavati River, and Siva married her. There is a shrine for Siva and Parvati under the Mango tree. The tree is 3500 years old, but the present one is its offshoot.

Sri Kailasnath Temple

Narasimha II, or Raja Simha, built this Siva temple (700-728 AD). The Siva Lingam is more than 10 feet in height. Devotees believe that visiting this Lord is 'Janma Rahityam', and the process of visiting is very difficult, including crawling. Siva is worshipped as Nataraja. The temple is under the control of the Archeological Survey of India. Astabhuji Durga is seen here.

Sri Varadaraja Swamy Temple

Sri Varadaraja Perumal temple is the most famous temple in Vishnu Kanchi. The temple is situated on the top of Hastagiri Hills. There are 24 steps to reach the Sanctum Sanctorium. The seven-tiered rajagopuram is quite impressive. It is said that Sri Varadaraja Swamy temple of Kanchi is one of the four most extraordinary Vaishnavite temples in India, which grants salvation. The other three temples are Sri Rangam, Tirumala and Tirunarayana Puram (Melkote). Lord Brahma worships the Swamy in Krutayuga, Gajendra in Tretayuga, Brihaspati in Dwaparayuga and Adisesha in Kaliyuga. Perumdevi Tayar is the consort of the Lord Perumal. There is a holy Pushkarini; a wooden replica of Sri Varadaraja Swamy was found in it. It is displayed once every 40 years. There is a 100-pillared hall full of sculptures of the Vijayanagara style.

<u>The Diety:</u>

Sri Varadaraja is enormous, has a standing posture facing the west, holds Sankha, Chakra, etc., and is richly decorated with jewels. The Brahmanda Purana says that Lord Brahma performed Yagna. Maha

Vishnu emerged in the form of Sri Varadaraja Swamy. At the request of Brahma, he remained in Vishnu Kanchi to bless devotees. In short, Sri Varadaraja is a self-manifestation of Sri Maha Vishnu. Several Vaishnavite gurus sang in praise of their Lord. Brahmotsavam and Garudotsavam are celebrated yearly from May to June, drawing lakhs of people. Vijayanagara rules contributed endowments, gifts and jewellery to the temple. Robert Clive was so impressed by looking at the Garudotsava that he presented his wife's necklace to the Lord. The district collector of Chengulput presented a set of beautiful jewels (used in the Lord's crown).

There are several sub-shrines like Yoga Narasimha. The temple has a large area of 23 acres. The Chola and Vijayanagara Kings evinced particular interest in the growth of the temple. The Dhwaja Sthambha is over 100 feet tall and made of single stone.

In addition to the holy tank (Ananda Tirtha), there is a beautiful flower garden, and the shrines of Alwars are placed there. Sri Ramanujacharya spent several years in this Kshetra. There is a gold and silver-plated carving of two lizards in the temple. The taint of a lizard falling on our bodies is believed to be removed by the mere touch of the carvings.

Significance of the Kshetra and Kanchi:

The shrine of the Varadaraja Swamy is supposed to be the second tallest shrine in India. The Rajagopuram is 100 feet high. On the western side of the temple and the northern side, there is 'Nooru Kalla Mandapa' (100 pillar hall) of the Vijayanagara style. Special mention may be made of its sculptural splendour. The Vijayanagara handiwork is visible when looking at the number of horse riders figures. The Vijayanagara rules lavished their attention on this 23-acre temple. The sculptors were past masters in depicting life-like figures using black granite, and they remain a marvel to the sightseers even centuries after. In short, the temple of Sri Varadaraja Perumal is called the Museum of Vijayanagara Art and Sculpture.

Sri Vaikuntha Perumal Temple

Sri Vaikuntha Perumal temple is famous for its architecture. While Sri Varadaraja Swamy is in a standing posture, Sri Vaikuntha Perumal is in a sitting posture. Vaikunthavalli Tayar is the Goddess. The temple is said to be from the 7th century AD during the reign of the Pallavas. Nandivarma Pallava Malla (731-795 AD) built this temple after the completion of Kailasanath temple. Inscriptions and carvings around the 'Prakaram' reveal the history of the times: Lord Vishnu appeared in the form of Vaikunthavasa to the king in a dream, and hence the name of the God is known as Vaikuntha Perumal. The Archeological Survey of India maintains the temple.

Perumal Temple of Vilakkoli

The temple is situated where Sri Vedanta Desika was born in 1268 AD. Sri Perumal, along with Sridevi and Bhudevi, is also called Deepa Prakasa or Lustre of the Lamp. The Goddess is Marakatavalli Tayar.

Astabhuja Perumal Temple

Ashtabhuja Perumal temple is 1.5 kilometres from Sri Varadaraja Swamy temple. The Rajagopuram is 3 tiered. The diety is also known as Adikesav Perumal, Gajendra Varadan Perumal, and Chakradhar. The deity appears in a standing posture. In his eight arms, he holds eight objects: a discus, Sword, Flower, Bow, Arrow, Shield, Conch, and Mace.

There is a Pushkarini, and it is here Gajendra sought the help of Sri Maha Vishnu to save him from a crocodile. The deity saved Gajendra from Crocodile with his discus.

Sri Sthanu Malayan Temple Suchindram

Suchindram is a famous pilgrimage centre in South India situated 13 kilometres from Kanyakumari. This temple of the 9th century is dedicated to the Trinity: Siva (Sthanu), Vishnu (Mal), and Brahma (Ayan). Therefore, the temple is known as Sri Sthanu Malayan Temple.

Suchindram was a dense forest in ancient times and popular as Jnanaranya, where sages attained salvation by meditating and obtaining supreme knowledge or Jnana. The two episodes of Ahalya and Anasuya are attached to Suchindram.

Ahalya Episode:

Ahalya was the wife of sage Gautama. She was purified after bathing in the Tirtha (Sodhana Tirtha) here. Indra was cleansed of his sins here by thrusting his hand into boiling Ghee for his misbehaviour towards Ahalya. Thus, 'Suchindram' denotes 'Suchi' for purification and 'Indram' for Indra.

Anasuya Episode:

Anasuya was a pious wife of sage Atri. They lived in an Ashram here. Sage was away in the Himalayas to perform a Yagna. In this context, Narada played an important role. Narada wanted to humble down the pride of goddesses Lakshmi, Parvati and Sarasvati. He revealed Anasuya's greatness and purity. These three goddesses urged their consorts to test her (Anasuya's) greatness. In the guise of mendicants, the Trinity proceeded to ANasuya's Ashram, pretended to be hungry and asked for food. She promised to feed them after they had bathed. The Trinity came up with a new demand, i.e., to serve them food nakedly. Anasuya obliged the request, brought the Padatirtha of her husband, and sprinkled it on the Trinity.

Consequently, Brahma, Vishnu, and Siva became infants. Anasuya removed her clothes, began soothing them, put them in cradles and sang lullabies. The Trinity slept. Narada narrated the story to sage Atri, who became angry. The three divine ladies came to Anasuya and requested Anasuya to hand over their husbands. Anasuya's power of prayer transformed the Trinity into their original form. Sage Atri asked them to be their children. They obliged, and Attri and Anasuya had children, namely Chandra, Dattatreya and Durvasa.

<u>Suchindram Temple and the Lingam:</u>

The Lingam represents the Trinity as per the wishes of sage Atri and Anasuya. This may be the only temple in India representing Brahma, Vishnu and Siva in Linga form at Suchindram. Brahma is at the bottom of the Linga, and Vishnu and Siva are at the top in the middle. There is a Nandi that is 13 feet tall, 21 feet long, and 10 feet wide.

<u>Regarding Puja:</u>

Puja activity is performed during the day but stopped after dusk, anticipating Indra's arrival to offer prayers at night.

<u>The Temple Architecture:</u>

The temple architecture of Suchindram is one of the richest in the world. The Gopuram, which is 134 feet high, is a gigantic structure containing beautiful sculptures based on scripture themes.

A hollow trunk of a 2500-year-old tree contains Brahma, Vishnu, and Siva in the form of Lingas. A milky white bull 800 years old has ceremonial carvings around its neck. The Dwarapalaka images are big and inspiring to look at. In front of the sanctum is a Mandapa of 32 pillars with beautiful carvings of the stories of the great epics of Ramayana and Anasuya.

There is a processional deity of Suchindra Perumal, a beautiful one in silver casing. In the temple corridors, there are many images of women carrying lamps, known popularly as 'Deepa Lakshmi'. Unfortunately, the images were damaged by Tippu Sultan and his followers, who plundered the temple. Later, some of them were renovated. The art is so fine that minute details of the sculptures are visible. The four musical pillars in the northern corridor catch the eyes of art lovers, producing different sounds and creating an atmosphere as if a musical party is providing a symphony of the music dedicated to the Lord of the Temple.

Vasanta Mandapam is dedicated to Vinayaka. In a small temple, the image of Umadevi appears to be a promoter of 'dharma' named 'Dharma Samvardhini'. Carvings on pillars are realistic, and the portrayal of Hanuman in Asoka forest is one such.

Another sculptured corridor is called Chitra Sabha, where Nataraj's idol is, and another depicts Siva as a mendicant. Another carving relates to Lord Krishna and Gopikas' episode with meticulous details.

There are numerous idols of Ganesh, the God of success, such as Maya Ganapathi, Sakti Ganapati, Vallabha Ganapati, etc. There is also a small wood temple containing Rama and Sita. Thus, the Suchindram temple, its mandapas, pillars, and carvings are the most beautiful. One can only see and enjoy them.

Brihadiswara Temple of Tanjore

Tanjore, also known as 'Tajavur', is the district headquarters of Tamilnadu. Thanjavur is a Tamil name. Tanjore's former name was Tanjai. 'Tanjum' was a demon who became a problem for the locals. Hence, Lord Vishnu destroyed the demon. The latter requested Vishnu to name the place after him, and his request was granted.

<u>Background of the Temple:</u>

The Chola emperor Rajaraja (984-1014 AD) had a dream in which the Lord commanded him to build a temple. Hence, this was a dream project. The temple, also known as Rajarajeswaram, was built using granite transported from a long distance. The temple construction began in 1003 AD and was completed in 1008 AD, i.e., five years duration; some say it was 12 years for completion.

<u>The Temple:</u>

This magnificent temple of Brihadiswara or Rajarajeswara is the sole work of the Chola ruler to eliminate black leprosy. Siva Lingam was brought from the Narmada River by 64 merchants. The temple is the tallest in South India, akin to the Orissan style, and has been a holy place since sage Naimisaranya lived in meditation here.

<u>The Vimana:</u>

The Vimana built over the sanctum Santorum is 216 feet high with 14 stories.

<u>Gopurams:</u>

The towers of the temple are the Gopurams. In South India, there are four entrances and four Gopurams. Generally, the Vimana usually overshadows the Gopurams as they are high. But in the context of this Tanjore Temple, the main temple is above the Gopuram, similar to the Bhuvaneswar or Orissan temples.

Brihadiswara temple, popularly known as the big temple, is a testimony of the grandeur of the Chola emperors. The two short Gopurams at the entrance contain beautiful sculptures like that of Krishna with Gopikas.

Figure 16: Brihadeeswara Temple of Tanjore

<u>Nandi:</u>

Nandi is placed separately in a Mandapa in the front part of the temple. It is enormous. Its height is 12 feet, length is 19 ½ feet, breadth is 8 ½ feet, and weight is 25 tons. It is made of a single stone. It is considered the second largest in India, the first being the biggest, situated in Lepakshi temple of Anantapur district of Andhra Pradesh. The Main Temple:

In the sanctum sanctorum of the main temple, one can have the darshan of 'Maha Linga Murthy' glowing with lustre. The tilak is beautiful, and the white cloth around the Linga denotes purity of heart. The gigantic 3.7-meter Lingam is one of the biggest in India and is made with granite procured from Narmada. Elegant sculptures are depicted. Beautiful Fresco paintings relating to Chola and Pandya times with the themes of mythological stories have been discovered recently.

The Goddess of the temple is Brihannayaki. The other sub-shrines are Ganesa, Subramanya, and Nataraja. Nataraja's figure is best in the south.

<u>Festivals:</u>

1. Raja Raja's birth star is celebrated one day every month
2. Krithika in Karthik Masa
3. 9-day annual festival celebrated in Vaisakha Masa

The Lord's services include the supply of Champaka flowers, Ghee for burning lamps, cooked rice, vegetable dishes, Ghee, Dal, rice boiled in milk, and Pan supari.

Brihadiswara temple is recognized as a World Heritage Centre, and the art, Fresco paintings and sculptures are protected by the Archeological Department of India.

Temples of Chennai

Sri Partha Sarathi Swamy Temple

This temple has been a vital place for Vaishnavite pilgrimage. We come to know about several saints singing about the deity. Sri Partha Sarathy Swamy temple is dedicated to Lord Krishna. The temple is in the Triplicane of Chennai near the seashore and is said to be one of the 108 Divyadhamas. The mythological name of the place is 'Vrindaranya'. In the 18 days of the Kurukshetra war, Sri Krishna played the role of a Charioteer or Saradhi to Arjuna or Partha. According to Brahmanda Purana, King Sumati had prayed to the Lord of Tirumala Sri Venkatesa worship to see him as Partha Sarathi. The Lord fulfilled the king's desire and came to Vrindavan. Vyasa presented Krishna's idol to the king. The same idol was installed as per the Agama sastras. Sri Krishna is in the temple with Balarama, Rukmini, Satyabhama, his son Pradyumna, and his grandson Aniruddha. This temple is the only one in India where Krishna appears with his family. Krishna is without Chakra and holds Conch (per the promise to Arjuna). The idol is 9 feet tall. There is a Pushkarini named Kairavi opposite the temple.

Festivals:

Bhahmotsavams are celebrated during April-May.

Sri Narasimha Swamy is worshipped in this temple named Sri Pellia-Singa-Perimal. A separate shrine is for Andal, the incarnation of Bhoodevi. Festivals (monthly and annual) are celebrated in the temple. Sri Ramanujacharya is given special prominence.

Sri Kapaleswara Temple

This temple is situated in Mylapur, Chennai. Goddess Parvathi, who is in the form of a 'Mayil' (peacock), performed penance here, so the name Mylapur is derived from it.

Kapaleswar temple is the most important shrine of Lord Siva in Chennai. It is located south of the Partha Sarathy temple near the beach. Presently, the region is the Santhome cathedral area. The temple suffered destruction due to the Portuguese capture of the region. A fragmentary inscription is found here. The present temple was rebuilt during Vijayanagar's time. Of course, the monuments were utilized in the new temple. 13th-century inscriptions reveal the history.

Siva appeared before Parvati with a begging bowl shaped like a Kapala. Hence, he is known as Kapaleswara. Dhwajastambha and Nandi are in between the sanctum and a Gopuram. Other structures are Vinayaka, Subramanya, and Navagrahas are present. In the sanctum, Vishnu, Brahma and Durga exist. Southern Mandapam is used for religious discourses, and the western contains Siva Lingam.

Brahmotsavams are celebrated from March to April. Parvati is known as Karpagamba. On this occasion, the deities are taken out in procession. It is said that Lord Sri Rama performed Brahmotsavam while visiting the place. Thus, the Kapaleswara temple of Chennai provides Bhakti, Spiritualism, and stories of epics related to the region.

Subramanyeswara Swamy Temples

Subramanya is often present with his family of Siva, Parvati and Ganesa. Subramanya is a many-titled deity. The devotees popularly worship him as Skanda, Kumara Swamy, Subramanya, Kartikeya etc. There are several temples in south India to this God. He was worshipped during the early centuries (A.D). Kartikeya is represented by one head and two arms. But he is also represented with six heads and 12 arms, and this form is called Shadanana Subramanya. He rides on a peacock with his two wives, Devasena on the left and Valli on the right. In his hands, he holds a Shakti kind of spear, arrow, sword, discus, noose, cock, bow, shield, conch and plough. He appears with one hand in Varada and the other in Abhaya mudra.

Further, he is described as an army commander (siding devatas) endowed with great strength and skill. He is regarded as a god of war. He appears as a guardian deity in many Siva temples.

In Tamilnadu state, Subramanya temples appear in large numbers next to Siva and Vishnu. Especially mention is made of six famous temples:

1. Palani Subramanyeswara
2. Tiruchendur Subramanyeswara
3. Tiruttani Subramanyeswara
4. Swamimalai Subramanyeswara
5. Tiruppara Kusram – Devasena – Kartikeya
6. Pazhamuthin cholai – Murugan Temple

Subramanyeswara Swamy temple of Palani

This temple is the most famous one in the Madurai district of South India. Subramanyeswara is the most revered god and is held in great adoration. There cannot be a temple in South India without a separate place allotted to Sri Subramanyeswara.

Location and Significance:

The temple is conspicuously located on a hill 450 feet in height, with 659 steps. The location is beautiful, and the western ghats are visible from the top of the hill. Subramanya is also mentioned as Murugan in ancient Sangam literature.

Composition of the Idol:

The idol comprises Navapashanams, or nine different kinds of minerals, by a sage called Bhoga. The posture of the deity is standing with a stout stick in the right hand (Dandam). Therefore, the deity is called Dandayudhapani. There are Rudraksha beads at the neck in the form of a garland. The Lord appears as an ascetic. Abhishekams are made to the Lord from sunrise to sunset in the following manner of ten types:

1. With gingelly oil
2. Trivaipodi
3. Rice powder
4. Turmeric powder
5. Pancha Amritam
6. Coconut water
7. Milk and honey
8. Rose water
9. Sandal paste
10. Vibhuti

After performing Abhishekam, the decoration and dressing of the Lord follow. Alankarams are varied:

1. Raja Alankara
2. Hunters (Vedan)
3. Sandal paste
4. Bala Subramanya
5. Vibhuti

Darshan starts from 6 AM. Pujas are performed in the morning, midday, evening and midnight(10 PM).

<u>Festivals</u>:

The main temple festivals are performed in January (Tai Poosam), April (Panguri Uttaram), May (Agni Nakshatra), June (Vaikuntham), and November (Skanda Shasti). In addition to these, there are regular festivals.

The car festival and Silver Car festival are attended by many people, not only from Tamilnadu but also from Kerala. Mohammadans also pray to him and regard him as Palani Baba. They perform the prayer on the veranda around the Sanctum-Sanctorum.

<u>Sthala Purana or Legend:</u>

A legend defines the name of the place Palani, and the story is related to Subramanya or Kumara Swamy and his clash with his parents, Siva and Parvati, in the context of "Jnana phala". Sage Agastya once created two separate hills called 'Sivagiri' and 'Saktigiri'. The sage prayed for Siva and Parvati to appear as the divine couple on the top of these hills. Agastya became happy to fulfil his desire. The sage commissioned his disciple Idumban to carry the hills to further south. Idumban carried the hills in a 'Kavadi' (A pole kept on shoulders with weights on either side). On the way, he took a rest at Palani, where Lord Subramanyam was present being upset with his divine parents due to his brother who outwitted him in the competition held by his parents, which tells that a rare fruit will be gifted to one who goes round the world and returns first. Subramanyam started on his peacock and came back thinking he came first. In the meantime, Ganesh went around his parents saying that all the worlds were within his parents and got the prize. Bala Subramanyam got angry, but Siva pacified him, saying he (Subramanyam) was the fruit (Jnana Phala). Hence, the place, Palani, became significant and remained a great pilgrimage centre.

There are several Mandapams on the steps leading to the temple. On the other hill (nearby) is the figure of Idumban, who brought in Kavadi. The Kadamba tree, which is supposed to be the 'Sthala Vriksha,' is holy here. The flowers are Subramanya Swamy's favourites. A tank called Saravana Tirtham is present where the Lord took his six-faced form (Shanmukha).

<u>Peoples Belief:</u>

Devotees strongly believe they will be relieved from Leukoderma and Asthma by a dip in Saravana Tirtha and receiving Abhisekha Tirtham. Further on the vow, they carry miniature Kavadis, a daily sight in the temple. This temple is one of the wealthiest in South India. Nearby this temple, there is another temple of Nava Durga (Sri Bhuvaneswari) and

Marakatha Lingam. Next to Tamilians, Malayalis also visit the temple in large numbers. The deity sits on a peacock throne in a Padmasana posture (Bala Subramanyam).

Subramnya Temple of Tiruchendur

Tiruchendur is 700 km from Chennai, 100 km from Kanyakumari, and 60 km from Tirunelveli. The temple is situated in the extreme southeast part of India and has been a famous pilgrimage centre for more than 2000 years. Subramanyeswar temple is a seashore temple (On the Gulf of Mannar). The tides of the sea wash the foot of the temple. It would not be an exaggeration to say that no other temple has such a beautiful appearance. The pilgrims bathe in one of the 9 Tirthams here to attain miraculous benefits. According to a source, Lord Brahma restored his lost head (One of the five heads lost due to Siva's anger) here. The temple of Tiruchendur, which is supposed to be the second one next to Palani, is mainly liked by Subramanya.

This shore temple was originally for Lord Siva. However, the shrine commemorates Subramanya's victory over the demons Sura Padma and Tarakasura. At the request of the devatas, Siva sent his son Karthikeya / Murugan / Skanda / Subramanya to fight with the asuras (6 days). Subramanya fought with them, and the Asuric forces were defeated, relieving the devatas.

The temple and the Lord:

The temple construction was a very modest one. But during the past 1000 years, many additions were made by successive rules like the Pandyas and Cheras.

The Gopuram is on the west instead of the east. This 300-year-old temple is nine stories high and 137 feet wide. In the 9th storey, a giant bell was fixed between 1832 and 1839.

<u>Dutch raids on the temple:</u>

In 1648 AD, the Dutch raided the temple and carried away the idol of the Lord. A storm created havoc, and they threw away the image. The local ruler ordered a Panchaloha idol, and it was ready. However, the original one was traced and reinstalled in the temple (1653 AD). Subramanya here is in a standing posture facing east. Near him is the Siva Lingam. There is a pillared corridor with a prominent figure of Karthikeya seated on a peacock.

In northern Prakara, there is a shrine to Lord Vishnu (Venkatesa Perumal), along with Gaja Lakshmi, Rangamathi, Sridevi, and Bhudevi.

Inside the temple, a series of murals depict the Dutch incursions into Tiruchendur (During the reign of Tirumalanayaka, Madurai ruler).

<u>Festivals:</u>

Several festivals are celebrated throughout the year, and Tiruchendur has become the busiest pilgrimage centre. Brahmotsavams are celebrated for six days. The temple owns enough properties for its maintenance and celebrations.

Sri Subramanya Swamy temple – Tiruttani

Sri Subramanya Swamy temple in Tiruttani is on a small hill with 365 masonry steps. Explaining its importance, some say it is the first of the six great temples of the Lord, while others say it is the second one. However, it is noted that Swamy resides here in bliss after his marriage with Valli. The mission of the Lord is completed with the suppression of the demons. Peace and tranquillity were established.

Tiruttani is the place where Subramanya was cooled down. 'Tiru' means sacred, and 'Tani' means cooling down. Tiruttani was also known as 'Cheruttani' – 'Cheru' means anger, and 'Tani' means cooling down. As Kailas is the abode of Siva, Tiruttani is the chosen place of Subramanya Swamy, otherwise known as Skandagiri.

<u>The greatness of the Lord:</u>

After killing Ravana, Sri Rama rediscovered this holy place and worshipped the Lord. Arjuna visited during his pilgrimage. Lord Indra worshipped the Lord thrice daily and got back his wealth. Vasuki, the serpent king, was healed of his injuries when he was used as a rope to churn Amrita from the sea (Ksheera Sagara). Sages like Agastya worshipped.

<u>The uniqueness of the Temple:</u>

The distribution of food to people experiencing poverty is unique. Feeding those who are in need is considered a holy activity. The devotees' requests are fulfilled immediately; hence, the Temple is known as 'Kshanikachalam'.

There is a sacred tank at the foot of the hill where the float festival is celebrated for three days. Thousands of devotees attend with 'Kavadis'. Sage Narada liked this place, which is known as 'Naradapriyam'.

Swami Malai Temple

This temple on a hillock near Kumbhakonam and Subramanya Swamy is worshipped as Swaminatha Swamy.

<u>The Story:</u>

Lord Siva forgot the 'Pranava Mantra' due to a curse by sage Bhriga. Siva asked Subramanya about the mantra, and he said he knew it. He said he would say it on the condition that Siva should accept him as his Guru. Siva agreed and learned the mantra, treating his son as a 'Guru'. The temple of Swaminatha is on the hillock, and the temple of Siva is at the foot of the hillock.

<u>The Temple:</u>

The temple measures 300 feet by 296 feet and has three Prakarams. There are three beautiful gopurams on the eastern, western and southern sides. The southern Gopuram is the biggest (Rajagopuram). Pandyan king Varaguna Pandya installed Sundareswar and Meenakshi Amman in Swamimalai, worshipped the divine couple, and constructed a big temple on the ground floor. The hillock is about 60 feet high, with 60 steps.

<u>The Deity:</u>

Sri Swaminatha is 6 feet tall, majestic and beautiful (Granite idol). The idol is quite captivating.

<u>Other Shrines:</u>

Vinayaka, Lakshmi, Sarasvati, and Visalakshi are the other deities.

The temple has one more speciality: the Lord is present with Devayani (this is the only temple). Swaminatha is known by names such as Jnana Pandita and Jnana Desika Guru. Indra's white elephant (Iravata) is present before the Lord instead of the peacock.

<u>Property of the Temple:</u>

This temple is supposed to be from the 2nd century BC during Paranthaka Chola. Its property consists of lands and valuable jewels, such as gold, diamonds, and rubies.

Worship on Krittika every month is compulsory in the temple calendar.

<u>Festivals celebrated:</u>

Festivals celebrated are Brahmotsava, Skanda Shasti, and Subramanya's marriage with Valli. Kanakabhishekam and Koti Archana are also performed. Devotees from far and near attend.

Tirupparan Kundram

Sri Subramanya Swamy temple is an ancient shrine in Tirupparan Kundram, 7 km southwest of Madurai. This temple's importance is that the marriage of Subramanya Swamy was celebrated here with the daughter of Indra, Devayani. Iravatam, Indra's elephant, took care of Amritavalli or Devayani. In Tamil, 'Deva' means celestial and 'Yani' means elephant.

Six sons of Parasura, the sage, had been cursed to become fish in Saravana pond (Poigai). For redemption, they prayed to Lord Subramanyam. They learned that the Lord would come to Tirupparan Kundram after defeating the demon Surapadma. They waited eagerly and received Subramanya. The Lord accepted to stay there. Viswakarma built a beautiful abode for his stay.

Indra, the king of angels, as a mark of his gratitude for relieving all devatas from 'asuras', desired to get his daughter Devayani married to Subramanya. The Lord agreed. Indrani (wife of Indra) and Devayani came from Mount Meru. The marriage, held in Tiruppan Kundram, was attended by Brahma, Vishnu and Siva, and their consorts. This marriage is said to be the spiritual fusion of the divine with a human, leading to bliss.

<u>The Temple:</u>

The temple is at the foothill. The innermost Prakaram is carved out of a single rock and is a cave temple. Pandyas built the temple. The Nayaks completed the outer portion of the temple. The present temple owes its existence to the efforts of the Tirumalanayaka and later Ravi Manganamma (Late 17th century). The sanctum is rectangular.

The other deities are Vishnu, Durga and Ganesa. Narasimha and Nataraj are present outside the sanctum. Abhishekam is performed to his trident and not the moola virat. Rajagopuram is quite impressive. Tirtham (Saravana) is essential in the context of the Lord's pooja activities, and devotees dip in it.

Murugan temple of Pazhamuthircholai

Skanda Purana and Nakkeevar's 'Tiru Murugatrupadai' are the sources of information about this Murugan temple situated just 4 km up the hill of 'Azagar'.

<u>Sthala Purana:</u>

An old saint 'Avvaiyar' was resting under a tree. Murugan wanted to test the saint and assumed the form of a small boy. He sat on one of the tree branches and asked the saint his willingness to taste the fruits (roasted). After tasting, the saint (female) was surprised to know that they were warm as if freshly roasted. The lady looked up, but the boy disappeared. Avvaiyar realized that it was the Leela of the Lord.

The temple is the smallest. The gopuram is four-tiered. Lord Subrahmanya/Murugan is present with his trident (Vel). He is depicted with four hands; Valli and Devayani are by his side. It is said that with the darshan of this Lord, one would be blessed with wealth and health.

Dandayudhapani Temple(Chennai)

This temple is one of the most famous temples in Chennai. He is the God of Vadapalani, otherwise known as Vadapalani andavar. Lord Subrahmanya Swamy is the God of the temple.

If we go back to the temple's history, there are interesting, informative stories. Annaswamy Nayagar is a devotee of the Swamy but has no money to buy a picture of God and God appeared in the dream of the shop owner who sells photos of the Lord and directed him to present a picture to Annaswamy, who treasured the picture and worshipped at home. Growing old, he searched for his successor to worship and conduct pooja to the image. God showed Ratnavel Chettiyar to be his successor. God appeared to Chettiyar in a dream and ordered him to go to Annaswamy. Chetty was happy and celebrated 'Shasti' day (the 6th day of the bright fortnight) and met Annaswamy. After his death, Chetty constructed a tomb for him. The house of Annaswamy Nayagar is converted into a temple. A sculptor was called for the image of the Subrahmanya. The sculptor observed fast and silent for 40 days and completed carving the stone image of the Lord.

Ratnavali performed Lord Subrahmanya's Kumbhabhishekam ceremony at Vadapalani on an auspicious day. After Ratnavali, God showed another successor named Tambiran. He performed poojas and collected funds for the construction of the temple. His dream came true, and the temple was completed. That is the beautiful temple of Vadapalani.

Apart from the God Subrahmanya Swamy, are many sannidhis devoted to Vinayaka, Siva, Parvati, Shanmukha with Valli and Devayani, etc. Dandayudhapani is a replica of his original in Palani.

Sri Ranganatha Swamy Temple – Srirangam

Sri Ranganatha Swamy temple is the biggest temple in India. The consort of the Lord is Ranganayaki. This temple is one of the great Vaishnavite temples, and others being Lord Venkateswara of Tirumala-Tirupati, Govindaraja Swamy of Tirupati, Ranganayaka Swamy of Nellore in AP, Sri Ananta Padmanabha Swamy of Trivandrum. Further, the Lord of Srirangam is one of the 108 Divya Desams. Tirupati is the richest temple in the South, or maybe in India, and Srirangam is the most visited temple in the South.

Srirangam is a 600-acre island town surrounded by the Cauvery water. The temple area occupies 156 acres. The details of the temple are amazing to know. It is 240 feet tall, and the 13-tiered Raja Gopuram, weighing nearly 25000 tons, is quite appealing. There are 21 gopurams. The temple is so big that whoever enters the temple needs help finding their way out.

According to a book on '108Divya Desams' (Vaishnavas) published in Telugu, the Srirangam temple consisted of 7 prakaras known as 'Sapta prakaras' (enclosures).

- In the first Prakara, there is 'Garbhalaya', known as 'Dharma Prakara', with a length of 240 feet and width of 180 feet. Sriranganatha is seen in a reclining posture. In this prakara, one may find dwarapalakas, yagasala, 'Vinaja Bhavi', 'Viswaksena's sannidhi', 'Pagalpattu Mandapa', 'Chilukala Mandapa' and 'Kannan Sannidhi'.

- 'Pavitrotsava Mandapa' also consists of Sannidhis of Hayagriva, Sarasvati devi and Perumal. Unjala Mandapa and Dhajarohana mandapa are the other ones.
- There is Garudan sannidhi, Vali, Sugriva sannidhi are in the 3rd prakara.
- Sannidhis of Kuntalwar, Garudalwar prevails. Sri Ranga Nachiyar, the Jagannatha sannidhi is to be seen. 1000-pillared hall (Veyi Kalla mandapam) is where Sri Ranganatha rests. Sannidhis of Kodandarama, Parthasaradhi, Dasavataras and Ramanujacharya (Udayalwar) are in this prakara.
- The 5th prakara is known as Uttara Veedhi. During Brahmotsavas, the Swamy passes through the crowds, giving darshan and blessings.
- Chitra Veedhi is the 6th prakara. Sannidhis of Vedanta Desikar and Jagannadh exist, and during Brahmotsavam, this is also busy.
- Adavalanjan Veedhi is the 7th Prakara, the outer wall (like a fort). One can go to Teppotsav, passing through the western Dwara through this.

<u>The historicity of Srirangam:</u>

According to the epigraphical sources, the temple's history dates back to the 10th century. Almost all the major dynasties, the Cholas, the Cheras, the Pandyas, and the Hoyasalas, contributed to the development of the temple, making it the biggest temple in India. Later, the great Vijayanagara rulers elevated the prominence of the temple to its present position. The Nayakas contribution is also, nonetheless. Sculptural splendour goes to these rulers.

Figure 17: Sri Ranganatha Swamy Temple of Sri Rangam

14th-century Muslim invasions caused damage to the temple. Malik Kafur's and Ulug Khan's raids severely damaged the growth of the temple. However, in 1371, the Vijayanagara troops stormed the Muslim invaders and restored worship. The glory made the people feel the temple as 'Bhooloka Vaikuntham'.

<u>Sthala Purana:</u>

1. Lord Brahma worshipped the idol of Ranganatha, keeping it in his possession.
2. It was given to the Suryavamshis of Ikshwakur. Lord Sri Rama worshipped it and kept it in his palace.
3. After Ravana Samhara, Vibheeshana proceeded to Ayodhya and saw the idol, requested Rama to give it, and the latter gave it to Vibheeshana on condition that it should not be kept on the ground. Vibhishana accepted, and while carrying, when he was in Srirangam, the idol became heaviest. Vibhishana was forced to keep it on the ground and installed it.
4. The shikhara appeared to be 'Om', which is interesting.

<u>Festivals of the Temple:</u>

Srirangam is said to be an extraordinary pilgrimage centre because of three things:

1. Importance of the place
2. Importance of the Lord and
3. Tirtha Pradhanyam.

Among the Tirthas, Chandra Pushkarini is situated in the temple complex, and the others are within a three—or four-km radius.

1. Lord Sri Rama started the Brahmotsavam as Tirthotsava (Punarvasu – Makara Masa)
2. Ramanuja started on Suddha Ekadasi (Kumbha masa)
3. Lord Brahma started
4. Chitri Brahmotsava (or) Viruppan Tirumal
5. 22 days Adhyayanotsav
6. Vaikunta Dwara Darsan (Dhana Sudha Ekadasi)
7. Tiruvaradhana Utsav (Kaikasi Dwadasi)

Lord Ranganadha is decorated on all occasions. Abhishekam is performed to the deity with Kaveri water brought in a silver vessel and placed on the Devasthanam elephant in a procession. The scholars chant Vedic mantras. Adi Sankaracharya installed a Janakarshana Yantra at Srirangam to attract pilgrims, just as he did in Tirumala, where he installed the Dhanakarshana Yantra. Sankara influenced power in the yantras, and it is a proven fact.

Ganesha Temples

Rock Fort Temple of Ganesha (Uchi Pillayar Temple)

Tiruchirapalli, or Trichy, is located south of Chennai and is well known for its famous rock, which is 275 feet high. The region is known as 'Dakshina Kailash'. Trichy was the seat of the Chola kings. The rock fort is the pride of this place. It is one of the oldest in the world, approximately 3800 million years, as old as the rocks of Green Land and older than the Himalayas.

The Rock Fort Temple had a temple complex consisting of three temples, namely Manikka Vinayaka Temple (at the foot of the hill), the Uchhi Pillayar (at the top of the hill), and the Thayumanavar or Mathru Butheswarar, Siva Temple in the middle of the hill.

The temple view is lovely, with eagles wheeling beneath and Trichi sprawling around.

Sri Uchhi Pillayar Temple:

This temple is dedicated to Lord Ganesh.

Legends:

Two interesting legends are connected with the 'rock' – one relating to Adisesha and the other to Vibhishana.

1. Once, when Lord Siva was doing penance on Mount Meru, the heavenly powers like Brahma, Vishnu, Indra and Adisesha were waiting at the entrance to get a darshan of the Lord. Adisesha was praised by one and all for carrying the seven worlds on his

head, which enraged 'Vayu'. He became jealous and challenged Adisesha for a trial of strength. Adisesha took up the challenge. In the competition, Adisesha coiled around Mount Meru with all his might, and Vayu tried to unloose. In this fight, the whole world suffered from hurricanes and storms. Vayu could not loosen the grip of Adisesha. Finally, Siva intervened and asked Adisesha to slacken the grip a bit. Vayu threw in all his might, resulting in the split of Mount Meru into three pieces. One fell in Sri Kalahasti, the second in Trichy (Rock Fort), and the third in Ceylon.

2. Vibhishana episode: When Vibhishana was carrying the Ranga Vimana (special chariot-like conveyance). Lord Vishnu is inside, and Nagaraja holds the umbrella. Narada, Tumbura, Vishvaksena, sages, and saints follow. This was Ikshvakus. Vibhishana halted at Trichy to perform religious rights) presented by Rama to Srilanka, Vinayaka intervened in the guise of a Brahmachari and placed the vimana on the ground, which got rooted. Vibhishana became angry and chased the boy. He ran to the rock's summit and transformed himself into Lord Vinayaka. There is another Vinayaka temple at the foot of the steps of the rock.

Avvayyar

Avvayyar is a staunch devotee of Ganesh. According to a local legend, Avvayyar, the great lady devotee of Ganesh, was given 'Swarga Prapti' by Lord Ganesh. He blessed her by listing his trunk. People believe they will get salvation by worshipping Ganapati, also known as Avvayyar.

Ankola Ganesh

The temple is located near Ponneri in Chennai. The region is known as Chaturveda Puram since ancient times. Lord Siva appeared before sage Agastya and said he was in the Chaturvedapura under an 'Ankola tree'. Further, the sage was ordered to prepare 108 Saikata Lingas. The sage prepared byt surprisingly all the Lingas took the shape of Ganesa. Agastya was shocked and prayed Siva, and the latter reminded him that he had forgotten to pray Ganesa before starting the work. The sage prayed to Ganesa, made one more Saikata Linga, and installed it with Ganesa.

The other idols in the temple are Tandava Krishna, Anjaneya, Sivakami Amman, Astottara Valli and Subramanyeswara.

Vinayaka of Kanyakumari

The temple of Vinayaka was the 'pratista' of Parasurama in Kanya Kumari on the seashore, and hence, this is known to be a Parasurama Vinayaka. The pratista was done just before the establishment of Kanyakumari Amman. This was done with a specific purpose: Vinayaka would help retain the deity there with all glory. Lord Indra also established another Vinayaka called Indrakantha Vinayaka.

Vaatapi Ganapati Temple (Tiruchengattam)

The temple is 23 km away from Maayavaram of Tiruvayur. It is said to be from Pallan times, probably during the 7th century AD, and was built by a general of Pallava kings named Chiru Tondar. The idol is said to have been brought from Badami or Vaatapi; hence, God is known as Vaatapi Ganapati.

Vinayaka Temple of Kumbakonam

There is a temple of Vinayaka on the bank of a tank. According to legend, once, a sugarcane vendor came to the bank of the tank with 1000 sugarcanes and rested for some time. Vinayaka, in the guise of a Brahmin boy, went to the vendor and asked for a sugarcane, but the latter being a miser, refused to give the sugarcane. But Vinayaka pulled one out of the bundle and ran away. The vendor chased him but failed to catch him, and the boy ran fast and disappeared into the temple complex.

Further, all the sugarcanes became tasteless. Having realized this, the vendor prayed Vinayaka. Since then, Vinayaka has been known as 'Karumbayiram' – 'Karumba' means sugarcane, and 'Airam' means 1000.

Another temple in Kumbakonam is known as 'Sweta Ganapati', an ancient one. At the time of Ksheera Sagara Madhanam, angels installed Sweta Ganapati on the banks of the Kaveri River, and it was white because of milk and foam.

Karpaga Vinayaka

This temple is an ancient one. The Lord is said to be 'Karpaga' because he is related to 'Kalpavriksha'. This temple is considered to have been built by the Pallava rulers. The trunk of Vinayaka turns right side here, a rare one. The idol is carved in a cave, and its height is 6 feet.

Mukti Ganapati of Tiruppavanam

The temple is situated on the banks of the river Vaigai. This temple of the Sivaganga region is holy and thus is considered Kasi and Rameswaram. Devotees visit this place to perform 'Pitru Karyams'.

Ganesh Temple of Pillayar Patti

This temple is around 12 km from Karaikudi. Pillayar means Ganesh, and Patti denotes village. This temple is quite famous in Tamil Nadu. This temple is said to be of 400 AD. There is also an idol of Mushika, Lord's vehicle. Devotees express their desires in the ear of the Mushika.

Ganesa shrines of Mayavaram

'Mayavaram' is considered the Benaras of southern India, situated in the Chennai – Tiruchirapally line. There are three shrines of Vinayaka under different names:

1. Periya Vinayaka (Big) – Sthala Vinayaka is enshrined on the southern side.
2. Agasthya Vinayaka: Sage Agasthya installed and conducted worship.
3. Kalanjiya Pillaiar or Granary Vinayaka or the Guard of the Granary.

Chidambaram (Sri Nataraja Temple)

The famous Sri Nataraja Swamy temple is situated at Chidambaram. This temple is also known as Ponnambalam and Tillai. The other names for this place are 'Pulliur', 'Vyaghrapuram', etc., or referred to as 'Koil' (The house of God).

The temple is dedicated to Lord Siva, who is seen in the dancing posture (Cosmic dance of bliss), otherwise known as 'Ananda Tandavam'. The speciality of the Chidambaram temple is that an idol, rather than the Lingam, represents Siva. Therefore, this is a rare temple.

Nataraja performed the 'Ananda Tandavam', or the dance of bliss, in the presence of Sivakama Sundari and all the Gods and sages. Devotees Patanjali and Vyaghrapada, too, attended to witness. The sages requested Siva to continue the Cosmic dance at 'Ponnambalam' ('Pon' means God, and 'Ambalam' means temple) forever. Siva or Nataraja obliged the request of the rishis and performed the cosmic dance at 'Chit Sabha' (innermost portion of the temple). Another dance form of Siva is 'Urdhwa Tandavam', in which Siva defeated Kalikadevi.

Chidambaram temple is known as 'Akasa Lingam' (embodiment of Siva in space). The Sangam literature, which is 2000 years old, quotes references to this. People often speak about 'Chidambara Rahasyam', meaning no image or Lingam exists. Devotees worship Siva as Akasa Linga.

The Temple:

The existing temple owes its greatness to the Cholas. The roof is gold-plated. The Pandyas and Vijayanagara rulers made handsome endowments. The image of Sri Krishnadevaraya can be seen in the northern gopuram.

Siva's form of Nataraja is a symbol of good interpretation. He performs fivefold activities:

1. Creation
2. Preservation
3. Destruction
4. Veiling and
5. Blessing

Siva is represented by three eyes, symbols of the Sun, Moon, and Fire, and of time past, present, and future. The third eye is located between the eyebrows (eye of wisdom). He wears a necklace of skulls, symbolizing he is the Lod of destruction. He wears ahes on his body. He also wears Rudrakshas. He also wears Upavita (thread).

Sivakami Amman's temple is a separate temple in the outermost prakaram. The walls contain several carvings, and the ceiling contains murals (Nayaka period). There is a thousand pillared hall that looks like a chariot with elephants.

There is another temple of Govindaraja Swamy (one of the 108 Vaishnava Divya Desams). It appears to be a fusion of Saivism and Vaishnavism. Pundarikavalli Thayar, too, had a separate shrine.

Dr Ananda Kumara Swamy describes the form of Nataraja as the synthesis of religion, science and art.

Worship or puja is performed daily six times to the Lord.

- Puja to the 'Spatika Linga' with ghee, milk, curd, rice, sandal and Bhasma (ash) abhisheka.
- Abhisheka to Nataraja's Ratna vigraha
- Puja is performed by noon, and the temple is closed by 4:30 PM
- Puja by 6:00 PM
- Puja by 8:00 PM
- The last puja at 10:00 PM

With Pavalimpu seva, the daily puja activity comes to an end.

Chidambaram is thus famous in central Tamilnadu since Siva as Nataraja has established as the 'Dancer of the Universe'. Chidambaram is India's holiest Siva shrine, and the temple style is Dravidian. Siva and Kali got into a dance-off, which Vishnu judged. Siva won and finally got the title of Nataraja, Lord of Dance. Big Nandi and Suvarna Koneru are attracting pilgrims.

Tiruvannamalai (Teju Lingam) – Arunachaleswar

Sri Arunachaleswar temple is one of the biggest in southern India, around 217 feet tall. Its Rajagopuram is imposing, with 11 stories, and is one of the tallest Gopurams in our country. Sri Krishnadevara Raya started the work that Sevvappa Nayak I (1532-1560), Nayak of Tanjore, completed.

<u>Historical backdrop of the Temple:</u>

History is inseparable from the origin of the temple and its growth. Without the mention of the Cholas, it would be incomplete to speak of the temple. The Cholas, the Vijayanagar, and Nayak kings did most of the renovation and extension of the temple. The services of the Pandyas and Hoyasalas are also memorable, including financial support for the temple's upkeep. The epigraphical sources in Sanskrit, Tamil, Telugu and Kannada provide ample information.

<u>The Legend or Sthala Purana:</u>

Once, Lord Brahma and Lord Vishnu argued to ascertain superiority over the other. The issue was brought to Lord Siva for resolution. Siva appeared before them in the form of 'Jyoti'. They were instructed to find out the beginning and end of the Jyoti. Brahma took the form of a swan, and Vishnu took the form of a Boar and tried to find the truth. Brahma and Vishnu failed in this mission and prayed that the Jyoti would take a concrete form.

Being pleased, Siva took the form of a Linga at the foot of a hill, Arunachala Hill, which later became the location of the temple.

<u>Umadevi Episode:</u>

Umadevi was engaged in penance but disturbed by Mahishasura. Hence, she slew him in the month of Karthika; Siva appeared as a flame on the Tiruvannamalai hill and merged Umadevi / Parvati into the left half of his body. Siva is, therefore, Arthanareeswara Murthy and Jyoti Swarupa.

Ancient Tamil classics mention that this temple dates back to 3000 years. Spread over 25 acres of land, it consists of seven prakaras or enclosures. Umadevi's shrine is situated in the third Prakara. The images of Ganesa and Subramanya, along with Dwarapalakas, are present in the same Prakara. In the first Prakara, Arunachaleswar exists.

The architectural and sculptural importance is high. There is a 1000-pillared mandapa and tank. Patala Lingam is said to be a basement shrine.

The chief festival of Tiruvannamalai is held in Karthika month on Krithika nakshatra. On this day, Jyoti appears at the top of the hill.

Tiruvallur (Sri Veera Raghava Perumal Temple)

This temple is one of the 108 Divya Desams. The temple originated in Kritayuga and was named Bhikksheswararanyam (Sages live on alms in the forest). The God, Sri Veera Raghava Perumal, is said to be a form of Lord Vishnu. Kanakavalli Thayar is the Goddess.

The deity facing est gives darshan as 'Bhujangasayana'. The gopuram is big with sculptural beauty. There is a kalyana mandapa. The other gods in the temple are Sita, Rama, Lakshmana and Sri Lakshmi Narasimha Swamy. Sri Chakralwar and Tirtheswara Swamy also exist here.

Tiruvaiyaru (or) Tiruvarur

<u>The prominence of the place:</u>

Turuvarur is a land of five rivers namely, Kaveri, Vennar, Kudamurutti, Vettar and Koleroon.

Tiruvarur is very famous for the birth of great Carnatic musicians. Although Carnatic music belonged to the four states of south India (Andhra Pradesh, Karnataka, Tamilnadu and Kerala), it flourished in Tamilnadu. Several Vaggeyakaras like Tyagaraja, Muttuswamy Dikshitar and Syama Sastry (The trinity of Carnatic music) composed their Kritis in Telugu. However, Tamilnadu is the homeland of Carnatic music.

The place is famous for the shrine of Tyagaraja – A Lord Shiva temple and Saint Tyagaraja of the Carnatic music trinity is named after this deity. Lord Shiva (Tyagaraja)'s consort, Parvathi is worshipped here as Kamalambika.

The temple is gigantic in structure. The annual festival of this saint singer is performed. The colossal construction of the temple is appealing, and the temple complex is in an area of around 20 acres, and the main shrine with a length of 846 feet and a breadth of 666 feet. Several tanks are attached to the temple. This temple is believed to have been initiated by Pavvavas, current temple is believed to be constructed during 9th century by Cholas and later expanded by Vijayanagara rulers.

Figure 18: Sri Tyagaraja Temple of Tiruvarur

Sri Panchanadeswara Temple

As cited above, the region is famous for its five rivers, so the temple's name is justified. It is the biggest temple complex, with a 15-acre area.

Sthala Purana:

The episodes of the great devotees are important. Sucharitan was a great devotee of Lord Siva. Siva saved him from death, as in the case of Markandeya.

Siva Lingam is powerful here. A visit to this temple is considered equivalent to a visit to Kailasa, the abode of Siva.

Royal Patronage:

The Cholas, Pandyas, and Vijayanagara monarchs patronized the temple as per the inscriptional sources.

The seven-tiered raja gopuram at the entrance is marvellous. Dharmasamvarthani is the divine consort. It is in a separate shrine with two prakaras named Dakshina and Uttara Kailasam. The trinity of music praised Amman.

Tyagaraja was a great devotee of Sri Rama and composed Kritis on him. He also composed songs on Vedas, Upanishads and the epics. The philosophy of life has been transmitted through his music, who lived and died in Tiruvaiyaru. 'Aradhanothsavams' will be celebrated here and in prominent places in south India for five days in January (Pushya Bahula Panchami – Samadhi day of Saint Tyagaraja). Thousands of musicians render performances.

The idol of the saint singer was installed in 1921, and in 1925, Kumbhabhishekam was held. In 1938, the shrine was completed.

Patteswaram (Siva Temple of Dhenupureswara and Durga Devi)

Patteswaram is eight km from Kumbhakonam in the temple belt of Tiruvaiyaru – Tanjore and Kumbhakonam.

Dhenupureswara:

'Dhenu' refers to 'Kamadhenu', the celestial cow. There is a storytelling about Kamadhenu. She had four daughters, one of whom was 'Patti', a great devotee of Lord Siva. The Lord is very pleased with her worship, and the place's name goes by 'Patti' and 'Iswara,' i.e., 'Patteswaram'. Siva, the chief deity, goes by Patteswara or Dhenupureswara.

The Temple:

The Patteswara temple is a vast campus with five towers and three prakaras. It is said that Parvati did penance here. A holy tank in front of the temple has an image of Vinayaka (Ajna Ganapati). Another sacred tirtha is named 'Gayatri Tirtha', which originates from sage Viswamitra, who received the Gayatri mantra from Goddess Gayatri.

Goddess Durga:

Goddess Durga is a powerful deity. The Chola kings installed and worshipped the God. After the fall of the Chola empire, Goddess Durga's idol was shifted to the Patteswaram temple. With the blessings of the Goddess, they have constructed 1000 Siva Linga kshetrams and performed Kumbhabhishekams. The Goddess (Black granite stone idol) is imposing and awe-inspiring. She is in a standing posture with a lion. The head of the buffalo and demon Mahishasura look in disguise. She holds Sankha and Chakra in her hands. Further, she has a parrot in her left hand and the mare of a lion in the right. She has different weapons in her hands.

Lord Sri Rama's visit:

Lord Sri Rama visited the temple to get rid of his Chayadosha for killing Ravana, though he is an incarnation of Vishnu. He installed a Lingam named Rama Lingam here.

Airavateerswar Temple of Darasuram

Darasuram is situated in the Tanjore district, which has become eminent due to the famous Temple of Airavateeswar, the Siva temple. Apart from the holy or spiritual aspect, the TempleTemple is well known for its architectural and sculptural excellence. The Temple's condition is deteriorating; it lacks a proper main entrance and is in poor financial condition.

<u>The Temple:</u>

The Temple was well built with seven walls and several prakaras. The TempleTemple remains in splendid isolation in a dilapidated condition with a beautifully carved entry gate. The ASI (Archeological Survey of India) rebuilt the TempleTemple, a world heritage monument. Regarding the appearance of the Temple, Percy Brown says: *"The Temple consists of a long rectangular building of no great height with a pyramidical tower or Vimana. Further, it had small but compact buildings of notable expressiveness."*

The original name of the Temple is Rajarajeswaram. According to some legendary sources, some stories were focused. One demon worshipped Siva with his 1000 wives. Secondly, Lord Yama bathed in the holy tank here to get rid of a disease caused by a curse. Later, the tank is known as 'Yama Tirtham'. The celestial elephant, too, worshipped here to get relief from sins. Hence, the Lord is known as Airavateeswara.

There is a small Nandi in a separate mandapa. The temple consists of the sanctum, antarala mandapa and raja gambhira mandapa. As cited above, the Temple is famous for architecture and sculpture. Durga, Nandi, and other carved figures can be seen. The Goddess in the Temple is Devanayaki. Further, all the carved poses of Bharata Natyam are inscribed on stone. Themes of social conditions are also presented. A stone image of Ravana carrying Kailas is a genuine specimen of artistry.

Sri Vaidyanatha Swamy Temple of Vaitheeswaran Koil

Vaitheeswaran Koil is one of the most important Saivaite temples on the northern Kaveri River. It is also known by several other names: Ialapuri, Vedapuri, Panarapuri, Pathiripuri, Angarakapuram, and Ambikapuram.

Lord Siva is worshipped here as a divine doctor. Hence, he is known as Vaideeswaran. He cured Angaraka of his leprosy and healed the wounds of the forces of Subramanya during his battle with demons. People believe that God can cure 5000 diseases. His consort assists Siva in this activity with medicated oil in her Sannidhi. So, she is called 'Taila Nayaki'. Skin diseases and mental illness are cured here by dipping in Tirtha and offering prayers.

The Temple:

The 5-tiered Rajagopuram invites devotees. Vaideeswaran Koil is important in different ways (Religious, medicinal, and astrological). It is famous for astrologers who practice Nadi Jyotishyam, which tells a person's past and future based on ancient manuscripts. Data about almost everybody on Earth is available.

The temple is beautiful, with architectural and sculptural elements (Old Pallaval). It has majestic towers on the east and western sides. From the entrance of the west, there are two Dhwajasthambas—one is Gold, and the other is silver.

The chief deity Vaidyanatha Eswarar and his consort is Taila Nayaki devi. There are many minor deities in the corridor. Dhanvantari, Murugan and Ganesa shrines also exist here. Sacred neem (Margosa) is the Sthalavriksha.

Tirthams:

1. The Siddhamruta tirtham is the most important and is in front of the Goddess temple. This Tirtha is called 'Goksheera Tirtha' (Kamadhenu bathed here).

2. Ikshasura tirtha tastes like cane juice.
3. Jatayu tirtham – Jatayu bathed here. Angaraka was released of his Leprosy.
4. Kodanda Tirtham – Sri Rama is enshrined here.

Lord Sri Rama and his brothers cremated Jatayu's body, known as 'Jatayu Kundam'. Sri Rama offered his prayers to his ancestors. There are several other tirthas which are supposed to be less important:

- Indrapati
- Sarvamukti
- Pinaka
- Mangala
- Durvasa
- Gautama
- Vilva
- Muri
- Sanga Santana

Madapams: There are mandapams to conduct various temple activities, such as Asthana, Alankara, Chitra, Vasantha, Tirthavayu and Kalanjia.

Some saints who visited the temple are Tirujnana Sambandar, Arunagiri Nathar, Veduganta Desikar, Sirajnana Desikar, Kumara Guru, and Chidambaram Muni.

<u>Valuable assets of the temple:</u>

The landed properties of the temple are 1176 acres of dryland and 6,105 acres of wetland. 1,60,750 Rs worth of jewels (old data) to adorn the deities during festivals. Gold and silver covers for the images, gemset crown, etc, are in possession of the temple.

Papanasam(Temple of Papa Vinaseswarar)

River Tamravarni is connected with this place. Papanasam is otherwise called as Papavinasanam. To get relief from the sins committed by human beings, they are relieved with the darshan and worship of the deity Papavinaseswar. Papavinasam is at the foot of the mountain ranges and the waterfall. Agasthya installed the divine couple of Siva and Parvati at the shrine. Hence, the deity is called as Agasthiswara.

According to a legend, during the time of a Pandya king, people were severely oppressed, and hence, they fled away. Among the captives was a man with a son and a daughter who were separated and reached Benaras. Not knowing each other, they fell in love and married. Later, they realized the sin and got the advice of learned men. They wore black clothes and wandered at pilgrimage centres. As Papanasam, they bathed in the river, and their black clothes turned white, which means they are relieved of their sin. God appeared and granted them everlasting happiness.

<u>Papanasam and Panoramic view:</u>

Though the place is a small village, it is beautiful, consisting of halls and resting rooms. The river and the waterfalls attract people. Papanasam is a picturesque spot providing a panoramic view. Fish of all sizes and golden hues abound in the water and are fed by the pilgrims in fulfilment of their vows. If the fish are caught, they turn into blood and injure the eyesight of those who eat them.

Srivilli Puthur (Sri Andal Temple and Sri Vatapatra Sayi Temple)

This temple is a divya desam and one of the most sacred Vaishnava temples. It is 78 km from Madurai. Vatapatra Sayi was the original deity of Srivilli Puthur before Andal was born. Lord Vishnu is in a reclining posture on Adisesha. Sridevi and Bhudevi are at his lotus feet. The Lord has to be seen from three doorways. Narada, Tumbura, Sanath Kumara, Kinnera, the Sun and the Moon are on the sides.

Vatapatra Sayi has a separate temple by the side of the Andals. By the side of the temple is the Tulasi garden of Vishnuchittar, the father of Andal.

The temple's Rajagopuram is majestic at 192 feet tall with 11-tiered Gopurams.

<u>Legend – Andal's Birth:</u>

There is a legend about Andal's birth. Her spiritual descent can be traced to three female divinities, Sri-Bhoo and Neela. The energy of God is personified as a female (Sakthi). Sakthi was of 3 types:

1.   Iccha Sakthi
2.   Kriya Sakti and
3.   Sakshat Sakti

Sri-Bhoo and Neela comes under the Iccha Sakti. A detailed explanation is found in Sri Sukta of Yajurveda.

Andal is compared to Sita, who is Ayoni Sambhava. But Sita is the counterpart of Rama and Andal of Sri Ranganatha. Andal's spirited descent is to be associated with the worldly one.

<u>Vishnuchittar and Andal:</u>

Vishnuchittar was a great devotee of Vishnu. He had a Tulasi vana from which he collected the fragrant flowers and made wreaths to offer Vatapatra Sayi. One day, while digging his garden, Vishnuchittar found a glorious child (Andal) like Sita to Janaka (cited above). This is seen in Divyasuri charitra. Andal is Godadevi, who showed devotion and love towards Vishnu / Krishna. Vishnuchittar used to offer garlands to Lord Vishnu every day. Goda used to wear the garlands during his absence and observed her reflection in the water of a well. One day, her father noticed this and was shocked. Lord Vishnu/Ranganatha appeared to Vishnuchittar in a dream and told him that he was pleased or delighted with the garlands worn by Goda. Vishnuchittar realized that Goda was none else but Sri Maha Lakshmi. From then on, he named her Andal(ruler of the Universe). The Lord was pleased to merge her here, i.e., Srivulliputhur. Some say the story happened in Srirangam. In Srivilliputhur, 'Sri' means Andal.

<u>Tiruppavai:</u>

Thirty lyrical stanzas praising Ranganatha, known as Tiruppavai, are an outstanding composition of Tamil literature concerning poetry, beautiful language, and philosophy.

Andal's temple consists of a 2-tiered sanctum. The epigraphical sources reveal the history since the 10th century. Later additions were made to the temple during the Nayaka rulers' reign. There are beautiful wood carvings like Dasavataras. By the 17th century, massive renovations were made.

<u>The wooden car (Ratham):</u>

This is used during festivals, and it is the biggest and heaviest in India, with nine massive wheels. The Festival is the 'Adi festival' (5-6 days). Pilgrims attend in large numbers.

Madhurantakam

Madhurantakam of Chengalput district in Tamilnadu was once known as Bakularanyam, deriving its name from 'Bakula' flowers (sweet smelling). Lord Sri Rama, Lakshmana and Sita are the principal deities of this modest temple. Sri Karunakara Murthy is also in the temple. In Kritayuga, some devotees of Sri Narayana desire to know the path to salvation. Sri Narayana gave them his image in the form of Karunakara Murthy to pray and meditate to find the means of salvation.

<u>The Temple:</u>

This temple consists of Sri Rama, Lakshmana, and Sita. Hanuman was away to inform Bharata about Sri Rama's arrival. He came later and took a bath in the Pushkarini known as Ramachandra Pushkarini and saw the deities already installed. Hence, Hanuman's temple is on the bank of Pushkarini.

Legend:

A legend tells about Sri Rama's halt during his journey to Lanka. Then, sage Vibhandaka requested to visit the place on his return trip to Ayodhya. It is said that the Pushpakavimana carrying Rama, Lakshmana, Sita, and others stopped here automatically. Sri Rama clasped Sita's hands and helped her get down the steps of Pushpaka Vimana. This picture is of a temple that is worshipped. The image of 'Hastavalambana Darsan' (holding each other's hands) is to be seen, which is quite realistic. Madhurantakam is thus a great pilgrimage centre. Vaishnavite saint cum philosopher Sri Ramanuja had his rebirth here. Vaishnavites of Sri Rangam sent Peria Nambi to invite Ramanujacharya. Nambi took Ramanuja to the 'Bakula Tree' in the temple, which is sacred, just like the Bodhi tree is to the Buddhists.

Excavations:

In 1937, an underground cave was discovered while renovating the temple walls. A 20-foot Mandapam with the copper image of Navanita Krishna and Sankha, Chakra, and Puja utensils, probably used by sages, were discovered.

Story of East India Company:

Leonel Blaze, the district collector of Chengalput, visited Madhurantakam and, during his morning walk (1798), had conversations with some local pundits. They expressed some funds for constructing a temple to Goddess Lord Rama, and Lakshmana gave darshan to him. By then, there is a breach of bund due to heavy rains. The collector could see Rama closing the breach with his arrows. News of his vision spread rapidly, and people gathered around. Mr. Blaze said the bund was safe with Rama's blessings. Devi's shrine was built under his supervision.

Sri Rama Navami celebrations last ten days during March-April. Karunakara Murthy's Brahmotsavam is also performed in June-July.

Vedaranyam

Vedaranyam is where sage Agastya had the darshan of Lord Siva in the form of his marriage with Parvati at Kailasa. Hence, Vedaranyam is called 'Dakshina Kailasam'. The sage requested the Lord to stay at Vedaranyam in the matrimonial form, and Siva granted his wish and enshrined behind the Linga as requested. Further, anybody who bathed in the holy waters of Vedatirtha and Manikantha will get salvation. This is how the place is known as Vedaranyam.

<u>The Temple:</u>

The temple faces the west and is surrounded by gopurams on the east and the west. There are two Prakarams inside. Ratha Veedhis are known as Dasaratha Maharaj streets.

<u>God & Goddess:</u>

Vedanayaka and Vedanayaki are the God and Goddess. Chaturvedas adored God, and hence, he is known as Vedanayaka.

<u>Enshrined deities in the outer Prakara:</u>

1. Kalabhairava
2. Sapta Kanyas
3. Viswanatha
4. Visalakshi
5. Setu Madhava
6. Vinayaka
7. Subramanya etc.

<u>Enshrined deities in the inner Prakara:</u>

1. Vedaranyeswara
2. Tyagaraja
3. Kalyana Sundara
4. Arthanareeswara
5. 63 Nayanars

6. The Lingas enshrined by Rama and Pandavas
7. Maha Lakshmi
8. Sarasvati
9. Durga
10. Nataraja etc.

Kings of Solar Dynasty:

1. Yuvanaswara
2. Mandhata

Narada's secret of happiness:

Narada clarified to a king's question that the secret of his cheerfulness and happiness is bathing in the lovely waters of Vedaranyam (Adi Setu).

Significance of Manikarnika:

Lord Sri Rama killed the asuras during his war with Ravana, equivalent to 'Brahma Hatya'. To get rid of this, he took a bath in Manikarnika, which is supposed to be comparable to 'Kasi Snana'.

Viswamitra – Vasistha clash:

Viswamitra asked Vashista to hand over Kamadhenu, but the latter declined to part with it, and hence, Viswamitra, being hurt, proceeded to do penance to become Brahmarshi. Viswamitra married Menaka and brought forth Sakuntala. Tilottama also tried to divert Viswamitra in Vedavana. The sage cursed her to become a deer, and she got her original form after drinking water from Vedanadi.

Vianayaka:

Sri Rama worshipped Veerahatti Vinayaka here after taking a bath in Manikarnika. There is also Vedavinayaka, where the Vedas worship. Sambandar and Appar, the two devotees, sang a song in praise of God and got the gate opened. Generally, Vedas lock the door until puja is completed.

<u>Siva's Standing Posture:</u>

In the inner Prakara is a shrine of Siva standing behind a bull with his consort on the left side. This is a rare pose to be seen in some of the South Indian temples.

<u>Other Goddesses:</u>

Gajalakshmi and Durga, with eight hands holding different weapons, are present here. The idols are beautifully carved. Siva in different forms and Rama padam are also to be seen here. The Archeological Department is the custodian of this.

Auspicious days of worship: Worship is performed every month on the new moon and full days on Mahasivaratri and on Fridays, etc.

Thus, Vedaranyam is famous in several aspects. Several sages, saints, and Purana purushas visited and worshipped a source of holiness for the pilgrims. The history of the place is known through Tamil and Sanskrit literature in the form of hundreds of verses.

Siva The Jambukeswar and Akhilandeswari Temple (Jambukeswaram)

The abode of Lord Siva, the Jambukeswaram, is near Trichi. His consort is Akhilandeswari Devi. At Jambukeswara, located on an island in the middle of the Kaveri River in Tiruchirapalli, Lord Siva is seen and known as Jala Linga. During the rainy season, the water level rises through the floor of the sanctum to flood the Linga. Regarding the island, it is the same one that contains the great temple of Srirangam, which is dedicated to Vishnu.

In ancient days, the area was a crab apple grove or Jambu. A story said that a sage went to Kailash to present the fruit to Siva, and God gave the seed to the sage as a gift. A tree started growing out of his head. Parvati did puja to the Lingam under the tree. In due course, an elephant brought Kaveri water to bathe the Linga. A spider also worshipped the

Lord by spinning a web over the Linga. Quarrel took place between the elephant and spider. Finally, both are dead. The story is similar to that of the Sri Kalahasthi temples episode. The first temple was built by a Chola king, Kotchangannan, who dedicated his life to the service of the Lord. The king built this temple and 70 temples, five of which were for Vishnu.

Visitors to the Temple:

Among the personalities who visited this temple, Lord Sri Rama, after the killing of Ravana, may be mentioned. Similarly, great sages Agasthya, Gautama, and Parasara also visited and worshipped the Lord.

Royal Patronage:

Chola, Pandya and Hoyasalas patronized the temple by all means. The sanctum was built by Kochengat Cholan, the walls of the 2nd Prakara were built by Vijayanagar rulers and the 3rd Prakara was built by Vikrama Cholan. Sundara Pandyan built the eastern tower in 4th prakara. The base of the Lingam is always in water. Goddess Akhilandeswari is in a separate shrine. She, too, worshipped the Lord here.

Architecture:

The artistry is impressive. The temple pillars are more perfectly clean and neat than the ones in the outer corridor in Rameswaram. There is a massive curtain-like pillar near Mother's shrine. Before entering the main temple, one has to go through gopurams and towers. The first and second ones had seven and four tiers, respectively.

Thus, the beautiful Siva temple steals the show from the enormous Ranganatha Swamy temple because of its architectural excellence. Jala Linga, under the ancient Jambu tree, represents Siva as water. Hence, Goddess Parvati created a Lingam out of water known as Appu Lingam. It is believed that Akhilandeswari Devi was furious. Therefore, when Adi Sankaracharya visited the temple, he offered Srichakra as Thaadanga or Thaatanka (earrings) to Akhilandeswari Devi to reduce her anger.

The temple had many mandapas namely Unjala mandapam, 100 pillared mandapam, 1000 pillared mandapam, Vasantha mandapam, and Somaskandar mandapam.

Siva and Vishnu Temples of Salem (Sri Sukavaneswar & Sri Alagirinatha Temples)

Sri Sukavaneswar temple of Salem is a 'Sivamsa' temple. Sri Suka muni worshipped the deity.

Sthalapurana:

Vedavyasa's son Suka worshipped here. Suka agreed with Brahma and said that Sarasvati created and gave voice to everyone in the universe. Brahma cursed the sage Suka to become a parrot and parroted what others said. Suka carried on his work and, at the same time, worshipped Siva Lingam here. A hunter threw an axe at the parrot and killed it. Siva Lingam was also damaged in this context. Suka's name continued to the forest as 'Sukavanam'.

The Temple:

The temple is said to be 2000 years old, and the Lingam is self-manifested. The divine consort is Swarnamalika. There is a Tirtham, which was frog-less. Adisesha was supposed to have stayed here. According to the Chola inscriptions, the temple was built during the 9th century. A mandapa known as Alankara mandapa was built by Davis, a British collector (1823). The other mandapas are Artha mandapa, Maha mandapa etc. The rajagopuram is 3-tiered one. There is also a small tank.

Sri Alagirinatha Swamy Temple:

This is a famous Vishnu temple of Salem near Sukavaneswar temple. Alagarinatha is otherwise called as Sunderaraja Perumal. Sri Sunderavalli Tayar is the divine consort. Davis also built a Kalyana mandapa here. There is a shrine of Vishnu, Durga (a Shakti form).

TELANGANA (TG)

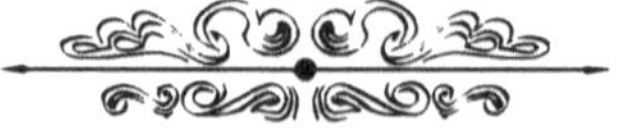

Telangana, India's newest state, was born on June 2, 2014. There are ten districts, including Hyderabad city, by the time of its formation, namely Hyderabad, Adilabad, Khammam, Karimnagar, Mahabubnagar, Medak, Nalgonda, Nizamabad, Ranga Reddy and Warangal. Later, the number of districts was increased to 31 from October 11, 2016. The state has an area of 1,12,077 Sq Km. The neighbouring states are Maharashtra and Chattisgarh in the north, Karnataka in the west and Andhra Pradesh in the south and east.

Figure 19: Telangana – Map of Major Cities and Temples

Telangana is situated on the Deccan plateau, bounded by the Nirmal-Balaghat, Kandikal, and Amarabad mountain ranges. The state's rivers are Musi, Krishna, Godavari, Bhima, and Manjeera.

During the early period, Telangana was known as 'Asmika'. The region was rich in pre-historic and megalithic cultures. Abul Fazal coined the term 'Telangana' in Ain-i-Akbari in the 16th century. It was said that Telanganites were the builders of Mesopotamia, Sumerian and Indus cultures. Satavahanas, Vishnukundins, Kakatiyas, Qutub Shahis and Asaf Jahis ruled the region. Sanskrit, Urdu, Persian and Bengali languages influenced the 'Desi Works'.

Several temples in Telangana are not only centres of devotion and religion but also unique, with rich architecture and beautiful sculptures.

Sri Ganesh Temple – Secunderabad

Sri Ganesh temple is near the railway station in the cantonment area of Secunderabad. During the English East India Company times, the British soldiers needed water; hence, they dug a well and found the idol of Sri Ganesh. The devotees of the region attempted to build a temple, but the British officials objected to the construction. As per the 'Sthala Purana', Sri Ganesh appeared in the dream of British officers and ordered the removal of obstacles in constructing the temple. Consequently, the temple construction activity proceeded uninterruptedly and since 1824, the devotees have worshipped Ganesha.

Rajagopuram at the entrance has 'Five Kalasas', and in the centre is the image of Ganesh. Omkaram and dwarapalakas are noticeable. Spacious Mukha mandapa and the temple complex are extensive and have various deities.

The main deity, Ganesh, is represented with four hands. Pasankusa and Modaka are also visible. The deity is highly decorative. Lord Venkateswara is the Kshetra palaka. Umamaheswara, Parvati, and Rajarajeswari idols are the other ones. Navaratri celebrations are done during 'Aasvija masa'. Subramanyeswara with Valli, Devasena, Anjaneya, and Navagraha temples also exist in the temple complex. All the temples are east-facing except Anjaneyas, which is south-facing.

Devotees believe that Sri Ganesh is a very powerful deity. The puja activities conducted by the temple are based on Vedic practices. Daily 'Panchamrutha Abhishekam', Satya Ganapathi Vratam, Mandala and Artha Mandala Deeksha (41 and 21 days) are the temple's activities. Vinayaka Chaturthi festival is celebrated on a grand scale, performing Navaratri Utsavam to Ganesh. Further, since there are other deities in the temple complex, the Navaratri festivals are being celebrated to Subramanyeswara Swamy (Krithika Nakshatra), Hanuman Jayanthi, Umamaheswara Swamy (Sivaratri). The vratas such as Kedareswara, Varalakshmi Devi, and Satyanarayana Swamy are also performed on respective occasions in Aswayuja masa, Sravana masa and Karthika masa. Devotees attend all the temple festivals and activities in large numbers, having profound devotion and faith in Lord Sri Ganesh of Secunderabad.

Alampur

Alampur has been famous as a temple town since historical times. It is also known as 'Alampuri Sima' (Srinivasachar—Epigraphical evidence) and Hemalapuri (Inscriptions of Krishnadevaraya). Alampur is in Jogulamba Gadwal district at the confluence of the Tungabhadra and the Krishna rivers. Alampur is often called 'Dakshina Kasi', 'Nava Brahmeswara Tirtha', and the 'Western gate of Srisailam'.

In addition to the inscriptional sources, there are literary sources to provide more about Alampur, like 'Palkuriki Somanathas', 'Panditaradhya Charitra' and 'Skanda Purana'. The Sthala Purana of Alampur is elaborately inscribed in Skandapurana in five chapters.

One interesting feature here is the comparison of Alampur with Kasi, according to Skandapurana. Similarities are:

1. Kasi is on the bank of the Ganges, and Alampur is on the bank of Tungabhadra
2. There are Ghats in Kasi as well as Alampur
3. Visweswara in Kasi and Brahmesvara in Alampur are worshipped.
4. Visalakshi and Jogulamba are the deities worshipped in both places.
5. Kalabrairava and Dantibhairava exist in Kasi and Alampur.
6. The main temple at Kasi is between Varana and Asi rivers, and at Alampur, it is between Vedavati and Nadavati.

Dynasties that promoted Alampur's glory were:

- Chalukyas of Badani
- The Rashtrakutas
- The Chalukyas of Kalyani
- The Kakatiyas and
- The Vijayanagars

The Temple of Alampur:

Alampur, the temple town, focuses on several temples, their styles, art, architecture, sculpture, etc. The principal deities are Nava Brahmas, situated in the fortress (Bala Brahma, the main shrine) dedicated to Lord Siva and Jogulamba, one of 'Astadasa Shakti Peethams' surrounded by the Nallamala hills.

The temples of Alampur date back to the 7th century AD and were built by the Badani Chalukyas, who were great patrons of art and architecture.

Nava Brahma Temples:

1. **Bala Brahma**: Bala Brahma temple is the principal temple. The Temple structure has been repaired and modified over several centuries. Regular puja is performed in the temple today. The deities of the temple are 'Durga', 'Arthanareeswara', 'Veerabhadra', 'Jogulamba', 'Saptamatrikas', 'Narasimha' etc. Sculptures of

Mahishasuramardini, Sahasra Linga and Mukhalinga are in the temple courtyard. The sikharas of the small shrines are of different styles.

2. **Kumara Brahma**: The porch pillars are noteworthy, and the carvings are delicate.

3. **Arka Brahma**: This is a roofless temple in decay.

4. **Veera Brahma**: There is no speciality except commonness like the other temples.

5. **Visva Brahma**: This is similar to Svarga Brahma temple except for the porch found in Svarga Brahma temple, which has rich carvings and sculptures.

6. **Taraka Brahma**: The style of architecture is akin to the southern. The temple faces east, and Garbhagriha, antarala, and a porch are there.

7. **Garuda Brahma**: This temple is similar to Padma Brahma temple.

8. **Svarga Brahma**: Inscriptional sources say that the temple was constructed during the last quarter of the 7th century AD facing east. The temple is known for its art, history and sculptures. This temple hall has beautiful carvings on the walls, like the Krishna Leela episode, Matrumurthi, animals, Lingodhbhava, Gangavatarana, Trivikrama, and Siva Tandava.

9. **Padma Brahma**: Beautiful sculptures are found on the temple's walls, but unfortunately, they are subjected to vandalism.

One interesting and informative thing is the linkage of six Brahma temples out of the nine with medical herbs used by Rasa Sidhas with God's blessings (Ramakrishna Sarma's writings of 1958).

Deity	Herb	Botanical Name
Bala Brahma	Abhaya (Sanskrit) / Kuruveru (Telugu)	Chrysopogon zizanioides
Kumara Brahma	Kumara (Sanskrit) / Kalabanda (Telugu) / Aloe Vera (English)	Aloe barbadensis miller

Arka Brahma	Arka (Sanskrit) / Jilledu (Telugu) / Crown Flower (English)	Calotropis gigantea
Veera Brahma	Gajanimma (Telugu)	Citrus Maxima
Viswa Brahma	Allamu (Telugu) / Ginger (English)	Zingiber officinale Roscoe
Padma Brahma	Tamara (Telugu) / Lotus (English)	Nelumbo

Table 1: Table explaining association of each deity with Herbs

The equivalent herbs for the remaining three – Garuda, Svarga and Taraka Brahmas – are unknown.

<u>Jogulamba Temple:</u>

Out of 31 districts of Telangana, the 7th is Jogulamba – Gadwal district. Alampur Jogulamba temple is one of the 18 'Shakthi Peethams'.

Figure 20: Jogulamba Temple

Goddess Jogulamba is a synonym for Parvati, the counterpart of Siva and daughter of Daksha. On being insulted by her father during Dakshayagna, she sacrificed her life. Her body was cut into pieces by Vishnu to save Siva's agony, and they fell in 51 places, out of which 18 are considered 'Ashtadasa Shakti Peethas'. Adi Sankaracharya visited the Jogulamba temple and prayed. It is said that once the icon of Jogulamba existed in the sanctum sanctorum of Bala Brahmeswara temple along with 'Chandi', 'Mundi', and 'Saptamatrikas' carved on a single stone. Over time, the icon was reinstalled. Devotees believe they will be blessed with children, wealth and reputation. As per the legend, Lord Brahma installed Siva and his consort Jogulamba. Alampur Jogulamba temple is on the banks of Tungabhadra, and it has become famous and influential. Therefore, pilgrims from all over the country visit it every day. During the Bahamanis, the temple was plundered and attacked. For some centuries, this Shaktipeetha lost its glory. During Krishnadeveraya, the Jogulamba temple was renovated.

Other Temples and Tirthas:

Surya Narayana and Narasimha temples are the other important temples of Alampur.

Suryanarayana, Parasurama, Saptamatrikas, and Ganapati figures are exemplary art pieces.

Papavinasa Tirtha is one of the three holy places near the Brahmeswara temple. The virtue of bathing in this Tirtha is said to be equivalent to the bath in the Ganges.

Ganika Siddheswara Temple is a holy place where Gandharvas and Sidhas took baths in Tungabhadra and worshipped Siva.

Rajarajesvari Tirtha – Kubera performed penance and pleased Siva

Other Gods on the campus are Kamakshi and Venkateswara. Outside, Ganesha and three-headed Dattatreya exist. Inside the fort are beautiful Hanuman and Madhavi Shakti idols. Salagrams around Bala

Brahmeswara temple are worshipped with 'Nityabhishekams' and Tungabhadra water chanting with Namaka Chamakams.

<u>Style and Architecture of Temples:</u>

Nava Brahma temples externally resemble Orissa temples, but they are similar to some of the rock-cut temples of western India. Nine temples are square. There is a Pradakshina passage. Carvings on pillars (similar to temples in West India). The hunter and deer carving on the Brahma temple's main entrance is beautiful.

The architecture of the temples is notable in three different styles. First, the towers were influenced by Northern India. Second, the Western Indian influence on the internal plan and third, the grace of the Guptas on the sculptures.

<u>Stories of Yellamma – Bhudevi and Punyavati:</u>

1. Yellamma and Bhudevi Story: Yellamma and Bhudevi are two Goddesses of Alampur, described in the Sthalapurana. The legend connected with the stories is as follows - Renuka was the wife of sage Jamadagni. She used to bring water from the Tungabhadra River daily for her husband's puja. Water is to be brought in a pot made out of river clay every day. She could do this with her 'Pati Bhakti' power. One day, she glanced at a king and queen bathing in the river during this process. This incident caused a disturbance in her mind, and she could not make a pot and returned to the Ashram without bringing water. Sage Jamadagni could visualize what had happened and ordered his sons to kill her. All of them kept quiet, and Parasurama obeyed his father's orders and beheaded her. The sage gave him a boon, whatever he needed. Parasurama asks his father to bring back his mother. Jamadagni said it was impossible since the head fell into some impure place. But he said the head would be worshipped by all people with the name of 'Yellamma', the 'Grama devata'. The body is to be renowned as 'Bhudevi'. Thus, these Goddesses appear only at Alampur.

2. Punyavati Story: (Connected with the construction of Alampur temples) The story is mentioned in the Sthalapurana, referring to a widow of Benaras named Punyavati, a devotee of Lord Siva. Siva granted her a boon to get a male child at her request. Villagers abused her, getting a child who had no father. It was the same insult the child faced when he began to grow. The mother instructed him to approach Lord Siva. The boy did penance, and Siva instructed him to go to Brahmeswara Kshetra and construct temples for all the Goddesses there. The boy was known as 'Rasa Siddha'. He came to Alampur and built the temples. During this process, a nastika king named Vilasat Raja invaded this place and destroyed many temples. Further, he tried to snatch away the pot containing 'Siddha Rasa' (miracle juice – stone can be converted to Gold) from the Rasa Siddha. Siddha knew this and cursed the king. He lost all his army and wealth. One day, the king was wandering, suffering from hunger and thirst. A hunter came to his rescue to bring a deer to appease his hunger. He caught hold of a deer, but the deer requested a permit to return soon after giving milk to its younger ones. The deer was left, and the king was informed of the news. The deer came back but turned its face because he was a sinful face. The king begged the deer to get rid of his sins. The deer told him to go to Alampur Brahmeswara temples, do penance, and reconstruct the temples. This story of the hunter, deer and Vilasat king is to be seen in beautiful sculptures. The deer further said that his sins will be lost when the king's sculpture is spoiled.

Vemulavada

As per the inscriptions, Vemulavada is called 'Lembula Vatika' and 'Lembulavada'. Vemulavada is presently in the Rajanna Siricilla district, which was in the erstwhile district of Karimnagar. Vemulavada is famous for its Sri Rajarajeswara Swamy temple, one of India's ancient and famous Siva temples. The region was historically significant since Vemulavada happened to be the capital of the Chalukyas (750-973 AD), who were feudatories of Rashtrakutas. There is also another temple, Baddegeswara Swamy temple, which is also in a good state of preservation. This temple is also known as Bheemeswara temple.

Origin of the Temple:

Narasimha I (his title is Rajaditya) of the Chalukyas of Vemulavada, the grandson of Yuddhamalla I, built the Rajarajeswara temple. Inscriptional evidence states that Rajaditya had done the Pratishtapana of this God and constructed the temple. In another inscription, King Anikesa, the lion of Chalukya Vemulavada, had the title of Rajaditya. These kings lived about the 9th and 10th centuries AD; the temple is 1000 years old.

The Temples:

Historians give a significant explanation regarding Vemulavada. In Prakrit, 'Vemudu' means 'Deity', and Vemulavada means 'Place of Deities'. According to Nelaturi Venkataramanaiah, in his 1953 writings, Plate 6 said that Vemulavada has extensive remains of temples and sculptures.

1. Rajarajeswara Temple
2. Nageswara Temple
3. Bheemeswara Temple
4. Venugopala Swamy Temple
5. Kedareswara Temple
6. Maha Lakshmi Temple
7. Kanaka Durga Temple
8. Narasimha Swamy Temple
9. Sitala (Baddi Pochamma) Temple etc.

Rajarajeswara Temple is the most famous temple. Vemulavada Bheemakavi received the grace of this God. There is a Sthalapurana of this temple known as 'Vemulavada Rajeswara Mahatyam'. A king named Narendra constructed the later temple, which contained structural and sculptural additions.

<u>Importance of Dharmagundam:</u>

To the north of the temple is a large tank and a special portion called 'Dharmagundam'. Narendra constructed the steps. It is said that one gets liberation by the darshan of Srisailam, death at Kasi, and penance at some other holy temples. Out mere name and bath in Dharmagundam will confer liberation.

In the temple's courtyard, there are shrines of Kumaraswamy (6 faces – Shanmukha), Ananta Padmanabha Swamy, Vishnu (Satyanarayana Swamy), Chanikeswari, Siva, Annapurna, Saptamatrikas, Varahi and Lakshmi Maha Ganapati. The Garbhagriha of the temple has a fine door frame of the Kalyani Chalukya type. The image of Sitala devi (Pochamma Temple) with four hands, with Trisula, Broomstick, Agnikundam, and Dhamaru in them, is to be seen in the courtyard. According to Venkataramanaiah (1953: Plates 7-12), the Antarala of the temple contains a good sculpture of Mahishasura Mardhini. The more important ones for the art historians are the Rajarajeswara, Bheemeswara and Kedareswara temples at Vemulavada.

<u>Stories focused by the Sthala Puranam:</u>

'Vemulavada Rajeswara Mahatyam' is called the Sthala puranam. Puranic stories have to be traced from Bhavishyottara Puranam stories or legends are as follows:

1. There was a great king named Narendra, who was Arjuna's grandson. One day, he went for hunting, and by mistake, he shot dead a sage who went to a pond to fetch water. The king wanted to get rid of 'Bhahma Hatya Dosha'. He came to Vemulavada and was relieved of his sin by taking three handfuls of water from 'Dharmagundam'. The same night, God appeared before him and told him that the Rajeswara shrine was at the bottom of Dharmagundam and he should bring it up and consecrate it on the tank's bank for the people's worship. The king implemented Lord Siva's orders.

2. Indra suffered from 'Brahma Hatya Dosham' because he killed Vritrasura, the demon. He took a bath in Dharmagundam and got relieved from his sin.

3. Another story is related to Dakshaprajapali, who performed yagna to excel all Gods. To prevent the success of yagna, the Sun god tried to snatch away the 'Havis'. In the trial, he lost his hands. Other Gods advised him to go to 'Dharmagundam' and perform penance for 100 years. The Sun God did penance and got his hands.

The importance of 'Dharmagundam' has already been quoted above. 'Kalyanotsavam' is celebrated yearly on Mahasivaratri to the Lord Siva (Purnima of Phalguna masa).

<u>The unique custom of the temple:</u>

'Sahasra Swarnabhishekam' (1000 golden pieces) and the offerings of Bulls (Nandeeswara) – Kodelu are the unique customs of Vemulavada Rajeswara's Temple by the devotees in addition to the normal Pujas, Abhishekams etc.

Kaleswaram

Kaleswaram is in the Mahadevpur Mandal, Bhoopalapalli (Acharya Jayashankar) district, carved out of the erstwhile Warangal district with the annexation of some parts of Karimnagar. Kaleswaram is on the right bank of the pious Godavari river and is confluent with the rivulet Pranahita. It is in the interior of a thick forest. 'Mukteswara Swamy' temple is the chief place of worship for the villagers. Of course, there are many other temples in a dilapidated condition. Kaleswaram has been a great Saivite centre from early times. There is a saying:

"Kaleswara Nivasova
Kaleswara Nirikshanam
Kaleswara Smaranam
Sarvapapa Pranasanam"

<u>Two Siva Lingas:</u>

One is Mukteswara, and the other is Kaleswara. The region is holy and famous as 'Dakshina Gangotri' and 'Dakshina Triveni'.

<u>Worship of Ganesa:</u>

Worship of Ganesa is compulsory before entering Kaleswara and Mukteswara Temples. Devotees worship Kaleswara first, then Mukteswara. At the entrance, Srungi and Bhrungi are there, as Dwarapalakas.

<u>Story of Yama:</u>

There are no sinners in this region because they are leading a dharmic life, enchanting 'Panchakshari Mantra'. Chitragupta never found anybody to be punished by Yama. Hence, Yama appealed to Siva to wind up Yamaloka. Then Siva promised that Yama would be given a holy place at Kaleswaram. Devotees should worship him first and then other deities. At Yama's request, Maya built a beautiful town named Kaleswaram (Kaladeva is Yamadharmaraja), which is equivalent to heaven.

<u>Other Temples:</u>

In addition to Kaleswara and Mukteswara temples, there are other temples, namely Somesvara, Sangamesvara, Chandikesvara, Adimuktesvara, Chandrasekhara, Subramanyesvara and Vijaya Ganapati.

Goddess Sarasvati temple is Maha Sarasvati, also known as Proudha Sarasvati. Bala Sarasvati (Kashmir) and Gnana Sarasvati (Basara) are the other famous temples. Pujas are performed daily, and special pujas will be celebrated on auspicious days.

Thousand Pillar Temple (Hanumakonda / Warangal Urban) – Rudresvar Temple:

Hanumakonda was the capital of Kakatiyas before Ganapati transferred his capital to Warangal. Hanumakonda is the land between the Godavari and Krishna rivers in the Dandaka forest. Hanumadri is another name for Hanumakonda. Hidimba Asram is also nearby (Kazipet). There are references to Bhadresvari or Bhadrakali. There is a Kalyana mandapa adjacent to Rudresvara Temple with 1000 pillars. According to inscriptional sources, the temple was built in 1163 AD. The temple is known as 'Trikuntalayam'.

<u>The Trikunta: (1000 pillared temple – Not to be taken literally)</u>

The three shrines are dedicated to Rudresvara, Vasudeva and Suryadevara. The temple is constructed on an Upapitha. A beautifully carved Nandi of black stone is placed on this platform. The temple reflects the Kakatiya style of architecture, culture and traditions. Beautiful 'Torana Silpas' welcomes the entrance of the temple. Devotees visit in large numbers on auspicious days like Mahasivaratri and Kartika Purnima. Abhishekams and Deepalankarams are special offerings of devotees. The renovation work of the temple injected freshness into the ruined one. This is recognised by UNESCO as a World Heritage site.

Ramappa Temple – Palampet

The temple is just 50 km from Warangal. This temple is also a Siva temple but named after sculptor Ramappa. Ramalingeswara is the deity. The military commander of Ganapatideva, Recharla Rudra, built this (inscriptional source). The dancing Nagini sculptures are beautifully engraved. From the architectural viewpoint and high sculptural standards of the Kakatiyas, the temple may be cited rather than the puja systems.

Panagal

The village of Panagal is near Nalgonda town, the district headquarters. The inscriptions refer to it as 'Panungallu' or 'Panugallu'. It has been a historical place since Kalyani Chalukyas, and Panagal remained an essential place under the Kakatiyas.

There are three important temples in the village:

1. The Paccala Someswara Temple or the Nalla Gudi
2. The Venkateswara Temple and
3. The Chaya Somesvara Tempe

The Paccala Somesvara Temple was the finest sculptural work. The Venkateswara temple is architecturally devoid of much significance. The Chaya Somesvara temple is an example of Trikuta.

<u>The Paccala Somesvara Temple:</u>

From the inscriptional evidence, this temple is found in Panagal. Its architectural style may be assigned to the 11th century AD. The grand plan of the temple is different from that of other temples of Telangana.

Paccala Somesvara, Rajarajesvari Devi, and Nandiswara can be seen. The Sikharas rise in storeys. Nagadevata sculptures are also present. Daily worship is performed. During Kartika masam and Maha Sivaratri occasions, special archanas and abhishekams are performed.

The wall sculptures are beautiful. Ganesa is riding a mouse, seated, and Nrutya Ganesa's sculptures are beautiful. Siva as Nataraja, 'Anugrahamurthi', 'Lingodbhava', and Devi sculptures are some more.

Pillar sculptures like Gajasura Samharamurti, Ravana shaking Kailasa, Narasimha killing Hiranyakasipa, and battle scenes from Ramayana and Mahabharata are notable.

<u>Venkateswara Temple:</u>

This temple was likely constructed during the 13th century AD under Kakatiya rule. The temple faces the eastern side. Venkatesvara along with Padmavati and Alamelmanga are seen. Opposite to the deity, the tortoise reminds Kurmatara of Lord Vishnu. Daily pujas and special pujas on festive days are being celebrated.

<u>The Chaya Somessvara Temple:</u>

This temple is a triple shrine (Chaya Somesvara—Dattatreya and Isvara). It comprises a mandapa, porch, and shrines to the north, east, and west of the mandapa. The shrines have superstructures of the stepped pyramidal type. In the sanctum Santorum of the Temple on 'Siva Linga', Chaya or shade is to be seen daily, and this is a wonder.

Narasimha Temples

Dharmapuri

Dharmapuri is in the newly formed district of Jagityal, which was a part of the Karimnagar district before the state reorganized the districts. Dharmapuri Lakshmi Narasimha Swamy temple and Kondagattu Anjaneya Swamy temple are the famous places of pilgrimage in this district, and some more temples exist in this region. Dharmapuri is one of the oldest villages renowned as a centre of Vedic and Sanskrit studies. Dharmapuri is on the right bank of the river, southwards flowing Godavari. The most important temple in Dharmapuri is dedicated to Lord Vishnu as Narasimha Swamy.

The puranic story and the greatness of the deity are detailed in the 'Brahmanda Purana' and an unpublished palm leaf manuscript in Sanskrit named 'Dharmapuri Kshetra Mahatyam'.

To save Prahlada, Lord Vishnu took on the incarnation of Narasimha and killed Hiranyakasipa, a Siva devotee. Siva, in the form of Sarabha, fought with Narasimha, but of course, he could not succeed. Narasimha was wandering in the Dandakaranya forest with a fearful appearance. In other words, this was the form of 'Ugra Narasimha'. All the Gods became frightened and approached Lord Brahma to suggest ways of appeasing the Ugra form of Vishnu. Lord Brahma did penance to pacify Vishnu. A king by the name of Dharma Varma, on the advice of Vishnu Sarma, also did penance to appease Brahma and, through him, wished to approach Vishnu in Narasimha's form. Brahma was finally appeased. The place is known as 'Brahma Pushkarini'. Vishnu also appeared before Brahma and Dharma Varma. Then Brahma requested Vishnu to remain there permanently in 'Sowmya Rupa'. Narasimha complied with Brahma's request at the same spot as Dharmapuri.

The Lord is seated in the Padmasana posture in the yogic form, not in the Ugra Rupa. The kshetra after Dharma Varma is called Dharmapuri. Brahma is also worshipped in the temple, a rare phenomenon in the temples.

Other important deities:

- A giant idol of Yama is at the gate. There is a story in this context. Yama, on his pilgrimage to get rid of his sins, came to Dharmapuri, bathed in Godavari, got peace of mind, and visited the deity of Dharmapuri Narasimha. There is a belief that devotees light the 'Ganda Deepam' to get rid of 'Apamrutyu Dosham' and be free from the fear of death. Yamakundam is the place where Lord Yama took his bath.
- At the inner gate, there are idols of Murali Krishna and Balarama. There are also four other temples at this place.
- Ramalingeswara Temple, Nutana Narasimha Temple, Dattatreya Temple, and one Rama Temple are on the banks of Godavari.

While returning from Lanka after the conquest of Ravana, Lord Rama visited this place of Dandakaranya and consecrated Siva as he did in Rameswaram (Saikata Linga Pratishta). Daily worship to Siva is being done.

Sage Goutama brought Godavari to this place; hence, a temple called Gautamesvara exists. Dharmapuri Kshetra is also famous for 'Kujagraha Dosha' relief to get married, and Pitrukarmas are also performed here. Narasimha is worshipped here as Prahlada – Narasimha, Yoga Narasimha, Ugra Narasimha, Lakshmi Narasimha etc.

Yadadri (Yadigiri Gutta)

Yadadri (formerly known as Yadagiri Gutta) was originally in Nalgonda district and is now in an independent district, Yadadri-Bhongir district. This temple is one of the holy places in the state of Telangana. Yadadri is named after sage Yada, son of Rishyasringa and Santa (Tretayuga), son of Vibhandaka, son of Kashipa Prajapathi.

There are no inscriptions or written and recorded material to give the history of this temple. However, literary sources focus on Yadadri. Valmiki Ramayana, Vyasa's Narasimhapurana, Skanda and Brahmanda Puranas mentioned some legends or Sthala Purana of this holy place as follows:

The deity of Yadadri is Lakshmi Narasimha Swamy. After killing Hiranyakasipa to save Prahlada at Ahobila, Narasimha appeared in 'Ugra Rupa'. Hence, all the sages requested Goddess Lakshmi to appease the Lord, and consequently, Narasimha appeared as Lakshmi Narasimha of Yadadri, situated on the top of a 300-foot hillock.

Yada, son of the great sage Rishyasrunga and Santa Devi, did penance and made Vishnu appear before him to confer boons. Yada prayed to the Lord to show him the three forms of Narasimha: Gandabherunda, Jwala and Yoga Narasimha. Vishnu appeared before Yada in three forms. Then, the latter begged the Lord to remain permanently on the hill in three forms. The Lord acceded to Yada's prayers. Since then, the hill has been named Yadagiri Gutta or Yadadri.

The Lord appeared in a dream to a village officer and told him that arrangements would be made for regular worship of the idol on the hill. Under a huge rock, people found the images of Narasimha. Since then, daily poojas have been performed.

According to another legend, one old Narasimha Swamy temple is two miles from the hill.

<u>The three forms of Narasimha:</u>

1. Gandabherunda Narasimha: An oil lamp is always burning here, indicating the importance of the holy site.
2. Jwala Narasimha: The image is shaped like a Serpent's head and ends like its tail.
3. Yoga Narasimha: The image of a figure seated in meditation

The Garbhagudi is a natural cave formed under a huge rock. Here, devotees bow involuntarily to the Lord.

<u>The Silver icons of Goddess Lakshmi and Narasimha:</u>

Since the images here are not visible, the silver icons of Goddess Laksmi and Narasimha are kept near the original idol for darshan and puja.

The power of the Lord is so great that pilgrims visit and worship the Lord with a strong belief that incurable diseases get cured. Thus, the temple's importance has been propagated for decades. A Siva temple on the hill also establishes that Hari and Hara are the same.

<u>Festivals:</u>

From Suddha Dwiteeya to Suddha Dwadasi in Phalguna masa, the Kalyana Mahotsavam is celebrated yearly, and pilgrims flock to have darshan of the Lord. The Pancharatna system of the agamas is adopted for temple activities.

Yadadri is thus a great pilgrimage centre, and people from all over the country visit. There is a strong belief that sages worship the Lord in disguise and 'Brahmadi Devatas'.

The Government of Telangana rebuilt the temple in the Krishna Sila (Black stone). The renovation was initiated in 2016 and was inaugurated on 28 March 2022, after the completion of construction.

Naacharam Gutta (Si Lakshmi Narasimha Swamy Temple)

Sri Lakshmi Narasimha Swamy Temple in Naacharam is in the district of Siddipet, carved out of the erstwhile Medak district. The term Naacharam is derived from 'Naachagiri', a hillock. This place is known as Svetagiri or Tapogiri. Sage Gargeya did penance.

The temple had an ancient origin. Here, Narasimha Swamy is said to be 'Svayambhu' at the beginning of 'Kaliyuga'. According to a story, Lord Vishnu deputed nine members to control the calamities during the beginning of Kaliyuga, and they are:

1. Hari
2. Antarakshaka
3. Prabuddha
4. Pippalada
5. Avirhotra
6. Drumila
7. Chavana
8. Karabhajana and
9. Kali

The divine deputies of Vishnu came and stayed here in a cave and did penance. Narasimha Swamy gave his darshan to them and blessed them. This way, the people of this region could know about this Svayambhu Narasimha.

The temple's Galipopuram had three storeys. Jaya and Vijaya idols are on either side of the entrance of the sanctum Sanctorum. The main temple faces southwards. In the Mukha mandapa, separate allotments are there for Lakshmi Devi, Goda Devi, and Garuda. Laksmi Devi is on the left side of the Lord to reduce the Ugrarupa.

On the left side of the temple, idols of Alwars exist, and on the right side, 'Utsava Vigrahas' are kept. On the campus, images of other Gods and Goddesses, like Kalabhairava, Navagrahas, Siva, Satyanaraya Swamy, Sita Rama, Anjaneya, Dattatreya, and Saibaba, are visible.

Sevas of the Temple: Kumkumarchana, Abhishekas and Vahanas are daily services. The annual function is Brahmotsavam on a grand scale (10 days), followed by Radhotsavam.

Mattapalli (Lakshmi Narasimha Swamy)

The Sri Lakshmi Narasimha Swamy temple is in the newly formed district of Suryapet, formerly in Nalgonda district. This Svayambhu Swamy of 'Mattapalli', otherwise known as 'Matampalli', is on the banks of the holy river Krishna. Matampalli happened to be the abode of sages like Bharadvaja. This temple is one of the 'Panchanarasimha' Kshetras, and it has over a thousand years of history.

Temple's background:

'Tangeda' is a small village in the Guntur district of the present Andhra Pradesh state. Swamy appeared in a dream to a devotee named Machi Reddy of the village. He revealed his idol form (Swayambhu) in a cave and asked him to install and construct a temple and perform puja with Dhoopa-Deepa-Naivedyam. The idol's height is 6 feet, and it has four hands: Sankhu, Chakra, and Gada. Abhayamudra is seen. The idol of Anjaneya, found in the Krishna River, is opposite Narasimha.

Devotees visit in large numbers. Thirty-two Pradakshinas are suggested to fulfil devotees' wants, such as health, children, and relief from planetary effects. It is said that Lord Yama also did 32 Pradakshinas; hence, the temple is also known as 'Yama Mohita Kshetra'. Another exciting thing is the use of 'Aare Leaf', which is dear to God, similar to 'Tulasi' to Vishnu.

Other deities: Rajya Lakshmi and Chenchu Lakshmi are being installed.

Vaadapalli (Sri Lakshmi Narasimha Swamy Temple)

Vaadapalli, or Vajeerabad, is in Nalgonda district, the seat of Lakshmi Narasimha and Agastisvara with Meenakshi Devi. Vaadapalli is a holy place where the two sacred rivers of Krishna and Musi (Muchukunda) flow jointly. Further, as per a story, sage Agastya stayed here after giving a curse to the Vindhya mountains. To reveal no discrimination between Vishnua and Siva, he installed Narasimha and Siva temples here.

Sri Lakshmi Narasimha temple faces southwards. The deity is represented with four hands. The temple complex is divided into Sanctum Sanctorum, 'Antaralayam', and Mandapa. There is a lamp post in Antaralaya and in the mandapas. The mother Goddess Adi Lakshmi, Alwar idols, inscriptions, Anjaneya, and Gautama idols are found.

Temple's Importance:

It is said that an oil lamp is kept just before the face of Swamy. The lamp flickers due to the air coming out of the Lord's breathing, and there is no scope for air coming from outside.

Festivals:

Nitya Pujas, or daily worship, are performed. Kalyanotsavam is celebrated during the month of Maagha masa. Special pujas are also performed on occasions like Narasimha Jayanthi, Toli Ekadasai, and Vaikunta Ekadasi.

Matsyagiri (Vemulakonda) Sri Lakshmi Narasimha Swamy Temple

Matsyagiri is in Yadadri-Bhongir district. Sri Lakshmi Narasimha Swamy temple mandapa is one of the ancient temples on the top of the hill— Vemulakonda, 500 feet high. The exact time of the temple is unknown. The deity is in a mandapa with a Pushkarini. There are several beautiful fish of the same category with three lines (Naamalu). There is plenty of water at Pushkarini.

Khammam – Sri Lakshmi Narasimha Swamy Temple

The name of Khammam is derived from the name of a local hill, 'Stambhadri'. There is an ancient temple called Narasimha Swamy (since Tretayuga). Stambhadri later became known as Kambhadri and Khammamet. Nearby, there is Munneru, a tributary of the river Krishna.

There are references to sages like Maudgalya. The temple came to light during Reddi Rajas's time.

The temple had three parts: Sanctum Sanctorum, Antaralayam and Mandapa. Apart from the main deity, there are other deities in the mandapa: Rajya Lakshmi, Kesava Swamy and Andal. In this Vaishnava temple, all the pujas and festivals are per the tradition.

Gajagiri Narasimhalaya

This temple is a cave where the Lord is present. Details are known little. Jaya and Vijaya are seen here, and images of Sri Raghunadha and Varaha exist. Pujas and festivals are celebrated on all days and festive days.

The peculiarity of this temple is that Jaggery water (Panaka) is given as an offering to Narasimha. The Jaggery water is poured into the mouth of the God. Half of the water is thrown back, as in the case of Mangalagiri Panakala Swamy in AP State.

Malluru Lakshmi Narasimha

This temple is on a small hill and 130 km from Warangal. The Lord is Svayambhu, who is 6 feet tall and in a standing pose with Sankhu, Chakra, and Gada.

The Lord's peculiarity is that his body is smooth/soft from the chest to the nave. He married Chenchu Lakshmi here. Sagas Bharadvaja and Angirasa stayed here. The Lord appeared to them in a dream and told them about his existence here.

Palakurti Sri Lakshmi Narasimha Swamy

Palakurti is on the Hyderabad—Warangal railway route, under the Ghanapur railway station's purview. The region is known for its scenic beauty.

Narasimha Swamy and Somesvara in the same cave appear as Svayambus, indicating the oneness of 'Siva Kesavas'. Earlier, it was difficult for the devotees to go by 365 steps to reach the hill. However, transportation problems are resolved now.

During 'Karthika Masam," the twin temples are busy with pilgrims. 'Laksha Deeparadhanotsavam', 'Gopuja,' and prayers are celebrated.

Bejjanki

Sri Lakshmi Narasimha Swamy temple at Bejjanki is just 35 Km from Karimnagar. The Swamy is Svayambhu, a cave temple. Siva Temple is also there, which existed even before Narasimha Swamy temple, with four central pillars of the mandapa nicely carved.

Banjara Hills, Hyderabad

Situated in Banjara Hills Road No 12, Hyderabad, the colony is new, but the old temple is Svayambhu Lakshmi Narasimha Swamy Temple. As per the local story, the temple existed even before Yadadri.

Palem – Sri Lakshmi Narasimha Temple

Palem is situated on the banks of 'Musi' on the Vijayawada – Hyderabad highway. It is said to have existed since the 13th century. This 'Svayambhu' deity on a 'Saalagrama sila' is Narasimha. The Lord appeared to a zamindar Gundamaraju in a dream and narrated his existence in a bush.

Anjaneya is the Kshetrapalaka of the temple. The temple was built according to Pancharatna Agama Sastra – Alwars are given importance. Goda Devi is known as 'Kalyana Kalpavalli'. Daily pujas and special pujas are performed on festive occasions.

Bhadrachalam

Bhadrachalam is in the Kottagudem district of Telangana state, situated on the banks of the holy river Godavari. The region shares its significance with the life of Sri Sita Ramachandra Swamy during exile. The famous temple is dedicated to Lord Sri Rama. Sri Ramachandra lived for some time in Bhadrachalam along with Sita and Lakshmana before Ravana carried away Sita. The story brings us back to the Ramayana era.

Mythological significance of Bhadrachalam:

Bhadrachalam is also known as 'Bhadragiri' or 'Bhadradri'. Bhadra's name is associated with this holy place. The boon child of Meru and Meru Devi was Bhadra, a sage and a great devotee of Vishnu. Sri Rama is said to have appeared in a vision to him along with Sita and Lakshmana. Acceding to Bhadra's request, Rama seated himself with Sita and Lakshmana on the Bhadragiri mountain or sage's head.

Source of the Bhadragiri Episode:

Veda Vyasa, the author of 'Ashtadasa Puranas', quoted the sequence of events related to Bhadragiri in one of his texts, Brahma Purana, in the chapter 'Gautami Mahatyam'.

The character of the Lord:

Lord Rama is the incarnation of Lord Vishnu in the process of Dasavataras. Rama never said, 'I am God'. He assumed the human form. He is said to be the embodiment of Dharma. As Valmiki said, 'Ramo Vigrahavan Dharmaha'. Sri Ramachandra is a role model to all human beings and shows the path of an ideal life. Respect for parents, affection towards brothers, ideal love towards Dharmapatni, following 'Eka Patnivrata', truthfulness, etc., are only some of the tenets of his character.

Bhadragiri Temple:

The origin and development of this Vaishnavite temple are to be enunciated in this context stage by stage.

The idols or Vigrahas of Rama, Lakshmana, and Sita are Svayambu, a beautiful sculpture. In India, there are thousands of temples dedicated to Sri Rama. Among them, around 25 are famous, and Bhadradri Sri Sira Ramachandra Swamy temple is one among them:

1. Rama Tirtham
2. Parnasala on the banks of Godavari
3. Ayodhya
4. Mithila
5. Nasik
6. Panchavati
7. Ramagiri
8. Lakshmana Puram
9. Gandhamadanam
10. Pampatiram
11. Kishkindha
12. Yamunatiram
13. Chitrakutam
14. Nandigrama
15. Bhadragiri
16. Hampi
17. Jeedikallu
18. Ontimitta
19. Tiruvallur
20. Tirupati
21. Madurantakam
22. Sri Rangam
23. Darbha Sayanam
24. Tiruppalnodi

The image of Sri Rama differs from the images found in other temples. Usually, the Lord is depicted in Tribhanga or Samabhanga pose with two hands – one holding the bow and the other arrow. Sri Rama at the sanctum of Bhadradri has four hands and is called 'Chathurbhuja Rama'. The Lord in his front has two hands and holds a bow and arrow (Kodanda bow and bana). The Sankha (Conch) and Chakra (discus) are held in the two rear hands. Sita stands by Rama's side in other temples, but it is different here. She sits on the left thigh of the Lord, and Lakshmana stands on the left side of the Lord. Another thing is both the primary deities are in the same stone carving.

<u>Role of Devotees (Bhaktas) and Rulers in the process of Temple Construction and Development:</u>

<u>Pokala Dammakka:</u>

Pokala Dammakka was an ardent devotee of Sri Rama. She was a resident of a village near Bhadrachalam. She collected roots, fruits and flowers in the forest, chanting 'Rama nama'. She found the deity of Lord Rama, Sita and Lakshmana. Sage Bhadra blessed Dammakka and said she was with his mother Meruka's Amsa. She used to worship the Lord and offered Nivedana of Palmyrah fruit daily. In a dream, she was told that a Mahatma would come to continue the task of the temple's construction. She narrated her experiences and dreams to Kancharla Gopanna or Ramadas, Tahasildar of the region (Palvancha). She constructed a mandapa for the housing of the idols.

<u>Bhakta Ramadas:</u>

Kancharla Gopanna, later known as Bhakta Ramadas, was born in Nelakondapalli in about 1630 AD. He was the nephew of Akkanna and Madanna, who were under the services of Golkonda Nawab Abdul Hasan Tanisha. Gopanna was well-versed in four languages: Sanskrit, Telugu, Persian and Urdu. This enabled him to get the post of Peshkar, whose duty is to collect revenues in the Palvancha area.

Gopanna was a great devotee of Sri Rama. One day, his son fell into a hot gruel and died. He took the dead child to the deity and prayed to him to restore life to his child. Accordingly, his prayers were fulfilled, and his boy was returned to life. Since then, Gopanna's devotion to the Lord multiplied, and he constructed a temple. He requested Tanisha's permission to build the temple with the available revenue collection of six lakh rupees. In anticipation of the consent, he started the construction. Another miracle is when he bathed in Godavari, found the holy Sudarshana Chakra, and fixed or installed it in the temple. Tanisha imprisoned Gopanna for spending Government money for 12 years at Golkonda Fort. During his prison life, he faced humiliation and torture. Despite this, he never compromised with circumstances. He wrote the famous 'Dasarathi Satakam'.

Gopanna was released after Rama and Lakshmana appeared before Tanisha and paid six lakh rupees in gold coins. The Nawab was surprised by whether the incident was a dream or reality. He felt that he saw Lord Rama and his joy knew no bounds. Tanisha placed the gold coins (Rama Maadas) at the feet of Gopanna, who took only two coins as divine mementoes. Since then, the ruler has allotted a portion of land revenue to the maintenance of the temple. He also sent pearls to the Lord during Kalyana Utsavam. The later Asafjahi rulers and the state government continued this practice after the independence.

Gopanna believed in sincerity and devotion rather than external propaganda in the form of worship. Further, he opined that religion is no bar for the prayer of Rama. Thereupon, he requested Archakas to permit Kabir into the temple. Gopanna then received Upadesam from Kabir and assumed the name of Ramadas (servant of Rama). Tumu Narasimhadas succeeded Saint Ramadas in his office.

<u>Tumu Narasimhadas (1790-1833):</u>

Being the successor of Gopanna or Ramadas in official responsibilities, he succeeded in all the spiritual activities of Bhadragiri Temple. He was a contemporary of Tyagaraja and a great scholar of the Sanskrit and Telugu languages. He was also a great musician and pilgrim who visited many temples by walking throughout India. His friend, Bhadragiri Varada, was a wealthy man from Madras. Ramadas was also a great devotee of Rama. Tumu Narasimha and Varada are said to be born with the Amsa's (spirit) of Kabir and Ramadas. Their efforts in the temple renovation work were successful.

Contribution of Bhakti Sangeetam:

In the Bradragiri temple, Bhakti-based Kritis or Kirthanas, coupled with music, are regularly chanted daily in the morning and evening. They are widely popular throughout Telugu-speaking areas. Hundreds of songs on festive occasions, lullabies and philosophical tattvas of Ramadas and Tumu Narasimhadas have been popular for centuries. A few are mentioned here:

- "Adigo Bhadradri, Gauthami Idigo Chudandi…"
- "Nanubrovamani Cheppave Sitamma Talli…."
- "Anta Ramamayam, Jagamanta Ramamayam…" (Ramadas)
- "Rama Namame Jeevanamu…"
- Ramachandra, Sita Manohara…"
- Bhajana Chesi vidhamu…" (Tumu Narasimha)

Temple view – Gopurams & Art:

The temple's main entrance is crowned by a tall gopuram (surrounded by 24 other temples), which takes us to the inner Prakara of the temple. The main shrines and Utsavigrahas of Lord Rama, Sita, and Lakshmana are present. The deity's image differs from that of other Rama temples, as cited above. Around the sanctum are shrines for Alwars and Sri Ramanuja, the founder of Vaishnavism. Siva Lingam from Kasi (during Ramadas times) is said to be the Kshetrapalaka.

Ornaments:

The sacred treasure of jewellery is preserved and protected by the authorities of the temple, and they are also displayed. They are 'Chitaku Patakamu' (Sita's), 'Mutyala Patakamu' (Lakshmana's), 'Pachchala Patakamu' (Bharata's) and 'Bangaru Molatadu' (Satrughna's).

<u>Sevas:</u>

The Archanas are being done as per "Sri Pancharatnaganam". Daily seva and special ones are performed on auspicious days, and annual functions are as follows:

1. Brabhata seva (By 5:00 AM)
2. Abhishekam (7:00 AM)
3. Darbaru Seva (9:30 PM)
4. Pavalimpu Seva (9:00 PM)

Vaikunta Ekadasi is being celebrated on a grand scale in January. Sri Rama Navami and Kalyanam (April) are celebrated with pomp, glory, and devotion and are attended by thousands of pilgrims.

Parnasala

Parnasala Sri Rama temple is located in the Kottagudem district, carved out of the Khammam district of Telangana state. In Parnasala, Lord Sri Rama built a hermitage to live with Sita and Lakshmana during his Vanavasa. Hence, this place gained importance. Rakshasa, by the name of Maricha, came in the guise of a golden deer and provided an opportunity for Ravana to take away Sita from the hermitage. In the temple campus, the footprints of the deer and Sita are preserved. After visiting Bhadradri, pilgrims also visit Parnasala.

'Sitavagu', a freshwater stream, was used for Lord Rama and Sita's bath. On a rock are marks of the divine couple's clothes (drying). Pranasala temple contains the deities of Sita, Rama, and Lakshmana. Here, Rama is said to be 'Soka Rama'.

Devotees find impressions of Ravana's chariot on the mountain range just opposite the Godavari river. Thus, Parnasala attained historical and mythological significance, in addition to being one of the 25 famous temples of Sri Rama in India.

Jeedikal – Ramachandra Swamy Temple

Jeedikal, located in the new district of 'Jangaon' or 'Jain gaon', is a holy place for Jains and Hindus. Here, devotees worship Sri Rama–Lakshmana and Sita along with Hanuman. Sri Rama passed through this place of 'Jeedikal' in search of Golden deer. In the temple, Sri Rama is said to be 'Swayambhu'. The place is also known as Veerachalam since 'Veera' was a great devotee of Rama. In the temple, there are 'Utsava Murthis' of the deities.

The temple possesses a gali gopuram, Maha mandapam, Navagraha Mandapam and Mandir of the Alwars. The puja activities are performed according to Vaishnavite traditions. Sri Rama Kalyanam is celebrated twice here (Sri Rama Navami and Kartika Masam). One speciality of this place is 'Jaatara'—people from all over Telangana attend in large numbers.

Dichpalli

Dichpalli temple of Sri Rama is a fine temple known for its architecture, which is solid in construction and graceful in finish. The temple was probably constructed during the middle of the 16th century, during the time of Vijayanagara ruler Ramaraya. Later, it was renovated in 1949.

A koneru (tank) and a mandapa are south of the temple. Sita, Lakshmana and Rama idols, along with Hanuman, are worshipped. In addition to the daily pujas, once in two years, special festivals are also celebrated, especially during Dasarah. Brahmotsavams (7 days) are a special attraction, followed by Radhotsavams.

In this region, the 'Dutch People' lived in large numbers; hence, it is known as 'Dutch Palli', later called 'Dichpalli' by the commoners. Special mention of the temple is to be made about the beautiful ornamentation of the walls reflecting the Dravidian style.

Sri Ramalayam (Sitarambagh – Hyderabad)

The Sitarambagh temple of Lord Sri Rama is built over 25 acres, having 50-foot wall wall, giving the temple a fort-like look. It is a centuries-old temple. One has to reach Darussalam to visit the temple (the place is near Mallepally on the way to Asif Nagar). The temple is situated in the middle of the most crowded localities of Hyderabad, the home of the Hindus and Muslims in equal numbers.

Architects of the Temple:

Puranmalji Ganeriwal, a member of the Ganeriwal family from Rajasthan, is said to have designed the temple of Sri Rama, which was built in 1835. Aravind Ghanerwal, presumably looking after the temple affairs, said a forest-like area surrounds the temple. Giant trees stand sentinel to this old temple structure, birds chirp, and pigeons coo from the many noons.

In the temple complex, there is a 16-pillar mandapa. After the darshan of Ganesa, devotees look at the Lord Sri Rama, the primary deity here. Adjacent to the Dhvajastambha, Anjaneya and Garudalwar are meant for darshan. Garudalwar's idol is also there in a special entrance. Opposite to this, Tayaru and Perumal are there.

The main deities are Sri Rama, Sita, Lakshmana, Bharata, and Satrughna. The temples of Siva, Anjaneya, Ganesa, Brahma, Andal, Varadaraja, Radhakrishna, and five Alwars are built separately here.

A shrine dedicated to Lord Hanuman to be seen now is a discovery. Worship is done only to the knee, and the rest had been buried over a period of time, said Aravind Ghanerwal. Idon of Hanuman was 6.5 feet tall, 4 feet wide and 3.5 feet thick.

Resources of the Temple:

Though the temple is under the Government of Telangana endowments department, there is no funding for its development. During the performance of 'Aarati' to the deities, people give 'Nazarana', which is utilized for the priests and their welfare. There are no 'Hundis', and the money given by the devotees is distributed among the 40 priests or Brahmins who are in the temple's service. The priests and their families live in rooms formerly used as 'Gosala'.

Temple Architecture:

The temple's doors are imposing. Its style is Kakatiya with a Rajasthani touch. Though the colour has faded, the richness of the art is still visible on the walls, doors, and sanctum sanctorum. Some say that the first gate of the temple shows European influence.

The Mughul touch is visible in 'Naubatkhana', where drums and shehanais are played. Chandeliers and fountains, too, remind us of the Mughul look.

Festivals:

Festivals are celebrated with great pomp in Sri Rama Navami, Dasara, Mukkoti Ekadasi, Godha Utsavam, and Janmashtami. The temple hosts the main deity, Sri Rama, in the Pattabhishekam arrangements with Sita, Rama, Lakshmana, Bharata, Satrughna and Hanuman. 'Utsava Idols' are also prepared and kept together. The puja activities are done every day.

Temple Management:

As said above, a Rajasthani family of Ganeriwal (who came from a village about 250 km from Ajmeer) is looking after the temple in Hyderabad. In addition, another temple – Rangaji temple in Pushkar, Rajasthan is also maintained by the same family. Thus, the temple is governed by three states – Maharashtra, Rajasthan and Telangana.

In short, Sitarambagh Sri Rama's temple in Hyderabad is reminiscent of the history of Telangana.

Ranganadha Swamy Temple of Jiyaguda

A famous Vaishnavism temple is Sri Ranganadha Swamy temple of Jiyaguda in Hyderabad. For four hundred years, devotees have considered it the 'Vaikunthadhamam'. One can reach the temple from 'Puranapool'.

History of the Temple:

Jiyaguda is otherwise known as Jiyarguda. Jiyar Swamis used to live in the Deccan region of Hyderabad 400 years ago. 'Visistadvaita Peethaddhipathi' Vanamamalai Jiyar selected this place on the banks of the river Musi or 'Muchi Kunda' to establish Ranganadha Swamy Temple.

Jiyar brought the idol from Sri Rangam, and the temple is said to be on the line of Sri Rangam temple. God Srimannarayana is lying on 'Seshatalpa' along with Sridevi and Bhudevi, and the idol sculptures are on a single stone (Yekasila). Of course, moola virat is small. Brahma is also to be seen near Ranganatha. The temple and temple complex seem beautiful, and the 'Dasavatara' scenes are portrayed.

Pujas and festivals are celebrated on a grand scale. Abhishekas to Swamy in the form of 'Salagrama' are performed. There is a special temple for Lakshmi Devi known as Tayaru. Anjaneya, Navagraha mandapa, and other deities are found on the campus.

Festivals like Vaikunta Ekadasi (Uttaradwara Darsan) and Goda Devi 'Karinomu Utsavams' (5 days – Sankranti) are the most popular. Nowadays, flowers and fruits are transported from Calcutta and Maharashtra.

Karmanghat Dhyananjaneya Swamy Temple

Karmanghat is in Saroornagar Mandal of Ranga Reddy district and is very famous and popular because of Dhyananjaneya Swamy temple, which has been in existence for more than nine centuries. Dhyananjaneya is also known as Abhayanjaneya since pilgrims or devotees strongly believe he is the protector to fulfil their wishes.

<u>Local Legend:</u>

Karmanghat area was known as Lakshmipuram in those days. Prataparudra II, the ruler of Golkonda, was a lover of hunting, so he was hunting in the forest area. He happened to listen to the roaring sounds of a tiger but could not find the tiger there. After some time, he could hear the chanting of 'Sri Ram… Sri Ram'. To his surprise, he found the idol of Dhananjaneya. The king saw the Lord in dreams the same day, ordering the construction of a temple.

Prataparudra II built the temple in 1143 AD. On the day of Hanuman Jayanthi, he offered prayers with his father, Prola. Since then, all the Kakatiya kings have continued the puja systems and extended the temple complex.

Other temple deities are Kodanda Rama, Viswanadha, Ganapati, Nagesvara, Sarasvati, Santoshimata, Durga Devi, Venugopala Swamy and Jagannadha Swamy.

During 1687, Aurangazeb occupied the Golkonda fort, capturing Abdul Hasan Tanisha. Under his project of demolition of Hindu temples, he proceeded to demolish Dhyananjaneya Swamy temple. The soldiers failed in their attempt. Aurangazeb got angry and tried to destroy it by entering the main gate. He was afraid of the sounding words of Hanuman:

"Hey Rajan, Mandir todna hai to pahale tum karo man ghat"— Karmanghat's present name derives from this incident.

<u>Aurangazeb said:</u>

"Hey Bhagavan, Tum sach hai to tumhara sachayi batav".

It is said that Hanuman appeared with a flood of light in a gigantic form. The Aurangazeb retreated.

<u>Festivals of the Temple:</u>

Temple festivals include Ugadi, Sri Rama Navami, Hanuman Jayanthi, Valmiki Jayanthi, Naga Panchami, Ganesh Chaturthi, Vijaya Dasami, Kartika Pournami, Maha Sivaratri, etc.

Kodagattu

Kondagattu, situated in Karimnagar district, is a holy place from the Ramayana. It is said that there is proof of Sita and Rama during their 'Vanavasa' there.

Sages installed Anjaneya and worshipped Narasimha Vaktra, one of Anjaneya's 'Pancha Mukhas', along with Sankha and Chakra, which are to be seen. There is Pushkarini also. God blesses the devotees, freeing them from all the planetary effects. Further, Alwar idols are found in a well here.

Taadubandu Veeranjaneya Temple – Secunderabad

The temple is in Secunderabad. As per local legend, the temple belonged to Tretayuga of Ramayana times. Sage Jaabali installed this Hanuman here and two more at Rishikesh and Tirupati. It is believed that Veeranjaneya Swamy is very powerful. The idol appeared in 1927 when Secunderabad was plunged into Plague disease.

The temple had Sanctum Sanctorum, Mukha Mandapa, Rajagopura and Vimana. A Hanuman named Dasanjaneya, along with Sri Rama, Sita, and Lakshmana, is to be seen and worshipped. Camel, Hanuman's vehicle, and Siva and Navagrahas were also installed. Different types of worship (Abhishekams, Archanas, etc.) are done with great devotion. Devotees attend the temple in large numbers on Tuesdays and Saturdays.

Sarasvati Temple of Basara

Basara was a part of the Adilabad district before the reorganization of the districts of Telangana state. Presently, it is in the Nirmal district.

There are two famous Sarasvati temples in India, one in Kashmir and the other in Basara. The presiding deity is Goddess Sarasvati or Sri Gnana Sarasvati Devi. The Temple is on the banks of Godavari. Basara, the seat of Goddess Sarasvati, is believed to be a place consecrated by the penance (Tapas) of Sri Veda Vyasa. Hence, Vyasa installed the deity or 'Pratista'. There is a story saying that after the completion of the battle of Kurukshetra, Vyasa came here for penance for the sake of peace. He bathed in Godavari in the early morning, brought three handfuls of sand from Godavari daily, and worshipped Sarasvati, Lakshmi and Kali. People believe that the caves where Vyasa lived and did penance exist, as well as the 'Samadhi' of Vyasa.

The Temple is situated with the north-facing Goddess Sarasvati in the sanctum sanctorum and opposite the deity Goddess Lakshmi's idol. Western side Goddess Kali is installed. There is a holy tank, and Vyasa's Temple is present here. Datta mandir is also there. There are also eight Tirthams: Indra Tirtham, Surya Tirtham, Vyasa Tirtham, Valmiki Tirtham, Vishnu Tirtham, Ganesh Tirtham, Putra Tirtham and Siva Tirtham. There is a Siva temple here.

The important festivals of the Temple are Vasantha Panchami, Devi Navaratrulu, Sivaratri, Vyasa Purnima etc.

Aksharabhyasam:

Parents devote their children to the 'Aksharabhyasa' program to receive the blessings of the Goddess, the mother of 'Vidya'.

Bhadrakali Temple of Warangal

Warangal Urban is a newly formed district of Telangana. Warangal is also called as 'Orugallu'. References are there to Bhadresvari, who is identified with Bhadrakali of the Bhadrakali temple on the Hanumakonda or Bhadrakali Tank. Hidimba Asrama, Hanumadri, or Hanumakonda are mentioned and are the abodes of Siddhas and Gods. The sacred soil between the Godavari and Krishna rivers is in the Dandaka forest. Sri

Rama, along with Sita and Lakshmana during his Vanavasam, stayed here for some time and saved Rishis from the Rakshasas. According to some sources, Sugreeva and other Vanaras also lived here.

<u>Bhadrakali's Idol:</u>

The idol of this mother goddess is 9 feet tall and 9 feet wide and is sitting facing west. She had eight hands – four on the right side bearing Sword, Churika, Japamala and Dhamaruka. Four hands are on the left, bearing Bell, Trisula, and Head of Asura and Panapatra. Historically, it was built, or the idol was installed during Pulakesin II (625 AD). Ganapati Deva, the Kakatiya king, dug a tank and allotted funds for the maintenance of the temple. Rudrama Devi has also continued the traditions of worship. Vijayanagara kings, too, continued. After 1565, the glory began to vanish. However, devotees strongly believe that her grace protects them. The face of the Goddess was in Ugrarupini, but later it came to be Santaswarupini.

<u>Celebrations:</u>

Daily worships and Sarannavaratri, Vasantaratrulu in Asvayuja, Chaitra masams and 'Pournami' in Ashadha masam. The Goddess is decorated as 'Sakambari Devi'. On Janmashtami day, she is decorated as Sri Krishna. The Kalyanotsavams or Brahmotsavams are celebrated on a grand scale on Sankara Jayanti (Vaisakha Suddha Panchami). After 1940, animal slaughter was prohibited. Pujas are allowed only on traditional lines of the Vedic formula.

Cult of Village Goddesses and Telangana State Temples

The panorama of Goddesses of Hinduism extended well beyond the significant deities like Sarasvati, Lakshmi and Parvati. Hinduism incorporates many minor gods who are supposed to regulate matters of personal interest for worshippers.

According to Rigveda, the Mother Goddess is boundless or 'Aditi'. The worship of the mother Goddess is otherwise known as 'Shakti Worship', which might have led to the cult of village Goddesses worshipped in every Indian village. These Goddesses are the various forms of divine mother Goddesses cited above.

Maisamma

Maisamma is a 'Gramadevata' (Village deity). Lakshmi, Parvati, or Kali Mata are said to be in the form of Maisamma in different places in the Telangana region. To mention a few of them, the temples at Hyderabad, Mahaboobnagar, Ranga Reddy regions are to be cited.

In the Begumpet area of Hyderabad, there is one ancient temple of Kanakala Katta Maisamma. She is said to be the incarnation of Maha Lakshmi. She is 'Svayambhu', existing since Nizams (1835-40). The Goddess became popular during the time of floods in 1907. Devotees believe that the Mother Goddess saved them. Presently, it is under the endowments department. The temple form came into existence in a century. Special pujas are celebrated only on Tuesdays and Fridays. During 'Ashada masam', last Sunday, the festival of 'Bonalu' will be celebrated.

At Balkampet in Hyderabad Maisamma is worshipped as 'Yellamma' is also popular. It is said the story goes back to 'Krutayuga' and Jamadagni. Her 'Shakti' came into a big stone here. The speciality here is that no idol or temple has existed for a long time.

Gandi Maisamma as Svayambhu, located in a wall of a fort or 'Buruju' (Hyderabad – Kurnool route), has been worshipped for hundreds of years as 'Grama Devata'. People believe her to be the form of 'Kali'. There is also a tank or 'Gandi' opposite the temple. Pujas are done daily and on 'Dasarah', especially during Navaratri celebrations.

At Nainapalli (Mahbubnagar-Kolhapur route), the Svayambhu Maisamma deity is located, and pujas have been celebrated there for a hundred years. On Sunday, people visit in large numbers.

'Katta Maisamma' of Kutbullapur region of Rangareddy region is famous as a village deity known for 'Jatara' (festival). Dances of 'Poturajulu', 'Deeparadhanas' and 'Pongali Naivedyams' are done with devotion and dedication to fulfil their wants (Abhishtams).

Maisamma is worshipped in old forts and is known as 'Khilla Maisamma'.

Renuka Yellamma – Pochamma

In Hyderabad, at Balkampet, people worship the deity for peace, happiness, and prosperity. The deity is also known as 'Balkamma' (Jalambika). Renuka Devi was the mother of Parasurama. She was 'Svayambu' 700 years ago. Near the idol, there is a well. In 1919, the Temple was renovated. Pochamma or Sitala Devi is the 'Kshetrapalakuralu'. The Bonalu festival is celebrated here. Devi Navaratrulu is a special occasion for the Temple's activities.

At Siddipet is a temple of Renuka – Yellamma, the village deity. The Puja system is as per 'Sakterya'. She appears as 'Santamurthi'. Abhishekams are performed on Tuesday and Friday.

Yellamma temple of Bodhan (Nizamabad) has existed since the 14th century. 'Jantu Bali' is given importance here.

Peddamma Temple – Hederabad

Peddamma Temple of Jubilee Hills in Hyderabad is thousands of years old in the seven-acre spacious area but appears modern after renovation. Sanctum Sanctorum and Rajagopuram are attractive, with five and seven stories, respectively. Ganapati, Sarasvati, Lakshmi and Durga temples also exist here.

Peddamma has four hands: Sankhu, Trishula, Kumkum Bharina in the left hand, and Chakra, Khadga in the right hand. Utsava Murthi is present. Every day Archanas, Abhishekams and Alamkarams are done. Navaratri celebrations during Dasarah are performed. The offering of Bonalu to the deity is usual.

Palvancha Peddamma Talli: (On the way to Bhadradri)

The mother goddess, Kanaka Durga, is worshipped as Peddamma Talli under a tamarind tree. Nitya pujas and festivals are celebrated on auspicious occasions.

Rampur Peddamma Talli of the Medak region is also a famous temple where pilgrims pay for their offerings.

Yedupayala Bhavani Temple (Medak)

Yedupayala temple is a Vana Durga Devi temple or Bhavani temple. Seven sub-rivers mingle with Manjeera here. In this stream, the Kanaka Durga deity appears as Svayambhu in a cave. Yedupayalu is named after famous sages Jamadagni, Atri, Kasyapa, Visvamitra, Vasista, Bharadvaja and Gautama.

According to a Puranic story, 'Sarpayaga' was performed here to eradicate the race of Sarpas. Parikshit and his son Janamejaya are reminded of this context. Garutmanta brought the Bhagavati River from 'Patala Loka' to purify the snake race. This is known as 'Garuda Ganga'. Yedupayala Jatara is famous for its connection with Maha Sivaratri.

Chamundesvari Temple in Medak region on the banks of Manjeera is a powerful deity. Every day, the Devi performs abhishekam with Manjeera water. Chamundesvari, one of the mother goddesses of 'Ashtadasa Shaktipeethas', had a few temples, one at Mysore and another in a village called 'Chitkul'. The deity has 18 hands on a monolith. The Navaratri festival is celebrated with pomp.

Mahankali Temples of Old City of Hederabad

Mahankali Temples of 'Meeralam Mandi' and 'Lal Darwaj' are highly powerful, attracting devotees in large numbers. They staunchly believed in the Goddess who protected people during floods to Musi (1908). Lal Darwaj temple is 400 years old. Bonaala Jataras or festivals are celebrated with folk dance to date by people with great devotion and enthusiasm.

During Nizam's time, Salar Jang took a particular interest in temple activities and upkeep.

Bhagya Lakshmi Amma's Temple

In the old city of Hyderabad, near Charminar, is the temple of Bhagya Lakshmi. The city of Hyderabad is also known as 'Bhagyanagar' because of this deity. She is none other than 'Maha Lakshmi'. This old temple was renovated in 1975.

Festivals of Telangana

'Bonaalu Utsavas' and 'Sammakka-Saarakka Jaataras' are Telangana's glorious festivals and are part of Telangana's culture.

Bonaalu Utsavas

It is estimated that in 272 temples, Bonaalu celebrations with processions carrying 'Ghatas' are held with grandeur every year. People attend in large numbers from Telangana, Andhra, Maharashtra, Karnataka, and other places. Even foreigners attend these celebrations. Laldarwaj and Mahankali Bonaalu Utsavams are famous.

The deity is decorated as 'Sakambari Devi' with all vegetables and green leaves. Mutyalamma temple, Haribouli Akkanna-Madanna Mahankali temple, Uppuguda Mahankali temple, Meeralam Mandi's temple, Sultan Shahi's Jagadamba temple, Gaulipura Mahankali temple etc., are well-known for 'Bonaalu Utsavams'.

Medaaram (Sammakka-Saarakka) Jaatara

The biggest 'Jaatara' or tribal festival of Medaaram (Sammakka-Saarakka) is not only of Telangana's culture but also the biggest in the Asian continent. Large numbers of people from different states participate. The government of Telangana recognizes this festival.

The story belongs to the 12th century. In the Karimnagar-Jagityal region, a place named Polavaasa was ruled by a tribal Lord named 'Medaraju'.

His daughter Sammakka was grown under his care (she was not his daughter). She was married to his nephew Pagidiraju, and they had three children: Saaralamma, Nagulamma and Jampanna. Kakati Prataparudra I invaded on Polavaasa. Medaraju, Tribal Lord escaped to Medaram.. Kakatiya's king faced guerilla warfare by Pagidiraju, Sammakka-Saarakka, Jampanna, and Nagulamma. But they died in the battle of Kakatiyas. Jampanna jumped into a vaagu, later known as 'Jampanna Vaagu'.

Sammakka stood like a rock and fought against the enemy. She disappeared near 'Chilakala Gutta'. The tribals could not trace her but found turmeric and 'Kumkuma Bharinelu'. Since then, a big festival, 'Jaatara', has been celebrated in Maagha Suddha Purnima. 'Jaggery Nivedana' is a traditional offering to the heroic deities.

TRIPURA (TR)

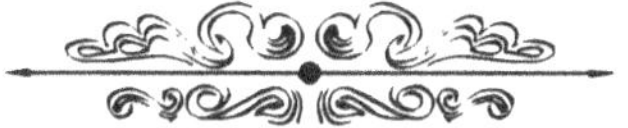

Hills, green valleys, flowing water, and dense forests surround Tripura, which has an area of 10,477 sq. Km. Agartala is the capital. Assam and Mizoram are neighbouring states, and Bangladesh is the neighbouring country. Tripura has unique sunrises and sunsets. The state was formed on 21 January 1972.

Tripura derived its name from the name of the deity, 'Tripuresvari' of 'Tripura'. According to the local dialect, 'Tri' means water and 'Pra' means near. Therefore, the land adjoining the water is the name of the state of Tripura.

Tripura's culture is composite – Tribal and Non-Tribal. The Tripuris worship 14 Gods and Goddesses (Chahhahas Devata). They follow tribal rituals and also various Hindu religious ceremonies.

Tripura Sundari Devi Temple

Tripura Sundari Devi temple is on a hill 57 Km from Agartala. The Goddess is also said to be one of the Shakti Peethams. The temple's shape is like a tortoise. It was constructed in the Bengali state in 1501. On Diwali day, celebrations are performed with grandeur, attended by lakhs of devotees. In 1681, the temple was renovated. The deity is 5 feet tall. Another small idol of 2 feet in height is also present there. There is also an idol of Kali in the same temple.

Kali Temple of Kamalasagar

Kali Temple of Kamalasagar, having 'Kund', is situated on a hill near Agartala (27 Km). The temple was built in the 15th century. The deity is also known as 'Mahishasuramardini'. The idol is represented with ten hands.

Unakoti

Unakoti means just one, which is less than one crore. There are sculptures from the 12th century and the Siva Temple from the 7th century. The idol of 'Kala Bhairava' is 30 feet high. Kala Bhairava festival is celebrated on 'Asokastami'.

UTTARAKHAND (UT)

Uttarakhand was initially formed as Uttaranchal on 9 November 2000 and renamed Uttarakhand in 2007. Uttar Pradesh and Himachal Pradesh are neighbouring states, and China and Nepal are neighbouring countries.

The rivers are Ganga, Yamuna, Bhagirathi, Ramganga. The great Himalayas and Shiwalik ranges are famous mountains. With the natural formation of Holy mountains, lakes, and rivers, Uttarakhand automatically became a powerful place, and it is thus said to be the best place to pursue spiritual activities. Hindus think of Uttarakhand as 'Dev Bhoomi', the land of Gods.

Figure 21: Uttarakhand – Map of Major Cities and Temples

Haridwar

Uttarakhand's holiest city is Haridwar, a much more significant place than Rishikesh. Haridwar is not only a sacred city but also beautiful. It is a strong belief that people will get salvation by entering heaven or the Kingdom of Gods. Haridwar is the gateway to this path. Holy Himalayas begin from this place, and the sacred Ganges begin downwards from Haridwar. The holy waters of the Ganges purify human being's sinful activities.

The flow of Ganges:

Kailasanath (Lord Siva) gave his blessings to Bhagirath to bring the Ganges down to the earth from heaven. Bhagirath succeeded in this task, and in fact, it was a spiritual miracle. In this process, the old Sivaliks have been cut off by the holy waters of the Ganges, making a significant passage having a one-mile breadth. Apart from the spiritual aspect of the flow of the Ganges, the other benefit of this work is that the barren lands that looked like deserts turned into fertile planes, enriching the lives of poor people.

According to statistical data, the length of the Ganges is 2525 Km. It flows through Uttarakhand, Uttar Pradesh, Bihar, Jharkhand, and West Bengal. The cities that the Ganges touch are Varanasi and Allahabad.

Ganga Aarti at Haridwar:

Ganga or Ganges is worshipped as the holy mother. From the early of the day to late at night, thousands of pilgrims take the holy dip and worship' Ganga mata'. Grand Aarti performed at 'Har-Ki-Pauri', a sacred experience for pilgrims. The ghat 'Har-Ki-Pauri' is significant because of the footprint of Vishnu (Hari) set into the upper wall of the ghat.

Asramas-Temples and Kumbha Mela:

Haridwar is the home to several ashrams and temples. Every day, a large number of pilgrims visit. Following are the important temples nearby:

1. Ganga
2. Shankaracharya
3. Navagraha
4. Sravan Nath
5. Maya Devi
6. Chandi Devi
7. Manasa Devi
8. Neeleswar etc.

Typically, Pandas arrange all facilities for the pilgrims, including puja and accommodation.

Yajmans are records kept verifying whether visitors' ancestors visited Haridwar. Kumbha Mela is held here once in 12 years.

The great trio of Gods, namely Brahma, Vishnu and Maheswara, descended from heaven to this place at the request of the devotees to satisfy this region. Further, when Raja Shwetu made penance to please Lord Brahma, the latter blessed him with a boon that the place be named after him as 'Brahma Kund'.

Similarly, Lord Vishnu set his feet at 'Har-Ki-Pauri', where the Ganges always touch Vishnu's feet (Haridwar).

In a story about Lord Siva, the legend says that Daksha Prajapati, son of Brahma, insulted his daughter Sati, Siva's consort. Therefore, the region of Daksha was destroyed. The place is named Daksheswara, Sivapuri, Neelparvat and Haridwar. Owing to the sacrifice of Sati, the place is also known as Mayapuri, the seat of rishis and saints.

<u>Visit of Epic Heroes:</u>

Bharata, brother of Lord Sri Rama, is said to have passed by this place to Rishikesh. Bharat Mandir is named after him later.

Pandavas had ascended to heaven (Swargarohana) from this place. Drutarastra, Vidura, Gandhari, and Kunti, too, visited this spot for salvation. Thus, Haridwar, known as Mayapuri, has been sacred since the Puranic times. Gangadwar and Tapovan are the other names.

Connection to History:

Hiuen Tsung, the Chinese pilgrim, visited Haridwar to witness the Kumbha Mela and beautifully described the grand ceremonious event.

Akbar came to Haridwar to merge the ashes of Raja Man Singh in the holy waters of the Ganges. At Brahma Kund, 'Man Singh ki Chhatri' has been placed, representing the beautiful masonry artistic work reflecting the Mughul style. A gallery was also established here in his memory.

Invaders attacked this place several times and caused heavy destruction of temples.

Under the British rule of Lord Dalhousie and Aukland, the sanctity of Haridwar was realized. Consequently, the 'Ganga Canal' scheme was launched and inaugurated in 1856.

Group of Temples and Shrines around the Brahma Kund:

- Manasa Devi Temple: This temple is situated on the top of Shivalik hills and is dedicated to Goddess Manasa Devi, the daughter of Lord Siva. She is supposed to be one of the 'Shakti Durga' forms. The temple's location is attractive and visible from any corner of Haridwar.
- Chandi Devi Temple: The temple of this Goddess is on the other side of the Ganges on top of the hills, 6 km away from the city.
- Maya Devi Temple: Haridwar's other name is 'Mayapuri', and the deity is Maya Devi. The three-headed Durga and the idols of Bhairava and Siva are seen here.
- Anjani Devi Temple: Pilgrims visit to fulfil their desires, and the temple is 6 km away from the city. The temples of Gauri Sankar and Neeleswar are also at the foot of Shiwaliks.
- Pashupatinath Temple: This is otherwise called as Sharwannath Temple.

- Navagraha Mandir: Near 'Har-Ki-Pauri', Maharaja Ranjit Singh constructed a magnificent Navagraha temple.
- Bhairon-Akhara: The black marble carvings show the idols of Bhairava, Siva, and three-headed Durga.
- Mahadeva Temple: This temple is situated near Gauri Kund. The practice of offering Bilwa leaves to Mahadeva is the same.
- Gayatri Temple: This temple near Sapta Rishi ashram is worth visiting.

Auspicious days at Haridwar:

Hindus from every nook and corner of India visit Haridwar to dip in the Ganges, perform pujas on auspicious days, and pay their respects to their ancestors by perming 'Pinda Shrardhas'.

Auspicious days are Ekadasi, Purnima, Amavasya, Sankranti, Solar and Lunar eclipses, and Baisakhi. People believe that on the first day of Baisakhi, on 13 April of every year, they will be blessed with an elixir (Amruth) at Brahma-Kund. After 12 years, Kumbha Parva starts on the same day.

Kushvart Ghat:

Kushvart Ghat is meant for 'Pind-dan' for ancestors and is near (South) Brahma Kund. 'Asti Visarjan' is also performed here.

Rishikesh

The abode of saints in Rishikesh is otherwise called 'Hrishikesh'. This holy place is just 24 Km from Haridwar on the banks of the Ganges and around the great Himalayas. A rishi named 'Raibhya' did penance and succeeded in getting Hrishikesh God's blessings. Rishikesh is the base for commencing the journey to the 'Chardham Yatra'.

Rishikesh is an excellent confluence centre between the Ganga, Yamuna, and Sarasvati rivers. Hence, the Ghat is popularly known as 'Triveni

Ghat'. In performing all religious rituals, it is similar to the Brahma Kund of Haridwar.

<u>Lakshman Jhoola:</u>

Lakshman Jhula is a hanging bridge across the Ganges that helps pedestrians, mules, and ponies cross. This is the spot where Lakshmana made penance. Later, Lakshmana's temple was erected. It is said that before 1889, the bridge was only a hanging jute rope bridge. Later, it was rebuilt with iron pillars. Lakshman Jhoola is thus an excellent bridge across the holy Ganges.

<u>Temples:</u>

The spiritual spectacle is visible along with natural scenic beauty since Rishikesh is an abode of temples and Ashrams.

- Raghunath Temple: Lord Sri Rama visited this place. This 13-story temple is a special attraction of the Lakshman Jhoola area. Every storey contains the idols of Gods and Goddesses.
- Kailash Niketan temple consists of Gods and Goddesses.
- Swarga-Ashram: The heavenly hermitage is 'Swarga-Ashram', opposite to Sivananda Ashram. This is the path to Badrinath temple.
- Gita Bhavan: The stories of Gita and Ramayana are beautifully inscribed on the walls. This Bhavan is affiliated with the famous Gita press of Gorakhpur.
- Satyanarayana Swamy temple: The temple is around 10 km from Haridwar and on the way to Rishikesh.
- Kanwa Maharshi Ashram: Kanwa lived with Sakuntala here (Abhignana Sakuntala of Kalidas).
- Other temples exist in Pushkar, Venkateswara, Chandra Mauleswara Satrughna, etc.

<u>Kankhal:</u>

This is a place of great significance, just 4 km from Har-Ki-Pauri. This is the place of King Daksha. 'Sati' was his daughter, and she performed self-immolation. There is a Sati Ghat on the banks of the Ganges. Sati Kund is a place where the wife of Siva, Sati, executed self-immolation in the sacred fire of 'Daksha Yagna'.

Confluence of Rivers – Way to Chardham and Existence of Six Prayags

1. On the way to Gangotri – Yamunotri, Kedarnath and Badrinath at the confluence of the holy rivers of Alakananda, Bhagiratha, Mandakini, Pindara, Vasuki, Son Ganga, Doli Ganga and Nanda, one finds spiritual pleasure in entering six Prayags.

2. Deva Prayag: Deva Prayag is a holy place near Srinagar at the juncture of Alakananda and Bhagiratha. It is related to the characters of the Ramayana. Lord Sri Rama, Sita Devi, Lakshmana, and Sugreeva stayed here for some time. Sri Rama installed the divine idols of black stone and paid offerings. To get the 'Punya Phalas', devotees perform three activities: 'Snana, Daana, and Tarpana. '

3. Rudra Prayag: Rudra Prayag is on the way to Gaurikund from Srinagar at the confluence of Mandakini and Alakananda rivers. There is a story about Narada's penance for the grace of Lord Siva to attain musical knowledge. Narada had Siva darshan, fulfilled his desire, and installed Rudradeva temple.

4. Karna Prayag: At the juncture of Alaka with Pindara, Karna, one of Mahabharat's heroes, performed Yagna to win the grace of 'Surya'. Ho got Kavacha, powerful bows and arrows from the Sun God.

5. Son Prayag: Son Prayag is on the way to Gaurikund. Son Ganga joins here with the Mandakini River, the nearest point to Kedarnath.

6. Vishnu Prayag: The confluence of Alaka with Doli Ganga is the place of Vishnu Prayag.

7. Nanda Prayag: This is the juncture point of the Nanda and Alakananda rivers, where King Nanda performed Yagnas. It is also on the way to Badrinath.

Chardham

The journey to the four holy places, believed to be the "abode of Gods" (Yamunotri, Gangotri, Kedarnath and Badrinath), nestled in the majestic Himalayan mountain ranges, is a pilgrimage of immense spiritual significance. These places, steeped in Puranic and Historic prominence, have drawn devotees for centuries, who visit with unwavering dedication, devotion, and a deep spiritual yearning, transcending the barriers of health or wealth.

The temples, a sacred haven, are open for a limited period of six months a year, from May to October – Vaisakha Suddha Trutiya (Akshaya Trutiya) to Aswiyuja Bahula Amavasya (Diwali). The pilgrimage, known as the Chardham trip, commences from the holy city of Haridwar, embarking on a nine-day journey with night halts. While Yamunotri, Gangotri, Kedarnath and Badrinath are considered Chardham, they are also known as Chota-Chardham, a testament to the unique pilgrimage experience they offer.

Yamunotri

The distance to Yamunotri from Haridwar is 235 km and 221 km from Rishikesh. The 6 km path is difficult; one should walk or travel by horse. It is a steep trek from approximately 9000 ft to 11500 ft. Before the Yamunotri yatra begins, one should cross through Hanuman Chatti, Pool Chatti, and Janaki Chatti. The pilgrims see the Goddess and daily special pujas are performed.

Gangotri River originates from Banderpoonch Mountain. The atmosphere is cold and freezing. But there is a natural hot spring. By bathing, one feels that life is back into one's cold bones before going into the temple for a darshan of Goddess Yamana.

<u>Puranic Story:</u>

Sun God's wife was Chayadevi. Yama and Yamuna were God's children. Chayadevi cursed her daughter Yamuna to stay in Bhooloka. Hence, she reached as a river.

<u>Historicity:</u>

Jaipur queen Gularia built the temple during 1892-93. But, due to the earthquake, the temple was demolished, and later, it was renovated. Adi Shankaracharya visited the place on foot when there were no transport facilities. Shankara's visit to Yamunotri made the place more holiest.

Gangotri

The journey from Yamunotri to Gangotri is a thrilling experience that offers spiritual and natural beauty. The lush greenery and the sight of snowcapped mountains are a treat for the eyes of pilgrims and tourists alike. Gangotri is located 99 km from Uttarkashi and is 3048 meters above sea level.

The temple is believed to have been constructed in the 18th century by Gorkha General Amar Singh Thapa and later renovated by the Jaipur kings. Gangotri is regarded as the birthplace of the Ganges, and for Hindus, the goddess 'Ganga Mata' is highly revered.

<u>Uttarakasi:</u>

'Trisul' in the mandir is said to be powerful as per the beliefs of the devotees.

<u>Gomukh:</u>

Bhagiratha brought 'Ganga', and the water flows for about 18 km, coming down to the earth through the face of a cow (Gomukh). The River Ganges from this spot, with a 50-60 ft width, travels to Gangotri. It is said that the holy waters from Gomukh to Gangotri are untouched by humans. Therefore, the water is carried to Rameswar for 'Abhishek' to the deity of Ramalingeswar or Ramanatha.

The present temple is built of white marble on a spacious campus with a western facing. 'Ganga mata' is the main deity of the temple. Adjacent to the temple are Goddesses Yamuna, Saraswati, Lakshmi and Annapurna Devi idols. One more speciality is the sitting Bhagiratha idol. Further, there are small mandirs of Ganesh, Hanuman and Lord Siva. Darshan to the temple is possible throughout the day with a lunch break (1:00-2:00 PM). This temple is closed on the day following Diwali and opens on Akshaya Trutiya (Vaisakha Suddha Tadiya). Yamunotri temple, too, follows the same closure and opening. Devotees strongly believe that a dip in the Ganges and darshan of Ganga mata will remove their sins. Some more Important Holy Places at Gangotri:

1. Siva Ling Mountains: One can see the twin snow mountains (Lord Siva and his consort Parvati) from Gomukh. The journey to Kedarnath starts from here.
2. Gupta Kasi: From this place to Gaurikund, the distance is just 34 km, and Kedarnath is 48 Km. Siddheswar Mahadev is in a cow's form here. Ganga and Yamuna waters are used for Abhishek of Swamy. The temple of Siva's consort is here.
3. Gaurikung: This is otherwise known as 'Gauri Tirth'. According to a legend, Parvati Amman did penance here and got her son Kumara Swamy.
4. Suryakund: Sun Gog bathed here to eliminate his sins.
5. Pandava's Cave: Located 1 ½ km from Gaurikund, and it is believed that five Pandavas spent some time here during their exile.
6. Vinayaka Dwaram: This place is located 3 Km from Gaurikund. It is believed that Parvatiputra Vinayaka's story of birth happened here.
7. Devaganga: This is a holy place, and Dharmaraja, his brothers and Draupadi bathed in the Ganges.

8. Cheed Baasa: This place is located 6 Km from Deva Ganga and is supposed to be where the trees (Cheed) are, with tents nearby for residing during the journey. Siva Ling Parvat is located 2 Km from here. The summit of this silver-like snowcapped mountain appears like a Conch and is glittering. The birth of Ganges is near the foot of this mountain.

9. Tapovan: This is said to be the birthplace of the Ganges, otherwise known as 'Vishnu Paadam'.

A journey to the Himalayan region's holy places is said to be the replica of 'Kailasa' and 'Vaikuntha'. Hence, devotees visit these places in their lifetime to get Moksha or Salvation.

Kedarnath

Kedarnath is one of the 12 Jyotirlingas of Lord Siva. It is a 12-km trek from Gaurikund on horseback or by Palanquin. The horse ride is tiring, as the roads are Kutcha. Snow and rainfall are common here most of the time.

Kedarnath temple is 3400 Km high amidst snow mountains and 11500 feet above sea level. The Hindu devotees strongly believe that Lord Siva or Nilakantha is present in this abode.

Establishment of the Temple:

It is believed that the Pandavas, the heroes of the Mahabharata, built the temple. Later, after thousands of years, the world preceptor Adi Shankaracharya rebuilt the temple. He made penance here and passed away at the age of 32. His 'Samadhi' is just 2 Km behind the temple.

Figure 22: Kedarnath Temple

Opening and Closure of the Temple:

Kedarnath temple opens during the last week of April or the first week of May (Surya Bhagavan enters Mesha Raasi on Mesha Sankraman day). The closure of the temple falls on October last week or November first week (during Kartika Maasa when Surya Bhagavan enters Vrischika Raasi). Thus, the temple is open only for six months for Swamy's worship. The Utsava Murti of Siva will be carried to 'Ukhi Math' (52 Km distance) for worship.

The Temple Complex:

When stepping into the complex from the entrance gate, there is a small 'Mukha Mandapa' and then the Sanctum Sanctorum, a square-shaped hall that measures 25 feet. The walls exhibit the sculptural work; on the left side wall is the 'Murthy of Badrinarayan'. According to the local legend, Kedarnath or Rudreswar is also the Lord of Badrinath temple. Swamy Badrinath made penance at the existing place of 'Badari' with Kedarinath's permission. Here, Kedarnath, the Swayambhu of 3 feet in height, is worshipped as 'Trigunarupa' unlike 'Siva Linga' worshipped in Siva temples.

When one enters the temple, there is the Murthy of Lord Ganesh on the right side and Siva's consort, Parvathi, on the left. Behind them, the main deity of Kedarnath is to be seen. In front of the temple, on the walls, there are sculptural forms of Kunti, Pandavas and Lord Krishna, which indicates their worship of the Lord Kedarnath.

<u>Procedure of Worship:</u>

Puja is performed twice a day, in the morning and evening. Morning puja is called 'Balbhoga' (Nirvana), comprising Ashtothara Sahasranama Archana and Abhishekha with 'Bilva Patra' and holy waters. Evening puja is called 'Sringara Puja' in the form of floral decoration, and devotees will not perform Archana between 6:00 and 7:00 PM. 'Visesha Harati' is given at this time, and Sadhus outside provides 'Sankhanada' (Conch) in praise of God.

<u>Other important places of significance:</u>

1. Adi Sankaracharya's Samadhi: Behind the Kedareswar temple is Adi Sankaracharya's Samadhi. No authentic sources provide the duration of this world philosopher's stay.
2. Agastheswara Temple: This is situated on the banks of Mandakini, where sage Agasthya meditated. The Vaisakhi festival is celebrated here.
3. 'Kunds' and 'Tirthas' – Rethakund, Sivakund, Brigukund, Vahini Tirth, Hanstirth, etc. – are situated here south of Kedareswar and symbolize holiness.
4. Doodh Ganga: At a distance of 2 Km, there are mountain ranges from where the 'Mandakini' flows. One waterfall resembles milk flowing from mountains and is a tributary river of the Mandakini.

It is approximately 5 Km in length and joins the Mandakini River 5 Km from its source. Doodh Ganga is part of four small streams that flow into the 'Mandakini'. The other three are Madhuganga, Swargaduari and Saraswati. Four sacred ponds are close to the temple: Retah, Udak, Rudra, and Rishi.

5. Five famous Mountains (Pancha Parvathas): These five mountains are situated behind Kedarnath:

   a. Rudra Himalayas
   b. Vishnupuri
   c. Brahmapuri
   d. Udgarukantha
   e. Swargaohana (via Mahapanth)

The last one is popular because only Dharmaraj reached Swarga, and the remaining Pandavas and Draupadi remained and passed away.

<u>Classification of Holy' Kedars':</u>

The holy Kedars are numbered five, and one should visit these five Kedars to attain salvation, as said by Bhishma to the Pandavas after the Kurukshetra battle. There is a story in this connection that runs as follows – After Pandavas won the Kurukshetra war, they wanted to seek the blessings of Lord Siva, and they visited Varanasi in search of Lord Siva. But Siva was not convinced that Pandavas should be blessed for the war sins committed and wanted to avoid meeting Pandavas. He took the form of a bull (Nandi) and hid in the Kedarnath region. However, Bhima was able to recognize Lord Siva and tried to capture the bull by its tail, and immediately Lord Siva disappeared and reappeared later in parts in five places, and they are:

1. Kedarnath – Hump
2. Madmaheshwar – Naabhi and Stomach
3. Rudranath – Face
4. Tunganath – Arms
5. Kalpeswar – Hair

Om Namasivaya Temple or Bugga Temple:

This is also just 2 km from the main temple. This place is known for 'Kunds' (similar to those cited above). Bugga Temple's kund is a square water pond. When devotees chant the mantra 'Om Namasivaya', bubbles will come up.

Floods of 2013 – Loss of Life and Properties:

During the second week of June 2013, Uttarakhand faced severe calamities, including floods and heavy rains that affected Kedarnath and caused loss of life and property. Flood waters rose up to 15 feet in height. Several buildings collapsed. Fortunately, the Kedarnath temple remained intact, and the walls were also not affected. Nearly 50,000 pilgrims were held up. The various states took up relief measures along with the central government.

Badrinath

Lord Sri Mahavishnu is the primary God of Badrinath. The temple is painted and is the most accessible and popular among all Chardham temples. From Haridwar or Rishikesh, one can easily reach Badrinath temple.

Alkananda and Taptakund are said to be holy. A dip in them (1/4 km from Badri temple, where there are hot springs) turns devotees pious, and then they are eligible to have darshan of Srimannarayan.

The devotees enter the Sanctum Sanctorum of the Lord and have darshan of Utsavamurthhis of Vishnu, Kubera, Garutmantha, Sridevi, Bhudevi and Nara Narayanulu, Narada, Udbhava and Paduka's of the Lord. At the Darshan Mandapa, celebrations like Visesha puja and Harati are done. Vishnu sahasraparayanas are goiong on in the Sabha mandapa.

Opening and Closure of the Temple:

April-May is fixed as per the Tithis for opening and closing during the third week of November. The same procedure applies to the Kedarnath temple.

<u>Pancha Badaris:</u>

Just like Pancha Kedars, Pancha Badaris classification is done. It is believed that Srimannarayana resides in all five places.

1. Badrinath
2. Yoga-Dhyana Badari
3. Bhavishya Badari
4. Aadi Badari and
5. Vriddha Badari

Yoga-Dhyana Badari is in a village called 'Pandukeswar' (in the name of Panduraj of Bharata); Panduraj performed Yoga and Dhyana here.

Bhavishya Badari is situated on the banks of 'Dhavalanidhi' and is at a height of 2744 meters near Joshimath in Subhain Village, which is 17 km from Joshimath. This place is known to be Badrinath›s future seat and hence is Bhavishya Badari.

Adi Badari: There are 16 small temples in Aadi Badari. Seven of these were installed by Aadi Sankaracharya. The temple of Srimannarayana, with the Lord sculptured in black stone, is one meter high and beautiful and attractive.

Vridha Badarai: 'Ani Matt' is another name for this place, which has a small Sri Maha Vishnu temple. When Badrinath is closed during winter for about six months, the Utsava murtis are carried to Joshi Matt for worship. Adi Sankaracharya made this arrangement. Before this arrangement, Aadi Sankaracharya started worshipping the Lord in the form of Utsava Murthi in this place. This temple is open throughout the year.

<u>Idols of Badrinath Temple – A Brief Explanation:</u>

- Sri Mahavishnu is carved in black stone. As the Swamy is 'Alankara priya,' he is decorated with Diamond jewellery, a crown, flowers, 'Srivatsa' and Brugulatha symbols on his chest, etc. He looks beautiful.

- Narada: Devarshi Narada's idol is on the main deity's left side. It is said that he had the right to worship the Lord from Vaisakha to Karthikam as Brahmachari.
- Nara-Narayana Idols: These idols appear on a single stone. Narayana is seen with Conch, Gada, Chakra, and Padma in his four hands, along with Sridevi and Bhoodevi. During Dwaparayuga, Nara is Arjuna and Narayana is Sri Krishna.
- Kubera's idol is also present.
- Garutmanta Idol: This is in standing posture with folded hands.
- Krishna's Devotee Udbhava's Idol: Krishna gave his Padukas to his devotee Udbhava and blessed him. The devotee took the golden Padukas to Badrinath Ashram and did penance. Afterwards, he got Moksha, and the Padukas were kept on a throne opposite Udbhava's idol.
- Sudarshan Chakra: It is kept on the southern side of the Murthy of Badrinath and covered with silver leaves.
- Akhanda Jyothi: On the left side of Swamy, Akanda Jyothi is to be seen, which lights throughout the year.

The other idols are Garuda, Hanuman, Vinayaka, and Lakshmi Devi (separate temple).

Places of importance to be visited:

Every pilgrim to Badrinath necessarily should visit some places as follows:

- Brahma Kapalam: Rudra cut off the head of Lord Brahma at this place. Hence, after taking a bath, pilgrims should offer Daana, Homas and Pindapradanas to their ancestors and forefathers to be seen at Brahmakapala. It is said that Pindapradanas at Gaya may be exempted if done at this place. There is an opportunity to perform 'Swa Pindapradan'. However, it is performed on the condition that they must stop all Puja activities at home after performing Swa Pindapradanam. If violated, Pitru devatas in heaven will be called back, which is considered a sin.

- Sesha Netra: This place is 1.5 km from Badari and is said to be the eye of Aadisesha.
- Charana Paduka: Lord Vishnu's charanams are to be seen here.
- Chakra Tirtha: There are two mountains, 'Nara' and 'Narayana'. The spot is known as Chakra Tirtha.
- Neelakantha Parvat: This snowcapped mountain is approximately 11,398 ft and is 9 km from Badrinath. According to a legend, there was no mountain initially at this place, and instead, there was a route between Kedarnath and Badrinath for priests to travel between the holy sites. However, Lord Shiva was upset over the sins of a priest and stood tall, blocking the way on this route in the form of Neelkantha mountain.

<u>Special features of Badrinath:</u>

The water is crystal clear and is believed to have the power to cure snake and scorpion bites. About 5 Km from Badrinath, there is a village called 'Mana', from which the border of India and China is just 23 Km away.

Some other places of interest to visit are the Valley of Flowers, Hema Kund Tirth, the Birthplace of the Alkananda river, Bhim pool, the Saraswati Devi temple, and Vyasa Guha (Cave), where it is believed that Vyasa recited the epic Mahabharata to Lord Ganesa.

UTTAR PRADESH (UP)

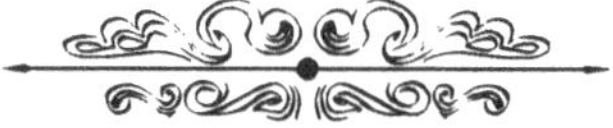

It was a united province by Aust 15, 1947 and later became Uttar Pradesh state on January 26, 1950. Nepal is the neighbouring country. The neighbouring states are Uttarakhand, Himachal Pradesh, Haryana, Delhi, Rajasthan, Madhya Pradesh, Chattisgarh, Jharkhand, and Bihar. Out of 75 districts of the state, Varanasi and Madhura occupy prominent places in the context of pilgrimages and Holy centres. Geographically, rivers like Ganga, Yamuna, and Gomti, as well as mountains like the lower hills of the Shiwalik range and Kaimur range, influence the history and religion of the region.

Figure 23: Uttar Pradesh – Map of Major Cities and Temples

Varanasi

One of the ancient cities of India is Varanasi, the holiest city of sanctity, spiritualism, and salvation, situated on the banks of the Ganges. 'Varuna' and 'Asi' are the two rivers that join the holy Ganges at Varanasi; hence, the city goes by the name of Varanasi. Varanasi has several names, like Kasi, Ananda Kanana, Siva Puri, Maha Sunsan, and Benaras.

According to the Siva Purana, Lord Shiva created this great city. According to Veda Vyas, Kasi had a glorious spiritual past, as explained in the Ashtadasa Puranas.

Kasi means ever shining. It is said to be the salvation centre (Mukti Kshetra). According to the Skanda Purana, if people say, "I will go to Kasi, live there, and die there," Lord Shiva will be happy and grant Moksha or 'Kaivalya'. Benaras is a continually inhabited city and one of Hinduism's seven holy cities.

Pilgrims dip in the Ganges to wash away a lifetime of sins or to cremate their loved ones. This practice makes us understand that Benaras is an auspicious place to die to get Moksha or salvation. The same thought has been expressed in the Skanda Purana, which is already cited above. Benaras is thus the beating heart of the Hindu universe. Here, the most intimate rituals of life and death occur, and the sights, sounds, and smells in and around the Ghats (estimated as 100) are also present.

Kasi Visveswara – The Jyothirlinga

Visvanatha or Visveswara means the happiest, and his dwelling place is therefore popularly known as 'Anandavana Varanasi'. Varanasi is one of the 'Dwadasa Jyotirlinga Kshetras'.

History of Viswanatha Temple and Varanasi:

Varanasi rose to prominence around 1200 BC. During the 8th century, the world preceptor 'Adi Sankaracharya' established Siva worship as the principal sect. This holy city was destroyed several times at different intervals by the Afghans and Mughals. Aurangzeb was the most destructive, looting and destroying several temples. The old city may look antique, but few buildings are over 200 years old. Viswanatha temple, the most famous, is dedicated to Lord Siva.

The present temple was built in 1776 by Ahilyabai of Indore. The 800 Kg of Gold plating on the tower and dome was supplied by Maharaja Rajit Singh of Lahore 50 years later.

<u>Timings of the Temple:</u>

The Viswanatha temple opens early, by 4:00 AM, and remains open until 11:00 PM. The linga form of Siva is small on one side in the Sanctum Sanctorum. Thousands of devotees visit daily to look at and perform 'Abhishekams'. Siva's three-pronged spear, the Trishul, is on the Sikhara. The city of Kasi is supposed to rest on this spear. Further, the river Ganga is supposed to flow from Siva's matted hair. Bhairava is the Kshetrapalaka of Kasi.

Figure 24: Ganga Aarthi in Varanasi

<u>Varanasi Ghats:</u>

Varanasi is at its brilliant best by the Ghats. One may find the long stretch of steps leading down to the water on the western bank of the Ganges. It looks like a theatre – the river's curve, the steps and people watching. Most of the Ghats (65-100) are used for bathing. A boat trip provides a chance to look at and listen to the ghats and learn about them. There are also several ghats meant for burning where bodies are created in public. The main ghat meant for the purpose is 'Manikarnika'.

- Manikarnika Ghat: This is a burning Ghat. Funeral processions take place. The disposal of the dead is done in the form of cremation with pathetic hearts, of course, with the belief that the soul has reached heaven since the death happened in Varanasi.

- Dasaswamedh Ghat: Puja to the rising Sun and at Sunset is performed. 'Ganga Aarathi' is the highlight in this context. Pilgrims gather on the steps to watch this, enlightening them spiritually.

- Assi Ghat: River 'Assi' meets the Ganges here. People attend to worship Mahadeva.

- Tulsi Ghat: Krishna's festival is celebrated on a grand scale. Karthika masam is important for pilgrims and devotees.

- Shivala Ghat: This was built by Maharaja of Benaras.

- Dandi Ghat and Hanuman Ghat: Both are used by ascetics.

- Harischandra Ghat: This is also a cremation ghat. This one is the oldest ghat and reminds us about Raja Harischandra's story, who stood for 'Satyam' or truthfulness despite the loss of kingdom and separation from family as per the word given to Sage Viswamitra.

- Kedar Ghat: This is busy with the South Indians and Bengalis.

- In the old city, the following Ghats exist:

  - Dasaswamedha Ghat: According to a legend, Lord Brahma sacrificed ten horses as part of the Dasa-Aswamedha Yaga performed here.

- ○ Someswar Ghat: This ghat is notable for healing diseases, and the Lord here is the Moon God.
- ○ Ahilyabai Ghat: This ghat was built in memory of the Queen of Indore, Ahilyabai.

Figure 25: View of Ghats as seen from a Boat Ride

Below is a list of all 88 Ghats:

No.	Ghat Name
1	Assi Ghat
2	Ganga Mahal Ghat (I)
3	Lassi Ghat
4	Tulsi Ghat
5	Bhadaini Ghat
6	Janaki Ghat

7	Mata Anandamai
8	Vaccharaja Ghat
9	Jain Ghat
10	Nishad Ghat
11	Prabhu Ghat
12	Panchkota Ghat
13	Chet Singh Ghat
14	Niranjani Ghat
15	Mahanirvani Ghat
16	Shivala Ghat
17	Gularia Ghat
18	Dandi Ghat
19	Hanuman Ghat
20	Prachina (Old) Hanumanana Ghat
21	Karnataka Ghat
22	Harish Chandra Ghat
23	Lali Ghat
24	Vijayanagaram Ghat
25	Kedar Ghat
26	Caowki (Chauki) Ghat
27	Ksemesvara / Somesvara Ghat
28	Mansarovar Ghat
29	Narad Ghat
30	Raja Ghat rebuilt by Amrut Rao Peshwa
31	Khori Ghat
32	Pandey Ghat
33	Sarvesvara Ghat
34	Digpatia Ghat

35	Causatthi Ghat
36	Rana Mahal Ghat
37	Darbhanga Ghat
38	Munshi Ghat
39	Ahilyabai Ghat
40	Sitala Ghat
41	Dashashwamedh Ghat
42	Prayag Ghat
43	Rajendra Prasad Ghat
44	Man Mandir Ghat
45	Tripura Bhairavi Ghat
46	Mir (Meer) Ghat
47	Phuta/ Naya Ghat
48	Nepali Ghat
49	Lalita Ghat
50	Bauli/ Umaraogiri/ Amroha Ghat
51	Jalasen (Jalasayi) Ghat
52	Khirki Gate
53	Manikarnika Ghat
54	Bajirao Ghat
55	Scindhia Ghat
56	Sankatha Ghat
57	Ganga Mahal Ghat (II)
58	Bhonsale Ghat
59	Naya Ghat
60	Genesa Ghat
61	Mehta Ghat
62	Rama Ghat

63	Jatara Ghat
64	Raja Gwalior Ghat
65	Mangala Gauri Ghat (also known as Bala Ghat)
66	Venimadhava Ghat
67	Pancaganga Ghat
68	Durga Ghat
69	Brahma Ghat
70	Bundi Parakota Ghat
71	(Adi)Sitala Ghat
72	Lal Ghat
73	Hanumanagardhi Ghat
74	Gaya/Gai Ghat
75	Badri Nayarana Ghat
76	Trilochan Ghat
77	Gola Ghat
78	Nandesvara /Nandu Ghat
79	Sakka Ghat
80	Telianala Ghat
81	Naya/Phuta Ghat
82	Prahalada Ghat
83	Raja Ghat (Bhaisasur Rajghat) / Lord Dufferin bridge / Malaviya Bridge
84	Adi Keshava Ghat
85	Sant Ravidas Ghat
86	Nishad Ghat (divided from Prahalada)
87	Rani Ghat
88	Shri Panch Agni Akhara Ghat

Table 2: List of all Ghats in Varanasi

Annapurna Devi Temple

On the same premises as Kasi Viswanatha temple is Annapurna Devi or Annapurneswari temple. Before the darshan of Annapurna Devi, one must first visit 'Hunthi Vinayaka' and get his permission before visiting Visweswara or Annapurneswari since he is said to be the chief executive of this city of Varanasi. Kalabhairava is the judicial officer.

<u>Episode of this Goddess:</u>

Annapurna Devi is another form of Parvathi or Gauri. Once, she closed Shiva's eyes, which resulted in complete darkness (Surya-Chandra and Agni are the three eyes of Shiva), causing calamities to all the living things. Due to her closing Shiva's eyes, she committed a sin and hence became black. She is known later as 'Kaatyayani' or 'Kaali'.

She made penance and appeared as Annapurna Devi with a golden vessel containing 'Annam'. She continuously made Annadaana to the people of Kaasi, and her colour was changed again to Gaura Varna and turned into 'Gauri' again.

<u>Sage Vyasa:</u>

Vyasa, along with his disciples, stayed comfortably in Kaasi. Shiva wanted to test Vyasa and the sage, but his disciples could not secure food (Anna) for about three days in Kaasi. Vyasa grew angry and tried to curse Kaasi. At this juncture, an old lady (Annapurna Devi in disguise) appeared before the sage and invited him and his disciples for lunch. To the surprise of the sage and his disciples, she gave a feast. Vyasa was surprised and shocked by this unbelievable incident. Vyasa realized his mistake and prayed to Shiva for pardon, but instead, he was ordered to leave Kaasinagara. Hence, he went to the other side of the Ganges, lived there, and continued his penance. That place is known as 'Vyasa Kaasi'.

Visaalakshi Devi Temple

Per puranic sources, Shiva said, "I wish to take up my abode as Kaasi. The Gods come to see me there, as well as the sages, the men, and the women of the world. I shall be known as Viswanatha, the Lord of the universe and Parvathi as 'Visaalakshi', the wide-eyed one. I will be Jyoti Linga or the light of life".

Kaasi is sacred as one of India's 'Astadasa Shaktipeethas' (18). Visaalakshi is said to be the super Goddess along with the other Super Goddesses like Kanchi Kamakshi and Madurai Meenakshi. Next to Benaras, Kanchi and Madurai in south India stand glorious. Devotees consider Varanasi and Visalakshi as greatly associated. They praise "Varanasyam Visalakshi".

Visalakshi and Annapurna are the names meant for 'Knowledge' and 'food'.

> *"Varanasyam Visalakshi, Annapurna Parakruti*
> *Annam, Gnanam cha Rakshati Nityam"*

The temple of Visalakshi is small. The Goddess's idol is just 2 – 2 ½ ft high and covered with Gold, which attracts devotees.

Other temples in Varanasi

- Durga Mandir: A Bengali queen constructed this temple during the 18th century. The deity is said to be 'Svayambhu'. The style of the temple is 'Nagari'. 'Durga Kund' is the sacred tank here. Navaratri celebrations are the highlight.
- Sankata Mochan Hanuman Temple: This temple is also famous here. It is a spiritual centre for devotees' gatherings.
- Thulasi Manas Mandir: This is a modern construction. Ramacharit Manas was portrayed on the walls of the Mandir.

Many more temples are at Varanasi to look at and pray.

Sites and Temples related to Ramayana and Mahabharata

Ayodhya

Ayodhya, the sacred birthplace of Lord Sri Rama, is on the banks of the Sarayu River. Putrakamesti yaga was celebrated by King Dasaratha, and the birth of Rama took place. Ayodhya is therefore known as 'Ram Janmabhoomi'. According to a Puranic story, 'Manu', son of Brahma, built and ruled Ayodhya. His eldest son was Ikshvaku. The dynasty of Rama is Ikshvaku. Mandhata, Harischandra, Dilipa, Raghu and others of great reputation ruled Ayodhya. Sri Rama is said to be of 65th generation. Kosala is attached to Ayodhya.

The construction of a mosque on the site of the Ram Mandir, a deeply contentious issue, has caused communal tensions between Hindus and Muslims. As per the Supreme Court's directive in 2019, the disputed land was given to Hindus to construct the Ram Mandir, while Muslims were given land in nearby Dhannipur to build a Mosque. A ground-breaking ceremony for the temple was performed on August 5, 2020, and a magnificent temple was inaugurated on January 22, 2024, after the Prana Pratishta Ceremony was held.

There are other monuments, such as the place where Rama lived along with Hanuman, Kaikeyi's Nanaka bhavan, Sita's residence, Dasrath's Mandir, Valmiki's Mandir, Chardharma Mandir, Govindaraj Mandir are there. Ananda Bhavan is the place where Rama and his brothers played during childhood days. 'Svargadwar' is a place where Rama completed his avatar situated here.

Naimisaranya

On the banks of the river 'Gomathi', Naimisaranya is a very famous place. Sage Suta and Saunaka stayed here and conducted puranic discussions. There are 'Kundas' like Bhahma Kund and Chakra Tirth (Vishnu created this with his Sudarsan Chakra). There is a temple for Lalita Devi where

Pandavas are said to have spent their time during 'Vanavasa'. Lord Siva narrated a story relating to the formation of Naimisaranya to Parvati (Brahma's creation). Lalita Devi played a vital role in this context. Hanuman Mandir, Pandava Khilla, Ramanuja Kutami, Vedavyas Mandir and many more exist.

Suka narrated the story of Bhagavata to Parikshit in 7 days here. 'Gaya' desired his death in the hands of Vishnu, and Sudarshana Chakra cut off his body into three parts, all of which fell in Naimisaranya. Therefore, 'Pitrukarmas' are celebrated here.

Chitrakuta Kshetra

125 Km from Allahabad, on the banks of the river Mandakini, this is a mountain area where Sri Rama spent some time during 'Vana Vaasa'. Sages Bhardvaja and Atri advised Rama from this place. Rama completed the 'Pinda Pradan' to Dasaratha during his Vanavas here. Hence, this region is called Ram Ghat.

Rama and Sita built a Parnasala here and lived. Now, there is a temple for them. Sri Rama gave his Padukas to Bharata (2 km from Bharat Milap). There is Sati Anasuya Asram (11 Km distance). Hanuman and Tulasidas Mandirs are also seen here.

Misrik Tirth

Located 90 Km from Lucknow, in this Tirth Kund, the holy waters of great rivers are mixed up (Misrik). Bath in this Tirth provides Mukti. This place is associated with Dadhuchi Maharshi. Further, this is where Luv and Kush catch hold of the 'Yagna Aswa' of Rama, and Sita is taken away from this place by her mother, Bhoodevi.

Madhura

Madhura is 150 km from Delhi on the banks of the Yamuna River. It is the birthplace of Sri Krishna Bhagawan, who was born in prison.

Local Legend: The Ramayana mentions Madhura. Satrughna killed Lavanasura, who belonged to the line of 'Madhu'; hence, the place is known as Madhura.

Madhura was ruined by the Mughul ruler Aurangzeb, who constructed a mosque by its side (Krishna Janma Bhoomi). The story of Krishna's birth and Devaki-Vasudewa are related to this place.

Brindavanam

Brindavan Kshetra is located on the banks of the Yamuna River (9 km from Madhura). Krishna Bhakti is the central theme here. Great devotees like Surdas and Meerabai popularized the Bhakti Geetas of Krishna and Radha (Radhe Shyam). Brindavan is full of Mandirs and peacocks. Chaitanya Prabhu is one of the propagators of this movement. Rangaji temple and Govind Dev Ji temples are noted temples in this context. Kali Mardan Ghat is well known here, where Krishna drove away the serpent.

Govardhan Giri

Krishna lifted Govardhan Giri with his little finger and protected cows and people when Indra grew angry and showered in the rain of stones, feeling neglected.

'Giri Pradakshina' is popular here during Sravana and Bhadrapada masas.

Vasudev Teerth

Lord Krishna took a rest here on the way to meet Pandavas. This place is located 100 Km from Delhi.

Triveni Sangam

The confluence of Ganga, Yamuna, and Saraswati (Antarvahini) is Triveni Sangam, located at Prayagaraj. Here, the Ganges water is clear white, whereas Yamuna water is greenish. Kumbh Mela is held every 12 years.

WEST BENGAL (WB)

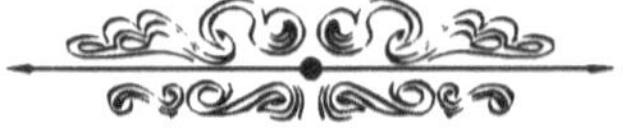

The area of West Bengal is 88,752 Sq. Km. Calcutta, or Kolkata, is the capital of West Bengal. Kolkata is the second largest city and is famous for its cultural and intellectual capital. Further, it was the former capital of British India. By 15 August 1947, it was a province and became a state on 26 January 1950. Odisha, Jharkhand, Bihar, and Sikkim are the neighbouring states, and Nepal, Bhutan, and Bangladesh are the neighbouring countries. Bengali is the chief language, and Hinduism, Islam, and Christianity are the major religions. Bhagirathi, Mayurakshi and Damodar are the famous rivers. Darjeeling is a well-known place.

West Bengal, a land of spiritual fervour, is renowned for its numerous temples dedicated to deities like Kali, Siva, Vishnu, and Shakti Peethams. The state comes alive during the festive seasons, with Durga and Kali pujas being celebrated with unparalleled zeal and enthusiasm, a testament to the vibrancy and liveliness of the culture.

Kali Temples

Kalighat Temple

The ancient temple of Kali or Kalighat is Calcutta's holiest spot for Hindus and probably the source of the city's name. The image of Kali is three-eyed. This temple is one of the 51 Shakti Peethams and is said to have been popular since the 5th or 6th century. The temple is not significant; the idol is not in its complete form. The head part of the deity (3 feet) is installed, and the tongue is stretched (2 feet). A legendary source reveals that Sati's upper part of the foot has fallen here. The story of Daksha is the source. The confluence of Ganga Sagar is the holy place of this Kali Kshetra. Devotees consider the deity one form of Durga, Lakshmi, and Saraswati.

Festivals: Daily pujas, pujas on auspicious days and Navaratri celebrations in Chaitramasa are performed here.

Dakshineswar Kali Temple

Another Kali temple in Calcutta is Dakshineswar, on the other side of the Hugli river. Here, Kali is otherwise known as Durgadevi. This temple is also quite ancient.

Ramakrishna Paramahamsa started his career as Pujari in childhood with the name of Gadadhara. Rani Rashmoni, a rich and pious lady, built this well-known temple at Dakshineswar, four miles from Calcutta, in 1855. Firstly, the elder brother of Ramakrishna Pandit, Ram Kumar, was the priest of the temple, and within a few days, Ramakrishna was employed as an assistant priest. Within a few days, a change came over Sri Rama Krishna. He used to sit for long hours in front of the image of Kali or consort of the Lord of eternity, called by him the 'Mother'. He attained excellent knowledge. This temple on the banks of the Ganges is holy, and the' Upalayas' are also on the campus. Radha Krishna and Sivalayas are twelve in number, and they are all similar. People consider them as 'Dwadasa Jyotirlingas'.

Shakti Temples

Background

In one of the Puranas, Kalki Purana, 'Daksha Yagna' is referred to. Parvati, or Sati, Consort of Lord Siva, was the daughter of Daksha. On the occasion of performing Yagna, Daksha did not invite his daughter and Son-in-law. Knowing about the Yagna through Narada, though uninvited, she attended the Yagna. Feeling insulted, she sat on the ground, closing her eyes and breathing her last. Siva destroyed the sacrifice and carried the dead body of his consort in fantastic sorrow. In this situation, Brahma and other Gods approached Vishnu for a solution. Vishnu cut off the body into a number of pieces, limb by limb. The parts of the body fell in different places numbered 51 styles as Shakli Peethams. Of 51,

18 are said to be 'Maha Shakti Preethams'. West Bengal is one of India's states, with some Shakti Peethams out of 51. Details are as follows:

It is observed that it is difficult to differentiate the 'Shakti Peethas' and 'Maha Shakthi Peethas' because there are no authentic proofs regarding the falling of body parts and limbs of Satidevi in the different parts of the country and Srilanka. Hence, those temples are upheld as Shakti or Maha Shakthi Peethams, who speak about parts of her body. Of course, one source, i.e., Sage Vyasa, narrated Sanskrit slokas to Janamejaya regarding these Peethams. They may need to be more comprehensive. Therefore, Confusion arises, and repetition of the narration of body parts of Satidevi occurs.

However, the table cited below attempts to provide some information in this regard. Vyasa said devotees attain Heavenly bliss or 'Sarvaloka Prapti' by 'Snana' (lakes before temples), 'Smarana', 'Darsana', and Puja of the 'Shakti Matas'.

Shakti Peethams of West Bengal:

S.No	Region	Name of Shakthi Mata	Limb/Body Part
1	Calcutta	Kali	Supposed to be source of Shakh prethas (51)
2	Kirit-Beda Nagar	Vimaladevi	Crown's place
3	Nandipur	Nandinidevi	Kanthahar
4	Nalhati	Nalateswari	Bone of the leg
5	Bakrisvar	Mahishamardini	Heart / manas
6	Betubrahna village	Chandidevi	Left Hand
7	Syalavadi Village	Bhramaramba	Left foot
8	Tamaluk Village	Kapalini	Ankle of the left leg
9	Ksheera Village	Bhutadhatri	Fingers of the right leg
10	Alipur	Kali	Fingers of the feet

11	Dakshinesvar (Calcutta)	Kali	-
12	Tarapith	Taradevi	Eyes
13	Bhirgam	Yogadhtadevi	Fingers of the right leg
14	Uchari	Mangalachandi	Right wrist
15	Howra Bridge (Calcutta)	Kali	Hair
16	Katuva	Bahuladevi	Left Hand
17	Bholpur	Kankali	Bone of the body
18	Attahas	Pullaradevi or Attahasadevi	Smiling lips of 18 ft

Table 3: Shakti Peethams of West Bengal

Devi Temples

1. Tripura Sundari Devi: This old temple is just 20km from Calcutta. Tripurasundari is famous here. In the same temple, the great trio of Gods, Brahma, Vishnu, and Mahesvara, can also be seen.

2. Mahishasura Mardini: At Bakresvar (cited above), there is the temple of Mahishasura Mardini in a standing pose with 18 hands containing weapons, giving darshan to the devotees. It is said Sage 'Asta Vakra' installed this idol. There are hot springs (Brahma Gundams) here.

3. Kapalinidevi (Vibhasa) – cited above. This is also a Shaktipeeth. The Swamy here is Sarvananda.

Siva Temples:

1. Siva Temple of Baraknath: One of the old Temples of Siva, built by Kalinga kings, is situated near Calcutta (Baraknath). The Temple is known for its sculpture. Hot springs attract devotees here. Maha Sivaratri is being celebrated on a grand scale.

2. The Syamalesvar (Siva) Temple of Dantan, situated on the way to Puri, is also ancient. Devotees worship Siva under the name Syamaleswar.

3. Yekapadesvar (Siva) Temple of Bankura is another ancient temple. The idol is represented with one foot and two hands here, which is rare.

4. Tarakeswar (Siva) of Pandale is near Calcutta (5 Km distance). The Temple belongs to the 18th century. Siva's Consort is known to be Tarakesvari. The Temple is a big Saiva kshetra. The God and Goddess are famous for relieving devotees from chronic diseases. Sivaratri festival is celebrated for about five days. There is a lake or Koneru where devotees can bathe before the darshan of God. There are many bells in the Temple for ringing by the devotees, which is unique.

5. Vaidyanath of Parli: This is the 5th Jyotirlinga Kshetra. There is a legend saying Ravana's association with this God.

6. Siva – Bamsapati: At a distance of 45 Km from Calcutta, this Temple is situated. Here, Siva's posture is unique and different. Sankara is lying on the lotus from Siva's navel. Parvathi is seated and named Hansesvaridevi.

7. Siva Temple of Gidhapahar: This Temple is situated in the mountain regions of Darjeeling, and devotees visit in large numbers to offer their prayers. The Sivaratri festival is celebrated grandly.

8. Dheerdham Temple of Darjeeling: This Temple is Darjeeling's most conspicuous Hindu temple and a replica of the Pashupatinath Temple in Kathmandu. In 1939, Purna Bahadur, the king of Nepal, built this Temple. It is a multistoried temple similar to the Tibetan style. Siva's marble idol is just before the entrance. The Maha Sivaratri festival is celebrated on a large scale.

Vishnu Temples:

1. Anantasayana Murthy – Bankura: Mahavishnu in the form of Anantasayana is the oldest Temple of Bankura. Devotees worship

on auspicious and regular days. This Temple is one of the famous Vaishnavite temples of West Bengal.

2. Jagannadh Temple – Howrah: Just 20 km from Howrah, Jagannadh Temple is like Puri Jagannadh temple. This Temple is situated at 'Vallabhapur Sri Rampur'. Puri Jagannadh reminds rath yatra, and this tradition is followed here also.

Krishna Temples:

1. Krishna Temple of Vishnupur: There is a Krishna Temple in Vishnupur, situated 130 km from Calcutta. During the 16th—17th centuries, Vaishnavism was in full swing, and the rulers were Staunch Vaishnavites. Hence, it is estimated that more than 20 Vishnu and Krishna temples appear to be Terracotta constructions.

2. Lalji Temple—Vishnupur: Radha and Krishna are the chief deities. According to a Bengali inscription, it was built in 1655 AD. There is also a sub-temple of Siva on the campus.

3. Radha Krishna Temple—Mayapur: This temple is located 115 Km from Calcutta, on the other bank of the Ganges. It is supposed to be the origin of the Hare Krishna movement. Sri Chaitanya Prabhu's nativity hails from this place. There are many Krishna Mandirs here. ISKCON's activities are prominent. 'Nam Sankirthan' and 'Bhajans' are the devotees' daily activities.

4. Krishna Kshetra near Howrah is organised by a mission called 'Gaudia', which was established by Goswami, a disciple of Sri Chaitanya, to propagate Krishna Bhakti.

5. Gopinath Temple is situated on a nock amid the holy Ganges.

6. Krishna Temples of Hugli: This temple is located 76 Km from Calcutta, Krishnadhamam, Radhagovind, and Vasudeva mandirs. All these Mandirs are supposed to be old ones that attract devotees.

7. Krishna Temples of Terrakot". Located 150 Km from Calcutta, there are temples of Madanmohan, Syama, Sridhar etc. (17th century)

8. Radha Madhav Temple of Kendur: This temple was constructed on the side of Bhakta Jayadev's house, and it is therefore known as the Jayadev temple.

Holy Confluence of Ganges and Bay of Bengal

Diamond Harbour of Calcutta is the place of the holy confluence of the Ganges and the sea, called 'Ganga Sugar'. There is also a temple for Gangedevi, Kapila Maharashti, Bhagiratha, and other sages. A three-day Mela on Makara Sankranti is being celebrated here. Bhagiratha brought the Ganges to the earth through Gangotri and Ganga Sagar and reached the seas, the origin being Siva's hair locks (Jata Juta).

Mahabharata Background:

1. Dharmaraja Temple: A temple was constructed for Dharmaraja in the Bardvan region of West Bengal. There is an episode of Dharmaraja and Yamadharmaraja in the context of testing Dharmanirati of Dharmaraja. Yama killed his four brothers. Dharmaraja answered the questions of Yama, and the latter promised to get back the life of only one brother. Then Dharmaja gave The option of Nakula (Panduraj had two wires, Kunti and Madri; Nakula was the son of Madri). Finally, Yama was satisfied with Dharmaraja's Dharmanirati and gave life to all his brothers. The speciality of the temple is Dharmaraja, who is in tortoise form.

2. Aditi Temple—Tamaluk: On the bank of the river Rupnarayan, there is a temple of Aditidevi. Krishna and Arjuna's idols are there. A war between Arjuna and a local king happened regarding Yaga Aswas's capture. Aswamedha Yaga was performed by the Pandavas. According to a legend, Krishna compromised between the two and released the horse.

EXPANSION OF HINDU TEMPLES AROUND THE WORLD

In ancient India, the concept of spiritual life was carved out by the sages and saints to facilitate the people's concentration on Gods and Goddesses to get relief from stress and strife. The oldest philosophy is said to be 'Hinduism' in the world, which stood in ecstasy because of its systematized ideals based on humanism.

Different versions of the definition of Hinduism have been put forward. Some say it is a religion, and others say it is a way of life. However, this philosophy attained the stamp of universality, followed by the construction of temples worldwide.

The focus is on the countries of the Far East, Southeast Asia, Malaya Peninsula, Cambodia, Java, Bali, Borneo, Burma, Siam, Indo-China, Indonesia, Philippines, Nepal, Sri Lanka, Malaysia, Thailand, Pakistan, etc., which have witnessed the wave. Temple construction and Puja activities began in Europe and the USA later in modern times (50 years ago).

During the 2nd century AD, Indians initiated maritime adventures and colonization activities and succeeded in settlements, followed by spiritual activities. The scope was widened by attaining political power and establishing cultural and religious institutions (2nd and 5th centuries AD). Kingdoms were established, and Brahmanical religion was patronized under the umbrella of Saivism. This wave swayed for nearly one thousand years. Splendid monuments of Indian art existed during the early times in these colonies.

Rise of Cultural and Religious Institutions in Asia

Indonesia Temples

Java

Java, Sumatra, Bali, and Borneo are part of the 'Malaya Archipelago' (the remains of Hindu culture have been discovered) or 'Suvarnaidvipa'.

Sailendra dynasty ruled this region who hail from the east coast of India or Kalinga in the 4th century AD. Sailendras were supposed to be the Lords of mountains. All The regions cited above (Including the Malaya peninsula) were under their sway. Some other islands of the East Indies were under them. The town 'Srivijaya' was founded by these rulers. The glory attained the peak in 8th century and continued till 11th century. The great South Indian king Rajendra Chola invaded the kingdom with his splendid fleet. Even then, Sailendras shook the Chola power and gave political power and unity to a large part of Indonesia.

<u>Prambanan Temple:</u>

The most beautiful and the biggest temple in Indonesia is the Prambanan Temple. A group of Hindu Temples here are named 'Roro Jonggrang'. The temple is built with one meter boundary walls. There are connected gates from all sides to the temple. Under the category of group of temples, there are four rows of temples numbering 240 (some are small, and some are big).

This temple (Prambanan) is situated in central Java, Indonesia. Perhaps this is not only the largest Hindu temple but also the biggest in Southeast Asia built in 850 CE consisting of eight main shrines. The towers or the gopurams are attractive (154 ft high). There are individual temples in the complex. The images of Brahma, Vishnu and Siva,the creator, the sustainer, and the destroyers are in existence. Indian art is behind the workmanship of the temples. As a part of Indian sculpture, episodes of Rama and Krishna are carved. The figures are dynamic and vital.

Bali

Bali situated in the far east is a Hindu colony, and kingdom was established in the 4th century AD continued to be rich and prosperous by the 6th century AD under Kaundinya Kshatriyas and in later times Bali come under the Javanese and the Dutch in 1839. For nearly 1500 years, Hindus felt that they have lost their political independence and hence they went to Indo-China and several islands of the Malaya Archipelago starting from Sumatra to New Guinea and Philippines in the Pacific Ocean.

Philippines: South Indian influence is profound here, and the people of South India have travelled and settled here. Religious, literary and cultural impact is strongly felt. The people of the Far East were attracted to Indian institutions. Idols of Ganesa are found here. Brahma, Vishnu, and Siva were worshipped by several gods and goddesses. Magnificent temples were constructed, and Hindu Gods and Goddesses were installed, Bali became a center of Hindu worshippers. Indra, Vishnu, Siva, and Durga are worshipped. Epics of Ramayana, Mahabharata, and Puranas are recited in the temples. Sanskrit being the base scholars flourished here and produced literary works. The Sanskrit language was sweet and flawless under their patronage. Writers had fond of knowledge of the language, literature and grammar; rhetoric to prosody, Kavyas, Vedantas, Smritis etc, outstanding works of Manu, Kalidas, and Panini were mastered.

Indian art, architecture, and sculpture have been adopted to construct the temples.

Borneo

Borneo is a big island east of Sumatra. According to epigraphical sources, Hinduism existed as early as the 1st century. Idols of Siva were unearthed some 60 or 70 years ago. Stone images of Siva, Nandiswara, Ganesa, and Brahma were found in a cave.

Myanmar

Sri Kali Hindu temple is situated in 'Little India' of Yangon downtown in Burma (British Province) and was built by Tamil migrants in 1871. Beautiful stone carvings of Hindu Gods are found here.

Thailand

'Mons' established an Indian kingdom during the 2nd and 3rd centuries AD. People were Indianized. Cambodia is a neighbouring Hindu colony. The Siamese language borrowed its script from India. Hindu rites, Samskaras, and festivals are a part of Siamese culture. The Dasarah festival is celebrated with great pomp to commemorate Rama's triumph over Ravana. Episodes of Ramayana and Mahabharata have a place in Siamese literature. Hindu influence is profound if we observe the names of the kings, people, and towns.

Indo – China

The region between India and China was used as a stop in the context of commercial and cultural activities between the two countries. Hindus established two powerful kingdoms, Champa and Kambuja.

Champa

The region flourished well for a period of 1300 years, from 150 AD to 1450 AD. Bhadravarma of Champa (387-413 AD) was the king who constructed a Siva temple at 'Myson', and the deity is known as Bhadreswara Swamy. Pilgrims from India visited the temple kings, and the people of the region were strong believers in Hindu philosophy and Saivaite doctrines. Though the region faced Mongol attacks, the kingdom, people, and temples were protected. Later in the 13th century, the attacks became inevitable.

Champa Temples:

There are many beautiful Temples. Among the Hindu Gods and Goddesses, Siva, Sakti, Ganesa, and Skanda are worshipped. Siva was worshipped in the Linga form. Bhadreswara was already mentioned above, and he was declared the national deity. Other Gods like Vishnu and Krishna are also worshipped. Indian elements of art are clearly seen in the temple constructions throughout the country. The Champa temple art is beautiful attaining a high level of excellence with and gorgeous ornamentations. The temple Toranas, entrances, and pillars are so beautiful that pilgrims cannot forget their memories once they leave the place.

Combodia

Kambuja is another kingdom south of Champa on the Mekong River, the passage to enter the kingdom. Present Cambodia is 'Kambuja'.

According to famous historian R.C. Majumdar, an Indian sage named Kaundinya landed here along with his wife Naga, Princess, and established this kingdom. He further said that the sage planted a spear obtained from Aswathama, son of Dronacharya. The kingdom's origin is dated to the 1st or 2nd century AD. The capital was Angkor, known for its world-famous architectural monuments.

<u>Angkor Wat:</u>

A temple complex in Cambodia, such as Angkor Wat, is popular in the Kher kingdom. King Suryavarman II of this kingdom built this temple in Cambodia in the early 12th century, putting in 27 years of effort. Siva and Vishnu Temples are wonderful. A shrine is dedicated to Siva, and it is said that it is the largest temple ever built by man. Both Saivism and Vaishnavism flourished well, though Saivism got prominence.

Varaha: The Vishnu temple of the temple complex is the world's largest religious monument, located on a 163-hectare site. By the end of the 12th century, it was transformed into a Buddhist temple. The capital of the Khmer kingdom was Yasodharmapura, later known as Angkor Thom.

Architecture:

The architecture styled as 'Khemar' is classical. Another interesting point is that the symbol of Cambodia is the Angkor Wat temple, which appears on their national flag.

The temple is galleried on a mountain, reminding Mount Meru that it is supposed to be the homeland of devatas. A deep defensive ditch, estimated 5 kilometres long, surrounds the castle and town, filled with water. The outer walls extend up to 3.6 km long and consist of 3 rectangular galleries. At the centre of the temple, there are towns.

This temple is universally known for its grandeur, incredible architecture, bas-reliefs, and representation of the devatas on temple walls, among other things, which have attracted millions of tourists. According to a mythological story, Lord Indra constructed this temple as a place for his son 'Precha Ket Mealea'. According to Zhou Daguan, a Chinese traveller, a divine architect constructed the temple in a single night.

The construction of the Vishnu temple commenced during the first half of the 12th century (1113-1150 AD) during the reign of Suryavarman II. The temple is declared a state temple, and the place is the capital. The temple's name is Varaha—Vishnu, and it was completed in 27 years (1177 AD).

The Chams (the enemies of the Khemars) sacked the temple.

Over time, Angkor Thom and Bayen emerged. The temple was later converted to a Buddhist (already cited above) temple. During the 16th – 17th centuries, the temple was neglected. Japanese have focused on Angkor Wat since it became a Buddhist centre. The Portuguese and the French also evinced great interest in Angkor Wat. They expressed the monument as an extraordinary construction, and it is impossible to describe its grandeur with a pen. Henry Mouhot, a French explorer and a nature lover, popularized this monument by publishing his travels. The monument is nonetheless inferior to those of Greece and Rome. The

French government evinced interest towards systematically studying the ruins from a historical perspective.

The epigraphical and the live stylistic evidence reveal the history of Angkor Wat. By 1885, The chronology of the rulers was listed out. By 1900, the French decided to allot funds for Angkor to preserve the monument for future generations. The 20th century witnessed the restoration work of Angkor Wat. The darkness of the temple was roosted out by illuminating the temple. Of course, some damage happened in the process at the time of the Cambodian civil war. Some bullet holes are found in a bas relief caused by the Vietnamese forces. The French adopted Angkor Wat to continue the artistic legacy of this world-famous monument. France stood as a protector of Cambodian monuments.

In 1992, it became a world monument (UNESCO's nomination). In 2015, a research team from Sydney University arrived to study the buried towers, which were built and demolished. The Archaeological Survey of India, too, played a vital role in continuing the restoration work. Countries like France, Japan, China, and Germany are also involved in the conservation projects like Angkor Wat.

Temples Of Nepal

Pasupatinath Temple

Shiva temple in Kathmandu, Nepal, is an important and world-famous temple. It is the oldest Hindu Temple in Nepal, constructed in 753 AD by King Jayadeva and reconstructed during the 12th and 17th centuries. The architecture is Pagoda style, which is different from the Indian style of temples. Only Hindus are allowed in this temple. This temple of Siva or Pashupatinath is listed as a World Heritage Center.

Changunarayana Temple

Situated in Khatmandu is another famous Nepalese temple. This temple is renowned from a historical and architectural point of view. Haridatta Varma, Liechavi king, built this richest temple in 325 AD. Like

Pasupatinath temple, this temple is also in the Pagoda style. This style is typical of all the Nepalese structures from the 5th to 12th centuries. There are references to this temple in several epigraphs. During 1585 – 1611, the temple was restored.

The Sanskrit language is the base, and literature and scholars flourished well. Sanskrit is sweet and flawless. Pandits were fond of Sanskrit knowledge.

Indian epics, Vedas, and other Sanskrit works were mastered. Indian art, architecture, and sculptural principles were followed in constructing Nepalese temples.

Malaysian Temples

Cave temple of Sri Subrahmanya Swamy

This temple is situated 13 km north of Kuala Lumpur. Batu caves are a series of limestone caves. The deity is the tallest and most popular outside India, at 427 meters. A Tamil trader, Thamboosamy Pillai, constructed the temple in 1890. The Festival of Thaipusam is celebrated in the temple and attracts many pilgrims from Malaysia, India, Australia, and Singapore.

Siva Temple – Tebrau

The Siva temple of Sri Raja Kaliyamman Temple, one of the most visited Hindu Temples outside India, stands out for its unique features. It is a glass temple, the oldest of its kind, and draws devotees in large numbers.

The temple, a testament to history and culture, was built beautifully using a mosaic of three lakh pieces of glass of different colours. Its beginnings date back to 1922. The 'Atma Lingam' of Siva, symbolized as a lotus, is a sight to behold. Rose water is poured on the Lord, and prayers are offered. The Siva Lingam is adorned with Rudraksha or Mukni beads. The wall sculptures, with their gold finishings, are a testament to the temple's beauty and grandeur.

Temples of Sri Lanka

Nallur Kandaswamy Kovil

This temple is also known as Murugan temple, a famous one in Jaffna in the town of Nallur. Murugan is the deity. The deity of the Goddess was given to the temple in the 10th century by the Chola queen Sembiyan Maha Devi.

Siva Temple of Konneswaram

This temple is on a rock overlooking Trincomalee, a fort town in Eastern Sri Lanka. It dates back to 2000 years and was destroyed by colonial invaders in the 17th century. On one side, there was the statue of Ravana, and on the other side, the Swamy rock.

Pakistan

Varun Dev Temple

Varun Dev temple, a thousand years old, is on the sandy beach of Manora in Pakistan. Although it is in a dilapidated state, it is a grand structure that attracts tourists. Its workmanship reminds us of its glorious history.

Temples in USA

After the 1st world War, the United States of America emerged as one of the superpowers, having an area of 9,826,630 sq. Km. Washington DC is the capital, and New York, Chicago, Houston, Philadelphia, Detroit, Dallas, Boston, Pittsburg, and San Francisco are the most significant cities. Educated Indians, since 50 or 60 years, have been going to the US for employment or to pursue higher studies. In this context, lakhs of the Indian population have settled or are staying. In this scenario, along with people, Indian religious beliefs and practices also travelled to America. Thus, the emergence of Hinduism followed by temples as centres of worship have been established in different parts of the US, including Washington DC, Florida, Illinois, Ashland, California, Atlanta, Pittsburg, New Jersey and other places from 1970 onwards.

Sri Maha Vallabha Ganapati Temple – New York

The first temple established in the US was Sri Maha Vallabha Ganapati Temple in New York in 1970. It took nearly seven years to complete. Traditional and religious activities have continued since then, and it has become one of the most famous temples in the USA.

Sri Siva and Vishnu Temple – Washington DC

In Washington, DC, a Siva and Vishnu temple was established, underlying the philosophy of oneness of Saivite and Vaishnavite cults of Hinduism. The architectural styles of Pallavan, Vijayanagara, and Canarese, as well as the southern styles, are being followed in the construction of the temples. The main deities in the temple complex consist of Ganesa, Siva, Parvati, Vishnu, Rama, and Krishna.

Siva – Vishnu Temple – Florida

Another Siva-Vishnu Temple was constructed in Florida, inviting architects from Mahabalipuram. Construction began after 29 years of effort in Washington, D.C. The temple is in the South Indian style and covers an area of 6,200 Sq ft. The chief architect was Ganapati Sthapati, who was behind the Sri Ramachandra Swamy temple of Bhadrachalam in Telangana state, India.

Balaji Temple – Illinois

The Balaji temple, dedicated to Lord Venkateshwara, was built as a part of the Vishnu group of temples during the first phase of temple construction in the USA. It is spread across a vast area of 20 acres. It has gained the interest of both Indian and American families who are keen on promoting various temple activities on par with the Tirupati Balaji temple in India. Apart from Lord Venkateshwara, the temple houses other deities such as Siva, Parvati, and Ganesa. Sculptors like Mutaia Stapati and others from Chicago have worked hard to promote this temple.

Sri Lakshmi Temple – Ashland, MA

Mutaia Stapati was the architect of the Sri Lakshmi Temple of Ashland, which was built in the 1980s. The temple is beautifully located in an area of 12 acres. Daily pujas, festivals, and all temple activities are conducted. Sri Maha Ganapati, Balaji, Nataraja, Subrahmanya, Navagrahas, and other deities are installed in the temple complex. On all festival occasions, special pujas are performed on all the deities.

Sri Venkateswara Swamy Temple – Malibu, California

Sri Venkateswara Swamy temple has been located in Calabasas, California, since 1981. It is also known as Malibu Hindu Temple and is organized by the Hindu Temple Society of Southern California. The Temple is South Indian in style.

Sri Venkateswara Swamy Temple – Pittsburg, Pennsylvania

Si Venkateswara Swarmy temple of Pittsburg is vast, beautiful, and amazing in South Indian style. Tirumala-Tirupati temple is the base for its construction. The temple was constructed during the early phase of 1975. The complex consists of Ganesa, Siva, and Parvati.

Siva and Balaji Temple – Atlanta, Georgia

This Siva-Vishnu temple was built in the 1980s in Atlanta, Georgia. The temple's architecture is not only traditional but beautiful—a feast for the eyes. Siva is worshipped as Rama Lingeswara and Vishnu as Venkateswara. Devotees worship Ganesa, Durga, Nageswara, Bhairava, and Hanuman in the complex.

Temples in UK

The United Kingdom constitutes the most significant part of the British Isles. Great Britain is the largest of the Islands forming the United Kingdom, comprising England, Scotland, Wales, and Ireland. There are the Channel Islands between Great Britain and France.

There are many beautiful Hindu temples in the United Kingdom.

Ganapati Temple

In 1981, Sri Ganapati temple was constructed in Wimbledon, London. All the traditional functions, Puja activities, religious discourses, Speeches, yoga, and meditation programs are conducted.

Balaji (or) Venkateswara Temples

Hindu Temples (stone) construction began in Europe and UK. Swami Narayan temple was constructed in UK-Neasden.

Birmingham

Sri Venkateswara temple is the first temple in the Midlands. The largest temple in Europe is the Balaji Temple at Tividale. Weekly pujas and daily pujas are performed between 11 AM to 7 PM, including Sunday.

Bradford Lakshmi Narayana Temple

This temple in Northern England was built and opened in 2007 by Queen Elizabeth and Prince Philip. All religions and cultural festivals are celebrated here.

London – Radhakrishna Temple

Faith, devotion, and dedication are strictly observed here, as in the case of all temples in the UK. In 1969, the Indian charitable trust established Radhakrishna Temple in Manchester. There is a Vaishnavite temple in Aldenham near Watford run by ISKCON, International Society for Krishna Consciousness is on a large campus of 70 acres of land. It is beautiful, with an artificial lake, flower gardens and lawns.

During the 1970s, a temple was constructed at Nottingham. Its activities include philosophical and religious discourses, charities, educational, social, cultural, and festivals.

Sri Murugan Temple

This temple is beautiful and unique. The temple was built with polished granite from India. The temple makes devotees feel that they are in Tamil Nadu. Puja systems are based on traditions and texts.

Sri Murugan Temple

APPENDIX

Jyotirlingas

<u>A Stotra in the context of Dwadasa Jyotirlingas:</u>

"Saurastre Somanathamcha (1), Srisaila (2) Mallikharjunam,
Ujjaenyam (3) Mahakale, Omkare (4) Paramesvaram, Prajvalyam
Vaidyanatham (5), Dhakinyam Bhima Sankaram (6), Sethubandhatu
Ramesam (7), Nagesam Darukavana (8), Varanasyanthu
Visvesvaram (9), Triyambakaun (10) Gauthamithate, Himalayetu
Kedaram (11), Gruhusnesamcha (12) Sivalaye"

It is said that those who pray the Jyotirlingas in the early morning and evening will be rid of the sins of seven births, free from all sufferings, and achieve all their wishes.

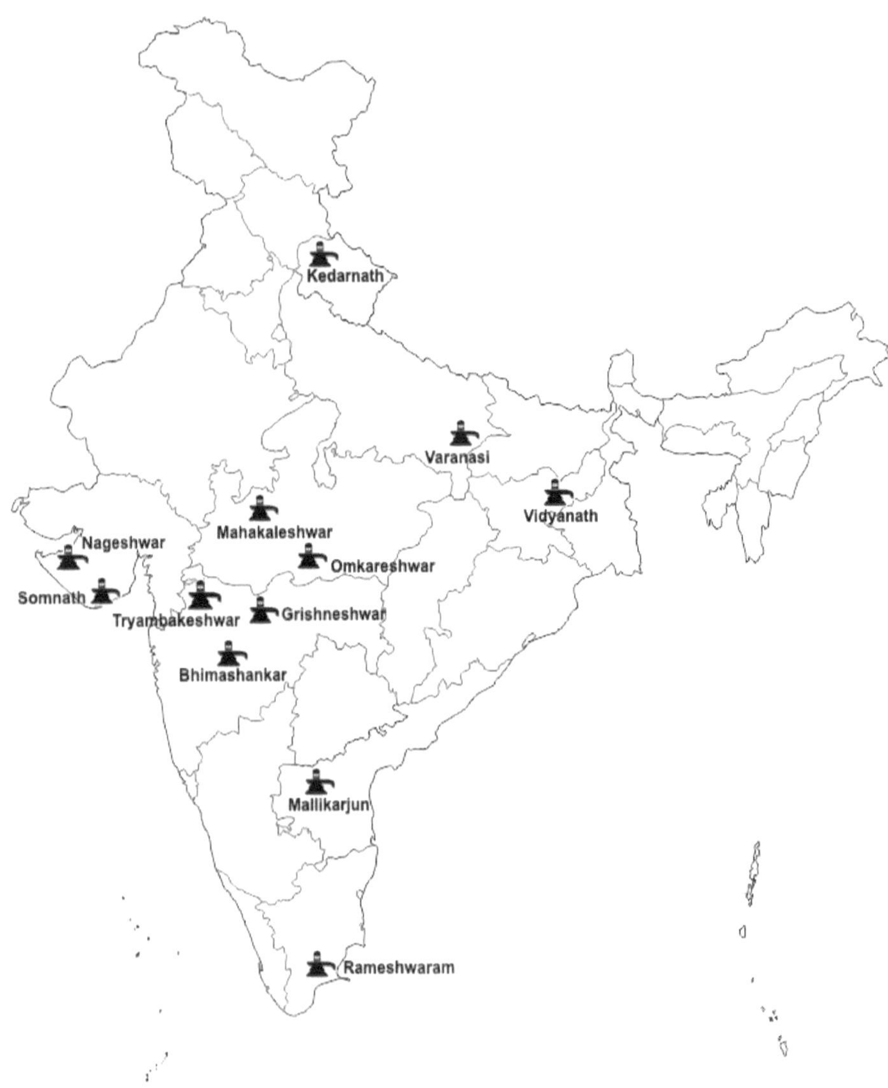

Figure 26: Map indicating approximate location of Jyothirlings across India

Ashtadasa Shakti Peethas

Ashtadasa Shakti Peethas are dedicated to various forms of Adi Shakti and are said to have come into existence after the death of the goddess Sati.

As per the 'Daksha Yagna' chapter in Kalika Purana, King Daksha, father of Parvathi (Sati), did not invite Siva to the yagna he proposed to perform. However, knowing about the yagna through Narada, Parvati attended the yagna though uninvited. Daksha started abusing Siva. At this discourtesy, Parvati sat on the ground, closed her eyes and reduced her body to ashes by the yogic fire. Siva's grief-stricken destroyed Daksha's sacrifice and wandered hither and thither in fantastic sorrow, carrying her dead body on his head. Brahma and other Gods were alarmed by the incident. They approached Vishnu and prayed to save them from the world's destruction. Brahma, Vishnu, and Sani entered the dead body of Sati and disposed of it limb by limb.

The body parts of Sati fell in 51 different places. Out of them, eighteen are important and are known as Ashtadasa or Maha Shakti Peethas. Below is a list of those Shakthi Peethas, their location, and the body parts associated with Sati Devi.

S.No	Shakthi Peetha	Location	Body Part
1	Kamakhya (Kamarupa Devi)	Kamakhya, Guwahati, Assam	Yoni khanda /Vulva/ Genital Organ
2	Avanti/ Mahakali Devi	Ujjain, Madhya Pradesh	Upper Lips
3	Lalita/ Madhaveswari Devi/ Alopi Mata	Prayag, Allahabad, Uttar Pradesh	Finger (Hand)
4	Vishalakshi	Varanasi, Uttar Pradesh	Earring
5	Bhramaramba Devi	Srisailam, Andhra Pradesh	Neck part

6	Biraja Devi	Jajpur, Odisha	Navel
7	Chamundeshwari Devi	Mysore, Karnataka	Hair
8	Ekaveerika Devi	Mahur, Maharashtra	Head
9	Jogulamba	Alampur, Telangana	Upper teeth
10	Kamakshi	Kanchi, Tamil Nadu	Back part
11	Mahalakshmi	Kolhapur, Maharashtra	Eyes
12	Manikyamba	Draksharamam, Andhra Pradesh	Left cheek
13	Puruhutika Devi	Pithapuram, Andhra Pradesh	Foot
14	Saraswathi Devi (Sharada Peeth)	Muzaffrabad, Pakistan Occupied Kashmir	Right hand
15	Sarvamangala Devi	Gaya, Bihar	Breast part
16	Shankari Devi	Trincomalee, Sri Lanka	Groin
17	Shrikkhala Devi	Pandua, West Bengal	Stomach
18	Vaishnavi Devi	Jwalamukhi, Himachal Pradesh	Tongue

Figure 27: Map indicating approximate location of Ashtadasa Shakti Peethas

AUTHOR BIO

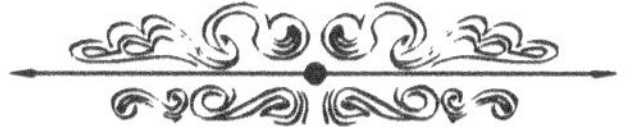

The book's author is Dr. K. Raghuram (Born in 1950), who has had a distinguished academic career. He is the recipient of the 'Sir R. Venkataratnam Gold Medal' from Andhra University, Visakhapatnam, for his academic excellence in 'Bachelor of Arts' (B.A.) in the year 1968 and is the topper in his 'Master of Arts' (M.A.) with a specialization in History & Archeology in the year 1970 from Osmania University, Hyderabad. He also received a Doctor of Philosophy (PhD) in History from Sri Venkateswara University, Tirupati, in 1993. He preferred teaching due to his passion and the zeal to serve and inspire future Historians. For about four decades (1971-2008), he served as Lecturer, Reader, Professor and Principal in NAAC Accredited Degree and Post-Graduation colleges in the composite state of Andhra Pradesh. Some of the honours and awards received include:

- 'State Best Teacher Award – Andhra Pradesh' for the year 2002
- Rashtriya Gaurav Award, New Delhi for Administration in the year 2005,
- 'Rajiv Gandhi Vidya Vikas Award' for distinguished services in Education from Union Ministry in the year 2007

Dr. K. Raghuram, as a researcher, has utilised extensive research material available at National Archives, States Archives of Andhra Pradesh, Tamil Nadu, National and state libraries, authored many Articles (Published in Proc. of History Congress, Triveni and Itihas Journals, Comprehensive History and Culture of Andhra Pradesh and Telangana – vol VIII Emeso, Hyderabad (2016), Comprehensive History & Culture of Guntur District (2008). To mention some:

- Buddhist Monastic education in Andhra – *Andhra Pradesh History congress (1999)*

- Education and learning in Guntur District under the East India company – *Itihas (2003)*
- Relations of Zamindars (Guntur) and East India Company (1996) – *Andhra Pradesh History congress*
- Financial Embezzlements under Zamindars of Guntur District and East India Company till 1857 – *Itihas (2015-16)*
- Foreigners by Birth, But Indians by choice– *Itihas (2007)*
- Journey of Kohinoor Diamond from India to UK – *Itihas (2012)*
- Indian Diamond in American Museum – *Itihas (2017-18)*
- Historical glimpses of Udayagiri – *Itihas (2009-11)*
- Women's Participation in the Freedom Struggle of India – *Itihas (2008)*
- Historical Monuments of Telangana's State capital – *Itihas (2020-21)*
- Equal opportunities for all (1960-62) – *Comprehensive History and Culture of AP & Telangana, Emeso, Hyd (2016)*
- Article on Pingali Venkaiah – "Architect of the Indian National Flag" – *Triveni (2003)*
- Brook Translation (Telugu to English): "Pingali Venkaiah – Architect if The Indian Tri-Colour" *(2021)*
- Translation (English to Telugu): "Relations of Zamindars of Guntur District and East India Company (1788-1857)" – Comprehensive History of Guntur District *(2008)*.

BIBLIOGRAPHY

Books in English:

- Arnold Edwin (1968), *"The song celestial"*, TTD, Tirupati.
- Banarsidas Motilal (1975), *"Puranic Encyclopaedia"*
- Bandopadhyay, P.K. (2005), *"The North East Saga"*. Government of India, Pub. Div.
- Barua, R.K. (1988), *"Temples of Assam"*, Bharatiya Vidya Bhavan, Bombay.
- Chaudhuri Nirad (1979), *"Hinduism – A Religion to live"*, New Delhi.
- Das, R.K. (2001), *"Temples of Tamilnad"*, Bharatiya Vidya Bhavan, Mumbai.
- Diana L. Eck (2012), *"India A Sacred Geography"*, New York.
- Diwakar, M. (2010), "Temples of South India", Chennai.
- Gopinath Rao T.A. (1914), *"Elements of Hindu Iconography"* (2 vols.), Madras.
- George Michell (1977), *"The Hindu Temples"*, Chicago, USA
- Kamala Mankekar (2004), "Culture and Religious Traditions – Temples of Goa", Pub. Div. GOl, New Delhi.
- Karuna Sagar Behera (2005), *"Konark – The Black Pagoda"* Pub. Div. Gol
- Kramrish Stella (1980), *"The Hindu Temple"*, Delhi
- Krishnadeva (1969), "Temples of North India", "National Book Trust of India, New Delhi Lalnitinga (1997), *"Mizoram"*, Pub. Div. Gol, New Delhi
- Mate, M.S. (1962), *"Temples and legends of Maharastra"* Bhavans, Mumbai.
- Mitchell, A.G. "Hindu gods and Goddesses", Pub. UBSPD
- Mohanlal Goyel (1987), "Pushkar Mahatyam", Pushkar, Ajmer.

- Rabindra Mohan Senapati (2004), *"Art and Culture of Orissa"* Pub. Div. GOl, New Delhi.
- Radha Kanth Bharati (2004), *"Rivers of India"*, National Book Trust of India, New Delhi.
- Radha Krishna Sarma (1972), *"Temples of Telangana"*, Hyderabad.
- Rajni Vyas (2003), *"Gujarat"*, Pub. Div, GOI, New Delhi.
- Rama Swamy N.S. (1984), *"Select Temples of South India"*, Madras
- Ramesan, N. (2000), *"Temples and Legends of Andhra Pradesh"*, Bharatiya Vidya Bhavan, Mumbai.
- Rao, G.V. (2003), *"Temples and legends of Karnataka"*, Bhavan's Pub.
- Roychoudhury P.C., (1988), *"Temples and Legends of Bihar"*, Bhavan's Pub., Bombay.
- Rawilson H.G. (1952), *"India: A Short Cultural History"*, New York.
- Rowland, B. (1956), *"The Art and Architecture of India"*, London.
- Sharma, B.R. (1997), *"Himachal Pradesh"*, Pub. Div., GOl.
- Sastri, H.K. (1916) *"South Indian Images of Gods and Goddesses"*, Madras.
- Saundararajan K.V. (1972), *"The Indian Temple Styles"*, New Delhi.
- Singh, A., *"The Gateways to Gods – Haridwar, Rishikesh"*
- Swamy Atma Shraddhananda (2013), *"Pilgrimage to Kanyakumari and Rameswaram"*, Sri Rama Krishna Math.
- Vaidyanathan K.R. (1988), *"Temples and Legends of Kerala"*, Bhavans, Bombay.

Books in Telugu:

- Lakshmi,P.S (2015) *"Sri Narasimha Kshetralu"*, Yaknadeepika, Hyderabad.
- Maidhili Venkateswararao (2011), *"Bharata Yatra darsini"*, Rajahmundry,
- Satyanarayana G (2013). *"Bharata Prasiddha Kshetralu"* Vijayawada.

- Veera Swamy (2009), *"Andhra Pradesh Puratana Devalayalu"*, Rajahmundry.
- *"Andhra Pradesh Darsini"* (1988). Pub. Vijayawada.
- *"Srisaila Charitra"* – Srisailam.
- Bhaskararaya Sarma, P, *"Dwadasa Jyotirlinga Charitra"*, Rajahmundry.
- Sanjeeva Naidu, MB (2015) (2015), *"Alampuram Kshetra Samagra Charitra"* And *"Astadasa Sakti Peetha Darsanam"*.
- Ramakrishna Sarma, G. (2011) *"Alampur Kshetramu"*, Kurnool.
- *"Sri Bhadrachala Kshetra Charitra"* (2005), SSRC Swamy Devasthanam, Bhadrachalam.
- Nagireddy N.S. (1999), *"Krishna zillalo Prasiddha Devalayalu"*, Vijayawada.
- *"108 Vaishnava Divya Kshetralu"* (2015), Vijayawada.

Journals:

- *Itihas* (Journal of Scate Archives & Research Institute – A.P.) Vols: XXXV, (2009-2011)
- *"Comprehensive History of A.P. and Telangana"* 1956-1990, Vol VIII, EMESCO (Hyd) 2016.
- "Comprehensive History and Culture of Guntur District" 2 Vols (2004, 2008)
- A.P. Souvenir (1987), *"Remains of Art and Architecture of Vijayawada"*
- *"Telangana State Information"* Planning Commission, (2017).
- Manorama year Books (Series)

News Papers – English and Telugu:

- Times of India, 11 Apr 2017
- Deccan Chronicle

    - 30 Apr, 2006
    - 10 sept, 2017

- Eenadu (Telugu Daily)

    - 04 Feb, 2001
    - 08 Aug, 2010
    - 11 Jul, 2012
    - 16 Jun, 2013
    - 25 Jun, 2013
    - 25 May, 2016
    - 29 Dec, 2017
    - 23 Apr, 2017
    - 04 Sep, 2017

Sources for Images:

All images specified in the book are personally photographed by family members of the authors. The following family members are acknowledged for the photographs: Vaidehi Kambhampati, Ramesh Kambhampati, Sreedhar Kambhampati and Rajani Kumar Khambhampati.

Sources for Maps:

All maps were sourced free from d-Maps.com and modified to mark the location of the major temples and cities by the author's son, Rajani Kumar Khambhampati. All maps were sourced and modified as per the terms and conditions of usage outlined by d-maps (https://d-maps.com/conditions.php?lang=en).

Below are the original sources of each outline map:

- Andhra Pradesh: https://d-maps.com/carte.php?num_car=16389&lang=en
- Karnataka: https://d-maps.com/carte.php?num_car=16747&lang=en
- Kerala: https://d-maps.com/carte.php?num_car=16767&lang=en
- Maharashtra: https://d-maps.com/carte.php?num_car=16853&lang=en
- Tamil Nadu: https://d-maps.com/carte.php?num_car=17045&lang=en

- Telangana: https://d-maps.com/carte.php?num_car=117963&lang=en
- Uttar Pradesh: https://d-maps.com/carte.php?num_car=17083&lang=en
- Uttarakhand: https://d-maps.com/carte.php?num_car=17099&lang=en
- India:
    - With State boundaries: https://d-maps.com/carte.php?num_car=24853&lang=en
    - With state and country boundaries: https://d-maps.com/carte.php?num_car=4183&lang=en